Sustainability, Growth, and Poverty Alleviation

Other Books Published in Cooperation with the International Food Policy Research Institute

Agricultural Change and Rural Poverty: Variations on a Theme by Dharm Narain
Edited by John W. Mellor and Gunvant M. Desai

Crop Insurance for Agricultural Development: Issues and Experience
Edited by Peter B. R. Hazell, Carlos Pomareda, and Alberto Valdés

Accelerating Food Production in Sub-Saharan Africa
Edited by John W. Mellor, Christopher L. Delgado, and Malcolm J. Blackie

Agricultural Price Policy for Developing Countries
Edited by John W. Mellor and Raisuddin Ahmed

Food Subsidies in Developing Countries: Costs, Benefits, and Policy Options
Edited by Per Pinstrup-Andersen

Variability in Grain Yields: Implications for Agricultural Research and Policy in Developing Countries
Edited by Jock R. Anderson and Peter B. R. Hazell

Seasonal Variability in Third World Agriculture: The Consequences for Food Security
Edited by David E. Sahn

The Green Revolution Reconsidered: The Impact of High-Yielding Rice Varieties in South India
By Peter B. R. Hazell and C. Ramasamy

The Political Economy of Food and Nutrition Policies
Edited by Per Pinstrup-Andersen

Agricultural Commercialization, Economic Development, and Nutrition
Edited by Joachim von Braun and Eileen Kennedy

Agriculture on the Road to Industrialization
Edited by John W. Mellor

Intrahousehold Resource Allocation in Developing Countries: Models, Methods, and Policy
Edited by Lawrence Haddad, John Hoddinott, and Harold Alderman

Sustainability, Growth, and Poverty Alleviation

A Policy and Agroecological Perspective

EDITED BY STEPHEN A. VOSTI AND THOMAS REARDON

Published for the International Food Policy Research Institute

The Johns Hopkins University Press
Baltimore and London

The Johns Hopkins University Press
2715 North Charles Street
Baltimore, Maryland 21218-4319
The Johns Hopkins Press Ltd., London

Library of Congress Cataloging-in-Publication Data will be found at the end of this book.
A catalog record for this book is available from the British Library.

ISBN 0-8018-5607-8

*To Yvonne, Daniela, Lia, and Gina, who supported the effort
completely and continuously, so that their counterparts
in the developing world might enjoy longer and better lives*

S.A.V.

*To my wife, Bonnie, whose encouragement was critical
at every step of this work*

T.R.

Contents

List of Tables and Figures   xiii

Foreword, by Per Pinstrup-Andersen   xvii

Preface   xxi

1   Introduction: The Critical Triangle of Links among
    Sustainability, Growth, and Poverty Alleviation   1
    STEPHEN A. VOSTI AND THOMAS REARDON

PART I   Concepts and Determinants of the Links among
         Sustainability, Growth, and Poverty Alleviation

2   Sustainable Growth in Agricultural Production:
    Poetry, Policy, and Science   19
    VERNON W. RUTTAN

3   Environmental Consequences of Agricultural Growth in
    Developing Countries   34
    HARTWIG DE HAEN

4   Poverty-Environment Links in Rural Areas of Developing Countries   47
    THOMAS REARDON AND STEPHEN A. VOSTI

5   The Links between Agricultural Growth, Environmental Degradation, and
    Nutrition and Health: Implications for Policy and Research   66
    JOACHIM VON BRAUN

6   Accelerated Resource Degradation by Agriculture in
    Developing Countries? The Role of Population Change and
    Responses to It   79
    MICHAEL LIPTON

7   Global Climate Change: Implications for the Links between
    Sustainability, Growth, and Poverty Alleviation   90
    THOMAS E. DOWNING AND MARTIN L. PARRY

8   The Relationship between Trade and Environment, with
     Special Reference to Agriculture   103
     AMMAR SIAMWALLA

9   Macroeconomic and Sectoral Policies, Natural Resources, and
     Sustainable Agricultural Growth   119
     EDWARD B. BARBIER

10   Policy Analysis of Conservation Investments: Extensions of
     Traditional Technology Adoption Research   135
     THOMAS REARDON AND STEPHEN A. VOSTI

11   "Exogenous" Interest Rates, Technology, and Farm Prices versus
     "Endogenous" Conservation Incentives and Policies   146
     MICHAEL LIPTON

12   Research Systems for Sustainable Agricultural Development   154
     PETER ORAM

PART II   **Links among Sustainability, Growth, and Poverty Alleviation
          by Agroecological Zone**

13   Agricultural Growth, Sustainability, and Poverty Alleviation in the
     Brazilian Amazon   179
     AÉRCIO S. CUNHA AND DONALD R. SAWYER

14   Agricultural Growth and Sustainability: Conditions for Their
     Compatibility in the Humid and Subhumid Tropics of Africa   191
     DUNSTAN S. C. SPENCER AND RUDOLPH A. POLSON

15   Agriculture-Environment-Poverty Interactions in the Southeast Asian
     Humid Tropics   208
     PRABHU L. PINGALI

16   Agricultural Growth and Sustainability: Prospects for
     Semi-Arid West Africa   229
     PETER J. MATLON AND AKINWUMI A. ADESINA

17   Prospects for Pastoralism in Semi-Arid Africa   246
     PATRICK WEBB AND D. LAYNE COPPOCK

18   Agricultural Sustainability, Growth, and Poverty Alleviation in the
     Indian Semi-Arid Tropics   261
     MERI L. WHITAKER, JOHN M. KERR, AND P. V. SHENOI

19   Agricultural Growth and Sustainability: Conditions for Their
     Compatibility in the Rainfed Production Systems of West Asia and
     North Africa   278
     RICHARD N. TUTWILER AND ELIZABETH BAILEY

20 Agricultural Growth and Sustainability: Perspectives and Experiences from the Himalayas 294
NARPAT S. JODHA

21 Institutional and Technological Perspectives on the Links between Agricultural Sustainability and Poverty: Illustrations from India 304
KANCHAN CHOPRA AND C. H. HANUMANTHA RAO

22 Agricultural Growth and Sustainability: Conditions for Their Compatibility in the East African Highlands 315
AMARE GETAHUN

23 A New Approach to Poverty Alleviation and Sustainability in the Dry Tropical Hillsides of Central America: A Guatemalan Case Study 328
RAFAEL CELIS, MARIO A. VEDOVA, AND SERGIO RUANO

24 Conclusions 339
STEPHEN A. VOSTI AND THOMAS REARDON

References 347

Contributors 389

Index 393

Tables and Figures

Tables

3.1 Soil degradation by type and cause (classified as moderately to excessively affected) 37

3.2 Net benefits from land use alternatives in the northern upland region of Thailand (million baht) 43

5.1 Links among agriculture, degradation, and health and nutrition when there is technical progress in agriculture 72

5.2 Links among agriculture, the environment, and health and nutrition without Green Revolution–type technical change in agriculture 74

7.1 Climate change and land use in Kenya 92

7.2 Linkages between climate change and sustainable agricultural development 98

7.3 Adaptive responses: timing and sector-specific strategies for agriculture 100

9.1 Typical environmental externalities in developing countries 123

9.2 Irrigation charges and costs for six Asian countries, 1987 131

12.1 CGIAR operational expenditures for essential activities, 1983, 1987, 1989, and 1991 158

12.2 Distribution of NARS research staff by disciplinary category for 92 developing countries, by region 164

12.3 Education and nationality of NARS research staff in Sub-Saharan Africa, 1980–1986 169

12.4 101 developing countries grouped by numbers of agricultural research scientists 172

13.1 Area harvested of food staples in Brazil's North region, selected years (thousands of hectares) 185

13.2 Total, urban, and rural population in Brazil's North region, by state, 1980 and 1991 (thousands) 186

13.3 Average yields of food staples for the North region and Brazil, selected years (metric tons per hectare) 186

13.4 Infant mortality rates for the North region and Brazil, 1980–1988
      (deaths under age one per thousand live births)   187
13.5 Indices of malnutrition, by region, 1975 and 1989 (percent)   188
14.1 Soils, population density, and market access of major agroecological
      subzones of the humid and subhumid tropics of West and
      Central Africa   194
14.2 Index of agricultural and forestry production in Africa   196
14.3 Agricultural and forestry production indexes in Côte d'Ivoire   198
15.1 Effects of soil conservation technologies, various slopes   212
15.2 Regional deforestation and poverty indicators, the Philippines   216
15.3 Determinants of irrigation infrastructure degradation in the Philippines:
      estimated elasticities   223
16.1 Land and population characteristics of the major agroclimatic zones in
      the West African semi-arid tropics   230
16.2 Sustainable and actual population densities in the major agroclimatic
      zones of West Africa (persons per square kilometer)   232
16.3 Prospects for different types of technical change in sorghum and millet
      production in the West African semi-arid tropics   240
18.1 Extent of dependence of poor and wealthy households on common
      property resources (CPRs) in dryland India   270
20.1 The sustainability implications of mountain conditions   296
20.2 Public intervention strategies and their effects on the sustainability
      prospects in mountain areas   300
22.1 Comparison of sustainability between the two farming systems and
      environments in the Ethiopian highlands   317
22.2 Estimated rates of soil loss in Ethiopia   318
22.3 Changes in population density in Kilimanjaro, Tanzania,
      1921–1978   318
22.4 Agriculture and the rural economy in the tropical and subtropical
      highlands   321
22.5 Farming systems in the western Usambara Mountains, Tanzania   324
23.1 Land use and population characteristics in Central America, by
      topographic class   329
23.2 Trends in land use and agricultural share of gross domestic product
      (GDP) in Central America (percent)   332
23.3 Percent change in crop yields per hectare in Central America,
      1981–1987   333

Figures

1.1 The critical triangle of development goals   2
A1.1 Agroecological zones of the developing world   14

3.1 Pesticide use, rice production, and pesticide subsidy, Indonesia, 1973–1990 42

4.1 Poverty and environment links 50

4.2 Household resource allocation 54

5.1 Links among agriculture, environmental degradation, nutrition and health, and policies 69

7.1 Sensitivity of world food poverty to global climate change, 2060 96

8.1 International trade and the environment 104

8.2 Cultivated area per agricultural worker, Thailand, 1961–1987 112

8.3 Area under forest in Thailand, 1975–1988 114

9.1 Economic policy and potential environmental impacts 122

10.1 Stylized nutrient presence and input use curve 139

15.1 Deforestation and poverty incidence in the Philippines, by region 217

15.2 Deforestation and expenditure patterns in the Philippines, by region 218

15.3 Deforestation and migration in the Philippines, by region 219

15.4 Deforestation and unemployment in the Philippines, by region 220

18.1 Area under irrigation by source, India, 1951–1986 267

22.1 Highlands of Sub-Saharan Africa 316

22.2 Major problem sequence in the agroecological system of the western Usambara Mountains 322

22.3 Likely development of land use in Ethiopia 322

22.4 Sustainable development of farm-household systems 325

Foreword

As this volume goes to press, 185 million children suffer from malnutrition, agricultural growth is stagnant in areas where many of these children live, and the natural resource base on which agriculture depends is being degraded. These facts are linked. In developing countries with rapid rates of population growth, and without appropriate agricultural technology for making the most of scarce natural resources, farmers are forced to deplete soils, watersheds, and forests in order to feed rural and urban populations. This degraded resource base, however, cannot be exploited indefinitely. Clearly, unless these resources are managed in sustainable ways, current as well as future generations will find their welfare threatened.

But what are the environmental goals, who should set them, and what policy instruments are available for achieving them? Policymakers in developing countries face growing frustration in trying to select realistic sustainability targets. The targets that are proposed often represent ideals. Either they are too general and therefore impossible to translate directly into policy action, or they are well defined but require difficult (and sometimes unrealistic) political decisions about how to balance the use of natural resources against the welfare of current and future generations and of various groups within the population. Frustration over this situation is compounded by the lack of solid information on the potential for various policies to bring about desired outcomes. In short, policymakers are often unsure which of the many sustainability targets to aim for, what the short- and long-term costs (both absolutely and vis-à-vis other goals) of various targets might be, and how to go about reaching these goals.

Policymakers cannot, and should not, abandon growth and poverty alleviation goals for the sake of environmental sustainability; the options are often wrongly cast in this way. Rather, the notion of sustainability must be practically introduced into policymakers' decisions and researchers' agendas. This means that more thought must be given to how to operationalize the concept of sustainability: What are we supposed to sustain? How do we measure it? When do we measure it? Where do we measure it? And more work is needed on how to weave it into a realistic, development-oriented framework, placing sustainability alongside established growth and poverty alleviation goals.

Much time and effort over the past 10 years have been devoted to drafting definitions of sustainability, and to a more limited extent, examining the effects of poverty and agricultural growth on environmental degradation. Despite this work, important knowledge gaps remain regarding the factors that create and condition the links among poverty, growth, and sustainability, and the extent to which these links represent opportunities for reversing current trends in natural resource degradation. For example, do rising levels of poverty or agricultural growth worsen degradation? If so, does this happen in all situations? Will such environmental degradation, in turn, limit prospects for poverty alleviation and agricultural growth in the future? If so, why and how? Can we expect poverty alleviation, however achieved, to reduce environmental degradation? Finally, but perhaps most importantly, what is the role of policy in altering or using these links to achieve objectives in all three outcomes simultaneously? Pinning down these causal links, their direction, and the mechanisms through which they work is critical for policy intervention to succeed. These gaps in our understanding constrain developed- and developing-country policymakers from taking informed action to achieve nationally and internationally mandated sustainability goals while also focusing on the long-accepted goals of poverty alleviation and agricultural growth.

This volume, with its policy focus, does not provide another definition of sustainability, principally because no single definition could possibly incorporate the ecological and political diversity in the developing world. In addition, the process of arriving at such a consensus definition (usually a voting scheme) would necessarily eliminate many concerns specific to individual countries and agroecological zones. Rather, the volume focuses on, first, identifying common factors that must be taken into account in deriving working definitions of sustainability (each applicable in a particular context), and second, providing specific recommendations about the ecological, socioeconomic, and cultural factors that must be continually monitored in order to chart progress in meeting sustainability objectives.

One of the principal shortcomings of the sustainability literature has been the incomplete appreciation of how other national goals complement or compete with sustainability goals. This volume begins with the premise that there are three desired outcomes of the policy-guided development process—environmental sustainability, growth, and poverty alleviation. What is needed is an improved understanding of potential complementarities and trade-offs among these outcomes, and the policy and other tools available for minimizing the trade-offs while exploiting the complementarities. Rigid adherence to narrowly defined sustainability conditions at the expense of policy actions affecting other goals is of little use.

The lack of an operational focus in previous work in this area has meant that the ultimate implementors of sustainable natural resource management practices—rural households and villages—have been largely overlooked. Without a clear understanding of the incentives and constraints faced by farmers and villages, and how these affect productivity and conservation investments, broad policy changes or technological innovations are unlikely to succeed. This micro-level focus has paid important research and policy dividends in the areas of poverty and growth; the same can be expected from sustainability research pursued at an equally disaggregated level.

This volume was designed to add operational vigor to the sustainability issue and to provide zone-specific reviews not only of how growth could affect sustainability and poverty could affect sustainability, but also of how sustainability could affect each of these. Particular emphasis was placed on the role of policy in determining and conditioning these links, while recognizing the limitations and possibilities associated with national sovereignty in defining and implementing policies.

It is my hope that the volume will spur additional, practical research aimed at providing policymakers with clear sets of objectives and methods for simultaneously addressing sustainability, growth, and poverty alleviation.

Per Pinstrup-Andersen
Director General
International Food Policy Research Institute

Preface

By the second half of the 1980s, debate had become heated on how to introduce environmental issues into agricultural and policy research in a practical way. The International Food Policy Research Institute (IFPRI) and the Deutsche Stiftung für internationale Entwicklung (DSE) were concerned that participants in that debate were failing to consider growth and poverty alleviation goals adequately and ignoring the links between these traditional objectives and environmental sustainability entirely.

That concern gave rise to an international conference that addressed these links. Held by IFPRI and DSE in September 1991 in Feldafing, Germany, the conference brought together social scientists, agricultural scientists, and policymakers from developing and developed countries. The conference focused on conceptualizing these links, clarifying their manifestations in the three major agroecological zones that are home to the vast majority of the world's poor, and drawing practical policy and research implications from the findings.

The papers and commentaries presented at the conference were published in a proceedings volume by DSE in 1992. In response to the wide-ranging debate generated by the proceedings, the present volume reflects a substantial revision and updating of the conference papers and the addition of several commissioned chapters to fill gaps in the proceedings.

We are grateful for the many contributions by IFPRI and DSE staff, as well as conference participants, to the success of the conference, the proceedings, and this book.

In particular, we thank John Mellor, Just Faaland, Per Pinstrup-Andersen, Peter Hazell, and Winfried von Urff (a coeditor of the 1992 proceedings volume) for their guidance and support from the conception of the idea for the conference in 1990 to the final publication of this book. We thank Engelbert Veelbehr and other members of the staff of DSE for planning and conference arrangements. We are particularly grateful to Lourdes Hinayon, Jay Willis, and Heidi Fritschel at IFPRI for their help in producing the book. Very special thanks go to Julie Witcover, whose tremendous contribution to the proceedings volume was underacknowledged. Finally, we are grateful to Laurie Goldberg, Julie Ruterbories, and Bridget Minietta for conference planning and support.

We are indebted to two external reviewers, whose comments helped focus the book's messages and trim it. Special thanks also go to the authors of the book's chapters, all of whom displayed unwavering support and great patience.

In addition to IFPRI core funding, for financial support for the conference and the preparation of this book we thank the German Ministry for Economic Cooperation, the Norwegian Ministry of Cooperation, the Government of Japan, and the U.S. Agency for International Development via the Food Security Cooperative Agreement with Michigan State University.

Sustainability, Growth, and Poverty Alleviation

1 Introduction: The Critical Triangle of Links among Sustainability, Growth, and Poverty Alleviation

STEPHEN A. VOSTI AND THOMAS REARDON

In many developing areas, populations are growing quickly and agriculture is growing slowly. The widening gap between food production and food needs can erode foreign exchange reserves and raise food prices, both of which hurt the poor and dampen overall economic growth. Agricultural growth thus remains central among policymakers' priorities in most developing countries: rapid increases in food and fiber output in the developing world are imperative.

Although successes in poverty alleviation have been achieved over the past three decades, partly because of successes in food-crop technology, rural poverty remains unacceptably high and is threatening to grow. This poverty ruins lives and undermines development, the environment, and political stability (see, for example, Lipton 1991; Cleaver and Schreiber 1994; Pinstrup-Andersen and Pandya-Lorch 1995).

In most of the developing world, increased crop output will have to come from higher yields, not more land under the plow. As the arable land frontier is closing or is closed in all but a few countries, higher yields will require the intensification of agriculture on land already cleared. Much progress in yields can be made with existing technologies, even in less favorable agroclimates and fragile areas such as the Sahel or the East African highlands (see Reardon et al. 1994a; Scherr et al. 1995). Nevertheless, yields per hectare for many crops in many areas are still well below potential. Output per workday can also rise, helping the poor. Yield increases in some areas will require technological innovations, for example, in areas of intensive lowland rice production (Plucknett 1993).

Whether it becomes more extensive or intensive, agriculture will transform the environment, as agriculture always has. An important issue is whether, and how, agricultural growth can be compatible with conservation of the farmland natural resource base and of the commons (the forests, wetlands, and bushlands). The environmental threat takes diverse forms across agroecological zones and countries. For example, biodiversity loss takes place in all agroecological zones but has drawn most international attention in the tropical

1

FIGURE 1.1 The critical triangle of development goals

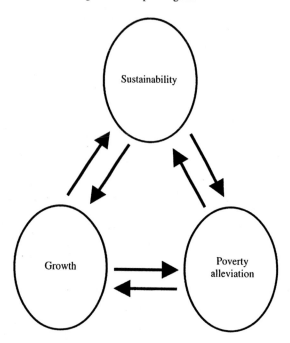

moist forests (Conservation International 1992). Some areas (in particular those having undergone a Green Revolution) have agricultural pollution problems (see Pingali, Chapter 15). But in most developing countries, the biggest problems are land and water degradation, which decrease crop yields and increase food costs, pushing many into poverty (World Bank 1992b; Reardon et al. 1994a).

A major challenge is to find policies, institutions, and technologies to make the three goals (growth, poverty alleviation, and sustainable natural resource use) more compatible. In the long term, it is easy to see that the three goals are complementary: for example, sustaining the natural resource base will help agricultural productivity growth. But these complementarities may take generations to play out, and many natural resources may be lost and many millions poorly fed in the meanwhile.

In the short term, there may be trade-offs among the three goals. These trade-offs will differ over policy contexts (countries) and agroecological zones. In agroclimatically unfavorable zones where agricultural intensification is difficult and expensive, reducing poverty may require putting more land under the plow—which can undermine poverty alleviation efforts over time by causing degradation of fragile margins—or finding alternative income sources. In agroclimatically more favorable zones, where cropping intensification is more practicable and sustainable, there is more potential to pursue growth without cultivating fragile hillsides, forests, or common grazing lands.

To make the three development goals more compatible, and do so over diverse zones and policy contexts, much more must be learned about the links between agricultural growth, poverty alleviation, and the sustainable use of natural resources, and the factors that condition these links (see Figure 1.1). Particularly little is known about two sides of this "critical triangle"—how agricultural growth interacts with the environment and how poverty interacts with the environment.[1]

Purpose and Structure of the Book

This book has four objectives:

1. to examine links among three critical development objectives—agricultural growth, poverty alleviation, and the sustainable[2] use of natural resources in rural areas of the developing world, especially the links between agricultural growth and sustainability and the links between poverty alleviation and sustainability;
2. to examine the nature and determinants of the links by agroecological zone and geopolitical area within major zones (the humid and subhumid tropics, the arid and semi-arid tropics, and the tropical highlands);

---

1. There is an established and growing literature on natural resource economics (see, for example, Carlson, Zilberman, and Miranowski 1993 and Dixon et al. 1994), which deals mainly with developed country issues (for example, pollution of groundwater from excessive use of chemicals, or erosion from tractor tillage). When this literature treats developing countries, the focus is generally on pollution in urban areas or runoff and salinization problems in large irrigation projects (for example, see Pearce and Warford 1993: chap. 7). Poverty and peasant-related issues are not commonly addressed. The more recent "sustainability" literature is developing concepts (theoretical and operational) of sustainability (what to sustain, how long to sustain it) (see, for example, Lynam and Herdt 1989; Lele 1991; Rapport 1992; Ruttan, Chapter 2, this volume; and Kruseman, Hengsdijk, and Ruben 1993 for a review of this literature). Economic and interdisciplinary perspectives on analyses of sustainability are also emerging (see, for example, Kuik and Verbruggen 1991; Chambers and Conway 1992; Fresco and Kroonenberg 1992; Pezzey 1992; Bebbington 1993; Ehui and Spencer 1993; Smit and Smithers 1993; and Stomph, Fresco, and van Keulen 1994). Relatively rare are systematic treatments of the links among agricultural growth, poverty alleviation, and environmental change, although contributions have been made (see, for example, Coxhead 1993; Kruseman, Hengsdijk, and Ruben 1993; Vosti 1993; and Cleaver and Schreiber 1994).

2. The Technical Advisory Committee of the Consultative Group on International Agricultural Research (TAC/CGIAR) defines sustainability as "the successful management of resources for agriculture to satisfy changing human needs while maintaining or enhancing the quality of the environment and conserving natural resources" (CGIAR/TAC 1989:3). Although the term "sustainability" has been used to describe the conservation of a vast array of biophysical and sociocultural processes (see Ruttan, Chapter 2), it is used here to refer specifically to the conservation of the natural resource base and the flows of services and outputs derived from that base.

3. to examine the policies, technologies, institutions, and other factors that condition these links;
4. to draw implications for the design and implementation of policies, technologies, and institutions to make as compatible as possible, and pursue as much as possible, all three objectives.

The book focuses on rural households and communities, key actors in natural resource management. Their behavior is the main determinant of the links between agricultural growth and sustainable use of the environment, and between poverty and the environment. The book does not address urban issues but does examine rural-urban relations pertinent to links among the three development objectives. The book also does not explore the links between growth and poverty alleviation, for which a large literature exists (see, for example, Lipton 1989; Hazell and Ramasamy 1991).

The present volume grew out of the proceedings of an international conference that addressed the links mentioned earlier. The conference was held in October 1991 in Germany, sponsored by the International Food Policy Research Institute (IFPRI) and the Deutsche Stiftung für Internationale Entwicklung (DSE), and brought together social and physical scientists and policymakers from developing and developed countries.[3] Several chapters were prepared subsequent to the conference to fill key gaps. The primary audience of the volume is policymakers, policy and technology researchers, and graduate and advanced undergraduate students.

Part I of this book (Chapters 2 through 12) addresses the concept and definitions of "sustainability" and examines the links between sustainability, growth, and poverty alleviation in rural areas of the developing world, touching on implications of and factors conditioning those links. Part II (Chapters 13 through 23) examines the nature of the links and the policy and technology implications thereof for particular agroecological zones and contexts. Chapter 24 discusses conclusions and gaps in current knowledge about the critical triangle goals and the links among them.

Overview of Findings

The Concept of Sustainability

Ruttan (Chapter 2) reviews the evolution of the concept of sustainability. He notes that an operational definition should focus on sustaining livelihoods of the rural poor, based on a variety of activities: cropping, livestock husbandry, agroforestry, resource extraction from the commons or open-access

---

3. The conference proceedings, with the papers as they were presented and discussants' comments, is Vosti, Reardon, and von Urff (1992).

areas, and nonagricultural activities. Sustainability does not necessarily imply "small-scale" or "low-input" agriculture, or any particular natural resource use, crop mix, production technique, or scale of operation. Sustainable livelihoods can be earned in activities that are large or small scale, with techniques intensive in external inputs or not.

Links among Sustainability, Growth, and Poverty Alleviation

SUSTAINABILITY-GROWTH LINKS.   Several points emerge from an examination of the effects of agricultural change on the environment and vice versa. First, the critical issue, as de Haen (Chapter 3) notes, is not whether there should be agricultural growth or how fast it should be, but how to undertake such growth so that the natural resource base is not degraded. Population pressure in many areas is forcing farmers to shift from extensive production systems to intensive systems that make use of more inputs, especially fertilizers. In other areas, failure to intensify agriculture has led to the extension of farming onto fragile margins (for example, hillsides) and consequent natural resource degradation (Celis, Vedova, and Ruano, Chapter 23, illustrate this for the Central American highlands). In Africa, where farmers have increased the intensity of land use by shortening fallows, the limits to yield growth are quickly reached (Spencer and Polson, Chapter 14). But there are justified worries in some areas of the developing world that increasing use of external inputs (such as chemical fertilizers and pesticides) can cause environmental damage. These concerns need to be addressed, but within the context of poverty-environment and growth-environment links.

Second, agricultural growth needs to combine sustainability—whereby private and common land and water resources are protected and degradation is stopped and reversed—with intensification where there are land constraints. Moreover, intensified use of privately held land for agriculture can reduce pressure on the commons and open-access areas, hence growth through intensification can even help the environment.

Third, diversifying economic activity and diversifying product mix on farms can be important to making growth and sustainability more compatible. Various chapters (such as de Haen, Chapter 3, and Reardon and Vosti, Chapter 10) note that diversification of income sources into nonagricultural activities is needed in some areas to reduce pressure on the land and to finance land improvements and buy inputs produced off-farm, especially where agricultural intensification is under way. In some cases it may be better to promote nonagricultural income generation activities in areas where agricultural growth is difficult to promote or where the environmental consequences of growth are severe. Working off-farm is then an "escape valve" that reduces reliance on fragile land and pays the food bill. Cunha and Sawyer (Chapter 13) make this point for the Amazon, as do Matlon and Adesina (Chapter 16) for the Sahel. Jodha (Chapter 20) and Getahun (Chapter 22) note that diversification of agricultural activities can also move farming away from production patterns that damage the environment toward niche production strategies better suited to fragile soils, such as horticultural and perennial crops.

Fourth, households and communities in a given region do not make decisions in a vacuum, and the results of their choices have repercussions beyond the boundaries of their farms or common areas. For example, Jodha (Chapter 20) and Celis, Vedova, and Ruano (Chapter 23) note that timber demand in far-off urban areas can affect land use on the hillsides of Nepal or Guatemala.

POVERTY-ENVIRONMENT LINKS. The links between poverty and the use of natural resources are the focal point of numerous chapters, and several key messages can be extracted. First, in the long run, if the resource base sustaining livelihoods is degraded and if restoration and conservation investments are not made, increased poverty is unavoidable. In the short to medium term, however, poverty-environment links are less clear. Reardon and Vosti (Chapter 4) present a framework for analyzing the links between poverty and the environment in rural areas. They distinguish poverty types by categories of assets, and environment by type of natural resource problem. The framework places particular emphasis on farm household income and investment strategies as determinants of the links. They find that a concept of "conservation investment poverty" is more relevant than the standard notion of "welfare poverty" in analysis of poverty-environment links. Moreover, they show that the strength and direction of the poverty-environment links can differ depending on the composition of the assets held by the rural poor, on the types of environmental problems they face, and on policies and extant natural resource management technologies and their costs. For example, if the poor are poor in farmland and depend on the commons for their livelihood, barring access to the commons (through regulations) will reduce degradation of the commons but hurt the poor. Or, where local externalities (such as agricultural pollution or overgrazing) exist, alleviating poverty may not be sufficient to avoid the degradation associated with these externalities. In the latter situation, poverty alleviation (wealth creation) can even increase degradation of the environment: richer farmers use more agricultural chemicals than do poor farmers, and richer landowners hold a greater proportion of wealth in cattle, putting additional pressure on remaining forested lands and hillsides for pasture formation. Similar increases in degradation occurring alongside poverty alleviation are evident among pastoralists in West Africa, where richer households hold larger herds of cattle and thus denude more bush area. In areas where poverty is pushing farmers into fragile lands, however, the vicious circle of poverty and degradation is often observed. Alleviating poverty in these cases can reduce pressure on the marginal lands, and degradation can be avoided, reduced, or even reversed.

In some cases, the unsustainable harvesting of resources can alleviate poverty, though not indefinitely (Cunha and Sawyer, Chapter 13). In such cases, barring the poor who depend on such resources from using them may exacerbate poverty, unless alternative strategies for income generation are promoted.

Health can be considered a component of wealth, hence illness an element of poverty. Von Braun (Chapter 5) examines the links between environmental degradation and human health in two scenarios: intensification via Green Revolution–type technical change in agriculture and intensification to raise output. In both, health and nutrition are affected by changes in food available per capita. If food output grows more slowly than population, nutrition declines. Certain technologies, beneficial if used correctly, can hurt health and nutrition if used incorrectly. For example, pesticides and irrigation can be important for agricultural intensification. But pesticides can harm farmers and consumers if excessively or incorrectly applied. Irrigation can provide breeding grounds for disease vectors. The poor health that results from these incorrect uses can in turn hurt agricultural productivity—undermining successful intensification—and increase poverty, which in turn hurts the environment. Policies, technologies, and institutional innovations that promote better sanitation, access to clean water, and control of tropical diseases are needed as agriculture is intensified. Thus increasing the complementarity among sustainability, growth, and poverty alleviation may require policy action outside the agricultural sector.

Factors Conditioning the Links

Policies, technologies, institutions, population pressure, agroclimatic conditions, and climate change can affect the links among sustainability, growth, and poverty alleviation by affecting the choices of rural households and communities, and the physical, social, and economic context in which these choices are made. These factors have the potential to increase the compatibility among the three objectives.

POLICIES. Relating specific policies to specific environmental, growth, or poverty alleviation outcomes is a complex task. Policy effects can be direct or not, intended or not, and quick or not. A given policy change can affect many different economic decisions and actors at once, and the aggregate of these can affect each of the critical development objectives. Four types of policies are discussed in this volume: (1) international trade policy; (2) macroeconomic, sectoral, and subsectoral policies; (3) natural resource policies; and (4) population policies.

A key point made by most authors in this volume is that the broader the policy instrument (say trade or macroeconomic policy), the broader and hence less predictable the effect will be on the environment or its links with growth or poverty alleviation. For example, Siamwalla (Chapter 8) points out that trade policies affect overall economic behavior of large groups of producers and consumers, which in turn affects the environment. He argues that such policies are too blunt to be relied upon for influencing the use of natural resources in desired ways. Policies that directly affect access to and use of natural resources will generally be more effective and efficient tools for such purposes. Misguided use of trade policies to try to achieve environmental goals can have unwanted consequences. Siamwalla illustrates with the case of Thailand, where use of policies to stem trade in cassava to address deforestation hurt the rural poor. A more appropriate set of policy instruments in that case would have included land titling laws, forest access regulations, and natural resource pricing reforms.

Yet most developing countries may have to take some broad policies as "givens." Lipton (Chapter 11) and Celis, Vedova, and Ruano (Chapter 23) note that developing countries are not always free to set their own trade policies and therefore may suffer the environmental consequences of the trade policies of others (mainly developed countries), for which national policy instruments cannot compensate. Perhaps the only trade policy with unambiguous consequences is a transfer policy—international debt relief—that reduces developing country debt burdens and is perhaps best achieved by a drop in international interest rates.

Barbier (Chapter 9) argues that macroeconomic and sectoral policies also affect natural resource use and degradation in farmlands and in the commons, but the size and nature of these effects will vary by context. Macroeconomic policies are generally more difficult or even dangerous to use expressly to influence natural resource use. Even sectoral policies can have unintended side effects. Barbier, like Siamwalla, advises caution in the use of such instruments for environmental improvement, especially when more targeted policies such as taxes, charges, and subsidies are available.

Barbier argues that priority should be given to the reform of government policies that appear to damage the environment and hurt welfare and equity. Counteracting such policy failures will often require complementary institutional reforms and subsector interventions. Moreover, public investments can influence—cause or redress—resource degradation and economic welfare; failure to account for these effects can be perilous. Improved economic analysis of the impacts and the causes of degradation is crucial, as is the integration of environmental objectives in policymaking. The key to success, once again, is to undertake this analysis in the context of poverty-environment and growth-environment links.

Nevertheless, expected environmental gains from policy change are often not realized because of structural impediments in the economy. Barbier (Chapter 9) points out that the conditions necessary for macroeconomic policies to have their desired effect on the environment—such as clearly defined and enforced property rights, efficient markets, corrective taxes and regulations, and the democratic allocation of public funds—are not generally met in rural areas of developing countries and are often notoriously difficult to realize in practice. Government interventions and private investments will be required to create proper enabling conditions, as will empowerment of local communities and the creation of stable and effective ways of defining and protecting property rights. At issue are what type of intervention, how much, when, and by whom—all of which have immediate implications for national action, local action (Chopra and Rao, Chapter 21), and development assistance.

Policy affects the environment via its effects on the actions of rural households and communities—the most important actors in the pursuit of sustainability, growth, and poverty alleviation. Households allocate their resources to meet food and livelihood security objectives. In the face of risky natural and economic environments, their planning horizons are often short and focused on immediate survival. Their economic decisions—including output mix, land use, and production technique—in turn affect the environment. Policy influences the incentives and constraints that shape these household decisions. Community investments in infrastructure (social and physical) influence household decisions, and communities' resources and actions can promote private food security and conservation initiatives (Chopra and Rao, Chapter 21).

Policy needs to aim first at helping farmers to meet food needs and then at encouraging and enabling them to fit into their income and investment strategies the natural resource management practices and investments needed to assure long-term sustainability. Policies that aim at natural resource conservation but undermine household food security strategies will fail.

Reardon and Vosti (Chapter 10) focus on how policy influences resource allocation decisions at the household and community levels and on what determines resource conservation investments (such as bunds, terraces, windbreaks, and practices such as organic matter application). They begin by comparing traditional "productivity investments" (such as irrigation, fertilizer, and modern seeds) with "conservation investments" and find that the latter have different requirements and characteristics. These differences point to the need for innovative policies beyond just "getting prices right" to encourage and enable farmers to make these investments. The three nonprice policies they recommend that stand out are (1) complementary public infrastructure investments (such as culverts to divert water flow from farm bunds) that make household investments more profitable, (2) institutional innovations that improve security and transferability of resource tenure, and (3) modified community-level arrangements that improve the management of the commons or watershed.

Chopra and Rao (Chapter 21) illustrate the latter in northwest India. They show how the national government encouraged community action through complementary infrastructure provision. Spencer and Polson (Chapter 14), Matlon and Adesina (Chapter 16), and Whitaker, Kerr, and Shenoi (Chapter 18) also provide examples of such institutional innovations in the semi-arid and humid zones.

However, authors disagree when assessing the impact on poverty of more "secure" resources. Siamwalla (Chapter 8), Pingali (Chapter 15), and Jodha (Chapter 20) point to instances where poverty was alleviated because the poor (especially the landless) appropriated common property in situations where use rights were ambiguous. More restrictive land tenure in such instances might have barred them from land, key to their survival, especially during times of stress.

Several implications for natural resource policy emerge. First, macroeconomic and sectoral policies that provide a stable platform for general economic growth and do not tax agriculture as a sector are necessary but not sufficient to promote good natural resource management by rural households and communities—sound natural resource policies and investments are needed.

Second, policymakers would do well to identify and implement systems of secure and transferable rights for natural resources that internalize negative production and consumption externalities—the environmental and other costs that result as by-products of production or consumption processes. These systems can be traditional or nontraditional, but the most successful policies will probably combine elements of both. An eye should be kept on the resource use rights of the poor, however. As land use systems intensify, the incentive to establish these rights will rise, and the poor's access to these resources will often be reduced.

Third, natural resource policies need to fit overall development (growth and poverty alleviation) objectives and vice versa. Policymakers in most developing countries treat growth and poverty alleviation as top priorities, and relegate environmental concerns to secondary status. Rather than argue that their priorities should be reversed (which would not long be politically sustainable), we argue that natural resource policies should not clash with development goals—instead, they should be mutually reinforcing.

Fourth, natural resources that are locally abundant but regionally or globally scarce are often underpriced and consequently overexploited. In such cases, governments can and should intervene to remove the disparity between the market value and the "scarcity value" of the resource, while making sure that such actions do not undermine food security strategies of households and communities depending on these resources. But the challenge lies in successfully intervening over long periods in settings where markets are poorly developed, infrastructure is poor, and enforcement is difficult (as discussed earlier).

Finally, policies affecting the prices of agricultural factors such as land and water can be of special value. Land taxes, for example, can promote the clear definition and potential transferability of property rights (Cunha and Sawyer, Chapter 13), as well as provide resources for local development (Celis, Vedova, and Ruano, Chapter 23). But land taxes, or any tax on natural resources held by the poor, can increase food insecurity (von Braun, Chapter 5).

TECHNOLOGIES. A key challenge is to design technologies that simultaneously meet growth and sustainability goals—"overlap technologies"—that can be adopted and efficiently used by farmers, including poor farmers. This will be a difficult task, but no substitute strategy is appropriate; low-input agriculture falls short of providing desperately needed output increases, and unmodified Green Revolution technologies or improved techniques not accompanied by resource conservation investments can eventually undermine the resource base.

To meet this challenge, Oram (Chapter 12) argues that traditional, commodity-based agricultural research and extension programs should be reoriented and restaffed to focus on agroecological zones and on a variety of products (crops, livestock, forests, and agroforestry). Extension needs to be a more helpful conduit among agricultural researchers, farmers, and policymakers. But these modifications should not supplant important plant and animal breeding and agronomic research needed to increase and stabilize yields. Research to raise and sustain yields and to conserve the natural resource base must coexist and be effectively integrated.

De Haen (Chapter 3) and Lipton (Chapter 6) warn that progress in finding technologies that combine growth and sustainability objectives will be slow for several reasons. Finding such technology packages that are also affordable and adoptable will be difficult. The task is made harder still as research budgets and support for agricultural research are cut. Developed country biases associated with traded technologies will become more severe, requiring more changes to make such technologies appropriate for developing country ecosystems and poor farmers.

For these overlap technologies to be adopted, Reardon and Vosti (Chapter 10), Spencer and Polson (Chapter 14), and Matlon and Adesina (Chapter 16) stress that they must be affordable to farmers. This can be achieved by (1) improving the technologies' short-term profitability; (2) promoting technologies that are consistent with farm households' short-term objectives for food security and income diversification, and consistent with labor availability, farm management skills, and cash constraints; (3) increasing access to rural credit; (4) increasing farmers' contribution to the design of technologies and improving the quality and coverage of extension services for these technologies; and (5) increasing the security and transferability of resource tenure, especially of those resources in danger of degradation.

Adoption and sustained use of overlap technologies may also require complementary public investments such as irrigation, wells, and culverts. Reardon and Vosti (Chapter 4) and Whitaker, Kerr, and Shenoi (Chapter 18) point out that this is especially important where economies of scale in public investments require large initial financial outlays and where maintenance expenditures cannot be met by households or communities.

The adoption of more sustainable agricultural practices will not be quick or uniform across farm households (Reardon and Vosti, Chapter 4), as many farmers lack the cash, labor, or managerial skills to adopt the more complicated forms of sustainable technologies, such as integrated pest management or nutrient cycling, or to make bulky conservation investments such as terraces or bunds. Therefore, equity issues linked to the early adoption of these technologies by better-off farmers may be a concern, and, where appropriate, this concern can be addressed by appropriate price policies and targeted extension, as well as public investments.

But the adoption of overlap technologies needs to be widespread. Unsustainable practices on nonadopting farms can harm neighbors and degrade the shared resource base, thereby creating negative externalities that undermine progress made by adopting farmers. The nonadopters may well be the poorest (in the conservation investment poverty sense discussed in Reardon and Vosti, Chapter 10). And von Braun (Chapter 5) notes that technical change that marginalizes the rural poor (especially the landless) can hurt the environment as the poor push onto marginal lands to meet food needs.

INSTITUTIONS. Institutions are the set of community and state organizations that set, enforce, and embody legal and social rules and norms that affect households' use of the environment, among other things. They also influence property rights, wealth distribution, and risk sharing in the community.

Reardon and Vosti (Chapter 4) note that generalized poverty erodes traditional community risk-sharing or insurance institutions by overtaxing them, forcing the poor to fend for themselves, often turning to resource mining and commons-dependent strategies. Von Braun (Chapter 5) points out that poor communities lack resources for community-level investments such as physical infrastructure, health, and education. Policies that strengthen traditional institutions and make them more flexible (particularly in the face of increasing population pressure) can reduce poverty and the dependence of the rural poor on resource mining, especially in response to droughts and floods.

Most authors note, however, that while traditional tenure systems may achieve development objectives under low population density (Jodha, Chapter 20; Chopra and Rao, Chapter 21; Getahun, Chapter 22), such systems may not be compatible with rapid economic change and large increases in population pressure (Lipton, Chapter 6). Therefore, merely strengthening traditional institutions will not be enough—substantial innovation is needed. Chopra and Rao note that governments can encourage and facilitate community institutional innovations for watershed management by linking public investments to these self-help innovations. Oram (Chapter 12) and Celis, Vedova, and Ruano (Chapter 23) highlight the roles of farmer groups and nongovernmental organizations (NGOs) in identifying, testing, and promoting overlap technologies.

POPULATION PRESSURE. Many chapters mention demographic issues, especially population growth, which increases pressure on resources and can spur processes that degrade the environment. Reducing population growth would reduce trade-offs between growth and sustainability. Lipton (Chapter 11) examines how population growth, and responses to it, affect the rural environment. He finds that decreasing population pressure in fragile areas is neither necessary nor sufficient to guarantee sustainable natural resource management. Fewer mouths to feed also means fewer able bodies to effect sustainable technical change. It must be through reductions in desired household fertility— or through outmigration—that population pressure can be eased. Sustainable and equitable development will reduce the number of children rural households want. Family planning and provision of contraceptives are complements to, not substitutes for, rural development.

AGROCLIMATIC CONDITIONS. Most chapters discuss the effects of agroclimate (soils, rainfall, ground- and surface water, sunshine) on the nature and potential, as well as the limits, of agriculture (particularly on product mix, technology choice, and productivity). Those characteristics of agriculture in turn affect labor use and incomes, hence poverty, and affect the environment both on- and off-farm, hence sustainability. Thus, agroclimate conditions the critical linkages among development goals. For example, the physical processes of resource degradation and recuperation, the externalities generated by agricultural production, the level and incidence of poverty and health problems, and population density may be similar within homogeneous agroclimatic zones. The effects of agroclimate can be assessed by dividing study areas geographically into agroclimatic or agroecological zones (AEZs). (See the appendix to this chapter for details and a map of AEZs of the developing world.) De Haen (Chapter 3) does this in his assessment of sustainability-growth links. Part II of this book examines all the links by presenting chapters that focus on each of the three zones that make up the majority of the tropics (the arid and semi-arid tropics, the humid and subhumid tropics, and the tropical highlands), while maintaining their emphasis on the nation-state, which is still the main unit of policy design and implementation.

CLIMATE CHANGE. At the most aggregate level, Downing and Parry (Chapter 7) show that potential increases in global mean temperatures and the increasing likelihood of extreme climatic events (like droughts and floods) can affect growth-environment-poverty links in the tropics. These effects differ by agroecological zone.

Conclusion

This volume's analysis of the links among sustainability, growth, and poverty alleviation highlights certain key approaches to development strategy and practice.

1. The agendas of environment and agricultural growth and poverty alleviation are *linked:* pursuing one without regard to the others is a path of failure in the long run.

FIGURE A1.1 Agroecological zones of the developing world

1. Warm arid and semi-arid tropics
2. Warm subhumid tropics
3. Warm humid tropics
4. Cool tropics (tropical highlands)
5. Warm arid and semi-arid subtropics
6. Warm subhumid subtropics
7. Warm/cool humid subtropics
8. Cool subtropics (summer rainfall)
9. Cool subtropics (winter rainfall)

SOURCE: Food and Agriculture Organization of the United Nations.

NOTE: The rainfed lengths of growing periods (LGPs) for the zones are as follows: arid, fewer than 75 days; semi-arid, 75–180 days; subhumid, 180–270 days; seasonally dry, fewer than 270 days; humid, more than 270 days. The thermal regimes for the zones during the rainfed LGPs are as follows: warm, average daily temperature greater than 20°C; cool, average daily temperature less than 20°C. Zones 5–9 include temperate areas. Zones 5–8 are characterized by summer rainfall; zone 9, by winter rainfall.

2. The links between poverty and environment and between growth and environment are conditioned by complex interactions among policies, technologies, and institutions. This complexity is exacerbated by differences in the links across agroecological zones. There is thus no simple solution such as low-input agriculture or local participation, or even renewals of Green Revolution approaches. Instead, there is a hard path ahead to seek combinations of innovative approaches that will find and promote "overlap technologies" that sustain the resource base while meeting ambitious but necessary growth goals.

3. The key actors are rural households and communities, who put as top priority today's survival and food security. Solutions that are aimed at helping the environment without helping rural economies to grow and become less poor will, in the end, neither meet environment goals nor be sustainable.

Appendix: Agroecological Zones of the Developing World

Identifying relatively homogeneous sets of natural resource characteristics is one way to delineate geographic areas that correspond to a certain level of agricultural potential. Such areas have been identified in the tropics based on climatic variables. The areas are termed "agroecological zones," or AEZs (CGIAR/TAC 1992).

In general, an AEZ is characterized by its rainfall and solar radiation patterns during the cropping season. In many cases, these climatic parameters are correlated with a broader set of natural resources (such as soil types and qualities), the quality and quantity of which influence the potential range of agricultural yields and product mixes (given available agricultural technologies and prices). Agricultural research institutions often find it practical to consider AEZ divisions in the tropics as clear and fixed (that is, not moving targets) to permit researchers to focus on the identification of policies, institutions, and technologies that affect the use of natural resources in given areas. Of course, in reality the borders of AEZs are not well-defined or stable (because the border depends on climatic variables, which fluctuate over years, and technologies and prices, which also change).

Figure A1.1 shows the nine major agroecological zones of the developing world. As mentioned, such a breakdown is somewhat arbitrary, involving selection of boundary levels of rainfall and solar radiation to separate the zones. Moreover, to address some issues, such as technology change or product mix, it can be helpful to further disaggregate into subzones or to aggregate to combinations of zones. Several chapters in Part II of this book do just that.

Concepts and Determinants of the Links among Sustainability, Growth, and Poverty Alleviation

2 Sustainable Growth in Agricultural Production: Poetry, Policy, and Science

VERNON W. RUTTAN

> Contemplation of the world's disappearing supplies of minerals, forests and other exhaustible assets has led to demands for regulation of their exploitation. The feeling that these products are now too cheap for the good of future generations, that they are being selfishly exploited at too rapid a rate, and that in consequence of their excessive cheapness they are being produced and consumed wastefully has given rise to the conservation movement.
>
> —Hotelling 1931

In this chapter I review the evolution of the sustainability concept and describe three "classical" systems of sustainable agriculture, none of which were or are capable of generating growth of output consistent with modern rates of growth in demand. The following sections discuss three unresolved analytical issues that divide the conventional resource economics and sustainable development communities, and then broaden the focus of the sustainability debate. The final sections discuss monitoring issues and argue that sustainable growth in agricultural production should be viewed as a research agenda rather than as a package of practices available to producers whether in developed or in developing countries.

When confronted with the task of defining sustainable agriculture, one's natural inclination is to finesse. "I don't think I can define it [sustainability] without unduly constraining the free flow of my thoughts" (Hopper 1987:5). Hopper's inclination to avoid the issue of definition reflects the emergence of sustainability as a banner under which many movements, with widely disparate reform agendas, have been able to march while avoiding confrontation over their often mutually inconsistent goals.

I am indebted to Randolph Barker, Yassir Islam, Richard Norgaard, C. Ford Runge, Robert M. Solow, Theodore Graham-Tomasi, and Stephen A. Vosti for comments on an earlier draft of this chapter.

19

Definitions of Sustainability

In spite of the advantages of avoiding defining a term that has apparently been adopted precisely because of its ambiguity, it is useful to trace the evolution of the concept. The term was first advanced in 1980 by the International Union for Conservation of Nature and Natural Resources (IUCN 1990; Lele 1991). Before the mid-1980s, the term had its widest currency among critics of what were viewed as "industrial" approaches to agricultural development (Harwood 1990:3–19). Proponents had traveled under rhetorical vehicles such as biodynamic agriculture, organic agriculture, farming systems, appropriate technology, and, more recently, regenerative and low-input agriculture (Dahlberg 1991).[1]

Gordon K. Douglass identified three alternative conceptual approaches to the definition of agricultural sustainability (Douglass 1984:3–29). *One group* (primarily mainstream agricultural and resource economists) defines sustainability primarily in technical and economic terms. It is the capacity to meet the expanding demand for agricultural commodities on increasingly favorable terms. The long-term decline in the real prices of agricultural commodities is viewed as evidence that the growth of agricultural production has been following a sustainable path. In contrast, a sustained rise in the real prices of agricultural commodities would be interpreted as evidence of unsustainable agriculture.

Douglass identifies a *second group* that regards agricultural sustainability primarily as an ecological issue for whom "an agricultural system which needlessly depletes, pollutes, or disrupts the ecological balance of natural systems is unsustainable" (Douglass 1984:2). This group believed that the present world population is already too large to be sustained at present per capita consumption (Goodland 1991).[2]

A *third group*, traveling under the banner of "alternative agriculture," places its primary emphasis on sustaining not just the physical resource base but a broad set of community values (Committee on the Role of Alternative Farming Methods in Modern Production Agriculture 1989). This group draws inspiration from the agroecological perspective. But it often views conventional science-based agriculture as an assault not only on the environment but on rural communities. Its adherents take as a major objective the strengthening or revitalization of rural culture and rural communities guided by the values of stewardship and self-reliance.

---

1. Sandra Batie regards the concept of sustainable development "as the latest step in a long evolution of public concern with respect both to natural resources and to the environment. . . . Prior to World War II those concerns . . . emphasized technically efficient development of such resources for use as commodities. After World War II, the emphasis shifted to the aesthetic and amenity use of natural resources" (Batie 1989:1083).

2. This view stems in part from a naive carrying capacity interpretation of the potential productivity of natural systems (Raup 1964).

By the mid-1980s, the sustainability concept was diffusing rapidly from the confines of its agroecological origins to include development in general. The term had been appropriated by the broader development community. A sampling of the definitions that have been advanced in support of particular agendas is listed in the appendix to this chapter. The definition that has achieved the widest currency is that adopted by the Brundtland Commission: "Sustainable development is development that meets the needs of the present without compromising the ability of future generations to meet their own needs" (World Commission on Environment and Development 1987:43).

The Brundtland Commission definition raises the possibility that it may be necessary for those alive today, particularly those living in the more affluent societies, to curb consumption to avoid an even more drastic decline in future generations' consumption. This is not a welcome message to societies that have found it difficult to use resources to address current poverty issues (Ruttan 1989). The historical experience, at least in the West, often causes skepticism about obligations to future generations. "We have actually done quite well at the hands of our ancestors. Given how poor they were and how rich we are, they might properly have saved less and consumed more" (Solow 1974:9). In most of the world, the ancestors have not been so kind. This suggests that the future may be too important to be left to either market forces or historical accident, even in the more affluent societies.

In spite of its challenge to current consumption in the developed countries, it is hard to avoid a conclusion that the popularity of the Brundtland Commission definition is due, at least in part, to the definition's being so broad that it is almost devoid of operational significance. The sustainability concept has undergone what has been referred to as "establishment appropriation." It is undergoing the same "natural history" as earlier reform efforts.

Initially, a "progressive" rhetoric is advanced by critics as a challenge to the legitimacy of dominant institutions and practices. If the groups and symbols involved are sufficiently threatening to the dominant institutions, these institutions will attempt to respond to these challenges by appropriating or embracing the symbols. "In so doing, these dominant institutions—such as the World Bank and the agricultural universities—are typically able to demobilize the movement" (Buttel 1991:7). Buttel argues that sustainability has been embraced by both radical reformers and neoconservatives because it moves the focus from achieving greater participation of the poor in the dividends from economic growth to protecting an impersonal nature from the destructive forces of growth (Buttel 1991:9). Lack of official attention to the issues of population policy and poverty alleviation at the 1992 Earth Summit in Rio de Janeiro would seem to provide evidence in support of Buttel's cynicism.

A more positive view might be that in a world that has become increasingly disillusioned about improving the well-being of the poorest, sustainability represents "a disguised method of keeping social justice on the political agenda of neo-conservative regimes" (Buttel 1991:17).

Sustainable Agricultural Systems in History

It is not uncommon for a social movement to achieve the status of an ideology while still in search of a methodology or a technology. If the reform movement is successful in directing scientific and technical effort in a productive direction, it becomes incorporated into normal scientific or technical practice. If it leads to a dead end, it slips into the underworld of science, often to be resurrected when the conditions that generated the concern again emerge on the social agenda.

Research on new uses for agricultural commodities is one example. It was promoted in the 1930s under the rubric of "chemurgy" and in the 1950s under the rubric of "utilization research" as a solution to the problem of agricultural surpluses. It lost both scientific and political credibility because it promised more than it could deliver. It emerged again in the late 1970s and early 1980s in the guise of enhancing "value-added."

Integrated pest management represents a more fortunate example. This term emerged in the 1960s to signify an alternative to chemical-intensive pest control and was appropriated in the 1970s as a rhetorical device to paper over the differences between ecologically oriented and economically oriented entomologists (Palladino 1989). At the time the terminology was adopted, there were few pest control technical packages that could credibly be regarded as either technologically or economically viable "integrated" pest control. After two decades of scientific research and technology development, there are now practices that meet the definition of integrated pest management as visualized by those who coined the term.

In the case of sustainable agricultural systems, several historical examples of systems that proved capable of achieving sustainable increases in agricultural production can be drawn upon. One example is the forest and bush fallow (or shifting cultivation) systems practiced in most areas of the world in premodern times in temperate areas and today in many tropical areas (Pingali, Bigot, and Binswanger 1987). At low population densities, these systems were sustainable over long periods. As population densities increased, short fallow systems emerged. Where the shift to short fallow systems was slow, as in western Europe and East Asia, farming systems emerged that permitted sustained output growth. Where the transition to short fallow has been quickened by population growth, the consequence has often been soil degradation and declining productivity.

A second example can be drawn from the history of East Asian wet rice cultivation (Hayami and Ruttan 1985). Traditional wet rice cultivation resembled farming in an aquarium. The rice grew tall and rank; it had a low grain-to-straw ratio. Most of what was produced, straw and grain, was recycled as human and animal manures. Mineral nutrients and organic matter were carried into the fields with the irrigation water. Rice yields rose continuously, though slowly, even under a monoculture system.

A third example of sustainable agriculture was the system of integrated crop-animal husbandry that emerged in western Europe in the late Middle Ages to replace the medieval two- and three-field systems (van Bath 1963; Boserup 1965a,b). The new husbandry system arose with the introduction and intensive use of new forage and green manure crops. These in turn permitted an increase in the availability and use of animal manures. This allowed the emergence of intensive crop-livestock systems of production that recycled plant nutrients in the form of animal manures to maintain and improve soil fertility.[3]

The three systems described, along with other similar systems based on indigenous technology, have provided an inspiration for the emerging field of agroecology. But none of these traditional systems has the capacity to respond to modern rates of growth in demand generated by rapid increases in population or income growth. Some traditional systems were able to sustain rates of growth of 0.5–1 percent per year. But modern rates of growth in demand are in the range of 1–2 percent per year in the developed countries. They often rise to the range of 3–5 percent per year in the less developed and newly in-dustrializing countries. Rates of growth in demand in this range lie outside the historical experience of even the presently developed countries!

In the developed world, the capacity to sustain the necessary increases in agricultural production will depend largely on the capacity for institutional innovation. If the capacity to sustain growth in agricultural production is lost, it will be a result of political and economic failure. In most tropical countries, however, it is quite clear that the scientific and technical knowledge is not yet available that will enable farmers to meet current demand or increases in that demand. Further, the research capacity has not yet been established to provide the necessary knowledge and technology. In these countries, achievement of sustainable agricultural surpluses is dependent on advances in scientific knowledge and on technical and institutional innovation (CGIAR/TAC 1989).

The Technological Challenge to Sustainability

Why has concern about the sustainability of modern agricultural systems emerged with such force toward the end of the twentieth century? The first

---

3. Jules N. Pretty notes: "Manorial estates survived many centuries of change and appear to have been highly sustainable agricultural systems. Yet this sustainability was not achieved because of high agricultural productivity—indeed it appears that farmers were trading off low productivity against the more highly valued goals of stability, sustainability, and equitability. These were promoted by the integrated nature of farming; the great diversity of produce, including wild resources; the diversity of livelihood strategies; the guaranteed source of labor; and the high degree of cooperation" (Pretty 1990:1).

reason is the unprecedented demands that growth of population and income are imposing on agricultural systems. One of the most remarkable transitions in the history of agriculture is being completed. Before this century, almost all increases in food production were obtained by bringing new land into production. Agricultural growth within this framework (the "resource exploitation" model) is no longer sustainable. By the first decades of the next century, almost all increases in food production must come from higher output per hectare. In most countries, the transition from a resource-based to a science-based system of agriculture is occurring within a single century. In a few countries this transition began in the nineteenth century, but for many developed countries it did not begin until the first half of this century. In contrast, most developing countries have been caught up in this transition only since midcentury. Among developing countries, this transition has proceeded further in South and Southeast Asia than in Latin America or Africa.

Historical trends in the production and consumption of the major food grains could easily be taken as evidence that one should not be too concerned about the capacity of farmers to meet future food demands. World wheat prices have declined since the 1850s. Rice prices have declined since the 1950s. These trends suggest that productivity growth has more than compensated for the rapid growth in demand from growth in population and income, particularly since World War II. But the past may not be an effective guide to the future. The demands that the developing countries will place on their agricultural producers from growth in population and in per capita consumption will be very high until well into the middle of the next century.

A second reason for concern about sustainability is that the sources of future productivity growth are not as apparent or as attainable now as they were a quarter century ago (Ruttan 1992). For example, incremental responses to increases in fertilizer use have declined. Expansion of irrigated area has become more costly. Maintenance research, the research required to prevent yields from declining, is rising as a share of total research (Plucknett and Smith 1976). The institutional capacity to respond to these concerns is limited, even in the countries with the most effective national agricultural research and extension systems. Indeed, during the 1980s there was considerable difficulty in many developing countries in maintaining the agricultural research capacity that had been established in the 1960s and 1970s (Cummings 1989; Eicher 1991).

It is possible that, within another decade, advances in basic knowledge will create new opportunities for advancing agricultural technology that will reverse the urgency of some of these concerns. The privatization of agricultural research in some developing countries is beginning to complement public sector capacity. Advances in molecular biology and genetic engineering are occurring rapidly. But the rate at which these promising advances will be translated into productive technology has been slower than anticipated.

It is only a slight overstatement to note that advances in crop yields have come about primarily by increasing plant populations per hectare and the ratio of grain to straw. Advances in animal feed efficiency have come about primarily by decreasing the share of feed consumed that is devoted to animal maintenance and by increasing the share devoted to the production of usable animal products. There are severe physiological constraints to continued improvement along these conventional paths. These constraints are most severe in the areas that have already achieved the highest productivity, as in western Europe, North America, and parts of East Asia. Advances in conventional technology will be inadequate to sustain the demands that will be placed on agriculture beyond 2020.

It seems reasonable to expect, however, that advances in molecular biology and genetic engineering will reduce the constraints on productivity growth in the major food- and feedgrains. But advances in agricultural technology will not be able to eliminate what some critics tend to view as a "subsidy" from outside the agricultural sector. Transfers of energy in the form of mineral fuels, pathogen and pest control chemicals, and mineral nutrients from outside the farm sector will continue to be needed to sustain growth in farm production—and in much larger quantities. Until population and demand growth rates fall below 1 percent per year, energy transfers can be expected to continue to expand. Over the long run, scarcity (reflected in rising real prices) of phosphate fertilizer and fossil fuels is likely to become the primary resource constraint on sustainable growth in farm output (Desai and Gandhi 1990; Chapman and Barker 1991).

This leads to what ought to be the primary concern about the sustainability of growth in agricultural production. This third set of concerns is with the environmental spillover from agricultural intensification. These spillover effects include the loss of soil resources due to erosion, waterlogging, and salinization; surface and groundwater contamination from plant nutrients and pesticides; resistance of insects, weeds, and pathogens to present methods of control; and the loss of land races and natural habitats (Conway and Pretty 1991). If agriculture is forced to continue to expand into more fragile environments because of lack of technical progress in more robust soil resource areas, problems such as soil erosion and desertification can be expected to become more severe. Additional deforestation will intensify problems of soil erosion, species loss, and degradation of water quality, and will contribute to climate change.

The sustainability of agricultural production will also be influenced by the impact of continued growth in industry and transportation. There can no longer be much doubt that the accumulation of carbon dioxide and other greenhouse gases—principally methane, nitrous oxide, and chlorofluorocarbons—has set in motion a process that will result in a rise in global average surface temperature over the next 30–60 years. There continues to be great uncertainty about the temperature and rainfall changes that can be expected at any particular date or location. But these changes can be expected to impose substantial adaptation demands on agriculture. The systems that will have the least capacity to adapt will be in countries with the weakest agricultural research and natural resource management capacity, mainly those in the humid and semi-arid tropics (Ruttan 1992). The effects of industrial growth can also be expected to impose substantial health problems on farmers and consumers. The effects of heavy-metal contamination have already affected the quality of crops and of animal and human health in many areas.

Sustainability Is Not Enough

A major issue over the next half-century for most developing countries, including the formerly centrally planned economies, will be how to generate and sustain the advances in agricultural technology that will be needed to meet the demands on their farm sectors. This objective appears to be in direct conflict with the world view of many of the leading advocates of sustainable development.

"Sustainable development" is a concept that implies limits to both the assimilative capacity of the environment and the capability of technology to enhance human welfare. To the sustainable development community, the capacity of the environment to assimilate pollution from human production and consumption activity is the ultimate limit to economic growth (Batie 1989). But this is not a problem that has emerged only during the second half of the twentieth century.[4]

I differ in one fundamental respect from those who are advancing the sustainability agenda. The capacity of a society to solve either the problem of sustenance or the problems posed by the production of residuals is inversely related to population density and the rate of population growth, and is positively related to its capacity for innovation in science and technology and in social institutions (Ruttan 1971). There is earnest concern that the bilateral and multilateral assistance agencies, in their rush to allocate resources in support of

---

4. "Man has throughout history been continuously challenged by the twin problems of (a) how to provide himself with adequate sustenance and (b) how to manage the disposal of what in recent literature has been referred to as 'residuals.' Failure to make balanced progress along both fronts has at times imposed serious constraints on societies' growth and development. The current environmental crisis represents one of those recurring times in history when technical and institutional change in the management of residuals has lagged relative to progress in the provision of sustenance, conceived in the broad sense of the material components of consumption. Furthermore, in relatively high income countries the demand for commodities and services related to sustenance is low and declines as income continues to rise, while the income elasticity of demand for more effective disposal of residuals and for environmental amenities is high and continues to rise. This is in sharp contrast to the situation in poor countries where the income elasticity of demand is high for sustenance and low for environmental amenities" (Ruttan 1971:707).

a sustainability agenda derived more from developed country than from developing country resource and environmental priorities, will fail to sustain the effort needed to build viable agricultural research institutions in the tropics. Africa, in particular, has been the victim of a succession of donor enthusiasms —integrated rural development, farming systems research, agroforestry programs, and others—for which program rhetoric has preceded the technical and institutional knowledge and capacity necessary for program implementation.

It is important that the sustainability community embrace an agenda that includes building (1) the capacity for improvement in the natural components of sustenance, particularly in low-income countries, and (2) the capacity to reduce the environmental stress associated with the production of residuals generated by agricultural and industrial production. Three unresolved issues are identified here that must be confronted before such a commitment can be translated into an internally consistent agenda for reform.

The Issue of Substitutability

There is inadequate knowledge in respect to the role of technology in widening the substitutability among natural resources and between natural resources and reproducible capital. Economists and technologists have traditionally viewed technical change as widening the possibility of substitution among resources—of fertilizer for land, for example (Solow 1974; Goeller and Weinberg 1976). The sustainability community rejects the "age of substitutability" argument. The loss of plant genetic resources is viewed as a permanent loss of capacity. The elasticity of substitution among natural factors and between natural and produced factors is viewed as very low (James, Nijkamp, and Opschoor 1989; Daly 1991). This is an argument, in economists' language, over the form of the production function. While the argument is often cast in philosophical terms, it is essentially an empirical issue of great importance. If, on the one hand, a combination of capital investment and technical change widens the opportunity for substitution, imposing constraints on present resource use could leave subsequent generations worse off. If, on the other hand, real output per unit of natural resource input is narrowly bounded—cannot exceed some upper limit that is not too far from where it is now—then catastrophe is unavoidable.

Obligations toward the Future

The second issue dividing the traditional resource economics and sustainability communities is how to deal analytically with the obligations of the present generation toward future generations. Intergenerational equity is at the center of the sustainability debate (Pearce, Barbier, and Markandya 1990; Solow 1991). Environmentalists have been critical of the approach used by resource and other economists in valuing future benefit and cost streams. The economists' approach involves the calculation of the "present value" of a resource development or protection project by discounting the cost and benefit stream by a "real interest rate" (the interest rate adjusted for inflation). It is World Bank policy (but not always practice) to require a 10–15 percent rate of return on projects. These rates are set well above long-term real interest rates (historically less than 4 percent) to reflect the effect of unanticipated inflation and other risks associated with project development and implementation.

The environmental critics insist that this approach results in a "dictatorship of the present" over the future. At conventional rates of interest, the present value of a dollar of benefits 50 years in the future approaches zero. "Discounting can make molehills out of even the biggest mountain" (Batie 1989: 1092). Solow has made the same point in more formal terms. He notes that if the marginal profit—marginal revenue less marginal cost—to resource owners rises slower than the rate of interest, resource production and consumption occur sooner and the resource is more quickly exhausted (Solow 1974; Lipton 1992).

A question that has not been adequately answered is whether, as a result of the adoption of a widely held sustainability "ethic," the market-determined discount rates would decline toward the rate preferred by those advancing the sustainability agenda.[5] Or will it be necessary to impose sumptuary regulations to induce society to shift the income distribution more strongly toward future generations? In most countries, efforts to achieve sustainable growth in agricultural production must involve some combination of (1) higher current rates of saving, that is, deferring present in favor of future consumption, and (2) more rapid technical change, particularly changes that enhance resource productivity and widen the range of substitutability among resources.

Incentive-Compatible Institutional Design

Third, improvement is needed in the design of institutions to make them capable of internalizing—within households, private firms, and public organizations—the costs of negative spillovers that create environmental stress. Under present institutional arrangements, important elements of the physical and social environment continue to be undervalued for purposes of both

---

5. The question of the impact of the use of a positive discount (or interest) rate on resource use decisions is more complex than is often implied in the sustainability literature. Simply lowering the discount rate to favor natural resource users will not assure slower drawdown of natural resources if the market rate of interest remains high. Recipients of the lower interest rates may transfer the revenue from resource use to investments that have higher rates of return rather than reinvesting to sustain the flow of resource benefits. Furthermore, high rates of resource use can be consistent with either high or low interest rates. In the case of forest use, for example, a low discount rate favors letting trees grow longer and planting trees. A low discount rate makes it profitable to invest in mining, land and water development, or other investment projects that might otherwise be unprofitable. That is why resource economists and environmentalists have argued for higher interest rates on public water resource projects (Graham-Tomasi 1991; Norgaard 1991; Price 1991). As an alternative to lower discount rates, Mikesell (1991) suggests taking resource depletion into account in project cost-benefit analysis.

market and nonmarket transactions. Traditional production theory implies that if the price of a resource is undervalued, it will be overused, even if that imposes large costs on society.

The dynamic consequences of failure to internalize spillover costs can be even more severe. In an environment characterized by rapid economic growth and changing relative factor prices, failure to internalize resource costs will bias the direction of technical change.

The process is apparent in agriculture. In the United States, federal farm programs have encouraged farmers to grow a few crops, to grow them continuously, and to use chemical-intensive methods in production (General Accounting Office 1990). Over the long run, one effect of U.S., European Community, and Japanese agricultural commodity programs has been to bias the direction of technical change by making land more expensive. Until very recently, the capacity of the environment to absorb the residuals from crop and livestock production has been treated as a free good. As a result, scientific and technical innovation in both the public and private sectors has been biased toward the development of land substitutes: plant nutrients, plant protection chemicals, and management systems that reflect the overvaluation of land and the undervaluation of the social costs of the disposal of residuals. In retrospect, it seems that the same biases in factor prices have led to underinvestment in pest and soil management technologies consistent with the social value of environmental services (Runge et al. 1990).

The design of incentive-compatible institutions—institutions capable of achieving compatibility between individual, organizational, and social objectives—remains an art rather than a science. The incentive-compatibility problem has not been solved even at the theoretical level.[6] There has been a failure to design institutions capable of achieving distributional equity anywhere in the world. If equity cannot be improved today, can intergenerational equity be promoted?

Monitoring Global Change

The three issues discussed here—substitutability, obligations to the future, and institutional design—remain unresolved at both the analytical and policy levels. This gap requires approaching the issues of technology and institutional design pragmatically. As noted earlier, indirect and aggregate measures—such as changes in relative prices of natural resource commodities and services, and partial and total productivity measures—have traditionally

---

6. The concept of incentive compatibility was introduced by Hurwicz (1972), who shows that it is not possible to specify an informationally decentralized mechanism for resource allocation that also generates efficient resource allocation and incentives for consumers to reveal their true preferences (see also Groves, Radner, and Reiter 1987).

been used to monitor changes in sustainability. Even these relatively gross measures are not available in many countries or regions. It is important that such data be developed and reported on annually for individual countries, for major regions within countries, and for major natural resource stocks and the services they provide.

But such measures will be incomplete. They capture the ex post consequences of resource availability, technological change, and environmental change. "Needed are data on the size and value of the resource base, its integrity and health, the wastes generated by production and consumption, and human influence—locally, nationally, and globally on resources and the environment" (Mathews and Turnstal 1991). It is important that a more sensitive set of resource, environmental, and health indicators be made available to analysts and to policymakers. These monitoring requirements are characterized here.[7]

Land and Water Resources

During the past several decades, there have been improvements in national and international capacity to observe and interpret global land-cover changes. An important start has been made in the estimation and mapping of indicators of soil degradation. But many of the data used for the indicators are subjective estimates. For example, U.S. estimates of the magnitude of soil erosion and the effects of soil erosion on land productivity come from only two sample surveys (Crosson 1986). In most countries the data used for such estimates come from a few studies that were not designed to generate estimates for the whole country. Capacity to monitor changes in the availability and quality of water resources, the erosion of genetic resources, and changes in other resource endowments relevant to agricultural sustainability is even less adequate than that for land resources.

Climate Change

The capacity to monitor and interpret the implications of projected climate changes on agricultural potential and on the production of other natural resource commodities and services globally, and in specific regions, is also severely limited and will remain so. Climate changes, in turn, affect temperatures and temperature extremes. These changes can also affect the seasonality, geographic distribution, frequency, and intensity of rainfall. Increased carbon dioxide concentration induces climate changes. More carbon dioxide can also stimulate the growth of some crops and weeds. But its effect under field conditions remains uncertain. Therefore, careful monitoring of the dimensions

---

7. For details, see WRI 1990a; Mathews and Turnstal 1991; and Ruttan 1994. Mathews and Turnstal and WRI assess efforts to develop environmental indicators.

of climate change and analysis of the implications of these changes for resource productivity will be important. The economic organization and technical conditions of agricultural production may be dramatically different several decades from now, when climate change may have proceeded far enough to induce significant response by agricultural producers.

Health

Changes in agricultural production associated with climate, resource, and technical change will affect human health. These include (1) the direct effects of agricultural practices, such as the trauma and toxic effects associated with the use of machinery and chemicals; (2) the indirect effects, related to changes in farming systems and income distribution; and (3) the effects of land conversion and more intensive farming on health.

In most countries, health indicators are highly subjective. Effective monitoring is dependent on carefully designed and conducted surveys. The establishment of links between changes in agricultural practices and health will require careful interdisciplinary research that relates changes in agricultural technology, farming systems, and land use to rural health and production. It is easier to measure pollution or contamination than to link the indicators to changes in either the ecosystem or human health.

An Uncertain Future

Mankind is far from being able to design adequate technological or institutional responses to issues of achieving sustainable growth in agricultural production or, put more generally, achieving sustainable growth of both the sustenance and amenity components of consumption.

At present, there is no package of technology available to transfer to producers that can assure the sustainability of growth in agricultural production at a rate that will enable agriculture, particularly in the developing countries, to meet the demands that are being placed on it.[8] Sustainability is appropriately viewed as a guide to future agricultural research agendas rather than as a guide to practice (Ruttan 1988; Graham-Tomasi 1991). As a guide to research, it seems useful to adhere to a definition that would include (1) development of technology and practices that maintain or enhance the quality of land and water resources, and (2) improvement in the performance of plant and animal production and in production practices that will ease the substitution of biological technology for chemical technology. The research agenda on sustainable agriculture

---

8. There is a large literature in agronomy, agricultural economics, and related fields that reports on research on developing or transferring sustainable agricultural practices. For examples, see other chapters in this volume; Board on Agriculture, National Research Council 1991; Board on Agriculture and Board on Science and Technology for Development 1992.

should be to explore what is biologically feasible without being too limited by present economic constraints.

Sustainability advocates have not been able to advance a program of institutional innovation or reform that can provide a credible guide to the organization of sustainable societies. Institutions that can assure intergenerational equity have not yet been designed. Few would challenge the assertion that future generations have rights to levels of sustenance and amenities that are at least equal to those enjoyed (or suffered) by the present generation. They also should inherit improvements in institutional capital—including scientific and cultural knowledge—needed to design more productive and healthy environments.

My conclusion on institutional design is similar to that advanced in the case of technology. Economists and other social scientists have made a good deal of progress in contributing the analysis needed for "course correction." But capacity to contribute to institutional design remains limited. That the problem of designing incentive-compatible institutions has not been solved, even in theory, means that institutional design proceeds on an ad hoc, trial-and-error basis. The errors are expensive. Institutional innovation and reform should be a high priority on the research agenda.

Appendix: Definitions of Sustainability

Ecological Sustainability

1. "Sustainable agriculture is both a philosophy and a system of farming. Sustainable agricultural systems rely on crop rotations, crop residues, animal manures, legumes and green manures, off-farm organic wastes, appropriate mechanical cultivation and mineral bearing rocks to maximize soil biological activity, and to maintain soil fertility and productivity. Natural, biological and cultural controls are used to manage pests, weeds and diseases. . . . We can no longer go on pretending that the energy-dependent, environmentally destructive systems of the past can be passed on as sustainable agriculture" (Hill 1990, quoted in Loyns and MacMillan 1990).

2. "Alternative agriculture is any system of food or fiber production that systematically pursues the following goals: more thorough incorporation of natural processes such as nutrient cycles, nitrogen fixation, and pest-predator relationships into the agricultural production process; reduction in the use of off farm inputs with the greatest potential to harm the environment or the health of farmers and consumers; greater productive use of biological and genetic potential of plant and animal species; improvement of the match between cropping patterns and the productive potential and physical limitations of agricultural lands to ensure long-term sustainability of current production levels; and profitable and efficient production with emphasis

on improved farm management, conservation of soil, water, energy and biological resources" (Committee on the Role of Alternative Farming Methods in Modern Production Agriculture 1989:4).

3. A sustainable system is "a system that can be maintained almost indefinitely in the same site, that over the long term enhances the environment and quality of life for farmers and society, and does not negatively affect the environmental system" (Gomez-Pompa et al. 1991:19).

4. "Sustainability should be treated as a dynamic concept, reflecting changing needs, especially those of a steadily increasing population. . . . The goal of a sustainable agriculture should be to maintain production at levels necessary to meet the increasing aspirations of an expanding world population without degrading the environment. It implies concern for the generation of income, the promotion of appropriate policies, and the conservation of natural resources" (CGIAR/TAC 1989:2–3).

Developmental Sustainability

5. "Sustainable development is not a fixed state of harmony but rather a balanced and adaptive process of change. . . . Sustainability takes for granted a balance between economic development—all quantitative and qualitative changes in the economy that offer positive contributions to welfare—and ecological sustainability—all quantitative and qualitative environmental strategies that seek to improve the quality of an ecosystem and hence also have a positive impact on welfare" (Nijkamp, van den Bergh, and Soeteman 1991:156).

6. "Sustainability has assumed particular importance because (of) the sharp drop in living standards that has accompanied adjustment programs in many countries. . . . We term real output growth sustainable if it exceeds population growth" (Faini and de Melo 1990:496).

7. "Project sustainability . . . [is] the maintenance of an acceptable net flow of benefits from the project's investments after its completion—after the project ceased to receive both financial and technical support" (Cernea 1987:118).

8. "Sustainability can be introduced into CBA [cost-benefit analysis] by setting a constraint on the depletion and degradation of the stock of natural capital. Essentially the economic efficacy objective is modified to mean that all projects that yield net benefits should be undertaken subject to the requirement that environmental damage (that is, natural capital depreciation) should be zero or negative. However, applied at the level of each project such a requirement would be stultifying. Few projects would be feasible. At the programme level, however, . . . it amounts to saying that netted out across a set of projects the sum of individual damages should be zero or negative" (Pearce, Barbier, and Markandya 1990:58–59).

3 Environmental Consequences of Agricultural Growth in Developing Countries

HARTWIG DE HAEN

All types of agriculture interfere with the ecosystems in which they are placed. The challenge is to undertake agriculture in such a way that there is an acceptable balance between short-term benefits from production and long-term benefits from preservation of the ecosystems and the conservation of the resource base for agriculture. The acceptable balance is determined by people's needs, preferences, and technological and economic options. These determinants change with demographic and social change, technical progress, and economic growth.

Much of the developing world has a great need for rapid agricultural growth to meet food and fiber needs for rapidly growing populations, industries, and foreign exchange requirements. Agricultural growth in these countries also spurs farm and nonfarm employment. Nonfarm growth is spurred through production and consumption linkages between agriculture and non-agriculture. Farm output increases also drive down the costs of food, which makes up a large share of the poor's budget in rural and urban areas (Mellor 1976; Hazell and Röell 1983).

The critical issue, then, is not *whether* there should be agricultural growth in developing countries or *how fast* it should be, but *how* to undertake such growth. Traditional low-input agriculture is not generally a solution for growth, as it typically allows only growth on the order of 1 percent annually, well below population growth rates in most of the developing world (Ruttan, Chapter 2, this volume). It also cannot be hailed as environment-friendly, as many of these agricultural systems are no longer in equilibrium with nature. The traditional

I am most grateful to David Norse, Reshma Saigal, and Timothy Aldington for their comments and very helpful assistance on an earlier draft of this chapter. The views expressed here are my own and do not necessarily reflect those of FAO or its member governments.

"co-evolutionary process" (Norgaard 1984), in which societies and ecosystems had sufficient time and space to adjust mutually through complex feedback mechanisms, is no longer adequate. Moreover, the land frontier has fully or nearly disappeared in much of the developing world, so farmers are choosing—or being forced—to move from extensive systems (where more land is brought under cultivation) to intensive systems (where more inputs are added to given land).[1] With population growth and farmers' rational quest to extend farming to meet immediate food security or income augmentation objectives, extensive systems have helped push farming, grazing, and gathering onto fragile margins (for example, hillsides), leading to erosion. This is particularly a problem in Africa, which has been relatively late in shifting from extensive to intensive systems.

Where farmers have intensified merely by adding more labor to fixed areas of land and by shortening fallows, limits to yield growth are quickly reached. For intensification to cause the land to yield more, improved seeds, irrigation, and fertilizer and other inputs are necessary. But there are justified worries in the developing world and many areas of the developed world that large increases in fertilizer, pesticide, and irrigation use can cause ecological damage such as biodiversity loss and salinization.

Thus the methods of agricultural growth in developing countries need to combine sustainability—whereby private and common land and water resources are protected and degradation is stopped and reversed—with intensification, whereby more production is induced from essentially static land resources. In turn, managing agricultural growth in a way that assures the quality and quantity of land and water resources, and biodiversity on- and off-farm, will ensure the resource base for productive agriculture into the future.

I argue here that there are a number of promising technologies that combine sustainability with intensification and a number of policy and institutional conditions that will promote their adoption. Even so, much more research is needed in national and international research systems to create more such technologies. Moreover, agroecologies across the tropics are so diverse that the paths to sustainable intensification will vary substantially and solutions will be highly location-specific. Finally, the solutions will need to involve public investments in infrastructure and training, include rural people as participants, and fit their objectives of food security and employment. Protection and rehabilitation of the natural resource base requires that rural people want to, and can, make the needed investments. Nations are no different: they will act if economic gain and environmental protection go together.

---

1. FAO (1988) estimates that over the next decade, on average, less than 20 percent of the increases in food production will come from area expansion and the rest from intensification through yield increases and multiple cropping in irrigated areas.

The first two sections of this chapter explore in more detail the problems related to combining growth and sustainability. First the extent and types of degradation of resources are described, and then the issues specific to four agroecological zones of the tropics are discussed. The next two sections discuss solutions: illustrations of technologies and strategies that combine growth and sustainability, and recommendations for technology and policy strategies.

Extent and Types of Resource Degradation

Land, water, biodiversity, and energy are key resources for agricultural production. There are limits to these resources under current costs and technologies, and degradation is making them even more limited. In this section, the state of these resources and their degradation are reviewed.

Land

The United Nations Environment Programme/International Soil Reference and Information Centre (UNEP/ISRIC 1991) notes that of 4,700 million hectares of agricultural land (including pasture) worldwide, some 900 million (19 percent) are moderately degraded and 300 million (6 percent) are very degraded (where the biotic functions are destroyed and the soil can again be productive only at high cost). Table 3.1 shows that deforestation is responsible for 32 percent, overgrazing for 33 percent, and mismanagement of arable land for 28 percent of land degradation. From another angle, water erosion is responsible for 62 percent, wind erosion for 23 percent, and chemical and physical degradation for 15 percent of degradation.

Stoorvogel and Smaling (1990) found, in a study of 38 countries of Sub-Saharan Africa, that 16 countries have average annual net nutrient losses per hectare of more than 20 kilograms of nitrogen, 10 kilograms of phosphorus 205, and 20 kilograms of potassium 20, and another 6 countries have double these losses. These losses occur in combination with high erosion and declining yields, and together may exceed the benefit from the use of the affected land. In Kenya, there was also loss of organic carbon in the soils, which partly explains why Stoorvogel and Smaling found that the highest maize yield response was from combined use of organic and mineral fertilizer.

Water

Water resources in developing countries suffer from several types of degradation. One important problem is salinization. Irrigated area has grown 50 percent over the past 20 years. Yet, of the 165 million hectares under irrigation in developing countries, some 20–30 million hectares are affected by salinity, and another 25 percent are threatened by it. The Food and Agriculture Organization of the United Nations (FAO) estimates that 1–1.5 million hectares of irrigated land are abandoned annually, mainly because of salt damage.

TABLE 3.1 Soil degradation by type and cause (classified as moderately to excessively affected)

| | Erosion | | | | Other Forms of Degradation | | | | Total | |
| | Water | | Wind | | Chemical | | Physical | | | |
	Million Hectares	Percentage of Total	Million Hectares	Percentage of Total	Million Hectares	Percentage of Total	Million Hectares	Percentage of Total	Million Hectares	Percentage of Total
Africa	170	53	98	31	36	11	17	5	321	100
Asia	315	70	90	20	41	9	6	1	452	100
South America	77	56	16	12	44	32	1	0	138	100
North and Central America	90	65	37	27	7	5	5	3	139	100
Europe	93	59	39	25	18	11	8	5	158	100
Australasia	3	50	—	—	1	17	2	33	6	100
Total	748	62	280	23	147	12	39	3	1,214	100

Major Causes by Type of Degradation (Percentage)

	Water	Wind	Chemical	Physical	Total
Deforestation	43	8	26	2	32
Overgrazing	29	60	6	16	33
Mismanagement of arable land	24	16	58	80	28
Other	4	16	12	2	7
Total	100	100	100	100	100

SOURCE: Adapted from UNEP/ISRIC 1991.

Another problem is that groundwater levels are sinking, and saltwater is intruding into coastal areas. Finally, where agriculture uses high levels of fertilizers and pesticides (a small share of developing country agriculture), aquifers are being polluted by nitrates and pesticide residues.

Biodiversity

Biological diversity is the genetic variety of plants and animals. This gene pool is useful in the pursuit of higher productivity and disease resistance through plant and animal breeding and biotechnology. Yet the widespread introduction of modern varieties of annual and perennial crops and livestock types has begun to narrow the range of domesticated breeds and species. Deforestation, the elimination of natural biotopes, and the use of nonspecific pesticides are accelerating the extinction of wild species. The rate of deforestation in developing countries increased from 10 to 17 million hectares annually over the period 1980–1990. Reversing these trends may mean short-term income loss for rural people but would be an investment in growth potential.

Energy

Agriculture in developing countries uses only 5 percent of total fossil fuel energy. If its use of fertilizers, pesticides, and farm machinery (which embody energy) rose substantially, so would the drain on global fossil energy. Yet a fundamental shift toward nonfossil fuels in a major way is not on the medium-run horizon. Costs of biomass energy production still well exceed those of fossil fuel. In addition, biomass fuel production might also increase pressure on the land, hence it might be preferable to use more gas or kerosene. Major efforts will be necessary to diversify the sources of energy, including solar and wind power, and to increase the efficiency of energy use.

Growth and Degradation Issues by Zone

The following subsections examine these issues more closely in four tropical agroecological zones.

Drylands and Areas of Uncertain Rainfall

Drylands are areas in the subtropical and cool climates with less than 500 millimeters of rainfall and a growing period of less than 120 days. Areas of uncertain rainfall are largely subhumid but with light, erratic rainfall. They make up almost half of the land area of developing countries (3.4 billion hectares, of which 2 billion are usable for agriculture) and support about 500 million people, including 50 million pastoralists. Crop production is constrained by soil moisture availability and irregularity of rainfall. Annual losses from desertification are 6 million hectares, caused mainly by overstocking of animals and conversion of pasture into arable land.

There are two options for growth in this zone: increase irrigation and increase the efficiency of use of rainfall. The latter includes (1) early warning and accurate short-term weather forecasting to ensure optimal adaptation of production and storage; and (2) soil and water conservation using, for example, contour bunds, minimum tillage, water harvesting, mulching, and agroforestry. Because of the frequently high fiscal and environmental costs of implementing new irrigation projects, increasing efficient use of rainfall may be more socially desirable than increasing irrigation in many locations.

The main challenge is to promote income-earning opportunities not only in agriculture but also in the nonagricultural sector, which will help relieve pressure on land. Agricultural technologies should focus on environmentally friendly technologies (such as conservation tillage, stress-tolerant varieties, and integrated pest management) given the fragility of the land and constraints on carrying capacity. Stabilizing farm income and increasing off-farm income will reduce the need for the poor in these areas to maintain excessively large livestock herds and misuse common property resources to survive. With more rapid nonagricultural growth, some of the marginal areas will be abandoned, and rehabilitation may then be too costly in comparison to alternative investments. But for now, even agricultural use of land with low economic returns contributes to the survival of millions of people and might continue to do so for the next generation.

Irrigated Areas

Sixty percent of grain production in developing countries is under irrigation, which increases yields relative to rainfed agriculture and reduces pressure to push onto marginal lands. FAO estimates the area under irrigation and naturally flooded lowland rice at about 200 million hectares by the end of the 1980s, having grown by 10 percent over the preceding decade.

Avoiding the problems engendered by irrigation (discussed earlier) may require lower water use intensity and thus lower yields. However, increasing costs of excessive water consumption can promote the use of more efficient water management techniques that do not necessarily lower yields. Subsidies and inefficiencies have sometimes led to excessive input use or excessive water consumption, particularly where water was provided at low or zero cost. Moreover, some large-scale irrigation schemes were not profitable from the outset, especially in Sub-Saharan Africa (see Matlon and Adesina, Chapter 16, this volume). Small-scale irrigation can be more economically viable and socially attractive because of the participation of local communities and better integration into natural ecosystems. Unfortunately, finding natural resource conditions conducive to the establishment and maintenance of small-scale irrigation is not easy. Shallow groundwater or drainage systems that permit irrigation in dry periods are requirements generally not met.

Humid and Subhumid Lowlands

More than 1 billion people live in the humid and subhumid lowlands, which cover about 3.1 billion hectares, most of them under forest, with 500 million hectares of arable land and 70 million hectares of cultivated perennials. These areas account for 80 percent of root and tuber production in developing countries. The major cause of their ecological instability is the reduction of tree cover, mainly as a result of the encroachment of agriculture. Population pressure has caused bush fallow periods to shorten substantially—a symptom as well as a cause of the decline in soil fertility.

To promote the intensification of agriculture in the limited area available, economic and institutional incentives are needed for increasing the use of fertilizer, the introduction of legume-based cropping systems and agroforestry, and the application of integrated pest management. Moreover, land use should be adjusted through appropriate mixes of regulations and incentives to safeguard the remaining natural biotopes and reduce unsustainable practices. More alternative income sources are needed, or migration into less vulnerable areas must take place.

Hill and Mountain Areas

These areas account for nearly 1 billion hectares. Many areas have slopes greater than 30 percent, where soil erosion is a severe problem. In general, they are relatively densely populated, and some have very high population densities, as much as 600 inhabitants per square kilometer in Rwanda or in the Himalayas. About 500 million people (approximately as many as in the dryland zone, and half as many as in the humid/subhumid zone) depend on agriculture as the primary income source in this zone—in an area one-third the size of the dryland zone.

Land protection measures and improvements in rural infrastructure may require costly investments in this zone. The more sustainable production systems tend to include cash crops, requiring commercialization, market outlets, and transportation. Yet in landlocked countries with limited competitiveness, families with only 0.5–1 hectare may find cash cropping too risky and instead prefer annual subsistence crops that are less ecologically viable. Moreover, von Braun, de Haen, and Blanken (1991) found that in Rwanda nonagricultural employment is also important to households in these areas, as it reduces pressure on fragile landholdings and allows families to maintain ecological sustainability of land use systems.

Complementarities between Growth and Sustainability: Illustrations

It is not easy to identify technologies that improve resource management in such a way that economic benefits exceed costs (leaving aside the possible gap between economic and farm-level benefits). Delays between causes and effects, and the variability of impacts over time, require long-term observation. Moreover, determining whether new technologies will be adopted is a complex undertaking, as adoption is a function of both household objectives (economic gain or food security) and constraints (such as credit limitations, risk aversion, lack of knowledge, and traditional land tenure rules). Objectives and constraints, as well as adoption rates and impact of practices, need to be monitored and analyzed if one is to be certain that a new technology is attractive and affordable and combines growth and sustainability elements. For such analysis and monitoring, farming systems research is needed (Byerlee and Collinson 1982; Chambers and Ghildyal 1985; FAO 1986; de Haen and Runge-Metzger 1989).

It is encouraging, however, that agricultural research has indeed found promising technologies that combine improved resource management with growth of agricultural incomes. Three examples—soil nutrient systems, integrated pest management, and land improvement investments—are described here.

Restoration of Soil Fertility

Integrated plant nutrition systems can be highly profitable at the farm level, even taking risk into account. An example from Kenya was discussed in a previous section. Yet fertilizer application rates are low in Sub-Saharan Africa. Modifications to extension services could contribute to some improvement in fertilizer use efficiency, but the key lies in both policy and farm level measures to overcome production risk, lack of farmer cash income, and distribution and marketing infrastructure constraints such as excessive margins, untimely deliveries, lack of transparency and competition, and low and unpredictable product prices.

Integrated Pest Management

Farmers sometimes use excessive doses of pesticides, despite the harm to the environment as well as loss of profits, both as a precaution and because of ignorance of the harm done to the ecosystem. Integrated pest management (IPM) campaigns therefore have had considerable success in a number of countries by persuading farmers to apply fewer sprays, to respect economic break-even points for pesticide use, and to replace toxic chemicals by biological or mechanical protection. The FAO's regional IPM program in Asia for rice systems has turned nearly 500,000 rice farmers into IPM experts through a system of "training the trainers." The program also persuaded governments to eliminate subsidies on pesticides. Figure 3.1 illustrates the effect: higher farm income, reduced use of chemicals, and even increased yields.

The adoption of IPM is helped by public investment in training and research institutions. The cost per trained farmer is relatively low (US$5–15 per farmer).

FIGURE 3.1 Pesticide use, rice production, and pesticide subsidy, Indonesia, 1973–1990

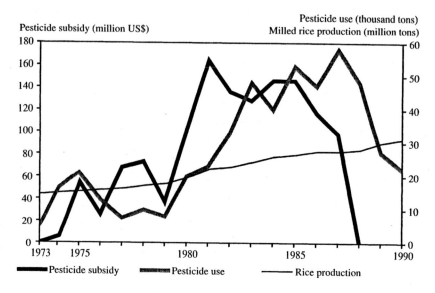

SOURCE: Indonesia, Ministry of Finance, various years.

NOTE: Pesticide production serves as a proxy for pesticide use.

Soil Protection

Slash-and-burn (cutting bush, burning residues, and then cropping without nutrient replacement) can provide immediate returns to farmers. But under conditions of short fallow, productive capacity declines rapidly starting in the second season. Attaviroz (1991) studied slash-and-burn in the northern uplands of Thailand. He calculated net benefits in the region (taking into account effects on downstream areas and water storage capacity). He then compared exploitative monocropping (slash-and-burn) with conservation farming (farming with contour plowing and mulching). He found that, except for the first year of land use, conservation farming was superior to the 15-year simulation (Table 3.2). Where land improvements (in which community labor builds contour bunds or wells to water live windbreaks) are added to the system, net benefits are similar but there is the added benefit of lower off-site erosion. This is an example of the role public investment can play in facilitating the adoption of technologies combining productivity and sustainability.

TABLE 3.2 Net benefits from land use alternatives in the northern upland region of Thailand (million baht)

Year	Exploitative Monocropping	Land Development Alone	Conservation Farming Alone	Conservation Farming + Land Development
1	3,367	−5,394	2,851	−8,272
2	2,374	4,151	4,790	4,838
3	1,608	2,975	4,788	4,836
4–6	1,190	854	4,783	4,465
7–9	−1,423	−1,299	4,777	4,829
10–11	−1,892	−1,536	4,770	4,457
13–15	−2,364	−1,406	4,763	4,452
Net present value[a]	−2,114	−4,244	47,757	35,582

SOURCE: Attaviroz 1991.
[a]5 percent discount rate.

Strategies for Minimizing the Trade-Offs between Agricultural Growth and Environmental Protection

Valuation of Resources

The starting point for reform is an appropriate valuation of environmental resources. The failure to account systematically for degradation has been caused largely by a general (false) belief that natural resources are abundant, free goods. A number of investment projects—for example, those proposing irrigation without proper drainage—would not have been approved if the present value of losses in natural resource capital through salinization had been taken into account.

Whatever the measures used for accounting, all factors that affect the quality and quantity of natural resources should be given due weight in private and public decisionmaking. Resource assessments should be used for land use planning and agroecological zoning, for design of input and resource price policies, and for evaluation of projects and investments.

Poverty Alleviation

Poverty makes the adoption of solutions that imply costs or lost income difficult, if not impossible, for low-income households. For the poor, immediate survival dictates all action. This implies a preference for production over protection. Poverty alleviation is thus essential, even if a direct causal relationship between poverty and environmental degradation does not exist. Many of the poor do not have access to land; much pollution, including global ecological destruction, results from the consumption habits of the rich, not the poor. Nevertheless, poverty alleviation is not only a precondition for the accumulation of resources for investment in resource protection, but also a human and social requirement for a sustainable development path.

Institutional Reform

Reform of the legal and social framework can lead to more equitable access to land and other resources, and clearly defined private responsibilities and rights to property and access (to farmland and common lands). The establishment of such rights is crucial to inducing investments in land improvements. Moreover, a regulatory framework can substitute for missing markets where externalities occur. The use of biodiversity and water resources must be subject to public policy.

Price and Trade Policies

It is well documented that macroeconomic and agricultural policies have often discriminated against sustainable land use practices in developing countries. Overvalued currencies, low procurement prices, and taxation have kept producer prices low in favor of consumers. In many cases, input pricing policies and tax exemptions (or subsidies) have encouraged the excessive use of potentially harmful inputs such as pesticides or the overuse of rangelands or irrigation (where water prices are set much lower than the true scarcity value of water).

Many governments have started to revise such policies as part of structural adjustment programs and more deliberate environmental policy. Although this trend is encouraging, much remains to be done toward an institutional and policy framework that encourages individuals and communities to adopt more sustainable techniques.

Research

Resource-rich as well as resource-poor regions need further research to improve environmental impact assessments and to develop production techniques that are adoptable, profitable, and less environmentally damaging. Such research cannot be promoted merely by setting priorities for public research budgets and by appeal to public-sector researchers. Many actors would thus not be reached, such as private industry researchers or in some cases the farmers themselves.

Environmental policies can encourage demand for more sustainable technologies from researchers—the theory of "induced innovation" applied to the externality problem (Runge 1986). For example, de Haen and Zimmer (1989) show that the ban on certain pesticides in Europe quickly led to the development of less harmful chemicals and to new forms of mechanical weeding.

Research themes need to cover the physical, institutional, and economic aspects of technological change in agriculture and its environmental consequences. Major gaps in knowledge remain, and close only slowly. For example, it is many years since various developed countries introduced legislation limiting soil degradation, but there is still only a partial understanding of the biotic and economic cost of soil erosion, so the effectiveness of such legislation cannot yet be measured. The effects of environmental change (for example, climate, biodiversity, resource degradation) on agricultural potential in developing countries are not well understood. Much of the adaptive and applied research must be conducted in a multidisciplinary way and by national agricultural research systems, given the complex and often site-specific nature of the problems.

Alternative Income Sources

Evidence shows that rural people are already much more engaged in off-farm employment than was previously assumed, but the potential for diversification of rural development needs to be further expanded.

Program and Resource Requirements

In conjunction with the United Nations Conference on Environment and Development's (UNCED) Agenda 21, efforts were made to estimate the additional financial requirement (beyond current spending) of pursuing sustained agriculture and rural development. The figure of US$35 billion for 1993–2000 was calculated. Some US$5 billion of this was estimated as an incremental need for international assistance. These figures may be daunting in today's climate of tight budgets. But such investments will produce substantial economic benefits. The World Watch Institute estimates that yearly losses of grain due to degradation total nearly US$7 billion.

Investments must be preceded by political will and public awareness of the relationship between environmental protection and socioeconomic development. Groups with vested interests must revise their stands, and actors must review their responsibilities in the national and international spheres.

What are the consequences for North-South transfers? First, farmers or rural people can be directly compensated for additional indigenous conservation activities through price increases for earmarked goods or services (for example, specific trademarks for "bioproducts") or through contractual arrangements (for example, debt-for-nature swaps). But we are a long way from

developing a suitable mechanism for such transfers. Second, formal development assistance can help, but it will remain a small proportion of the total cost
of shifting to a more sustainable agricultural growth path. Thus most of the
costs will be borne by developing country governments, communities, and
farmers.[2]

---

2. It is difficult to go beyond rough estimates of the costs and how much will have to be met
by development assistance, because there could be a major shift in the content of agricultural
growth and consequently in the pattern of fixed and variable costs. The proposed emphasis on more
knowledge-based interventions instead of physical capital-intensive approaches—for example,
IPM and biological interventions as opposed to engineering techniques for soil conservation—
implies a relative reduction in resource transfer needs for a given intervention. The IPM project
described in this chapter costs only about US$5–15 per farmer, substantially less than conventional
projects.

4 Poverty-Environment Links in Rural Areas of Developing Countries

THOMAS REARDON AND STEPHEN A. VOSTI

The link between poverty and environment is often mentioned in the "sustainable development" debate but is seldom systematically explored (Lele 1991). The literature that treats the link usually focuses on the "vicious circle" between poverty and degradation. The circle is Malthusian in inspiration: farmers, pushed by population increase and poverty, extend cropping onto fragile marginal lands, degrading them. The latter reduces yields, which further impoverishes farmers (for example, Mink 1993; Pearce and Warford 1993; Dasgupta and Mähler 1994; Celis, Vedova, and Ruano, Chapter 23, this volume). The implications of this focus on the vicious circle of poverty and degradation are that poverty alleviation will necessarily reduce degradation of the environment, and its inverse, that arresting and reversing environmental decline will help the poor (Leonard 1989; Cleaver and Schreiber 1994).

In this chapter we take issue with the narrow focus of the current poverty-environment debate, as well as its logical and practical implications. We outline five sets of gaps in this literature, previewing the main points with respect to each theme, and then introduce and discuss a new conceptual framework to explore poverty-environment links.

First, when the poverty-environment link is discussed for a range of zones and environmental problems, "poverty" is usually treated as a single concept (for example, Leonard 1989). Rarely asked is how the *type* of poverty influences the poverty-environment link. But the range of types of poverty is the range of lack of the various assets (and income flows derived from them): (1) natural

An earlier version of this chapter is Reardon and Vosti (1995). We are grateful to USAID/ Global Bureau, Office of Agriculture and Food Security via the Food Security II Cooperative Agreement at Michigan State University, and to the Government of Japan for support for this research. We are also grateful to Tim Frankenberger, Peter Hazell, Michael Lipton, James Oehmke, Per Pinstrup-Andersen, Sara Scherr, Scott Swinton, participants in the Uppsala Agricultural University Seminar Series, and Julie Witcover for useful comments.

resource assets, (2) human resource assets, (3) on-farm physical and financial assets, (4) off-farm physical and financial assets, (5) community-owned resources, and (6) political capital. A household might be well-endowed in one asset but poor in another, and the type of poverty can influence poverty-environment links. Note that the immediate implication of this decomposition of poverty by asset category is that there is no *single* poverty link, but rather many links that need to be explored.

Second, the literature usually does not differentiate types of environmental change when discussing the poverty-environment link, or it focuses on a particular type of change such as soil erosion. But the environment can be differentiated by the components of natural resources: soil, water, ground cover, biodiversity of wild and domesticated flora and fauna, and air. Expanding the debate to differentiate between types of environmental components, or problems associated with them, can have important implications for understanding the links.

Third, the environment literature does not usually treat poverty measurement issues—level, distribution (over households), and time path (whether it is transitory or chronic)—or how these can affect the poverty-environment links. We show that for poverty-environment analyses these poverty measurement issues matter, and that it is inadequate to limit the measurement of poverty to "welfare poverty," measured according to income, consumption, or nutrition criteria, as is common in the poverty and food security literature. Rather, we argue that the criterion for poverty in poverty-environment analyses should concern the ability to make minimum investments in resource improvements to maintain or enhance the quantity and quality of the resource base, to forestall or reverse resource degradation. A household below this line is termed "conservation-investment poor," to differentiate it from the welfare poor. Households or villages above a welfare-determined poverty line may still be too conservation-investment poor to make, for example, needed soil conservation investments.

Fourth, the strength and symmetry of the causal links between poverty and environment are rarely discussed in the literature. Is poverty alleviation necessary or sufficient to redress environmental problems? Does redressing environmental problems alleviate poverty? In what circumstances? The questions are critical for policy formulation and sequencing. We show that the answers can depend on the type and level of poverty and the type of conservation investments required to address particular environmental problems. Moreover, the dynamics of the links are relatively neglected in the literature, apart from recent treatment of population-environment dynamics (for example, Dasgupta and Mähler 1994). But the links are likely to change over time, and causal directions can change in unexpected ways. For example, the poor may "mine" the soil through intensive cropping without accompanying investments in soil conservation and then use the profits to diversify their incomes away from risky agriculture to protect their medium-term food security; this strategy might, in the longer run, reduce pressure on the land.

Fifth, insights from the literature on farm household economics and household food security strategies (for example, Ellis 1993) have not been brought sufficiently to bear on understanding poverty-environment links. Yet rural household and village income, land use, and investment strategies *determine* the links between poverty and environment. In turn, this behavior is conditioned by factors such as price and interest rate policy, village infrastructure, and technology; hence the practical link to policy and research strategies (see, for example, Reardon and Vosti 1992; Barbier, Chapter 9, this volume).

To address these shortcomings, a new conceptual framework is needed to move the debate on this link into a more practical and strategic domain. Such a framework should first differentiate types of poverty and types of environmental change into categories useful for guiding food security, poverty, and environment policies, and monitoring the effects of policies and projects. Such differentiation is taking place in the debate about the links between general economic growth and agricultural growth, on one hand, and environment, on the other (see, for example, de Haen, Chapter 3, this volume), and the debate about environment and poverty should be deepened and enriched in the same way. In addition, the framework should show the household and community behavioral determinants of the links and how this behavior is conditioned by policy and other factors.

We present such a conceptual framework as a flow diagram in Figure 4.1, relating four blocks of variables: (1) categories of assets of the rural poor; (2) household and village behavior pertinent to poverty-environment links (for example, income generation, investment, land use); (3) categories of natural resources (soil, water, and so forth); and (4) conditioning variables (market conditions, technologies, and so forth). There are several links between the boxes: the asset categories of poverty affect household and village behavior, which in turn affects the quality and quantity of natural resources as well as household and village assets. The conditioning variables influence the links between the types of poverty and behavior, as well as the links between behavior and natural resources.

The next section presents typologies of poverty and of the environment. This is followed by a discussion of behavior of households and communities (in particular, income, investment, and land use strategies). Typologies of poverty and of environment are then linked to household and community behavior, with illustrations from various agroecological zones. The next-to-last section discusses conditioning variables and their effects. A final section summarizes and draws policy implications. The discussion in this chapter is limited to rural areas and focused on resource degradation because it is the major environmental problem in most poor countries.

FIGURE 4.1 Poverty and environment links

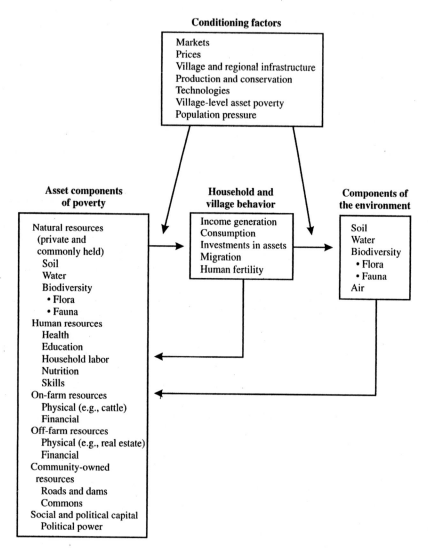

Typologies of Poverty and Environment Relevant to Their Links

Poverty Typology

The asset portfolio of the rural poor may be examined by asking the question, "poor in what?" Households and communities have the following assets: (1) natural resources, composed of water (ground and surface), ground cover, biodiversity of wild and domestic fauna and flora, and soil; (2) human resource endowment, composed of education, health, nutrition, skills, and number of people; (3) on-farm resources (livestock, farmland, pastures, reservoirs, buildings, equipment, financial resources); (4) off-farm resources (local off-farm physical and financial capital); (5) community-owned resources such as roads, dams, and commons; and (6) social and political capital (see Figure 4.1). These assets (stocks) are used to generate flows of products or cash income. The level and composition of that income determine whether households are poor and how poor they are.

An asset decomposition of poverty will be useful only where the fungibility of assets is limited. The existence, conduct, and performance of labor, capital, and product markets, and the distribution of political power condition this fungibility, which, in turn, determines how easily households can convert one form of wealth to another (for example, household labor into farm capital, or land into cash).

Where markets are absent or underdeveloped (even just seasonally), or where there are constraints on market access (tied to resource endowments), one asset market or holding can be isolated from another. Asset-specific poverty can influence livelihood activities and investment decisions with possible adverse implications for some components of the environment. For example, when a family is poor in land, but land is the collateral to obtain credit, the household's ability is limited to acquire cash to make farm and nonfarm capital investments, as well as land improvements to protect soils. This, in turn, limits its ability to diversify into nonfarm activities or to intensify farming. The household is left to resort to extensive farming, implying the need to push onto fragile lands. Or, if access to land is a political privilege, those lacking political clout may be forced to rely on wage labor to survive.

Criterion: Welfare Poverty versus Conservation-Investment Poverty

The literature treating households suffering from what is termed "welfare poverty" uses criteria based on income, consumption, and nutrition, for example, based on a benchmark minimum income sufficient to attain minimum caloric intake (below which one enters "ultra-poverty," according to Lipton [1983]), to meet an anthropometric standard (Lipton and van der Gaag 1994), or to buy a diet just sufficient, given a regional diet level and composition (Greer and Thorbecke 1986). These measures may be appropriate for assessing human misery, but for two reasons may not be the appropriate benchmark for use in assessing poverty levels in the context of analysis of poverty-environment links. First, purely welfare-poverty criteria can miss the potentially large group of households that are not "absolutely poor" by the usual consumption-oriented definition but are too poor—in that their surplus above the minimum diet line is still too small—to make key conservation or intensification investments necessary to prevent their land use practices from damaging the resource base or leading them to push onto fragile lands. Second, welfare poverty analysis generally focuses on households or individuals and is difficult to extend empirically to the community level. Head count and other methods for aggregating poverty have been devised, but these methods fail to capture the amount by which communities fall short of meeting consumption needs or the distribution within the community of surpluses that could be used to make conservation investments.

Rather, for analysis of poverty-environment links, we suggest the use of a measure of "conservation-investment poverty." This is the cutoff point defined as the ability to make minimum investments in resource improvements to maintain or enhance the quantity and quality of the resource base—to forestall or reverse resource degradation. Unlike welfare measures of poverty, the cutoff point for conservation-investment poverty is site specific, a function of local labor and nonlabor input costs and of the types of investment that are needed for the particular environmental problems or risks faced.

Of course, the welfare poor are usually also investment poor. The converse (that the conservation-investment poor are welfare poor) is not necessarily true. Hence anthropometric and welfare poverty maps would not necessarily detect the kind or level of poverty that may be important to poverty-environment links. If a household is above the welfare-poverty line, it can still be conservation-investment poor in four situations: (1) market conditions make it impossible for the household to convert its assets or products into enough cash to make conservation investments; (2) the household can obtain the cash but cannot buy labor or other inputs needed for conservation measures because these inputs are somehow rationed; (3) household income may be somewhat above the welfare-poverty line but is not sufficiently above it to generate an adequate surplus for conservation investment; or (4) the household may choose to use surpluses for consumption, savings, or investments of other types (for example, in education or improved housing).[1] Indeed, given the special requirements and consequences of conservation investments (discussed in Reardon and Vosti, Chapter 10, this volume), one may well expect other types of investments to have "first claim" on household surpluses (Vosti and Witcover 1993).

Moreover, in the long run, if a household is investment poor but not welfare poor, it may lead to natural resource degradation that eventually causes the household to become welfare poor—the vicious circle can be realized.

---

1. Poor farmers may have a high discount rate and may sacrifice long-term goals (for example, conservation investments) for immediate food security via land use mining or income diversification. This is not to suggest that households or communities are irrational or unreasonably myopic in their resource allocation or that opportunities for trading-off short-term welfare for long-term welfare (for example, consuming less to finance land improvement today to ensure sufficient production tomorrow) are not known and sometimes pursued. Rather, such intertemporal trade-offs may be constrained by the composition of household assets and the markets where they can be sold. Households can thus be rational but constrained in their investment and consumption.

Also, a household might be above a conservation-investment poverty line, on average, but have severely unstable income and thus be more averse to risky investments in land improvement.

Environment Typology

The natural environment can be decomposed into the following ecologically interdependent categories: soil, water (ground and surface), biodiversity (of flora and fauna), and air (see Figure 4.1). Depending on which attributes are valued by rural households and what these values are, a particular natural resource (a household asset) may be either harvested, left undisturbed, or even enhanced. Yet some attributes of particular natural resources may not matter to the rural poor, at least in the short to medium run, but may greatly concern policymakers monitoring natural resource stocks—that is, the resources may be valued differently and seen as serving different purposes when viewed from the perspective of the society in general and from that of the rural poor. For example, a large tree can be a valuable "carbon sink" to society, but the rural poor may view the same tree as a source of ash to enhance soils or as timber for sale. This is part of the general problem of negative environmental externalities of a particular farm household's behavior to the rest of society. Society may even view a household as rich in a resource that society values (for example, biodiversity), but this resource may not be considered valuable (at least under current conditions) by the poor household, as markets for converting social value into private wealth and income may not exist.

Behavior of the Poor: The Determinants of Poverty-Environment Links

Figure 4.2 shows the poor household's resource allocation to income-earning activities and investment, and the environmental consequences of this allocation, in a simple two-period dynamic framework. (1) The household starts with a set of household food security and livelihood objectives. (2) In period 1, the household has access to a set of natural resources, human capital, on-farm and off-farm physical and financial capital, community-owned resources, and social and political capital. (3) The household is also faced with a set of external conditioning factors (most notably, prices, policies, technologies, and institutions). (4) The household allocates its labor, land, and capital to income-earning activities and investments in two sectors, agriculture and non-agriculture. (5) The livelihood activities and investments have environmental consequences on-farm and, via externalities, off-farm. (6) The activities and investments, plus the environmental consequences, alter the household's access to resources and capital, hence the household has a new stock of assets as it enters period 2, and begins the allocation again.

Note that the level and type of poverty (in terms of asset categories) affect *what* income and investment strategies the household follows and *how* it carries

FIGURE 4.2 Household resource allocation

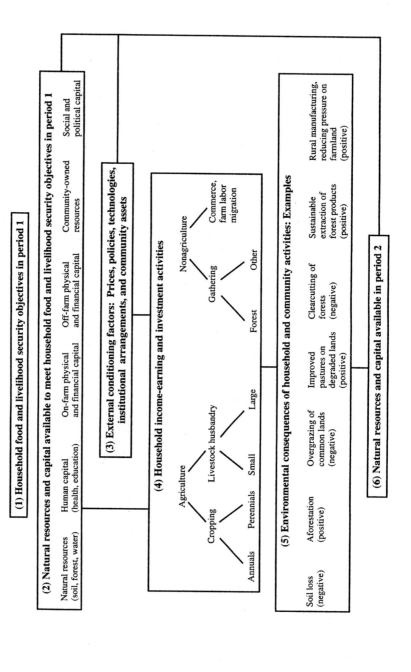

them out. These strategies and how they can affect poverty-environment links are discussed here.

Income-Earning Strategies

To manage the high risk (ex ante) and cope with consequent losses (ex post) that typify agriculture in environmentally fragile areas, the rural poor earn income from a variety of sources, shown in Figure 4.2: in farming and livestock husbandry, in the nonagricultural sector (both on-farm and off-farm), in gathering (local flora and fauna), and from community-owned resources and political capital that pay direct dividends or condition the returns from other investments. But the poor's strong incentive to diversify income across these sources is not always matched by capacity, which can be undermined by their asset poverty. This discussion examines what the poor do and how they do it and posits how this affects the environment.

NONAGRICULTURE. The rural poor in fragile areas diversify incomes and assets into the nonagricultural sector to manage risk and cope with cropping shortfall, as well as to alleviate poverty. Most nonagricultural activities in which the poor engage are labor intensive, with little use of capital, thus low entry barriers. Such activities include, for example, petty commerce, portage, farm labor, unskilled labor for construction, and long-haul or seasonal migration. Yet there can be an inverse relation between the fragility of the resource base and the availability of such wage-earning off-farm activities. Off-farm activities tend to be plentiful where they spin off from a dynamic agriculture (rural growth linkages) or urban-rural exchange (Matlon 1979; Haggblade, Hazell, and Brown 1989; Reardon et al. 1994b). Thus fragile areas that might benefit from increased off-farm activities may be less likely to create opportunities for them.

Diversification of activities and assets into the nonfarm sector can have implications for the environment, depending on the nature and severity of the environmental problem and on the nature of investments required to address the problem. The effect can be either positive or negative. On the one hand, where the poor successfully diversify into nonagricultural activities, they can become less directly dependent on land, hence less vulnerable to land degradation. Cash from nonfarm activities can also be used to finance soil conservation investments and use of fertility-enhancing inputs (see Reardon, Crawford, and Kelly 1994 for a review of evidence). On the other hand, resource conservation investments or allocation of labor to natural resource management may not be a priority use of investment funds or own-labor for the poor household. Investments in off-farm activity can compete with investments in land conservation, a competition exacerbated by the poor's lack of investable cash or available labor beyond their subsistence needs.

Whether diversification away from cropping or from livestock husbandry leads to less resource degradation also depends partly on whether past agricultural activities started a downward spiral of degradation (for example, removal of topsoil and bush cover) that would not naturally be reversed without resource conservation investments. If no critical threshold has been crossed (overwhelming the ecosystem's resilience), then reduction in pressure on the land from income diversification might reduce or arrest degradation of the environment. Hence both the degree and type of degradation *and* the degree and type of poverty matter to poverty-environment links.

LIVESTOCK HUSBANDRY AND WILD FOOD AND FUEL GATHERING. When the poor engage in small livestock husbandry and gathering of wild food and fuel, they do so mainly in the commons or in open-access lands, and the activities are usually labor intensive and require little capital. Income in cash or in kind from these activities tends to be more important to the poor than to richer rural households in their diversification and coping strategies (Webb and Coppock, Chapter 17; Jodha, Chapter 20, both in this volume). This greater importance makes the rural poor more vulnerable than the rich to the disappearance of edible or marketable wild fauna and flora and to removal of bush cover (but not necessarily biodiversity per se).

This greater reliance on livelihood activities based on use of the commons and on open-access lands has often led observers to blame the poor for overgrazing and overforesting open-access lands. Livestock indeed are important to the poor, but the poor household usually cannot afford to own many animals. For example, the poorest tercile of households owns far fewer animals per household than do richer households in West Africa (see Christensen 1989). Thus individual poor households put less pressure on semi-arid pasturelands than do individual rich households.

A conventional poverty-environment link is thus turned on its head: as absolute importance of livestock holding increases with household income, and as incomes rise in rural areas, households should be expected to invest in more livestock and place greater pressure on the commons. Analogously, reducing poverty in tropical forest areas such as the Amazon may induce technical change (for example, adoption of chain saws) in forest conversion, even among small farmers, thus increasing deforestation rates.

CROPPING. In general, poverty has the most direct effect on the environment via cropping, where poverty influences the household's technology and investment path in extensification or intensification of cropping. On the one hand, where there is still a sufficient extensive margin (such as forest), the conservation-investment poor can convert forest to farmland and offset land degradation with more land under cultivation—until they run up against the end of the land frontier. Extensification onto fragile lands such as hillsides can create erosion.

On the other hand, Boserup (1965a) outlines a number of technology and investment paths to agricultural intensification that farmers follow in the wake of increased land constraints and demand for land—conditions that result from population growth, increased demand for agricultural products, or reduced transportation costs (Boserup 1965a; Pingali, Bigot, and Binswanger 1987). Two broad paths can be distilled from Boserup's framework: (1) a *labor-led* intensification path where farmers merely add labor to the production process on given land, allowing them to crop more densely, and weed and harvest more intensively; and (2) a *capital-led* intensification path where farmers augment their labor with variable and capital inputs, in particular, fertilizer, organic matter, and capital that facilitates land improvement. Boserup identifies the second path as having higher land and labor productivity (and hence higher income levels) than the former. Similarly, Matlon and Spencer (1984) note that the capital-led path is more sustainable and productive in fragile, resource-poor areas as the fertility-enhancing input use helps the farmer avoid exhausting the soil during intensification and the capital (land improvement) helps avoid erosion and runoff. By contrast, in much of the African tropics, for example, the labor-led path to intensification is unsustainable and leads to land degradation, stagnation of land productivity, and even decreases in labor productivity. In situations such as the tropical highlands, where demographic pressure and degradation are severe, farm households that follow only the labor-led path are in for long-run ecological disaster and further immiseration (Cleaver and Schreiber 1994).

Therefore, in situations of fragile and degrading environments and land constraints, hence lack of opportunity to extensify, households too conservation-investment poor to make the requisite investments for the capital-led intensification path will find themselves both increasing the rate of degradation and becoming more vulnerable to its productivity consequences.

Illustrations from Rwanda show the divergent tendencies inherent in the poor's cash and land constraints coincident with their reliance on the land. Poorer households participate less than do richer households in coffee farming, partly because of land quality and input requirements. They fallow less because of pressure to crop all available land to meet food security needs. Yet poor farmers crop more intensively than do larger, wealthier farmers, protecting the soil from hard rainfall through denser planting. In addition, small and poor farmers tend to invest more in resource conservation measures (for example, terraces) when they have cash available from off-farm work (Clay et al. 1995).

Moreover, being poor can lead a priori to a distribution of assets skewed toward certain types and qualities of natural resources. Sometimes poorer families are constrained to take the most fragile land or to clear forest and work with easily eroded land. Sometimes they are relegated to the end of irrigation canals and suffer the combined residual silting problems of the other users (Yudelman 1989). Investments in political capital at the community level (vis-à-vis higher government levels), redistribution of political power over households (so that the poor are better represented), or changes in decision-making processes at the community level can address these issues.

Investment Strategies

Investments (such as in land improvements) embody land use strategies to enhance the environment, and investments in on-farm and off-farm assets affect crop choice and the type and rate of agricultural intensification (see Reardon and Vosti, Chapter 10, this volume). The focus here is on land improvements (such as bunds, terraces, windbreaks, culverts), because land is generally the most important natural resource available to poor rural households.

Land improvement investments are determined by three factors. First, there are incentives specific to the household, which include (1) net returns of the investment, which depend on yields and input requirements per investment unit, and the prices of inputs and outputs; (2) riskiness of the investment, which includes short- to medium-term risk associated with price and yield variability and long-term risk stemming from political and policy instability and insecure land tenure; (3) relative returns and risks—compared with alternative farm and nonfarm investments; and (4) the household-specific discount rate, proxied by household characteristics that heighten the importance of immediate survival to increase the discount rate; the poorer the household, the more immediate survival counts, for example.[2]

Second, there is capacity to invest, specific to the household, which includes (1) the categories of assets discussed and the flow of cash earned from them; and (2) complementary assets on-farm, such as a well (complementary asset) that provides water to maintain a live windbreak (investment).

Third, there are external conditioning variables common to households in a particular agroclimatic/policy context, which include (1) technologies for production and input or output processing, which affect the set of available investments and their profitability and riskiness; (2) agricultural and macroeconomic policies, which affect input and output prices; (3) the economic and institutional environment (legal system including land tenure customs and laws, markets, extension services), which affects not only the household's objective function (for example, how much food to grow versus to buy), but also the feasibility and relative profitability of nonfarm and farm activities (intersectoral terms of trade), through its effects on output and input prices (via output, input, credit, land, and labor markets), on the type of technology available, and on access to resources; (4) the physical environment (soils, rainfall, temperature, diseases, and pests), which affects the technical feasibility of potential investments and their profitability and riskiness; (5) transport and communication infrastructure, which determines the availability of information,

---

2. Even given similar assets and incomes, households may behave very differently because they have different discount rates. One could postulate that discount rates depend on age, number of children, income, education, gender, and so on.

access to markets, and costs and returns of investment; and (6) community-level infrastructure (such as dams, culverts, and farm-level bunds), which are key complementary investments (Christensen 1989; Reardon and Vosti 1992; Reardon, Crawford, and Kelly 1995).

The level and type (by asset category) of poverty affect the determinants of investment. The assets of poor households tend to be mainly labor. Land improvements that require inputs other than labor, or that require large amounts of capital or labor at particular times during the agricultural cycle, are less likely to be undertaken by the poor. The movement of a household from the category of being poor in an asset (such as land) to being conservation-investment poor in general depends on the level of risk (from price and rainfall instability, or from insecurity of land tenure, hence risk of appropriation of capital), on the nature of markets, on whether these translate into lack of sufficient liquidity (to buy labor or materials for certain land improvements), and on the willingness to use the liquidity for the investment in question.

Illustrations of Links between Types of Poverty, the Poor's Activities, and the Environment

This discussion of the links between types of poverty, the income activities and conservation investments of the poor, and the environment may be illustrated by the following three cases. (Each agroecological zone–geopolitical area is discussed in more detail elsewhere in this volume.)

The Poor in Tropical Rain Forests of Brazil: Rich in Biodiversity but Poor in Soil, Financial Assets, Labor, and Social Capital

Poor farmers in the Amazon region have access mainly to forest cover and biodiversity, both of which are locally abundant but globally scarce. Markets do not generally exist to translate global demand for these resources into secure income streams for farmers. The poor are also constrained by lack of soil nutrients, labor, good health, and cash to meet food production and purchase needs. Poverty in all asset categories but forest cover and biodiversity leads farmers to convert forests into farmland by burning trees to generate nutrients to enhance soils. That is, farmers use biophysical processes rather than markets to convert plentiful assets into in-kind income flows to meet food security needs. To break this cycle, the poor must move away from biophysical processes for converting their principal asset (forest cover) and reduce dependence on that asset. This diversification will require markets for forest cover and biodiversity, new technologies to increase the productivity of labor and of already-cleared land, and alternative off-farm income sources (Cunha and Sawyer, Chapter 13, this volume).

The resource mining process is exacerbated by the general absence of established communities, at least during the early stages of settlement. The gap in social capital creates a complete dependency on state and federal agencies (and funds) to provide key community-level investments. When the sources fail to provide or maintain these investments, community action can occur, but these responses are generally focused on production and not on natural resource management or poverty alleviation—two-thirds of the critical triangle are abandoned.

Much of the past deforestation in the Brazilian Amazon had little to do with poverty (although those responsible for future forest conversion and their motives might be quite different). In response to fiscal and other incentives, large landholders using sophisticated technology have laid waste millions of hectares of tropical forest—these actors were far from poor, by any definition (Hecht 1984; Mahar 1989).

The Poor in the Sahel: Rich in Land but Poor in Land Quality and On-Farm and Off-Farm Physical and Financial Assets

Sahel lands are fragile and degrading. Despite increasing constraints on land, the poor have good access to rangeland and cropland (though of poor carrying capacity) but are poor in livestock and off-farm income. Thus they are dependent for food security on their low-quality farmland and on open-access lands for gathering and small-scale animal husbandry in the commons, which are overgrazed. The responsibility for overgrazing is weighted toward richer households that own much more livestock than do poorer households. Moreover, there is a need to intensify cropping to reduce pressure on the fragile margins, but poor households lack cash and credit to purchase nonlabor variable inputs. Poor communities lack complementary infrastructure (such as roads or depots) to obtain these inputs (Lele and Stone 1989; Stryker 1989; Reardon et al. 1994b; Reardon 1995; Matlon and Adesina, Chapter 16).

Labor (the main asset of the poor) is a key input in the dry season for bund construction (a key land improvement to protect fields against flash floods and runoff over the hardpan surface). Capital to augment their labor (carts or trucks to haul rocks or laterite for bunds) is expensive. There is little investment in rock bunds except where government-supplied trucks have permitted. Labor is not easily substitutable for these key materials or equipment.

The Poor in the Rwanda Highlands: Rich in Labor but Poor in Land and Off-Farm Physical and Financial Assets

In Rwanda, there is intense pressure on the land: the poor depend on microplots to survive and have few animals. There is very skewed distribution of nonfarm income. Where the land-poor are also poor in off-farm capital, they can make few soil conservation investments because of lack of cash for materials and labor hire. Those with cash crops such as coffee or with nonfarm income have both the incentive (reliance on little land) and the cash to make conservation investments. Moreover, many of the poor practice labor-led intensification, lacking the means to buy fertilizer or mulch and owning few animals to generate manure. Limits to yield increases are reached early in such a system, and the soil can be exhausted from lack of amendments such as fertilizer. This gives rise to a vicious circle of poverty, labor-led intensification, degradation, and more poverty (Clay et al. 1995).

Conditioning Variables and Their Effects

The income and investment strategies of poor households, hence the links between poverty and environment, are conditioned by the following factors, which are relevant to policymakers.

First, the existence, structure, and performance of markets condition the prevalent type of poverty, as well as the substitutability of assets in investment and income generation, as discussed earlier.

Second, relative input prices, output prices, wages, and the interest rate affect farm resource use and investment. Raising the market price of a locally abundant asset (for example, biodiversity) can alter its use as well as reduce the incidence of poverty.

Third, complementary hard infrastructure (such as culverts, dams, wells, market facilities, and roads) and soft infrastructure (such as extension services, schools, and medical services) at the community level affect the cost of transactions and of inputs and outputs, and thus private costs of investment in resource conservation. Infrastructure also influences the development of non-farm activities, the commercialization of agriculture, and urban-rural links, which are important determinants of income opportunities for the poor.

Fourth, production and resource conservation technologies embody the substitutability among assets in both production and investment. Changing technical rates of substitution among assets, especially between humanmade assets and natural resources (Ruttan, Chapter 2, this volume) can alter household decisions and environmental consequences. For example, technological change in agriculture that increases land productivity can help relieve pressure on surrounding forests and hillsides.

Land improvement technology and input prices together define the cutoff point for conservation-investment poverty, and change in either can make such investments more accessible to the poor. For example, bunds may need to be built only with laterite pieces that are far from the farm, requiring trucks to fetch, and thereby making households that are rich in labor but poor in capital become conservation-investment poor. A change of technique that allows bunds to be built with local materials would eliminate this source of conservation-investment poverty, as would a decrease in the cost of transporting bund materials. Conversely, a macroeconomic change such as the recent devaluation of the Francophone West African currency increases transport costs and may drive some households into conservation-investment poverty by putting the costs of "transport-heavy" investments out of reach.

Fifth, community wealth (physical and social assets) conditions the poor household's options and behavior in four ways.

1. Community wealth affects insurance and wealth distribution mechanisms. Intracommunity distribution of wealth also conditions the level and incidence of poverty, as well as its effect on the environment. The distribution of poverty in the community can affect the cost faced by and the effectiveness of redistribution and joint-investment institutions in the community. The distribution is governed by rules related, for example, to land tenure and inheritance rights, and to credit collateral. Land tenure institutions can influence the perceived incentive and risk facing the poor who are weighing the decision to invest in land improvement.

2. The community may be forced to dedicate resources for welfare insurance to the welfare poor, which means diversion of resources from production and from resource conservation investments, as well as from enforcement of watershed management. On the one hand, the community can mitigate welfare poverty with community insurance mechanisms (for example, interhousehold transfers) and can mitigate investment poverty with transfers. These institutions and investments can help the poor to avoid coping activities or resource mining that degrades. Property rights set and enforced by communities are intimately linked to the externalities of farming and herding that affect the environment of the commons (Schmid 1987).

3. Community investments in physical and social infrastructure influence two key things related to the incidence of conservation-investment poverty. On the one hand, infrastructure affects economic opportunities for the poor by its effect on demand levels for the poor's farm products as well as products and services of activities off-farm. On the other hand, community complementary investments in a watershed, such as in culverts and dams or in trucks or carts to transport bund materials, affects the cost of natural resource management investments by the poor. These community and government complementary investments can make private land improvement investments more affordable to the poor.

4. The level and distribution of wealth in the community can also affect the enforceability of regulations that control access to the commons (Lipton, Chapter 6, this volume).

Sixth, the population growth rate determines pressure on the land and fuels degradation if there are not income alternatives or technological change available to relieve the pressure. Human fertility decisions at the household level, aggregated over households, determine this conditioning factor (Dasgupta and Mähler 1994; Lipton, Chapter 6, this volume).

Conclusions

Not all environmental degradation in developing countries is linked to poverty; for example, pollution as an externality of the agriculture of richer farmers, or forest or commons overexploitation by large and capital-intensive lumber and cattle operations can ravage the environment without the poor's lifting a hand. But where there are links between poverty and the environment, they are often complex, and to address them is challenging. To date, efforts to analyze the link between poverty and the environment have been too general on the poverty and on the environment sides, and thus have not been able to sort out seemingly conflicting evidence. In this chapter we addressed this issue by (1) decomposing poverty into asset categories; (2) decomposing the physical resource endowment and environment; (3) showing how poverty types and levels affect household livelihood activities and investment decisions, which, in turn, affect the environment; and (4) showing what factors external to the household condition the links.

Poverty-Environment Links

First, poverty is multifaceted, and the type of poverty affects the poverty-environment links. Poverty type is defined according to the asset category or categories in which households are poor. The potential for substitutability among assets in income generation and investment influences the relation between poverty in a given asset and household behavior.

Second, the environment is multifaceted, and the type of environmental problem affects the poverty-environment links. Poverty and soil degradation interact differently from the way poverty and rural pollution do, or the way poverty and loss of biodiversity do.

Third, since poverty and the environment are multifaceted, there is no *single* link between the two, but rather a series of links that may respond in different ways to policy and other changes.

Fourth, the income, investment, and land use strategies of the rural household and community determine the links. Poverty affects what kinds of activities and investments are undertaken and in what way, and thus how natural resources are used and enhanced.

Fifth, the level of poverty conditions the links. Households can have incomes above an established welfare poverty line—have enough to eat, have good health—but still be too poor in key assets and thus overall cash and human resources to be able to make critical investments or follow key land use practices to maintain or enhance their natural resource base. They might thus be better off than the welfare poor but still be conservation-investment poor; the former is usually also the latter. In any case, the important measure for poverty in the analysis of links is conservation-investment poverty.

Sixth, the distribution of poverty across households within a community also conditions the links. It does so directly as well as indirectly by affecting the wealth of the community and its ability to manage risk, to compensate the poor, and to build and maintain infrastructure that can help the poor to invest in natural resource enhancement.

Policy Implications and Research Gaps

First, the links between poverty and the environment in a given setting depend on the level, distribution, and type of poverty, the type of environmental problem, and conditioning variables. As these change over contexts, the direction of causality and the strength of the links can change. Given the diversity of types of poverty and types of environmental problems, policy prescription will be site specific, and the proposed conceptual framework can provide guidance in policy formulation and implementation.

Second, reducing poverty can reduce resource degradation where poverty is driving extensification onto fragile hillsides or forests, or where poverty is blocking the way to sustainable capital-led intensification. But alleviating poverty will not necessarily lead to less resource degradation where the only insurance available is investment in more livestock or more cleared land, and insurance demand increases with household income. Alleviating poverty will not reduce pollution from overuse of agricultural chemicals, the use of which increases with farmer wealth. Moreover, reducing poverty just to the point where households are above the welfare-poverty line may not be enough in many cases for households to be sufficiently well off to be able to afford key investments in natural resource management; such investments require that households be above the conservation-investment poverty line, a line that depends on the costs and types of investment needed and on the composition of assets of the poor household.

Third, enhancing the natural resource base can reduce poverty, where, for example, soil degradation reduces yields on the farms of the poor. But conserving natural resources can also increase poverty, for instance, in cases where poor households are barred from gathering wild flora and fauna but depend on this as a key income strategy for survival.

The upshot of the second and third implications is that, in the short term, reducing poverty will not necessarily protect the environment, nor will protecting the environment necessarily alleviate poverty. Specific policy action to affect the set of conditioning variables will be needed to maximize the achievement of both goals at once.

Fourth, the most effective way simultaneously to reduce poverty and enhance the resource base is to understand what categories of asset poverty and conditioning variables are driving households' behavior (for example, degrading land use practices or lack of conservation investments) and focus effort on these. Promotion of key markets, investment in complementary infrastructure, and research to make resource management technologies more productive and affordable are examples of such efforts. Policy should aim at affecting household and community behavior with the goal of helping poor households attain their main objective, food security, while, as much as possible, maintaining or enhancing the resource base.

Fifth, production and investment of households and communities can generate environmental externalities (both positive and negative). The latter can have a direct and large impact on the asset holdings of the rural poor's neighbors (who themselves might also be poor), thereby potentially reducing and changing the composition of their wealth and promoting compensatory income-earning activities and investment. Although they are not explicitly treated in this chapter, our conceptual framework can be extended to incorporate these externalities, and policy actions to address them can be analyzed in that framework.

Sixth, a key gap in research is understanding how complementary community and government investments (in physical and social infrastructure) can make private land improvement investments more affordable to the poor, and how policy might promote such community investments and the continued maintenance they often require.

5 The Links between Agricultural Growth, Environmental Degradation, and Nutrition and Health: Implications for Policy and Research

JOACHIM VON BRAUN

Environmental degradation undermines agricultural production potential and contributes to sustained poverty, as manifested by poor nutrition and health. Poor nutrition and health force poor people into environmentally unsustainable behavior. These harmful links are the central themes of this chapter, which aims to derive policy implications and major research needs.

In this chapter I first discuss a broad conceptual framework for the links between agricultural growth, environmental degradation, and nutrition and health. The second section examines agriculture, nutrition, and health linkages in two scenarios: (1) output growth with new agricultural technology, defined to be a Green Revolution package (irrigation, new seeds, fertilizer, pesticide, information); and (2) output increases only, by area expansion and resource mining. I show that policies are needed to avoid, mitigate, and compensate harm to nutrition and health from environmental degradation in both scenarios.

Conceptualizing the Linkages

Environmental versus Human Resources?

Difficult ethical and economic questions arise when competition and complementarity between natural resource preservation and human resource enhancement are considered jointly, as they have to be. These questions relate to whether human resources require special attention in policies for overall resource improvement. For instance, it could be argued that natural resource mining is justifiable for purposes of economic and social development. But could that argument ever be true for human resources? I answer no. An acceptance of environmental benefits at human cost diverts attention from the need for a global commitment to development that alleviates poverty. At the extreme, it blocks the road to human capital improvement as a foundation for accelerated technical change. Placing human capital development as a top priority is the only humane way to address the challenge of population pressure on natural resources in low-income countries. In the short run, as well as intergenerationally, basic health and nutrition standards can be viewed as constraints that need to be taken into account by environmental policies.

Basic human resource improvement through public action for education, nutrition, and health is both a precondition for and an accelerator of growth. How do nutrition and health influence agricultural growth and its effects on natural resources, and vice versa? To address these links, a broad array of aspects of the environment in which people live, not just the natural environment, need to be dealt with. A broad, people-focused definition of environment will comprise not only air, water, soil, and climate, but also household- and community-level conditions, such as shelter, food and water quality, health risks and pathogens, community health, and sanitation services.

Complex externalities, both positive and negative, can link human resources to natural resource use. For instance, a household may contribute to degradation of natural resources by excessive charcoal production, yet use the profits for improvement of human resources, such as by investing in a source of clean water. These effects in the two domains can have long-term implications that are difficult to evaluate. Identifying such externalities, and understanding the temporal links among natural resource use, technical change, and human resource improvement are challenging research issues that warrant attention. Positive and negative health and nutrition externalities of agricultural technologies are a case in point.

Internalizing externalities and integrating health and nutrition into cost-benefit analysis (CBA) are difficult issues, especially where many are in absolute poverty. First, the argument for using policy to internalize negative externalities of production cannot be directly applied to households in absolute poverty. Households pushed by poverty into nonsustainable production systems cannot be taxed to reduce environmental degradation when they are at the borderline of undernutrition and have no other coping options. In such cases, efforts to internalize negative environmental externalities have to be coupled at the very least with subsidies for social security, including food security for the poorest (von Braun 1991b).

Dealing with the potential health and nutrition externalities of agricultural technology requires attention from the many diverse actors in engineering, agricultural program planning, health services, and farm households. Major conceptual and methodological deficiencies remain (Bandaragoda 1986; Olivares 1987; Lipton and de Kadt 1988; Dixon, Talbot, and Le Moigne 1989; Oomen, de Wolf, and Jobin 1990). In addition, standard methods of economic appraisal generally continue to bypass the economic aspects of health problems, not to mention humanitarian aspects.[1]

---

1. The World Bank's list of suggested "Specialists Related to Environmental Assessment" includes no public health, tropical disease, or nutrition specialists (World Bank Environment Department 1991, vol. 1:22).

Second, including nutrition and health concerns in CBA will not be easy.[2] The estimation of health costs in CBA, using a "healthy days lost" (foregone earnings) approach, including prematurely lost lives, is unacceptable.[3] In some circumstances, technologies that are risky or that harm nutrition and health could be the most "acceptable" for the poorest countries.[4]

Health and nutrition concerns need to be directly included in participatory and research-based planning for improvements in design and construction of agricultural projects. The methods to be used include (1) cost-effectiveness assessments to determine ways to maintain preproject health risks in a project environment; (2) inclusion of long-term health benefits and costs in CBA; and (3) calculation of ex ante estimates of morbidity and mortality effects of policy and project alternatives. A first step in all three cases is to generate estimates of incidence and prevalence of disease in the context of a project (Rosenfield and Bower 1978).

A Conceptual Framework

The preceding discussion leads to a conceptual framework that emphasizes the explicit consideration of human welfare in the context of agricultural and natural resource policies and programs.

Links between agricultural growth and nutrition and health improvement are shown in Figure 5.1. These links are usually two-way. Agricultural growth (through supply, employment, and income effects) can affect nutrition and health. In turn, nutrition and health can affect agricultural growth (by their human capital and labor productivity effects) (Strauss 1986; Haddad and Bouis 1991). Degradation of the environment related to agricultural growth can hurt nutrition and health by lowering water quality, eroding soils, and increasing household time needed for farming and collecting water and firewood. Environmental degradation can also slow agricultural growth, thereby (indirectly) reducing growth's positive effect on nutrition and health by reducing resources for investment in institutions delivering related services.

Institutions, and the nature and pattern of technical change and the commercialization of agriculture, influence whether and how agricultural growth causes environmental degradation. Institutions and technical change are, in turn, influenced by population characteristics and human capital formation.

---

2. A World Bank publication argues, "Ideally, the monetary value of health impacts should be determined by the individuals' willingness to pay for improved health. In practice, 'second best' techniques may be necessary, such as valuing earnings that are foregone through premature death, sickness, or absenteeism" (World Bank Environment Department 1991, vol. 1:142). The publication acknowledges that the "approach is often questioned on ethical grounds" (p. 143).

3. For a review and critique of the approach, see Hufschmidt et al. 1983.

4. New evidence that rejects the conventional view that values are equivalent between gains and losses associated with components of the environment adds further conceptual complications (Knetsch 1990).

FIGURE 5.1 Links among agriculture, environmental degradation, nutrition and health, and policies

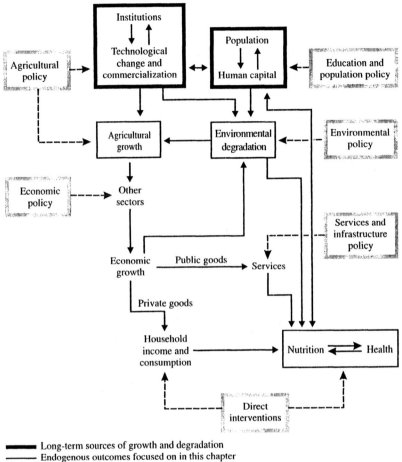

Long-term sources of growth and degradation
Endogenous outcomes focused on in this chapter
Policy interventions (with -----)
Not specifically lined = intermediate factors and linkages

Therefore, agricultural growth and environmental degradation are shown as endogenous in Figure 5.1.

Nutrition and health (and changes in them) are linked to the effects on private goods (mediated by household income, consumption, and health-related behavior) and on public goods (nutrition and health services) as shown in the lower half of Figure 5.1. Malnutrition-infection cycles are determined by the type of public and private goods available to the rural poor (Tomkins and Watson 1989).

Six broad sets of policies, not intended to be comprehensive, are shown in Figure 5.1 to highlight the range of policy interventions relevant to agricultural growth, environmental degradation, and nutrition and health. Finally, the effects shown in Figure 5.1 can occur quickly or slowly. Understanding the speed of the effects is important.

Intrahousehold-, Household-, and Community-Level Issues

How environmental degradation affects people's health and nutrition depends on the nature of the degradation and on the socioeconomic and demographic structures of communities, households, and their members. The environmental behavior of poor households is driven by their necessary concern for immediate food and health needs. The poor's high "time preference" rate can clash with environmental concerns.

Many studies show gender differences in consumption and nutrition behavior within households (Thomas 1990; Haddad and Hoddinott 1991). Other studies show a higher preference by women for food and nutrition security of children, a pattern that has led to targeting technology-transfer systems to women. Similarly, there may be scope for gender targeting of environmental measures (McGuire and Popkin 1988).

Community behavior can have complex effects on environment. Community provision of social security to households, for instance, can prevent the depletion of natural resources owned by households. A household has, however, little incentive to invest, for instance in sanitation, if the rest of the community does not. Often it is the community rather than the individual household that ought to be targeted with interventions for environmental, nutrition, and health improvement.

Quantifying the Linkages: Data Gaps

Recording of agricultural change is far ahead of recording of health and nutrition change in low-income countries. Only very rough estimates exist on the extent to which absolute poverty is concentrated in environmentally threatened environments. Leonard et al. (1989) conclude that 57 percent of the rural poor live on lands of low agricultural potential. Broca and Oram (1991) estimate that roughly 50 percent of the poor in Sub-Saharan Africa live in the arid and semi-arid zones. In South Asia, 69 percent of the poor are in the three driest agroecological zones. However, low potential does not necessarily equal ecological vulnerability (Kates and Haarmann 1992). Until poverty becomes adequately geo-referenced, linkages among agriculture, environmental degradation, and health and nutrition will not be comprehensively identified, and the ability to guide policy relevant to them will be limited.

Technology as a Determinant of Links among Agriculture, Degradation, and Health and Nutrition

Two types of linkages among agriculture, degradation, and health and nutrition are broadly distinguished here: (1) those that are established by typical new agricultural technologies and (2) those that occur in environments lacking technological change. This conceptualization emphasizes the extremes on a spectrum to highlight the need for sustainable agricultural technologies *and* public action for health and nutrition to overcome degradation and health and nutrition problems in *both* types of production systems.

Links When There Is Technical Change

Much has been written about Green Revolution technology, agricultural commercialization, and its nutrition effects (for example, Hazell and Röell 1983; Pinstrup-Andersen 1986; Lipton and Longhurst 1989; Binswanger and von Braun 1991). However, research on health effects of technology is less comprehensive (IIMI 1986; IRRI 1987; Lipton and de Kadt 1988; von Braun, Puetz, and Webb 1989; Kennedy 1989; Bouis and Haddad 1990; Ruttan 1990). The effects on health and nutrition of Green Revolution–type technological change fall into five broad categories.

1. Population concentration around project areas can lead to the spread of, for example, diarrhea, typhoid, cholera, tuberculosis—the typical diseases of poverty (Lopez 1990)—because of inadequate sanitation and the lack of immunity of residents to communicable diseases.
2. Changes in surface- and groundwater availability and quality as well as in drainage affect the incidence of waterborne diseases such as malaria, schistosomiasis, river blindness (onchocerciasis), and Japanese encephalitis.
3. Diet quality changes can be induced by changes in availability of types of foods as a result of crop mix changes or reduction of access to traditional foods, including nutritious wild foods.
4. Excessive use or inappropriate application of pesticides hurts workers and the consumers of treated crops.
5. Changes in household resource endowments, behavior, and time allocation can affect child care and sanitation.

Table 5.1 lists the debated linkages, including secondary effects, among elements of a typical technical package for agricultural growth, potential environmental degradation, and related disease risks. The focus in the following sections is on irrigation and pesticide use.

IRRIGATION. There appears to be no basis for a generalization that irrigation harms health and nutrition. Vector-borne diseases such as malaria, schistosomiasis, filariasis, and onchocerciasis, among others, should not be blamed on irrigated agriculture per se. Their spread is influenced by irrigation project design and by social and cultural factors in the area.

Although many case studies show increased prevalence and incidence of malaria and schistosomiasis due to irrigation (WHO 1980, 1983; Mills and Thomas 1984; Gratz 1987), it often appears that fields, not canals or drains, are

TABLE 5.1 Links among agriculture, degradation, and health and nutrition when there is technical progress in agriculture

Technology Element	Potential Environmental Degradation	Disease Risk and/or Nutrition Insecurity
Irrigation	Reduced water quality or quantity	Diarrhea, cholera, typhoid
	Increase in mosquitos	Malaria
	Increase in aquatic snails	Schistosomiasis
	Increase in blackflies	Onchocerciasis
Pesticides	Excessive and/or inappropriate pesticide use	Poisoning
Fertilizer	Leakage of nitrates into drinking water	Diseases of the circulatory system in infants
Secondary effects		
Crowding, sanitation deficiency		Communicable diseases
Diet change		Nutritional deficiencies
Vector control (inappropriate pesticide use)		Poisoning, resistance build-up

the major sources of vector breeding.[5] Vector breeding can be addressed by system design and disease eradication campaigns (IIMI 1986; Samarasinghe 1986).

But focusing exclusively on the impact of irrigation on the prevalence of a particular tropical disease excludes many of the indirect links between agriculture and health and nutrition hypothesized in Figure 5.1. For example, malaria prevalence in an irrigated area may be lower than in an upland area when the household's ability to buy malaria treatment drugs is enhanced because of higher income resulting from the irrigated agriculture. A study by the International Food Policy Research Institute in The Gambia found favorable consumption and child nutrition effects from irrigation due to the income and employment from irrigated rice production (von Braun, Puetz, and Webb 1989). Moreover, the effects of clean water availability on health and nutrition of preschoolers is well established (WHO Commission on Health and Environment 1992). The combined provision of safe water with health and nutrition education translates into effective reduction in water-related infectious disease (McJunkin 1982).

---

5. In areas with onchocerciasis (river blindness), this may not be true because blackflies are attracted to fast flowing, oxygen-rich water (Oomen, de Wolf, and Jobin 1990).

PESTICIDES. Population groups at risk of pesticide poisoning are those that have (1) brief but high exposure (for example, laborers working with pesticides in the field); (2) lengthy and high exposure (for example, pesticide manufacturers and crop harvesters); and (3) lengthy and low exposure (including many working in processing and distribution of treated crops). In low-income countries, the first and second are the main problems.

Accurate data on acute and chronic pesticide poisoning are scarce, particularly in developing countries. Studies in Indonesia, Malaysia, and Sri Lanka in the 1980s suggest that 13.8 percent, 14.5 percent, and 11.9 percent, respectively, of pesticide users have been poisoned at least once (Jeyaratnam, Lun, and Phoon 1987). Ministry of Health statistics in Sri Lanka show 13,000 hospital admissions for pesticide poisoning in 1988, with 1,500 deaths, many more than caused by malaria (Jeyaratnam, Lun, and Phoon 1987).

Although concerns have long been expressed about the effects of pesticides on people and the natural environment in developing countries, few studies have quantified these effects. There are even fewer studies on the productivity effects of pesticide application or full cost-benefit analyses that include health effects. The International Rice Research Institute (IRRI) monitored the production and health of a sample of farmers in the Philippines over two years. It found that the use of pesticides harmed health and harmed productivity via effects on the quantity and quality of labor, management, and supervision (Antle and Pingali 1992). The positive effects of pesticides were overwhelmed by their adverse health effects. Other studies in the Philippines found that long exposure to pesticides led to cardiopulmonary, neurological, and hematological problems (Marquez, Pingali, and Palis 1992).

The health effects of pesticides are not restricted to the user. The effects can be indirect. In cotton-growing regions of Guatemala and Nicaragua, some of the highest levels of DDT recorded in humans were found in breast milk of women (World Bank 1992b). In the Philippines, pesticide use in rice production reduced the population of frogs, fish, and other animals used for food, which reduced the variety of foods produced by the paddy and may have hurt diets of farmers and other rural poor (Marquez, Pingali, and Palis 1992).

Laws and regulations governing pesticide use must be passed and enforced. Protective clothing and other safety equipment must be made available and affordable. Safety training programs must be conducted and made accessible to farmers with little education. Subsidies must be eliminated, and the price of pesticides must be set to reflect their true cost.

Technical Progress, Environmental Degradation, and
Health and Nutrition Linkages: Summary Comments

None of the health and nutrition problems linked to technical change in agriculture needs to be accepted. Solutions can be found in technology improvement and complementary measures. A condition for solving health and

TABLE 5.2 Links among agriculture, the environment, and health and nutrition without Green Revolution–type technical change in agriculture

Agricultural Change/Practices	Environmental Effects		Household-Level Effects and Health and Nutrition Effects
	Primary	Secondary	
Expansion of area farmed	Desertification	Drought	Impoverishment/productivity decline
	Deforestation	Floods	Migration-related health stress
	Watershed degradation	Climate change (?)	Vector-borne disease (when moving into disease prone areas)
Resource mining (e.g., soil mining, overgrazing)	Soil erosion		Communicable diseases (when sanitation breaks down)
	Soil fertility decline		Chronic food insecurity
	Loss of pasture		Seasonal malnutrition
			Famines

nutrition problems caused directly or indirectly by agricultural change is a better understanding of the causes and effects.

Pesticide poisonings may have to be identified and treated (or eliminated) on a local or even case-by-case basis. However, there may be scale economies in preventing health problems from other technologies. For example, preventing the spreading of disease by irrigation may be less costly in large irrigation projects than in small schemes where overhead costs are higher. Integration of water management, education, health services, sanitation, and chemical control may be more effective, and less costly, than isolated "campaigns" and uncoordinated measures, and may be more sustainable by communities.[6]

Links When There Is No Technical Change

Agricultural growth without Green Revolution–type technical change is possible through soil mining and area expansion (where land is abundant), but such growth is not sustainable. It also has primary and secondary environmental deterioration effects and potential health and nutrition effects (Table 5.2). Primary environmental effects are desertification, deforestation, watershed deterioration, soil erosion, and soil fertility decline. Secondary effects include drought, floods, and, potentially, climate change.

The main household-level effect is productivity decline and consequently impoverishment—the cause of an array of nutrition and health problems.

---

6. See the guidelines for the incorporation of health safeguards into irrigation projects through intersectoral cooperation prepared for the joint WHO/FAO/UN panel on environmental management for vector control (Tiffen 1989).

Moreover, when agricultural growth falters in the least-developed countries, it slows the delivery of health and sanitation services. This limits progress in health and nutritional improvement.

The "disaster" secondary effects—droughts and floods—put countries' health and sanitation systems under stress, accelerating morbidity and mortality. Research on the link between deforestation and droughts, floods, and climate change is at an early stage and requires more attention. It appears, however, that deforestation in the watersheds of the Himalayas played a major role in the increased occurrence of floods downstream in Bangladesh in the 1980s (World Bank 1990b). Similarly, more frequent floods in the 1980s in Sudan can be traced to deforestation in the Ethiopian highlands. Floods such as those in 1988 in Sudan and in 1991 in Bangladesh can lead to drastic increases in communicable diseases if sanitation breaks down as a result of the flooding.

Two cases in this context are briefly discussed: (1) when agriculture presses uphill and (2) when agriculture presses toward the rain forest.

WHEN AGRICULTURE PRESSES UPHILL. Many hillside agricultural regions of low-income countries have high person-land ratios and are—because of limited infrastructure, missing markets, and food security risks—subsistence-oriented. Few hill areas have benefited from productivity-increasing technological change in food crops (potatoes seem an exception). Commercial export crops such as tea, coffee, spices (for example, cardamom), and vegetables are important income sources in some hill areas.

Indigenous mechanisms for increasing labor productivity under increased land scarcity can be effective but not enough to stem the overall productivity declines. In Rwanda's high-altitude zone (2,000–2,600 meters), von Braun, de Haen, and Blanken (1991) found that a 10 percent increase in the person-land ratio (which stands at 12 persons per hectare) results in a 3.6 percent decline in labor productivity. Such decreases in productivity of land and labor have to be compensated for by area expansion, hence increased degradation.

Sometimes the search for better health conditions can lead to environmental degradation. For example, high population density in some highland zones originated partly from settlers' desire for a better health environment (for example, in high-altitude zones of Ethiopia there were fewer waterborne diseases). High population growth led to movement uphill, with effects on forests, watersheds, and soils, as well as movement downhill into valleys, which are more prone to waterborne and waterwashed diseases.

The degradation of forests, watersheds, and soils in hillside areas have implications for health and nutrition. Indirect effects from floods were discussed earlier. Direct effects include reduced productivity of time allocated to home goods production, especially water and fuel acquisition. Deforestation leads to increased time for fuel acquisition, thus increasing food preparation costs. Moving uphill can reduce household access to water.

In Nepal, areas of rapid deforestation have poorer preschooler nutrition. The more involved older children are in fuelwood collection and agricultural activities, the worse their nutrition. The competition for women's time in agriculture versus fuelwood collection has become increasingly severe and has undermined family nutrition (Kumar and Hotchkiss 1988). In Rwanda, moving to hillsides gave women a heavier workload and caused them to be ill more often, so the work was passed to the children. In the most food-deficient households, children did 21 percent of the fuelwood collection and 53 percent of the water fetching (compared with 11 and 27 percent in non-food-deficient households) (von Braun, de Haen, and Blanken 1991).[7]

Weak infrastructure constrains agricultural input and output market integration in hill areas. It also limits the delivery of health and sanitation services. Water scarcity and lack of sanitation cause undernutrition. Lack of a clean latrine increases chronic malnutrition symptoms (weight-for-height) by 33 percent and severe infestation of intestinal worms—a major health environment problem—by 17 percent (von Braun, de Haen, and Blanken 1991). These causes of malnutrition were more powerful than calorie deficiency.

WHEN AGRICULTURE PRESSES INTO THE TROPICAL RAIN FORESTS. Expansion of agriculture into the rain forest zone (the causes of which are examined in Browder 1989 and Mahar 1989) can have nutrition and health effects for those who move there and for those who are already there. Diet can change, and diseases can be fostered by cultivation practices, human behavior, and differential lack of immunity to certain diseases.

While consumption patterns of rain forest populations are increasingly well studied (for example, Hladik, Bahuchet, and de Garine 1990), little is known about the effects of deforestation on nutrition and health. Studies in southern Cameroon show that seasonality of food intake by rain forest people is typically low, as is anthropometric status variation (for example, Froment 1990). Cassava provides 40–65 percent of calories in those communities. Much of the African rain forest population depends on cassava for food security. The potential nutritional drawbacks of cassava are low protein content, low energy density, and toxic effects from the natural content of cyanide-yielding compounds (Rosling 1987).

Malnutrition in rain forest communities is closely related to infectious diseases and vector-borne diseases (malaria and sleeping sickness). Malaria is the major vector-borne disease in the tropical forest. It affects both long-term residents and recent settlers. Settlers moving to the Amazon suffer disproportionately from malaria. Vosti and Loker (1990) reported malaria prevalence rates of up to 40 percent, especially in the initial stages of settlement.

---

7. Women, providing 80 percent of field labor time, were ill 14 percent of the time (von Braun, de Haen, and Blanken 1991).

The relationship between deforestation and malaria is complex. The density and type of mosquito populations can change with land use, with potentially important implications for malaria transmission (Sornmani 1987). Household behavior can also influence malaria incidence in rain forest settlement areas. Vosti (1990) found that agricultural occupation per se was not a significant determinant of malaria in a study area in the Amazon region of Brazil. However, distance of the house from the forest reduced malaria prevalence, as did use of insecticides and improved quality of housing. Malaria-stricken settler households face prohibitive costs of treatment that "can initiate a downward spiral of decapitalization as treatment costs outpace income and erode scant assets" (Vosti and Loker 1990:12). This downward spiral forces settler households to leave before their investment in land clearance begins to pay off. Agriculture's impact on health and nutrition in the rain forest depends on physical and social infrastructure.

Policy and Research Implications

Policy Implications

Five policy implications emerge. First, bad health and undernutrition render the poor inefficient. Morbidity impairs their labor productivity, and food insecurity leads to inefficient household strategies and damage to the environment. Hence public action for health and nutrition security in marginal areas is also "healthy" for the environment. Second, technology-driven agricultural growth, which contributes to general income growth, generally is good for nutrition and health. Third, the specific health and nutrition risks of technological change must be mitigated through appropriate technology design. Where this is infeasible, health and nutrition risks must be compensated by expansion of services. Not all nutrition and health risks can or should be addressed by agricultural policies. Fourth, healthy living environments can be produced. Scope exists for agricultural, public health, and nutrition workers and researchers to join in improved program design for health and nutrition. A condition for improved program designs is good monitoring of effects. Fifth, governments and donors must address the health and nutrition consequences of agricultural projects that change the environment. They need to acknowledge that the impacts of such projects on health and nutrition can be direct or indirect and can occur over the short or long run.

Research Implications

Several research implications also emerge. First, cost-benefit analyses and environmental impact assessments of agricultural projects must address not only changes in the environment, but also changes in the health and nutrition of rural people. Research is needed for the appropriate broadening of environmental impact assessment and cost-benefit analyses. Second, conceptual and empirical research is needed on the time lags and leads of critical linkages among agriculture, environment, and health and nutrition. Third, joint research by agriculturalists and health specialists, among other disciplines, must be conducted on the effects of agricultural policies and practices on human health and nutrition to address risks more effectively and comprehensively.

6 Accelerated Resource Degradation by Agriculture in Developing Countries? The Role of Population Change and Responses to It

MICHAEL LIPTON

Rural Development Modalities and Resource Depletion

When and where the rates, styles, or paths of agricultural and rural development in poor countries are to blame for accelerated degradation of global or local resources, why is this happening? No person would knowingly behave in ways that destroy resources necessary to the survival of that person, or of his or her offspring, unless very strong pressures to do so are present. Four such pressures merit review. First, there are national-level pressures associated with economic development. These include (1) increases in population as mortality falls but fertility declines lag and (2) declines in common property resources (CPRs).[1] In addition, there are international pressures, including (3) interest-rate changes and (4) technology transfers. I consider the first two pressures in this chapter and address the other two in Chapter 11 of this volume.

It is still common to blame the poor for destroying their environment by excessive production of children. Yet each couple's reproductive decisions are usually rational. Given the medical and economic circumstances, the rate of population growth in a country can well be regarded as endogenous (National Academy of Sciences 1985; Birdsall 1988). However, each couple's decisions were presumably rational during the thousands of years when fertility in developing countries hardly exceeded mortality. The economic and medical changes that have so accelerated "endogenous" population growth (and that are, of course, in many ways so desirable) were not themselves endogenous.

Local and global rates of resource degradation can be accelerated by rises in rural population (for example, as mortality falls as a result of endogenous or exogenous forces) in four ways. First, risk aversion or externalities associated

---

I am grateful to James Fairhead, Melissa Leach, Thomas Reardon, and Stephen A. Vosti for valuable comments on an earlier draft. Errors remain my own.

1. The focus here will be on natural population increase. Migration will enter the discussion as an effect of natural increase.

with "paradoxes of assurance" (Sen 1967) may mean that each rational couple produces more children than would be preferred by all couples if they had, and were assured that all couples would act upon, better information. Such over-shooting can lead to "excessive" rates of resource degradation. Second, techni-cal changes induced by population growth, in response to either higher labor-land ratios or increased demand for food (Lipton 1990), can affect resource degradation rates. Third, by a range of mechanisms, population increase may lead to rises in households' rate of time preference, in the market rate of interest, or in both. Fourth, increased population, even if the parental decisions causing it are privately optimal, raises the costs and diffuses the benefits of collective choices that might reduce degradation of CPRs (Lipton 1985).

Population Growth and Environment

The Research Consensus on Population Growth

There is a surprising amount of academic agreement about the causes and effects of population growth in poor countries. The research consensus (Schultz 1981; World Bank 1984a; Birdsall 1985, 1988; National Academy of Sciences 1985) is as follows. Subject to societal pressures, most couples act rationally in setting family size norms and in using traditional, and sometimes modern, means of birth prevention to implement them. That is, each couple—subject to physical and economic factors affecting the woman's lifetime supply of babies—sets its demand for babies by rationally using its information on (1) the costs and risks of producing and rearing children; (2) the benefits, both in pleasure and in future income streams, that flow from children; (3) the riskiness of such benefits; and (4) the costs (financial and psychic) of obtaining and using means of birth prevention (Easterlin and Crimmins 1985). In par-ticular, parents weigh the risk that a child will not support them in their old age owing to its premature death, its adult unemployment, or its refusal to transfer much of its earned adult income. They also weigh the costs, gains, and risks of "substituting quality for quantity" by producing fewer offspring but educating them better or longer so that they may earn and contribute more income (Becker and Lewis 1974; Schultz 1981).

Typically, these factors are associated with about 40 percent of inter-household or intergroup variance in measures of actual or desired fertility. The remainder is probably related, among other things, to community-level factors affecting norms about, for example, age of marriage, postpartum abstention from intercourse, and the use of contraception (Cain and McNicoll 1986), and to possible divergences of view, and of power, between wife and husband on family size norms and the means to secure them.

There is much quantitative evidence that family size decisions are private-ly rational for most couples. Yet this does not imply that the societal consequences, such as rapid population growth, would secure general assent if they could be "decided" by voters, markets, or "socially optimizing" setters of incentives that affect couples' fertility decisions. Each "poor" couple's extra child, in countries with high and rising person-land ratios, tends to reduce the wage or employment of each other "poor" couple's children. That transfers some income from often poor workers to generally nonpoor employers. Now suppose instead that each poor couple possessed assurance that all such couples would implement an agreement to have three children instead of four. Then, each poor couple would increase its expected remittances (and security) in old age by producing fewer but better-off "candidate worker" children. All poor couples and their children would be better off (Sen 1967) at the cost of the many fewer nonpoor couples who are net buyers of labor.

This is not the only such case admitted in the consensus. Lack of information about birth prevention, and the environment issues reviewed later in this chapter, strengthen the case for policies to spread and cheapen the means of birth prevention and to increase incentives to produce smaller families and more widely spaced births. Furthermore, the benefits from reducing fertility rates strengthen the case for more public spending to reduce incentives to fertility. For example, if there are favorable external effects from reducing the chosen levels of fertility (even though each fertility decision is individually optimal), there is a case for more public spending to increase the female share in secondary education and modern-sector employment, because such female participation is known to delay marriage and to decrease marital fertility (Cleland and Hobcraft 1985; Singh and Casterline 1985).

The consensus is muddied by advocates of two other positions. First, some people (usually politicians rather than academics) still believe that "improvident" parenthood is widespread and that there are communities, cultures, and clerics that pressure couples toward higher fertility by increasing the psychic costs of birth prevention. Second, at the other extreme, some researchers (notably Simon 1981)—and many politicians—argue that child-creating behavior is not only rational (as in the consensus position) but usually without significant negative externalities. The focus here is on the environmental implications of the consensus view.

Malthus's Two Pressures, the Four Responses, and Incentives

Extra population places claims upon resources. For Malthus, the limit to the level of population is set by the alleged eventual consequence of overpopulation: food deprivation, which compels a choice among paths to zero population growth. His hope is for "abstinence," principally by later marriage. Malthus's early work claims that, if such abstinence is not chosen, a growing population must eventually tolerate increasing famine and disease.

Malthus and his contemporary critics paid almost no attention to resource degradation. However, Malthus saw two mechanisms by which population growth leads to food deprivation. First, farmland yields diminishing returns of food as populations grow. Thus food availability grows more slowly than population. Second, growing labor surpluses drive down the wage, relative to the land component of food costs. Thus workers' food entitlements (Sen 1981) grow more slowly than their population.

There appear to be four responses by which growing populations react to avoid Malthusian crises. Response 1, not explicitly considered by Malthus, is the "Chayanovian response." As each household grows in size, the marginal utility of food relative to that of leisure increases. In response, the household raises workforce participation and duration.

The second and third responses were treated by Malthus, although neither he nor his critics discuss the implications for resource degradation. Response 2 is an expansion of the extensive land margin, including migration on a world scale to land-abundant areas. Response 3 is technical progress, in two senses: that of Boserup (1965b, 1981), in which intensification of land use and increases in yields accelerate food *availability,* and that of Ruttan and Binswanger (1978) and Hayami and Ruttan (1985), in which innovations that raise labor use per acre increase *entitlements.*

Malthus believed that responses 2 and 3 were bound to be exhausted eventually. Without "preventive checks," therefore, his gloomy forecasts seemed certain to happen if population continued to grow. However, in his later work (Malthus 1824 in Malthus and Pearce 1988), he placed increasing hope in another response, namely, an increasing willingness to restrain fertility if economic growth improved children's survival prospects, especially if education were free (response 4).

It is necessary to look at the effects of the challenges posed by the need for both food availability and food entitlements, as they are addressed by these four responses, on resource degradation. However, these effects take place, in part, via responses to changing incentives.

Neither Malthus nor his modern successors in the environment debate appear to give close attention to changes in incentives—whether due to changing relative prices or to changes in technology—caused by either the initial problem or the responses. This omission, noted by Beckerman (1974) and his successors, probably occurs because attention was (and to a certain extent, is) focused on limits to growth rather than on the speed of approach to (or avoidance of) such limits. In other words, both Malthus and his critics tended to underestimate the elasticity and plasticity of compensating behavior—including migration, appropriate innovation, and perhaps invention—in response to population change.

Extensive Margins and Population-Responsive Migration

The effect on resource degradation of response 2 to population growth (to increase land cultivation at the extensive margin) is perhaps the most analyzed.

Yet it is little known that in many countries, low-potential, even desert, areas are showing considerably faster population growth than areas of high potential for agricultural intensification. For instance, the Rajasthan Desert in India (between the Aravalli hills and the border with Pakistan) experienced 1.5 percent yearly population growth in 1901–1971—much faster than India as a whole. This rate rose to 3.3 percent in 1971–1981, compared with 2.2 percent for all India. The least densely populated, most arid districts (Jaisalmer and Bikaner) have among the fastest rates of rural population growth rates in India (Mathur 1988). Yet extending cultivation is seldom a sustainable response to continued population increase in the fragile areas. Net sown areas in this area of Rajasthan grew 14 percent in the 1950s, 12.5 percent in the 1960s, but only 4.4 percent in the 1970s. Nor are technical progress and agricultural research supporting increased land cultivation as a response to population pressure. At the same time, water scarcity and established crop mix precluded most of the yield-enhancing benefits of the Green Revolution (Mathur 1988).

Why is long-term population growth in fragile rural areas so rapid? Why is there not more outmigration to more fertile areas? In the short run, rural-to-rural migration (in response to population pressure) often involves labor migration to Green Revolution areas, for example, to the Indian Punjab in 1967–1973. When labor flows into Green Revolution areas, it sometimes causes a resumption of sharecrop tenancies by big landlords or direct amalgamation of smallholdings to create bigger, *less* labor-intensive commercial farms (Cohen 1975). These trends mean that rural-to-rural migration—in response to population growth and also to local Green Revolutions—often tends in the longer term to involve net movements *toward* sparsely populated, fragile areas, in search of new land to absorb their labor. For example, rural-to-rural migration occurred from southern to northwest Brazil, and in Bangladesh from Comilla to the Chittagong Hill Tracts. When people in these Green Revolution areas were displaced by demographic, agrotechnical, and land ownership changes tending to increase labor supply relative to demand, they poured into sparsely populated but environmentally fragile areas. There, they sometimes found themselves in sharp conflict with local populations who use trees and land more sustainably but who lack well-codified property rights. However, intensification in receiving areas often brings increases in labor skills, machines, and herbicides, and lower elasticity of employment with respect to output (Jayasuriya and Shand 1986; Bhalla 1987). This probably means that poverty reduction is less than would normally be associated with agricultural intensification.

Two sets of actions can reduce negative impacts in immigrant-receiving areas. First, the immigrants require appropriate technologies and price incentives if they are to preserve local resources by investing in tree cover, terracing, or contour plowing. Second, governments need to support—produce, provide, tender out, or perhaps subsidize—*appropriate* sorts of investment. These investments stretch well beyond conventional pure public goods. They include investments in communication, innovation, invention, and research, as faster population growth closes the extensive margin in formerly land-abundant areas. That process compels intensification, which is seldom sustainable either with the same technical means as prevailed in these areas when they were farmed at lower intensity, or with means suitable in more densely populated, water-controlled areas. The fruits of research and investment in the intensification of hitherto marginal land are often not public goods, being both rivalrous and price-excludable. However, such investments are often too uncertain, too long term at prevailing high interest rates, and too likely to be external and difficult for providers to capture to be adequately provided by private enterprise alone.

What about alleviating agro-Malthusian challenges by making land available to a larger proportion of rural residents in the sending zones as outmigration reduces population pressure there? Land redistribution has indeed been a major remedy in many parts of Asia (China, Taiwan, Kerala, and West Bengal in India) and Africa (Kenya, currently perhaps Zimbabwe and South Africa). It is, however, complementary with other measures to restrain population increase—which may even rise if poor couples come to believe their children will have more land to farm but do not face any new incentives to moderate their fertility. This was Malthus's serious, but only, objection to the land reform proposals of Alleyn Young.

In rural areas of low-income countries, the resource-degrading or resource-preserving impact of net rural-to-urban migration needs no extensive review, because such migration and its overall rural impact are known to be rather small. Moreover, there is an important countervailing factor to any positive impact that such net migration may have on farmland availability. Townward migration, together with the much more important effects of urban natural increase and rising urban income-per-person, pulls land (and associated water) into nonfarm uses. Such resources tend to have previously been especially well adapted to intensive farming. Their shift to nonfarm uses therefore impedes net agricultural expansion. In that sense, urbanization is like salinity: in both cases, past land loss, occurring when extra people degrade the environment because they face wrong price and technology incentives, reduces—perhaps below zero—the net present impact of type 2 responses.

Intensification and Technical Progress

Perhaps the main policy issue in low-income countries, raised by the need to respond to population growth with sustainable increases in output of food or food exchangeables, is the choice between expansion of farm area into increasingly marginal lands or intensification of currently farmed areas. The issues are well reviewed in Reardon and Islam (1989) and essentially rest on the balance and bias of price and technology incentives and on the prospects created by research and technology for sustaining the patterns of farming that emerge with each option. Reardon and Islam correctly emphasize the distinction between areas of low productivity and low sustainable potential and areas of low productivity and high potential. The latter areas must be identified and researched.

Such areas are crucial to responses 2 and 3. They, along with previously uncultivated areas, can become recipients for rural-to-rural migrants. Existing farming in these areas can be intensified to feed and employ more people in place.

To further examine the potential for technical progress to improve the prospects for environment-preserving type 3 responses to population growth, one needs to explore two different effects of population growth on the path of technical change.

First, population growth increases the pressure to invest, innovate, and even invent technologies and forms of agricultural production and resource use that raise per-person output of food or food exchangeables by intensifying land use (Boserup 1965b, 1981). Second, population growth cheapens labor relative to land and capital, creating incentives that raise labor-land ratios (Ruttan and Binswanger 1978; Hayami and Ruttan 1985). The two effects correspond, respectively, to technical responses to population growth that maintain or increase food *availability* and food *entitlements* in the sense of Sen (1981). Either set of responses can take place alone, and there is no guarantee that either or both sets of technical responses will suffice to permit continued real growth in welfare. Indeed, there are indications of rather weak Hayami-Ruttan-Binswanger (HRB) responses to rural population growth in parts of South Asia (Jayasuriya and Shand 1986; Bhalla 1987) and, alarmingly, of extremely weak Boserup responses in most of Sub-Saharan Africa (Timmer 1988).

Both problems arise partly because technological change (type 3 responses) cannot, economically, turn "this Island into a garden" in any sequence one wishes. The appropriate sequences usually require both public and private investments substantially higher than are likely. For example, early investments frequently need to embody some form of improved water control. These investments normally predate cost-effective innovation in agronomic, biological, chemical, or mechanical technology (Ishikawa 1968; Bray 1986). With some exceptions, biological, chemical, agronomic, and mechanical innovations—in the absence of improved structures for water management—have, since 1960, proved unable to support profitable farm decisions that permit yields to keep up with, let alone to outpace, rural population growth in developing countries. But, given water control, Green Revolution–type responses to population growth have been rapid in many areas. Therefore, the adequacy of technical change, as a type 3 response to population growth, has depended heavily on the willingness of farmers and governments to divert resources from current uses toward water control investments.

That willingness is heavily dependent on price and technology incentives—notably interest rates and water control techniques, infrastructure, and equipment—sufficiently attractive to persuade farmers and politicians to move cash and labor into water management investments. Lacking such incentives, poor people (and their governments) are induced to respond to population acceleration, not with technical responses requiring long-sighted investments, but with "mining" of soil, water, and other resources.

Now, consider the extent to which type 3 innovation-invention sequences, where affordable and profitable as private or public responses to population growth, are likely to reduce possible threats of accelerated resource degradation. There is nothing about intensifying (Boserup) or labor-using (HRB) type 3 responses that *need* reduce, or increase, resource depletion rates. Intensification can lead to eroded dust bowls—or to the use of fertilizers and composts to regenerate depleted soils. Extra labor can repair bunds and plow along contours—or harvest more and more high-yielding cassava until the soil is destroyed. However, if science is under heavy pressure from rapid population growth to raise yields of food for growing workforces, then researchers are less able to attend to longer-term conservation goals, even more so because anti-depletion research is costly.

Further, suppose that food or food-exchangeables were more available, that there were greater entitlements to food, and that there were slower depletion of natural resources. The basic Malthusian problem would still arise: will access to food and income merely stimulate more population growth, with ever-diminishing prospects of such good fortune with successive rounds of type 3 response?

Fertility Responses to Growth of Population and of the Economy

It is now known, as Malthus by 1824 was beginning to suspect, that the tendency of population to increase, in response to labor-using technical progress in food production, can be fairly short-term. As the poor become better off, they tend to substitute, plan, and use resources for a few, healthy, better-educated children. However, the length of this "short" term is critical to the resource-depleting impact. Vosti, Witcover, and Lipton (1995) show that Indian districts that enjoyed more Boserup and HRB technical progress in agriculture in 1960/61–1987/88 (almost all during the Green Revolution after 1965) experienced slower declines in 1971–1981 in total fertility rates, and hence faster population growth, than did the districts with less technical progress along Green Revolution lines, although the effects varied by crop.

There is evidence that changes in income, incentives, and information linked to rural modernization eventually bring total fertility rates sharply down. But the data from India suggest that this can be a long process. This is mainly because technical progress in the HRB style is, and ought to be, labor using—which raises the returns to child and adolescent labor well before it creates new work chances that raise the opportunity cost of child rearing for potential mothers and thus bring fertility down. The long delay also arises partly because, for the very poor, extra income at first brings significantly improved maternal nutrition and health care, and hence higher fertility (and fewer stillbirths) (Easterlin and Crimmins 1985). Only after income increases have pushed poor mothers over the "hump" of positive income effects (via biological supply of children) on fertility do the negative effects of extra earning prospects for women and their educated children—and hence the negative effects of "development" on the demand for children—begin to predominate.

The speed of the fall in fertility (response 4) due to the changed costs and benefits of childbirth, child rearing, contraception, prospects of child survival, and support for the couple in old age is central in assessing the effect of population growth on resource degradation rates. The story, however, is less simple than the popular paradigm that more people degrade resources more, while fewer people (slower population growth) degrade resources less. In general, more income (for mothers and for better-educated children) induces couples to "substitute quality for quantity," so that population growth rates fall (Becker and Lewis 1974). However, the way in which the extra income is earned may degrade local resources, perhaps faster than the avoided population growth would have done. Some resources, degraded by demands that increase with (or faster than) population growth, may be inadequately replaced, or may be nonrenewable, nonsubstitutable, and locally nondiscoverable. These resources may be used in near-fixed proportions to other resources in producing some key product. Some resources are used more than in proportion to the growth of income (for example, forest products). Research, if concerned with sustainability, should categorize resources by the rate at which depletion changes as income, as well as population, grows.

If one allows for incentive adjustments, even less is known about the impact of population, as compared with income growth associated with a population slowdown, on resource degradation rates. For example, little is known about the effect upon resource degradation of the demographic transition.

To understand better the effects of population change on the environment, the following questions must be answered: (1) How do relative prices, and production and consumption transformation technologies, respond to the demand created by more people, versus more income for a stable population? (2) How do resource use characteristics (prices and discovery, extraction, and technologies of uses) respond to more people, versus more income for a stable population? (3) How do resource use characteristics respond to incentive changes (new resource technologies or prices)? (4) Do the price and technology changes lead to changes in population and output?

These issues can be simplified if some key prices and technologies are largely exogenous ("imported") rather than endogenous (locally created).

Chapter 11 of this volume discusses the exogeneity of real interest rates and technical progress, two critical determinants of the choice between resource-saving and resource-degrading techniques.

Common Property Resources

Earlier, this chapter reported the evidence that fertility decisions are endogenous and privately rational. It has been shown that these decisions are not socially and environmentally optimal, and the prospects that induced technical progress will moderate rural resource degradation are uncertain. Doubts have been raised about whether Green Revolution types of technical progress will swiftly generate incentives for lower fertility. This section briefly evaluates the claim that population growth threatens rural resources mainly by its effect on the management of CPRs.

There is little doubt that CPRs are important in developing countries, especially in arid and semi-arid areas. In 21 groups of villages in India in 1982–1985, CPRs accounted for 20 percent of income for households cultivating less than 2 hectares (including landless households). However, the shares were only 1–2 percent among the other one-third, the nonpoor households (Jodha 1991a). CPR income is thus important to the rural poor and reduces inequality (Jodha 1986a). However, CPRs declined sharply in area (Jodha 1991a) and productivity (Jodha 1985) between the mid-1950s and the mid-1970s.

But does this decline in CPRs show that population growth degrades rural resources, especially those that benefit the poor? More people *in* a community means that more people have to be persuaded to respect the rules (of, say, common grazing, fishing, or fuel gathering) and decreases the benefits-per-person from the CPR. More people *outside* a community, but near one of the community's CPRs, increases the numbers likely to poach on that CPR and thus transform it into an open-access resource and use it rapidly. These factors combine to increase "contributors' dilemma" (Olson 1982); with population growth, the community entitled to access a CPR is under pressure to pay higher charges for the protection of the CPR against overuse, yet sees fewer per-person benefits, and more free-riding fellow users, of whom some may evade payment.

That population growth makes CPR management harder, however, does not imply that resource degradation need always accelerate. On the contrary, the risk of deterioration of CPR management, when population grows, leads people to avoid that risk. However, such response is incomplete and imperfect. This partly explains why population growth rates are positively correlated, across locations, with rates of decline in CPRs.

For example, Jodha (1986a) tabulates population densities for 1981, and shares of CPRs in total village area for 1982–1985, in 21 groups of villages in semi-arid or arid areas of India. Leaving aside the six districts of high population density (more than 200 people per square kilometer)—in which the share of CPR land in village area seems not to fall below 9–11 percent—higher density reduces the share of CPR in village area. For the remaining 15 districts, the R^2 of 1982–1984 CPR share in area upon 1981 population density per square kilometer is 0.40. It rises further if the two districts with villages of very low density (fewer than 82 people per square kilometer) are excluded—much of the nonprivate land there is too poor to be worth managing as CPRs. The strong positive correlation over the relevant range is important because—although it is a travesty to claim that CPRs normally lead to tragedies of the commons (as shown in Ostrom 1990)—many resources are better protected against overrapid degradation if such resources shift to other forms of ownership.

How much population growth spurs resource degradation does not depend mainly on the structure of property rights, partly because population growth leads to incentives to change those rights. Rather, the harmful resource impacts depend on the extent to which more people use or pollute particular resources—for want of price-mediated or technology-mediated invention, economization, discovery, or substitution. These responses—on common, state, or private property—can all be thwarted by exogenous or inappropriate influences on price or technology, or as a result of a range of available technologies or institutions that does not suffice to allow much response, or renders it blocked or infeasible.

Migot-Adholla et al. (1991) summarize African evidence that property rights, far from preventing development, strongly respond to person-land ratios. (A closely analogous responsiveness of the Indian caste system has been documented [Rudolph and Rudolph 1968].) It is suggested here that the population-property sequence, while (similarly) responding to resource degradation, is not a major cause of that degradation. It is the combination of more people, high interest rates and other "short-termist" incentives, scarce land, and inadequate technical progress that threatens to validate the claim that population growth in rural areas causes resource degradation—and to do so whatever the structure of property rights.

7 Global Climate Change: Implications for the Links between Sustainability, Growth, and Poverty Alleviation

THOMAS E. DOWNING AND MARTIN L. PARRY

Global climate change presents a significant threat to sustainable agricultural development. This threat has prompted increased research on the physical and human effects of climate change (see, for example, Kasperson et al. 1990). In this chapter we review the potential effect of climate change on agricultural systems through its effects on average rainfall and weather extremes, and, via increases in carbon dioxide concentration, on plant growth. We also discuss examples of recent research on potential effects at the national (Kenya) and world level.[1] We conclude with recommendations for policy and research aimed at promoting resilient systems for use of natural resources.

The effects of climate change on alleviation of poverty, economic growth, and sustainable development are uncertain. Insight is constrained by the long-term nature of climate change, the lack of reliable regional projections of new climates, and the rapid pace of social, political, economic, and demographic change.

Projections of Climate Change

Climate change is expected to result from increased concentrations of greenhouse gases. These gases, in order of importance, are carbon dioxide, methane, nitrous oxide, halocarbons, and sulfur dioxide. The emission of greenhouse gases depends on levels and types of economic activities, as well as on technology and policies to stabilize or reduce emissions. Whereas greenhouse gases are well mixed in the upper atmosphere, the regional effects of climate change brought about by these gases depend on local conditions such as topography and land surface.

---

1. This chapter draws upon research undertaken by the Climate Change and International Agriculture project funded by the U.S. Environmental Protection Agency and coordinated by Cynthia Rosenzweig (Goddard Institute for Space Studies) and the authors. See Downing (1992) and Rosenzweig et al. (1992) for a more complete summary of the project findings.

The most common sources of climate forecasts are general circulation models (GCMs) (Houghton, Jenkins, and Ephraums 1990; Houghton, Callander, and Varney 1992; Houghton et al. 1996). Although the details of the models vary, the current set of global warming experiments using GCMs remarkably reach the common conclusion that the global average temperature will increase 1.0–3.5 degrees centigrade by 2100, with a more vigorous hydrological cycle (Houghton et al. 1996; see also Cubasch and Cess 1990; Downing 1992; Gates et al. 1992).

However, GCMs have a number of limitations that restrict their ability to project regional impacts: low spatial resolution, sensitivity to parameterization schemes for hydrological processes (for example, cloud formation and surface fluxes), and lack of realistic coupling with dynamic ocean and biosphere models. Therefore, climate modelers have little confidence in projected changes for specific regions.

The GCM experiments are also inconclusive about whether the variability of climate will change with global warming. However, a shift in the average climate will change the distribution of extreme events, such as the number of hot days or frosts. Possible changes in the frequency and magnitude of tropical and midlatitude storms are also uncertain, although changes in their tracks could have serious regional effects.

Effects on Agricultural Productivity

Climate change can affect agricultural productivity (yields) in three ways: by changing average rainfall and sunshine; by increasing atmospheric concentrations of carbon dioxide; and by changing the frequency of extreme events (Tegart, Sheldon, and Griffiths 1990). More specifically, global climate change may (1) lengthen the growing season as a result of higher temperatures, (2) reduce soil moisture because of increased evaporative demand (with or without changes in precipitation), (3) alter the stages of plant growth by accelerating growth, (4) affect the partitioning and quality of plant biomass, and (5) affect crop pests and diseases—all of which can shift agricultural potential geographically. The magnitude of such changes is illustrated here with examples from Kenya.

Changes in Climatic Averages

Crop-climate relationships have been the focus of many studies using water balance models, statistical correlations, critical climatic parameters, and agroclimatological indices (see, for example, Parry 1990). Research for Kenya illustrates the significance of climate change for (1) shifts in agroclimatic potential, using the length of growing period; and (2) shifts in land use, as gauged by an optimization model (Downing 1992). Based on several GCM scenarios, future climate change in Kenya involves an

TABLE 7.1 Climate change and land use in Kenya

	Province							Total
	Central	Coast	Eastern	Northeastern	Nyanza	Rift Valley	Western	
Current arable land (hectares)	698	734	1,350	103	787	2,144	630	6,343
Current high-potential land[a] (hectares)	400	170	352	5	285	914	223	2,344
Change in arable land (percent)								
+2.5°C	1.0	-18.0	-28.4	-66.6	0.4	5.1	3.1	-6.9
+2.5°C, +10 percent precipitation	3.9	12.2	17.5	5.2	5.3	16.8	3.5	12.1
+2.5°C, +20 percent precipitation	6.7	50.1	65.8	44.9	7.6	40.0	3.7	35.5
+4°C	-0.6	-31.8	-43.5	-88.1	-1.4	3.5	3.1	-12.9
+4°C, +10 percent precipitation	5.5	0.0	1.5	-1.8	4.4	15.2	3.5	6.8
+4°C, +20 percent precipitation	6.9	36.3	41.3	21.9	7.4	32.2	3.7	25.8
Change in high-potential land (percent)								
+2.5°C	11.9	-25.4	-14.8	-27.5	26.4	27.8	66.7	18.0
+2.5°C, +10 percent precipitation	15.2	28.1	27.3	0.0	21.2	30.1	-8.3	22.1
+2.5°C, +20 percent precipitation	27.6	117.7	162.9	200.0	23.2	43.7	-31.1	54.9
+4°C	-2.1	-38.8	-31.0	-100.0	34.9	26.9	73.7	13.5
+4°C, +10 percent precipitation	20.0	3.7	10.3	0.0	42.6	31.1	56.2	29.6
+4°C, +20 percent precipitation	30.4	86.3	92.0	54.9	-3.3	33.8	-16.6	36.5
Change in calorie index[b] (percent)								
+2.5°C	22.5	-30.4	-17.2	-48.9	0.4	4.4	-7.9	-2.3
+2.5°C, +10 percent precipitation	45.4	8.4	5.3	-10.4	4.6	25.8	-3.9	16.2
+2.5°C, +20 percent precipitation	63.0	45.3	34.7	16.0	11.7	39.2	-12.3	32.0
+4°C	8.5	-37.5	-34.2	-60.7	-17.9	-2.2	-7.1	-13.1
+4°C, +10 percent precipitation	29.4	-8.4	-15.9	-15.1	-16.8	9.5	-8.4	-0.6
+4°C, +20 percent precipitation	55.1	20.3	3.5	3.2	-13.3	20.0	-18.1	11.7

SOURCE: Data from G. Fischer, International Institute for Applied Systems Analysis (IIASA), reported in Downing 1992.

[a]Includes classes C1 and C2, which are estimated to be able to achieve 60–100 percent of the maximum attainable yield.

[b]The calorie index is the weighted optimization criterion. In Western Province, expansion of coffee and tea depresses the calorie index, although food would presumably be purchased with higher farm incomes.

increase in mean annual temperature of 2.5–5 degrees centigrade with a 0–25 percent increase in precipitation. Incremental scenarios of +2.5 degrees centigrade and +4.0 degrees centigrade, along with a 0, +10, and +20 percent increase in precipitation, were used.

A growing season in Kenya is defined as the period during which rainfall exceeds 50 percent of potential evapotranspiration and temperatures are sufficient for crop growth (Kassam et al. 1991). The baseline length of growing periods (LGPs) was estimated from 437 weather stations in Kenya, using data on mean annual temperature, average potential evapotranspiration, and historical rainfall for about 30 years.

Scenarios of climate change were applied to the spatial climate data to derive new LGP zones and to reassess potential farm productivity. A 4-degree-centigrade increase in temperature in Kenya results in a dramatic shortening of the LGP. The arid region (no growing period) doubles in size, the limit of maize cultivation (LGP > 90 days) retreats to higher elevations, and the tea and dairy zone (LGP > 330 days) becomes drier or disappears in some places.

These changes, incorporated into an agroclimatic index, were then used in a more complex analysis of land use potential. The effects of climate change on land use were judged based on the agroecological database and method that involves (1) selection of land use types and input levels for 64 crops, each assessed for three levels of management; (2) description of crop requirements matched to the agroecological characteristics of each location; (3) specification of rotation options and constraints for crop and livestock systems; (4) description of the relationship between the crop, livestock, and fuelwood sectors; (5) quantification of potential arable land and crop production of each activity by agroecological cell; and (6) specification of district agricultural planning scenarios with objectives and constraints—all used as inputs to a linear programming model that optimizes the allocation of land (Fischer et al. 1991; Kassam et al. 1991; see also more recently Fischer et al. 1996). The optimization is based on the weighted sum of net calorie and protein production for human consumption available from each activity.

As expected, given the large range of agroecological environments in Kenya, the results show a wide range of impacts (Table 7.1). Currently, land in Kenya suitable for permanent cultivation exceeds 6,000 square kilometers. Most of the high-potential land is concentrated in the highlands of the Central, Eastern, and Rift Valley Provinces. Hence, in eastern and southern Kenya, increases in temperature, without corresponding increases in rainfall, would result in dramatic reductions in potential agricultural production. For example, in Eastern Province, the potential arable land decreases by 28 percent with an increase of 2.5 degrees centigrade in temperature, but increases 18–66 percent if precipitation increases 10–20 percent. In central and western Kenya, gains from increased arable land (as higher-altitude areas become more suitable) and increased intensity of farming (resulting from temperature increases and multiple crops per year) usually more than outweigh the negative effects of reduced soil moisture, even in scenarios assuming no change in precipitation.

Direct Enrichment of CO_2

Increased concentrations of carbon dioxide increase plant growth and water use efficiency but reduce nitrogen content and hence protein levels and nutritional quality. These direct effects depend on how carbon is used in photosynthesis: crops such as wheat, soybeans, and rice respond to increased CO_2 enrichment to a greater extent than crops such as millet, sorghum, and maize. These effects have been demonstrated in many experimental trials (Cure and Acock 1986). However, the effects on many crops and on actual farm plots remain uncertain.

The potential effects of CO_2 enrichment have been gauged by a number of crop-climate models. Potential productivity increases of 25 percent for crops such as wheat, soybeans, and rice and 7 percent for crops such as millet, sorghum, and maize have been forecasted. Increased water use efficiency related to CO_2 enrichment is particularly important for water resources. The crop models with direct enrichment, however, need further validation against field trials before the results warrant much confidence.

Changes in Weather Extremes

Even if climate variability remains at its current levels, episodes of extreme weather may increase in frequency, magnitude, and persistence. For example, drought frequency can shift dramatically (Rind et al. 1990). Based on an index of atmospheric demand for moisture, severe droughts, which currently have a frequency of 5 percent, will increase in frequency to 50 percent by the 2050s. Increased variability can affect wheat yields and the probability of crop failure more than changes in mean conditions (Mearns, Rosenzweig, and Goldberg 1991).

Implications for Agricultural Production and Food Poverty

The secondary effects of climate change on agricultural production depend on how changes in potential productivity affect agricultural systems: crop choice, area planted and harvested, availability and allocation of labor, level of inputs, adoption of existing agricultural technology, and development of new technology. Impoverishment may amplify the long-term effects of climate change: the poor must exploit their resources to survive, resulting in degradation and reduced resilience. This connection between the impacts of altered resource potential and poverty warrants analysis of specific vulnerable socioeconomic groups and places (see Downing 1996).

World Food System and Climate Change

The analysis of the biophysical effects of climate change and vulnerable socioeconomic groups lays the foundation for a more complete assessment of the sensitivity of the world food system to global change. The effect of climate change may be exacerbated, mitigated, or transferred as the impacts spread through space and time. These are difficult links to model. To begin to examine the impact of global climate change on global food security, the Basic Linked System (BLS) world trade model was used to look at the transient response of the world food system to scenarios of climate change (see Rosenzweig et al. 1992 and Fischer et al. 1996 for details).

The BLS links 34 national and regional models in a general equilibrium system that represents all economic sectors (through trade, world market prices, and financial flows). The links between sustainability, growth, and poverty alleviation were explicitly modeled. Summary indicators include cereal production, cereal prices, and risk of food poverty. Food poverty is defined as the proportion of the population with insufficient income to either produce or buy enough food to meet their requirements.

At each stage of the assessment there are large uncertainties. The results should be interpreted as a sensitivity test of the relative magnitudes of global environmental changes in climate, economy, and population. The relevant scenarios and results of the BLS simulations appear in Figure 7.1.

The *baseline reference scenario* is based on the following assumptions: the United Nations medium estimate of population growth (from 5.3 billion in 1990 to 10.3 billion by 2060), a 50 percent trade liberalization by 2020, moderate economic growth, and increased cereal yields (0.7 percent per year) owing to technological improvements. This reference scenario projects cereal production to grow from 1,795 million metric tons in 1990 to 3,286 million metric tons in 2060. Cereal prices increase 21 percent compared with 1990. The prevalence of food poverty decreases from about 13 percent of the population of developing countries to more than 7 percent in 2060. The absolute number of food-poor, however, increases from 530 million to 641 million.

The *low population growth scenario* includes the same assumptions as the baseline reference scenario but uses the United Nations low population estimate (8.6 billion by 2060, 17 percent lower than the medium estimate). Higher per capita incomes and slower population growth contribute to lower world cereal production (2,929 million metric tons, 89 percent of the baseline reference) and lower cereal prices (92 percent of 1970 prices). Both the rate of food poverty and the absolute number of food-poor would decline from the 1990 reference, reaching 6 percent of the population of developing countries (395 million people) in 2060.

The *low economic growth scenario* projects economic growth 10 percent lower than the baseline reference scenario. In 2060, production is near the level

FIGURE 7.1 Sensitivity of world food poverty to global climate change, 2060

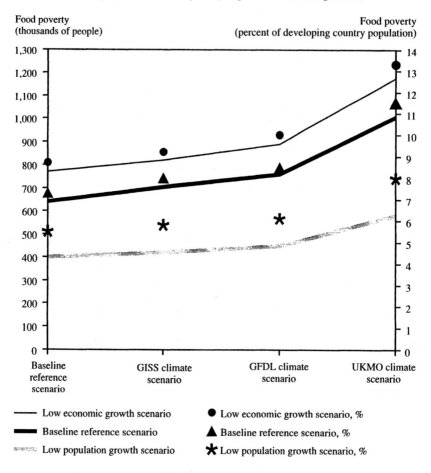

SOURCE: Data in Rosenzweig et al. 1992.

NOTES: Results for three climate scenarios (with CO_2 effects) are shown: GISS (Goddard Institute for Space Studies), GFDL (Geophysical Fluid Dynamics Laboratory), and UKMO (U.K. Meteorological Office).

of the reference scenario, but prices are 13 percent higher and the rate of food poverty is 18 percent higher.

The *climate change and baseline reference scenario* combines three climate change scenarios with the effects of CO_2 enrichment and the assumptions of the baseline reference scenario. Compared with the baseline reference projection, each of the three scenarios produces declines in world cereal production (from –1.2 to –7.6 percent in 2060) and increases in world cereal prices

(24–145 percent in 2060). However, the impacts are greatest in developing countries: production declines about 10 percent and food-poverty rates increase 10–58 percent in 2060.

The *climate change and low population growth scenario* uses the same climate scenarios but the low projection of population growth. Although world cereal production is less with lower population growth, the relative impact of climate change is much the same. World cereal prices increase but slightly less than in the medium population growth case (19–116 percent in 2060). Slowing the rate of population growth would also mitigate the impact of climate change on food poverty: prevalence rates would increase 5–47 percent, about 5 percent less than in the medium population growth scenario with climate change.

The *climate change and low economic growth scenario* results in percentage changes in global cereal production, prices, and food poverty that are similar to the effects of climate change in the baseline reference scenario. That is, the effect of climate change does not significantly exacerbate the impacts of lower economic growth.

Several important conclusions appear warranted by this exploratory analysis. (1) The effects of world climate change on yields are considerably mitigated as the model steps through each year of analysis and allows the system to respond through area planted, agricultural intensity, investment, and prices. (2) Changes in potential productivity and prices may significantly alter trade patterns, particularly between developed and developing countries. (3) The impact of climate change will make efforts to reduce food poverty more difficult, through altered agroecological potential in developing countries or through effects on the distribution of income, world food prices, and food imports. (4) Developing countries unable to purchase food at higher world prices may suffer significant reduction in consumption, with increased risk of widespread food shortages. (5) Slowing population growth, all other things being equal, reduces the prevalence of food poverty by almost 40 percent in 2060. (6) Climate change could offset the benefits from slower population growth, but policies to stabilize populations may be as desirable as efforts to stabilize greenhouse gas emissions.

Conclusion: Sustainability and Adaptation

Implications of Climate Change for Sustainable Agricultural Development

The potential importance of climate change for the key aspects of sustainable agricultural development listed earlier is summarized in Table 7.2. Climate change will alter agricultural productivity, or agroecological potential, through increased concentrations of carbon dioxide, shifts in average climatic patterns, changes in the frequency and magnitude of extreme events, and changes in other natural resources. The changes in agroecological potential

TABLE 7.2 Linkages between climate change and sustainable agricultural development

Effect of Climate Change	Human Activity		Valued Environmental Components				Consequences	
	Agricultural Production[a]	Material Flux	Soils	Water	Landscape	Vulnerable Populations	Pollution	Food Security
Increased CO_2	≈ increased productivity	≈	▲ nutrients	▲ water use efficiency	→ land use	▲ → farm productivity and income	▲ irrigation demand	▲ farm productivity
Altered mean climates	▲ global production can be sustained; regional and crop-specific changes likely	→ new cultivars and practices; pests, disease	▲ shorter growing season; → land use shifts	▲ evapotranspiraton; → land use shifts	→ shifts in cropping systems and land use	▲ → farm productivity and income, regional effects in marginal zones	▲ agronomic practices (control of pests and disease)	▲ growing season; → labor demands
Extreme episodes	▲ risk of drought, frost, flood	→ as above	▲ land cover; ≈ rainfall erosivity	▲ water reservoir levels, drought impacts on ecosystems	▲ cumulative stress	▲ → shift in risk, impoverishment during drought	≈	▲ shift in risk, storage needs
Effects on other natural resources	▲ → soil fertility, erosion, salinization, water for irrigation	→ as above	▲ land cover, salinization, waterlogging, flooding	▲ water budget and quality; → land use shifts	→ land use shifts	▲ → resource productivity and income	▲ water quality, erosion	→ farm productivity
Secondary economic effects	▲ prices, income, employment, inputs, regional trade	▲ e.g., trade volume and distances	▲ local land use intensification and expansion to achieve self-sufficiency relative to access to food from other regions			▲ → physical and economic access to food	▲ agro-chemical use, cultivated area and intensity	▲ related to access issues

NOTES: ▲, direct effect, as noted; →, indirect impact through other effects; ≈, uncertain relationship.
[a]Production is the realized harvest, that is, potential yield (productivity) times area harvested.

will come through reductions in yield and farmed area. Effects are uncertain. But it is possible that in the aggregate they may threaten food security at the global level and significantly reduce food security for specific vulnerable groups.

Potential Coping Strategies

The literature on the agricultural impacts of climate change has expanded dramatically. Yet few studies have systematically assessed the potential to mitigate the impacts through (1) soil and water management; (2) changes in crop and livestock product mix, technology, and land use; and (3) economic adjustments such as diversification, storage, and infrastructure at the farm, regional, and national levels (Table 7.3).

Four domains of adaptive options relevant to farmers, researchers, and policymakers need to be explored.

ACCOMMODATION. Socioeconomic systems can gradually adapt to small changes in climate at little cost. This is because the changes are below a threshold of noticeable economic impact or occur on a time scale that makes these changes easily absorbed by socioeconomic systems. Farmers and extension services can react to small changes in market signals prompted by climate change, production techniques, or crops mix. In addition, slow climate change, of up to perhaps 1 degree centigrade to the year 2020, could allow plant breeders time to develop new varieties in the altered environment in which they will be grown by farmers. Crop breeding could also address the problems posed by the higher temperatures and CO_2 concentrations.

PLANNED RESILIENCY. A set of adjustments can be envisioned that provides for greater resiliency to climatic variations, regardless of the eventual climate change. For example, improved seasonal forecasting and farmer and policymaker response would reduce the cost of agricultural production and supporting infrastructure. Farmers and extension services could be better equipped to predict the impact of short-term weather shocks, and policymakers could develop more effective programs for identifying and compensating those most affected by such shocks. Other examples include research into new varieties, more effective mechanisms to diversify farm income and risk, and integrated pest management that improves yields and soil moisture management.

PURPOSEFUL ADJUSTMENT. Specific practices designed primarily to cope with expected climate change, but not justified by short-term social and economic benefits, can be termed purposeful adjustments. They entail a higher cost than the responses already mentioned and a higher risk of error. Examples include development of crops that are sensitive to CO_2 enrichment, and interregional water transfers for irrigation.

CRISIS RESPONSE. After climate change has had significant impacts, societies may respond to crises with a further set of adjustments. These crisis responses entail bearing the full cost of the impact and the additional cost of

TABLE 7.3 Adaptive responses: timing and sector-specific strategies for agriculture

Timing Response	Type of Response		
	Soil and Water Management	Crop Choice, Husbandry, and Land Use	Economic Adjustments
Accommodation: acceleration of current trends to match rate of climate change	Soil conservation: e.g., increased use of terraces, zero tillage, mulching, dry season cover	Crop choice: e.g., use of new varieties of existing crops, some crop substitution, conversion to or from crops or pasture, use of nitrogen-fixing crops, changes in livestock types and levels	Investment: e.g., infrastructure, equipment and machinery, farm inputs, marketing and credit, agroclimatic information
	Water management: e.g., increased use of irrigation (with varying quantity and timing), soil drainage, mulching, fallowing, crop rotation	Husbandry: changes in rotations, timing of planting and harvest, mix of varieties, planting depth, plant density, herbicides, pesticides, fertilizer application Land use: e.g., changes in area, choice of location, specialization	Diversification of income: e.g., savings and storage, employment, regional development Economic integration: e.g., off-farm purchases, subsidies Altered consumption: e.g., food, education, health
Planned resiliency: strategies for coping with a range of current and potential climatic variations	As above, but with emphasis on experimentation in a wider variety of sites and climatic conditions	As above, but including development of and experimentation with new varieties and different crops, experimentation across a wide variety of climatic and soil conditions	As above, with effective national and international policies to prevent famine, promote regional food security, and enhance equitable regional economic development
Purposeful adjustment: specific responses in anticipation of forecast climate	Increased irrigation capacity, capital-intensive soil and water management	Breeding of crops specifically adapted to CO_2-enriched atmospheres, heat stress, and other projected changes	Mechanisms to share costs of mitigating the impacts of climate change
Crisis response: emergency measures adopted after the failure of previous responses	Importation of water, rehabilitation of degraded lands	Importation of and rapid experimentation with alternative crops and varieties	Disaster relief, bearing of the social and economic consequences (e.g., migration, political instability)

SOURCE: Downing 1992.

emergency actions that may or may not reduce vulnerability to additional impacts. For example, food insecurity due to crop failure caused by drought can be addressed by emergency food aid, but the vulnerability to drought remains.

Adaptive strategies will probably vary by agroecological zone and vulnerable socioeconomic group. For example, coping with extreme events such as drought is critically dependent on the ability to produce and market a surplus in a year of good rainfall, and this ability varies by agroclimatic zone, land use patterns, and household characteristics (Downing 1991).

Planned Responses and Research Needs

Suggestions for planned responses to climate change, including research needs, parallel the four domains of adaptive options suggested above. Clearly, enough research has been conducted to recommend precautionary policies to prevent crises. Research demonstrates that coping with climate change at levels currently projected will entail enormous costs at the global level, but the costs in terms of the livelihood of vulnerable populations of *not* undertaking at least some of these investments could be even higher (Tegart, Sheldon, and Griffiths 1990; Mintzer 1992).

Policymakers may seek to balance the cost of coping with climate change (including bearing the consequences) and the cost of limiting greenhouse gas emissions. In any case, limiting emissions of greenhouse gases is essential, although the targets and means for stabilizing carbon dioxide, nitrogen, halocarbon, and methane releases need to be further explored.

The difficulty of assessing the costs of climate change warrants undertaking a set of planned responses to promote resilient systems (natural resource, economic, political, and social) to promote global and regional food security. Given present knowledge, recommendations for purposeful local adaptation are premature. Over the next decade, scientific understanding of climate change should dramatically improve to the point where forecasts at the regional scale will provide a basis for targeted coping strategies.

Promoting resiliency requires improved databases and monitoring, increased understanding of climate-society relationships, and a wider range of potential adaptive strategies. (For example, see Higgins et al. 1982; Parry et al. 1990; Human Dimensions Programme 1992; IGBP 1992a,b; Mintzer 1992; Norse et al. 1992.) Data and monitoring needs on global change include (1) global, national, and local baseline data on resources, land use, and socioeconomic conditions; and (2) global, national, and local monitoring of the human dimensions of global environmental change, particularly land use, land degradation, and food poverty, to complement monitoring of the physical environment.

In addition, field assessment and model development need to be pursued to identify critical thresholds in climate-society relationships. Specific assessments should include (1) sectoral studies of crop-climate interactions, assessments of the range of practicable technical adjustments, and the social, economic, environmental, and political constraints to their adoption; (2) analysis of cross-sectoral linkages and the socioeconomic effects of climate change; (3) global, national, and local case studies and modeling of processes and driving forces of global change, including land transformation or degradation; (4) land use and land cover modeling to provide realistic representation of surface conditions for coupled atmosphere-ocean-biosphere general circulation models; and (5) theoretical and applied studies that integrate different levels of analysis, from the farm to community, nation, and world.

Finally, policies to promote resilient resource use are warranted. These include increasing the pace and focus of agricultural research in developing countries, investing in improved technology, and building institutions that are able to assess the implications of changing resources, develop and test practicable coping strategies, and implement policies to alleviate food poverty and promote sustainable development. Global environmental change can exacerbate the gulf between developed and developing countries—in levels of greenhouse gas emissions, scale of projected impacts, and the ability to cope with or take advantage of projected changes. Concerted action to limit emissions, reduce hunger, and plan for a range of possible futures is prudent.

8 The Relationship between Trade and Environment, with Special Reference to Agriculture

AMMAR SIAMWALLA

Trade and environment, the subjects joined in this chapter, do not have a direct relationship. They are both consequences of human economic activities. The volume of trade engaged in by a country is influenced by, among other things, its resource endowment, its taste idiosyncracies, and its technological capabilities— all relative to the same variables in other countries. Added to these as contributory factors are the policies that governments pursue regarding production, consumption, trade, and resource use.

At the same time, a country's economic activities (not just traded volume) directly impinge on its environment through the following pathways:

1. its production activities may cause the environment to be destroyed or irreversibly changed and effluents to be discharged into that environment;
2. its consumption activities may cause similar damage;
3. less important, its trading activities may allow movement of pollutants to accompany, surreptitiously, movement of goods (this aspect will be ignored in the rest of the chapter).

The levels and direction of these basic economic activities are in turn affected by the level of technology in the country, by its consumers' taste, by its resource endowments, and by government interventions in the various goods and factor markets. These variables also influence how much impact a given level of production, consumption, and trade will have on the environment of a country. At least of equal importance, resource policies exert influence on this interaction. Resource policies include property rights, tort law, pollution regulation, and government investments that influence resource availability either positively or negatively (storage dams, desalinization, afforestation, sewage treatment, and the like).

It is a poor strategy to ask how much one endogenous variable, trade, affects another, the environmental spillover. It is more appropriate to ask how different trade policy configurations influence the extent of environmental spillover, given resource and other nontrade policies (see Figure 8.1). This will

FIGURE 8.1 International trade and the environment

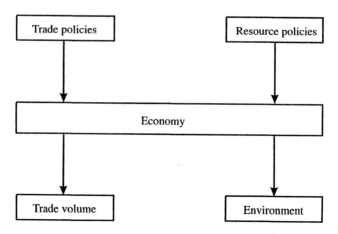

be the first step of this analysis. The next step is to ask how resource policies can affect both the volume of trade and the extent of the environmental spillover, and to weigh the effectiveness of trade versus resource policies. Throughout, the impact of both sets of policies on the welfare of the poor will be touched upon.

I have followed the economist's convention in not modeling the interaction in the formulation of the two sets of policies, thus ignoring politico-economic considerations that may lead to such interaction. Therefore an extremely powerful export sector created, for example, by a colonial trading regime may prevent the implementation of a particular set of resource policies. Of course, the two sets of policies do not have independent consequences—that is the whole point of this chapter. I shall follow these two steps of analysis by a case study before proceeding to international policy implications.

The Impact of Trade Policies, Given Resource Policies

In this section I take as given the resource policies followed in a "typical" developing country, which will be characterized as follows. It will be assumed that while property rights in older settled lands may be assured by the state, the extension of private cultivation into new lands (which are sometimes theoretically publicly owned) is not subject to any clear rules. The discharge of effluents from both industrial and agricultural activities is only tenuously regulated. Recourse to tort law as a means of disciplining or regulating spillover effects will be assumed to be sufficiently difficult and time-consuming as not to be worth anyone's while. It is possible to summarize the various aspects of such a set of resource policies by saying that natural resources in such a country are generally underpriced. Users of resources, which may also include public authorities, are not sufficiently induced to take account of the consequences of their action on the availability and quality of resources.

Given these policies, it is important to distinguish between measured income that ignores the environmental spillovers that affect the economy's sustainability and true welfare that incorporates these effects. I maintain two hypotheses in this chapter: (1) it is possible to evaluate the level of true welfare, in a way that is commensurate with measured income, so that one can compare the two measures; and (2) an increase in measured income will, other things (particularly policies) being equal, increase the spillover effects, so that a given increase in measured income will increase true welfare by less, or may even reduce true welfare.

I also assume that this "typical" developing country conducts the bulk of its trade with "typical" developed countries with greener policies than those outlined here. Thus the developed countries have better enforcement of property rights, tort law is an effective disciplinary device, effluents are strictly policed, and so on. Second, in its international trade, this developing country competes with other developing countries following resource policies similar to it. Occasionally it would be necessary to distinguish between two types of developing countries, namely, those with land surplus, for example, in Latin America and parts of Sub-Saharan Africa, and those with severe land constraint, mostly in Asia.

How would the trade policies of a developing country with these resource policies influence its environment? Given limited space, I focus on two contrasting trade regimes: a relatively open trading regime and a relatively closed one.[1] The policy instruments deployed to close an economy to trade may include overvalued exchange rates, border taxes, or regulations on domestic production and consumption. The total effect of these policies is to reduce the volume of goods and services crossing the border. I also assume that, among the tradable goods, the "typical" closed developing country tends to protect its industry and disprotect its agriculture, and that opening up the economy entails a correction of this bias.

This simplified characterization of trade policies implies that a more open trade regime will have a higher real exchange rate (home currency per unit of foreign currency) than a closed one. Equivalently, tradable goods prices in general will have higher relative prices in an open trade regime, and prices of nontradable goods and wages will be relatively lower.[2] Given the bias in favor of industry and against agriculture, prices of agricultural tradables relative to in-

---

1. An open economy need not imply laissez-faire, although the latter implies the former.
2. Here the assumption is that the nontradable sector is generally more labor-intensive than the tradable sector.

dustrial tradables may end up higher in a more open trading regime, whereas industrial tradables may or may not have higher prices relative to the non-tradables.

I shall trace the long-run end result of an opening of the economy, ignoring the intervening period of adjustment. To obtain results, assumptions will have to be made at each step along the way, which may or may not be valid for any given developing country. Indeed, the links in each step of the chain of arguments are weak. The main conclusion of this section is that no clear and simple conclusion to the question of the impact of trade policy on the environment is possible, even if the resource policy is fixed.

An opening up of the economy will have the following consequences: (1) it will increase measured income (gains from trade); (2) it will lead to a different production structure; (3) the production technology of existing industries may be changed; and (4) it will lead to a different consumption pattern.

In the following, I track the results of the first three of these changes on the environment and on the welfare of the poor. I ignore the impact of the change in the consumption pattern on the environment, although its impact on poverty and income distribution is significant and will be touched upon where appropriate.

International trade theory tells us that opening up a closed economy will result in an increase in aggregate measured income. Such an increase in measured income would ipso facto lead to higher environmental spillover effects.[3]

The impact on income distribution and on the level of poverty is unclear, however. The improvement in the agricultural prices relative to industrial prices may reduce rural/urban income disparities and reduce one major contributor of income inequality. But if food prices have been kept artificially low in a closed economy regime, its impact on nonfood-producing poor households can be extremely important and may indeed reverse the improvement from other policies.

Within the industrial sector, empirical studies indicate quite strongly that the protected sectors tend to be more capital-intensive. Such a pattern of protection would cause a unit of investment to have a lower impact on the demand for labor than would a less protected regime. Measured income of the poorer households could therefore be expected to be somewhat better in an open regime.

The higher relative prices for agriculture consequent upon the opening of the economy would cause the agricultural sector to expand. The industrial sector may contract (unless the exchange rate distortion in the closed regime is enormous). One would therefore expect environmental damage from industrial

---

3. It is possible and even likely that the increase in measured income yields the public sector more revenues to pursue "greener" resource policies.

plants to decline, but there would be increased strains on improperly priced resources in agriculture, for example, forestland. Where such extra resources are not readily available, the environmental damage from agricultural intensification, for example, from agricultural chemicals, would increase. In general, one would expect the mix of adverse spillover effects to change. There is as yet no reason to expect such a change in the mix to increase or decrease aggregate true welfare. Even if the question is disaggregated to ask what the impact on the true welfare of rural and urban households is, it is not possible to state clearly whether the true welfare of each of these groups will improve or decline.

In addition to the impact on producers themselves, the fiscal impact needs to be considered. A more open trade regime may increase the effective tax base of a country—border taxes are the easiest for a developing country to collect. To the extent that a major portion of resource policies would involve public expenditures, trade may give public authorities the resources to clean up the mess that it created.

Nevertheless, there are two reasons why inadequate resource policies may make the impact on total welfare of an opening of the economy worse than what would be indicated by an increase in measured income. First, the underpricing of natural resources would lead to a misperception by private agents of the country's true comparative advantage. Many activities that are natural resource–intensive would be perceived to be relatively profitable and would be expanded beyond the "optimal" level, and this tendency may well be stronger in a more open trading regime than in a closed one. This would be the case if, as assumed, the country's trading partners (that is, the developed countries) follow greener policies than it. If the developing country has an open investment climate as well, there would be a strong incentive to move some of the dirtier industries from developed countries to it.

The second reason for true welfare to be adversely affected by a more open trading regime is offered somewhat more tentatively. Trade implies production specialization, and it could be argued that specialization, particularly in agriculture, would be more adverse to the environment than a more diverse production mix.[4]

This point, however, is controversial. It has been generally observed that, among developing countries, poverty tends to cause most closed developing economies to concentrate on the production of basic food staples, and the more open an economy is, the more diverse is its crop mix. But this is true only at the aggregate level. At the farm level, on the other hand, commercialization tends to lead to monocropping. For very small island economies, monocropping is also the consequence.

---

4. In industry, specialization in production can also lead to a heavier (and therefore more harmful) concentration of toxic substances, which may be more difficult to disperse.

Furthermore, the opening of a land-surplus economy, by making land valuable, leads to large-scale expansion of cultivation and a consequent reduction in forested areas. For land-short economies, it is not clear what the impact of an opening of the economy is. The key element needed to draw a conclusion is the country's agricultural pricing policies. Typically, for most developing countries that are not exporters of food staples, Krueger, Schiff, and Valdés (1988) have shown there is a bias in favor of food staples and against cash agriculture generally. An opening of the economy would lead to a shift toward cash cropping and perhaps somewhat away from food staples. Inasmuch as such cash-cropping activities may be relatively labor-intensive, and thus more suited to the endowments of a land-short economy, this shift would tend to benefit the poor. Whether such a shift would lead to a greater burden on the environment is difficult to establish a priori. Once upon a time, one could safely generalize that food production uses less agricultural chemicals than cash cropping. But with the introduction of high-yielding varieties of the major cereals in the past two decades, it would be hazardous to make any such claim.

Looking somewhat beyond agriculture, however, East Asian experience suggests that an opening of the economy, particularly if that economy has plentiful supplies of labor, tends to accelerate the pace of industrialization, which, in turn, implies that the resource pressure on agriculture can be considerably reduced. However, the same East Asian experience also indicates that, unless firm action is taken at an early stage, industrial pollution can rapidly increase and can be very expensive to clean up post facto.

The East Asian experience also raises a key question. In conventional economic theory, opening a country to trade will lead to a one-shot increase in the level of measured income. There may, however, be some grounds to believe that opening a trade regime will increase the growth of measured income. In a more open trading regime, producers are then subject to a stricter discipline of international competition and induced to invest more in learning, adopting, and, eventually, inventing new technology. If this is the case, then the effects (desirable and undesirable) I have been discussing would be cumulative. The questions that a society will have to address would also become more dynamic. For example, people in East Asia, after suffering from adverse environmental conditions, are paying for a cleanup of that environment (even though it may be very expensive). Much higher levels of measured income after years of continuous growth allow them to afford such cleanups.

It is therefore difficult to have clear and conclusive answers on how an opening of the economy affects the distribution of true welfare. I stated earlier that there is some ground to argue that an opening of the economy will improve the distribution of measured income. But if, as I have been assuming, in a "typical" developing country, natural resources are underpriced, then it is no longer applicable to use the conventional Walrasian mode of analysis whereby each household has a clear endowment of resources, which determines its share of total income, after the determination of factor prices in a general equilibrium interaction. With the price mechanism held in abeyance or at least severely distorted, institutional questions pertaining to the access of rich and poor households to the underpriced resources will have to be modeled, and different results can be obtained depending on how these questions are answered.

Many links form the chain of argument leading to the conclusion that trade policies may or may not affect the resources and environment of a country. Each of the links may add to, or subtract from, the effect. Knowledge of each of the links is still extremely sketchy. It is not surprising therefore that there is no clear conclusion. To assess the impact on the true welfare of the poor would require further links, about which knowledge is equally sketchy. I can only summarize some of the issues that remain unresolved.

1. Does production restructuring, with industry (perhaps) contracting and agriculture expanding, lead to a net increase or decrease in environmental damage?
2. How does one value the different sorts of environmental damages, for example, deforestation versus industrial effluents?
3. Does trade always lead to increased specialization for the economy as a whole?
4. Does specialization lead to more environmental damage than does diversification?
5. When a resource is underpriced, what rules allow one person rather than another to gain access to it?
6. If trade allows a government to raise more taxes, how does it spend the money?
7. Does trade increase the growth as well as the level of measured incomes?

With all these uncertainties, to blame trade policy for, or to deploy it to minimize, adverse environmental effects would be dangerous. The next section argues that if the government of a developing country is seriously concerned with its environmental problems, it would be more profitable to address the resource policy issues directly, rather than to use trade policy as a proxy to solve these problems.

Reforming Resource Policies

"Getting prices right" has been applied to output pricing policies, particularly agricultural prices. The central theme of this chapter is that many developing countries have got their *resource* prices wrong, and this will probably end up being more costly for them than getting output prices wrong. If resource prices are wrong, to place the burden of correction on adjustment of output prices alone can be counterproductive. Trade policy is little more than a cheap way for governments to induce large changes in tradable output prices.

Given the administrative constraints that governments of developing countries face, can it not be argued that output price policies (that is, trade policies) can be used to substitute for inadequate resource policies? This can be done to a certain extent, but since administrative constraints are cited as the reason for this action, it is important to point out an unavoidable trade-off. In view of the extreme complexity discussed in the previous section, to use trade policies as substitutes for resource policies requires sophisticated capabilities in policy design. To implement resource policies, on the other hand, requires a capability in policy implementation. It is by no means obvious in which area a developing country's government is more deficient.

I have used as an intellectual device the summary notion that, in most developing countries, resources are underpriced. There is, however, no need to be committed to the idea of using the price mechanism to solve all environmental and resource problems. Alternative means may be used to steer the economy toward a more efficient use of its natural resources.[5] Once these are in place, then it is clearly better to have an open trade policy. Some of the problems of having an open trade policy with a poor set of resource policies would then simply disappear. For example, the import of dirty industries producing goods for export to developed countries would be more difficult if the developing country has a fairly firm but appropriate set of policies against, say, effluent discharges.[6]

How would changes in resource policies affect the distribution of welfare in a country? Consider the following concrete examples:

1. the enclosures in Europe from the end of the Middle Ages to the beginning of the Industrial Revolution, as a result of increasing commerce within Europe;
2. the homesteading by pioneers in North America during the nineteenth century when the continent was opened for international trade by the advent of the railroads;
3. the distribution of public lands for plantation production by the colonial governments in countries such as Malaysia; and
4. the expansion of cultivation by small farmers into forested areas without the granting of clear property rights in countries such as Thailand (see the following section).

Each of these cases (except the last) is a clear assignment of property rights. Some of them may have been close to optimal from a resource manage-

---

5. See Weitzman (1974) for a theoretical discussion of whether price or quantity manipulation will yield the better result.

6. "Appropriate" here would mean that the standards used take into account the absorptive capacity of the environment and are not just a copy of the standards adopted in developed countries.

ment point of view, and some not. More to the point, each of these cases is nothing less than a wholesale redistribution of property rights, whose outcome depends heavily on the social and political preconditions in the relevant country. Theorizing or generalizing from these and other experiences is well beyond the scope of this chapter. For normative purposes, one can conceivably design a set of resource policies for a well-meaning technocrat oblivious to his country's political stresses and strains, such that the welfare of the poorer households is protected. The only problem such a designer would face is a lack of clients!

Cassava in Thailand: A Case Study

Since a series of economic reforms in the late 1950s, Thailand has generally enjoyed a period of macroeconomic stability and a relatively open trading regime. True, there were rather hefty export taxes on the country's most important commodities, namely, rice (ended in 1986) and rubber. But production and exports of other agricultural commodities have not been seriously hindered. On the contrary, throughout the 1960s and 1970s, the Thai government invested heavily in constructing a road network, which allows much of the country to have access to overseas markets.

At the same time, Thailand is one of the few Asian countries that had surplus land until as late as 1980, access to which has been quite easy. The easy availability of land with good access to the seaports and an open trading regime together led to an enormous expansion of the area under cultivation. Outside Japan and the newly industrialized countries, Thailand must be the only country in Asia that saw an increase in cultivated area per agricultural worker as late as 1978 (Figure 8.2). This increase in land per worker ratio is a reflection of the very low marginal cost of land, created by the lax land and forestry policy of the Thai government. Because land has an artificially low price, Thailand began to grow increasing quantities of crops that require relatively little labor per unit of land, such as maize and cassava (Siamwalla 1995).[7]

I shall focus on the expansion of cassava production in northeast Thailand. The cassava story is full of ironies. Its growth and indeed its very existence is dependent on the monumental distortion of the European Community's Common Agricultural Policy (CAP). As a result of this policy, cereal prices in the European Community (EC) were very high, while at the same time, as a result of concessions granted during the Dillon and the Kennedy rounds, protein crops and root crops could enter the EC with very low tariffs. It did not take traders long to realize that a combination of the two latter crops

---

7. Sugarcane is an exception in this respect, but then the Thai government had a highly protective policy toward sugar.

FIGURE 8.2 Cultivated area per agricultural worker, Thailand, 1961–1987

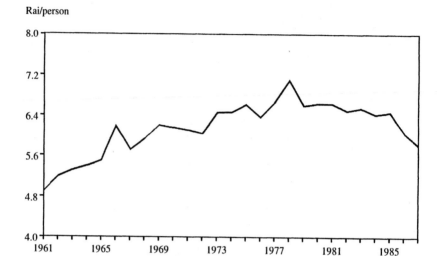

SOURCE: Cultivated area figures from the Office of Agricultural Economics, Thailand, for the 22 most important crops, compiled by Thailand Development Research Institute (TDRI); population figures from the Agricultural Workers Population Census.

NOTE: 1 rai = 0.16 hectare.

could provide European feedmills with almost as good a substitute for cereals, at a much lower price.

Cassava must be one of the world's easiest crops to grow. It requires little labor and attention. In Asia, it is relatively disease-free. Insects do not attack the crop because the roots have a high enough concentration of cyanic acid to kill them. It can be harvested at any time between about four to fourteen months, so farmers are freer to choose the harvest time. It can be grown on relatively poor soils, and it is drought tolerant. Most tropical countries can grow cassava, even on some of their worst lands.

The comparative advantage in cassava production is therefore dependent not so much on the resources required to grow the crop itself, but rather on the resources required to transport the product to the market. The latter resources are extremely important, inasmuch as the product is relatively low-valued— when it leaves the farm, it fetches a price of merely three cents per kilogram or US$30 a metric ton.

The combination of the newly built road system and the availability of land gave Thailand enormous comparative advantage in cassava production and led to a rapid expansion of the area under cassava cultivation. Between 1968 and 1980, cassava production doubled every four years, until the tonnage of cassava pellets exported reached 6 million.[8] From 1980 on, the earnings from cassava exports (almost entirely from the European Community) totaled US\$0.8–1 billion and rivaled the earnings from rice exports.

It can hardly be denied that cassava production and exports have increased the measured income of some of the poor in Thailand and thus have lifted them out of poverty. A total of 84.3 percent of the poor of Thailand live in the rural areas,[9] and more than half of them are in the northeastern region (which has a third of the overall population). The percentage of people deemed to be living in poverty steadily declined between 1963 and 1981. Poverty in the northeast declined along with that in the rest of the country.

The decline in poverty is intimately connected with the expansion of the area under cultivation—recall the increase in the amount of land per agricultural worker. This expansion absorbed a considerable proportion of the rapid increase in the labor force. In the 1970s the share of labor force in agriculture during the wet season actually increased despite the increase in gross national product per capita. To this day, there are relatively few landless laborers (about 15 percent) in the Thai agricultural labor force.

What has been the impact of these developments on the natural environment in Thailand and in the northeast in particular? Most visibly, there has been a steep decline in forested areas, with the forested area in the northeast halving from close to 30 percent of the area in a period of less than 15 years (Figure 8.3). The process by which the forests have been removed and the land converted to agricultural use is of some interest.

By law, this surplus land is designated as public land, much of it claimed by the Royal Forestry Department (RFD). In fact, neither the department nor the rest of the bureaucracy was able to prevent its lands from being encroached on by settlers who used the land they acquired to grow a variety of crops, mostly to feed the export markets.

In most instances, the process of acquisition would proceed as follows. A forest concession would be granted to private companies. In all contracts, the concessionaire would be expected to cut the trees designated as removable by RFD and to replant them so that when the 30-year concession expires, the forest would return to its original state. No one followed this rule. Farmers, observing that the forest was not being protected, moved into the cleared lands and began farming them. Regarded as squatters by the government, they were never issued titles for the lands they thus acquired. Nevertheless, these lands were bought and sold by them, with protection sometimes provided by private enforcers (Hirsch 1990). Because no titles were issued, land was cheap. But it

---

8. To minimize shipping costs, the cassava root is first cut, dried, and then pressed into cigarette-shaped pellets. The pelletization is done in order to be able to fit a larger tonnage into bulk carriers (50,000–100,000 metric tons) used to transport the cassava to Europe.

9. This is the 1988 figure; the corresponding figure in 1980 was 90 percent.

FIGURE 8.3 Area under forest in Thailand, 1975–1988

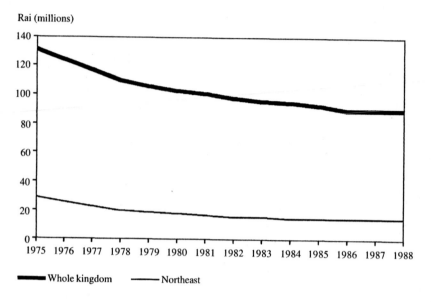

SOURCE: Office of Agricultural Economics, Thailand.

NOTE: 1 rai = 0.16 hectare.

also meant that it could not be placed as collateral with the banks, so long-term investment to improve the land could not be made (Feder et al. 1988). A land-extensive method of cultivation and choice of crops (such as cassava and maize) resulted. This, of course, increased the demand for land and quickened the pace of deforestation.

It is difficult to estimate the damage done to the environment because of the deforestation. There have been claims that rainfall has decreased as a result. An unpublished statistical analysis done by Direk Patamasiriwat at the Thailand Development Research Institute indicates generally that there has been a decline of rainfall in the majority of the stations, but in most cases the decline is statistically insignificant. An area of less doubt is the increasing soil salinity observed in some areas because of the increased fluctuations in the water table. Watershed areas and areas with steep slopes in the northeast are relatively rare, so soil erosion problems are somewhat minor. Finally, there is one area of concern where there is little doubt. Northeasterners, like rural people elsewhere, do some hunting and gathering in addition to farming. The decline in the forested area has undoubtedly severely diminished this supplementary source of food.

Do all these changes indicate that northeastern agriculture is unsustainable? It is probably impossible to know the answer. The end to the cassava boom came in the 1980s as a consequence of two developments. First, there is no more forest to be removed. Second, European tolerance of what the EC considered to be an undermining of the CAP came to an end. In 1982 the EC and Thailand agreed to limit exports of cassava to the Community to about 5 million metric tons per year, although the EC was unable to bully the United States into agreeing to limit its exports of corn gluten and citrus pulp, two other cereal substitutes.

These two developments had a palpable impact on the northeast. The incidence of poverty in the northeast increased noticeably between 1981 and 1985.[10] Northeasterners have had a tradition of migrating outside their villages for seasonal jobs—probably dictated by the fact that their agricultural season lasts only six months. This tradition intensified in the 1980s. Young northeasterners can now be found in large numbers in industrial plants. But unlike the earlier migrants, many of these young migrants do not return seasonally to farm in their home villages. Complaints by the remaining, older farmers of labor shortage in agriculture are now quite common.

With the departure of so much labor, it is clear that northeastern agriculture as previously practiced is no longer sustainable, but that unsustainability has relatively little to do with the deterioration of the natural environment. Whatever impact this deterioration may have had is greatly overshadowed by the change in the economic context that northeasterners face.

Regardless of the extraneous developments, it is clear that the main problem arising from the development of the cassava industry is the decline in the area under forest cover in Thailand. The Thai government appears to have followed a very strict resource policy design: it owns all the areas under forest cover and will not allow any cutting down of the trees. It also has a very lax policy implementation: the forests were cut down and the land occupied by cassava growers. A more realistic policy design that takes account of its own implementation capabilities, as well as farmers' needs, would have prevented much of the adverse environmental impact of the growth of the cassava industry.

International Policies on Trade and Environment

Environmental issues are beginning to creep into international trade discussions, despite the tenuous link between the two issues. As there is a clear danger that these discussions can lead to antitrade action and, more important, to unilateral action that hurts the interest of the weaker developing countries, it

---

10. This development affects all of rural Thailand, on account of the worldwide agricultural depression in 1985.

is important to keep separate issues that should be subject to international control and regulation and those that should not.

The economic theory of externalities tells us that government intervention may be called for when one party's production or consumption activities impinge on the profitability of another party's. The matter comes under international jurisdiction if the two parties are separated by an international boundary. There are now clearly many issues that display such characteristics. At the global level are ozone depletion and consequent climate change problems. Less global, but still international, are the acid rain problem and the division of riparian water resources. That these are externalities is not in doubt, although the scientific evidence for their presence or their impact may be questioned. In some of these cases, international treaties have been signed or are under negotiation, and may involve the use of trade sanctions against deviant signatories.

More problematic is the argument that the global community has an interest in maintaining its genetic resources and its biological diversity, even though it cannot be proven how these can affect welfare of people across international boundary lines. Nonetheless, if the preferences of the global community have been revealed in an internationally negotiated treaty (for example, the Convention on International Trade in Endangered Species, CITES), then trade sanctions may be applied against deviant countries.

It is when unilateral action is taken by a country to express its preferences about environmental policies in another country that the way is open for trade sanctions to be abused. Not only is one country imposing its preferences on another, but it can also dress what is essentially a protectionist policy in respectably green clothes. Even here, it is important to distinguish clearly between what really needs control and regulation and what is a Pandora's box that will open all sorts of protectionist claims.

Currently, Article XX of the General Agreement on Tariffs and Trade (GATT) allows measures to be taken by importing countries on a wide variety of grounds, as long as the same standards apply to both imported and domestic products (Article III, National Treatment). In the case of cassava, if the Netherlands decides that the consumption of concentrated animal feed and the intensive production of livestock can lead to severe environmental damage, then it may undertake action to limit the consumption of the feed, which may entail a limitation on cassava imports.

Even though this exception has not been without its problems (Jackson 1989:206–208), there have been attempts to expand the regulations to cover production processes in the exporting country as well. The following example is taken from Jackson (1989:208).

> Take, as an example, the production of a certain type of plastic toy. The toy itself, let us suppose, is perfectly safe, poses no health hazard, and cannot burn or

emit gases. Thus neither the domestic nor the imported models of this toy will constitute a hazard to be guarded against. However, assume that the manufacture of these toys can be quite hazardous, perhaps because the processing of chemicals to make and mold the plastic involves noxious fumes, danger of explosion, or inhalation of carcinogenic gases.

Likewise, assume that the domestic factory producing this toy emits noxious smoke, affecting the environment. In such a case governments will impose requirements to protect health and safety of the workers and the environs on the manufacturing company, and these will have costs that must be included in the price of the product. Now suppose that imports of identical toys occur from a country which is not so careful about the health of its employees or environs and imposes no such regulation. The imports, all other things being equal, can be priced cheaper and could cause competitive distress to the domestic producers. Is this fair?

It is this expansion from products to processes that could lead to various protectionist devices. Jackson's example can be used to argue that a lax environmental standard constitutes an implicit export subsidy. Since there is a tradition in GATT against such a subsidy, international action seems to be called for. But consider what has to be proven to show that differing environmental standards constitute an unjustifiable export subsidy.

All human activities impinge on the environment. But the abuse that a community or a country can inflict on its environment will be more or less damaging depending on the capacity of that environment to absorb pollutants. This absorptive capacity depends not only on the level of abuse that is currently being directed at the environment, but also on the cumulative effects of past abuses. At any time, a country's sustainable comparative advantage depends on that absorptive capacity of the environment. A country that still has an unused environmental absorptive capacity may decide that it can have a laxer set of standards in its environmental policies than another that has been abusing its environment for a longer period of time. For the latter to insist that the better-endowed country adopt the same standards cannot be justified, unless the production process affects the environment across an international boundary.

What if it can be incontrovertibly proven that the exporting country is indeed abusing its own (and only its own) environment, and doing so unsustainably, but nonetheless claims the sovereign right to weigh the long-term consequence less than its desire for current economic growth? Does another country have a right to say that this constitutes an unfair export subsidy? These questions enter into something close to philosophical realms now, and it is difficult for a mere economist to weigh in. I would venture only to make the following plea, on behalf of consistency rather than on the rights and wrongs of the issue.

The argument that willingness to abuse the environment is an unfair subsidy can be sustained only if one regards the inhabitants of a country as "paying" a tax by suffering from the consequences of that abuse. The tax is then used to sustain the polluting industry. If this is to be constituted an unfair subsidy, then any action taken by the government to clean the environment that does not impose an equal burden on the polluting industry must also be considered an unfair subsidy.

Conclusion

The central argument of this chapter is simple but negative: the links between trade and the environment are extremely tenuous. To ensure sustainability of their economic growth, it is far more helpful for developing countries to attack their resource policies directly than to address environmental woes by tinkering with their trade policies. This is not to say that the trade policies are unimportant, but rather that their importance and impact lie elsewhere.

9 Macroeconomic and Sectoral Policies, Natural Resources, and Sustainable Agricultural Growth

EDWARD B. BARBIER

In this chapter I discuss, both generally and with illustrations, the effects of macroeconomic and sectoral policies on the development and use of key natural resources (forests, arable land, water resources, wetlands) for agricultural and overall growth in developing countries. I review the mechanisms through which these effects occur and the role of macroeconomic and sectoral policies in influencing these mechanisms. Of particular interest are the policy trade-offs between promoting agricultural growth and environmental degradation, in both the short and long run.

Market Failures, Policy Failures, and the Incentives for Resource Degradation

Defining the Problem

Excessive natural resource degradation in developing countries is often a direct outcome of individuals' and governments' not fully recognizing and integrating environmental values into decisionmaking processes. If markets do not reflect environmental values adequately, a failure of the market is said to exist. It usually occurs because of (1) open-access exploitation or public goods, (2) externalities or other nonmarketed goods and services, (3) uncertainty and risk, or (4) imperfect competition. Where government decisions or policies do not fully reflect environmental values, there is policy failure. Policy failure arises through (1) failure to correct market failures, or (2) government interventions that exacerbate resource degradation.[1] Throughout the developing

---

1. A policy failure can also arise if governments *overvalue* resources. For example, governments may choose to set aside natural resources that ought to be exploited for development purposes. A World Bank (1990a) study of protected areas in Malawi concluded that the benefits of protecting so much land were not worth the opportunity costs of foregone agricultural production, thus suggesting that some land should be "de-gazetted."

119

world, the existence of poorly formulated input- and output-pricing policies, insecure land titling and registration, tax thresholds and rebates, cheap and restricted credit facilities, overvalued exchange rates, and other policy distortions has exacerbated problems of natural resource management. By failing to make markets and private decisionmakers accountable for foregone environmental values, these policies may contribute to market failure. At worst, the direct private costs of resource-using activities are subsidized or distorted, thus encouraging unnecessary environmental degradation.

The uncompensated loss of nonmarketed environmental services, resource systems, and biodiversity through large-scale resource depletion and degradation in developing countries may call for the increased use of regulatory instruments to attain an improvement in the environment directly, or for the increased use of taxes, subsidies, and other market-based instruments to alter private costs and benefits so as to "internalize" the unaccounted social costs (and benefits) of environmental degradation. However, in developing countries, the effectiveness of regulatory instruments is often limited by (1) poorly functioning judicial, administrative, and monitoring and enforcement procedures; (2) the scarce financial resources available for environmental regulation, especially for mitigating risk and variability; and (3) the high transport and transaction costs that undermine enforcement of environmental regulations. The effectiveness of market-based instruments in internalizing the social costs of environmental degradation may depend on how well market systems reflect private costs in the first instance. The pervasiveness of market and policy failures underlying many of the environmental degradation problems in developing economies suggests many instances in which public policies and incomplete markets reduce the direct costs to individuals of using the environment.

Thus many authors stress the need for developing countries to use policy reform as an economic instrument, that is, to remove subsidies and other public policy interventions that distort the private costs of resource use and pollution discharge.[2] Similarly, institutional reforms, such as the improvement or establishment of property and resource right regimes, legal titling, environmental sanctions, contract enforcement, and so forth, are equally important policy instruments for improved natural resource management in developing countries in that they assist or even establish markets for environmental goods and services.

Although regulatory and market-based instruments for environmental improvement are important to developing economies, in this chapter I focus on the role of policy reforms, particularly in the areas of macroeconomic and trade policies, sectoral policies, and public investment, for improving natural resource management in these economies.[3]

---

2. For discussions of policy reform in correcting the agricultural and environmental problems of developing countries, see Stiglitz (1987), Repetto (1988), Panayotou (1990), Pearce (1990), and Barbier (1991a,b).

3. For a discussion of the relative merits of regulatory and market-based instruments to correct environmental problems in developing countries, see Panayotou (1990) and Pearce (1990).

The Role of Macroeconomic and Sectoral Policies

Macroeconomic, trade, and sectoral policies can alter the incentives governing the use of natural resources indirectly by changing aggregate demand, as well as directly by distorting the relative prices of natural resources and related goods and services. Figure 9.1 shows some of the potential economic policy–environmental linkages that exist in developing countries. Such linkages suggest that important opportunities exist for what Repetto (1988) has called "complementary" policy reforms: those that raise current economic welfare and reduce long-term environmental degradation. In other words, correcting government policies that generate perverse economic incentives through taxes, subsidies, and other market interventions may not only improve economic efficiency but also generate larger savings in terms of reduced environmental costs.

However, "getting the prices right" for resource management is not a simple process in developing economies and requires careful economic analysis of the problem. In some instances, such as in the presence of environmental externalities, more rather than less government intervention may be required (Table 9.1). More common is the problem of insufficient data and information to allow precise estimation of the economic and environmental costs arising from market and policy failures. In most cases, cost estimates consisting of orders of magnitude and indicators of the direction of change may be sufficient for policy analysis. But with many natural resource problems in developing countries, even this state of "optimal ignorance" has not been achieved (Barbier 1991b). The challenge for economists is to improve analysis and understanding of how economic policies affect the resource base while avoiding the temptation to oversimplify the links between policies and resource effects.

The Role of Public Investment

Public investment in, for example, infrastructure and agriculture projects can also directly induce resource degradation by failing to take into account the opportunity costs of foregoing alternative uses of natural resources and the possible loss of important environmental services. Government-financed investment programs, such as road building and rural development programs, may indirectly be encouraging resource degradation by opening up inaccessible frontier areas or open-access resources to exploitation. On the other hand, public investments can also have beneficial effects. For example, agricultural infrastructure investments can increase productivity and thus reduce pressure on the land. Roads often reduce marketing costs, thus improving income-earning opportunities from agriculture and promoting land-conserving investments. Again, careful analysis of the environmental benefits and costs associated with all public investments is required.

The remaining sections focus on more specific examples of the macroeconomic and sectoral policies, as well as public investments, affecting natural resource use in developing countries.

FIGURE 9.1 Economic policy and potential environmental impacts

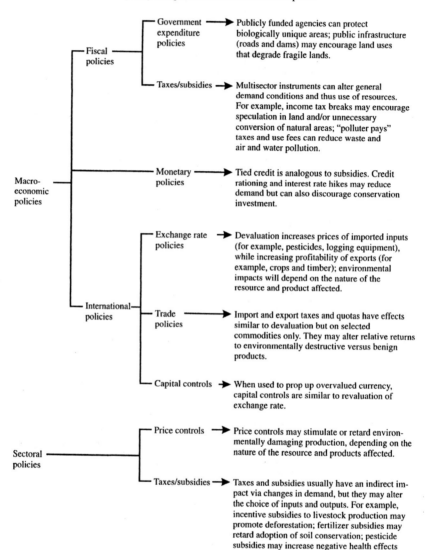

SOURCE: Bishop, Aylward, and Barbier 1991.

122

TABLE 9.1 Typical environmental externalities in developing countries

Externality and Source	Uncompensated Effects	Analysis and Valuation	Common Policy Responses
Air pollution (industrial, commercial, and automotive emissions)	Respiratory ailments	Medical treatment costs; days of work lost	Set emissions standards or taxes; restricted licenses to pollute; subsidize control
Water pollution (industrial, commercial, and private effluent)	Diverse health effects (poisoning, genetic damage); destruction of fish stocks	Medical treatment costs; days of work lost; reduced fish production; potable water treatment costs	As above
Soil erosion (deforestation, agriculture)	Siltation and sedimentation of reservoirs, irrigation infrastructure, river channels, ports, and harbors; destruction of fisheries; increased flood damage; reduced groundwater recharge; reduced reliability of river flows	Reduced hydroelectric and irrigation capacity and useful life; increased dredging costs; reduced fish production; flood damage costs; increased water supply costs	Increase land rent or tax and timber stumpage fee or tax; subsidize soil and water conservation
Watershed protection (natural and plantation forest, reserves)	Protection of above	Avoidance of damage costs listed above	Modify relative returns to perennial versus annual crops (subsidy or tax); subsidize protection of watersheds
Water regulation (wetland, mangrove swamps)	Natural waste recycling and water purification; maintenance of water flows; protection from storm surges	Avoidance of damage costs listed above	Remove implicit and explicit subsidies for draining and filling wetland; subsidize conservation

SOURCE: Bishop, Aylward, and Barbier 1991.

Macroeconomic and Trade Policies

The impacts of macroeconomic and trade policies on natural resource degradation are often difficult to discern because the effects are usually indirect, influencing effective rates of protection, interest rates and credit markets, terms of trade between sectors, and overall aggregate demand (see Figure 9.1). Developing countries usually are price takers in international commodity markets and therefore must be aware of the vagaries of these markets in designing trade and macroeconomic policies. Increased indebtedness and economic imbalance may compound resource problems if they cause long-term management to be sacrificed for short-term revenue and export earnings. This does not necessarily imply that all macroeconomic policies promoting immediate growth and poverty alleviation objectives should be held subordinate to environmental considerations. What it does imply is that there must be "correct" economic signals informing public choice between any immediate and long-term policy goals. Thus the economic relationships influencing resource degradation need to be clarified if sound macroeconomic and trade policies are to be designed and if economic development is ultimately to be sustained in low-income countries.

A recent analysis has indicated how the profitability of gum arabic and other crops in Sudan is distorted through overvalued exchange rates (Barbier 1990a). Not only is gum arabic an important export crop for Sudan, but maintenance of the "gum belt" across northern Sudan also protects against desertification and land degradation. However, the government currently maintains an artificially low exchange rate, which in the case of gum arabic cultivation is especially detrimental because of its low use of external inputs. The analysis shows that gum arabic would be more economically profitable compared with its rival substitute crops if devaluation brought farmgate prices more in line with border-equivalent prices. Furthermore, an econometric analysis has shown that a devaluation would raise gum arabic export earnings while at the same time allowing the possibility for the domestic price of gum to be raised or at least held constant (IIED/IES 1990).

Not all devaluations and complementary macroeconomic and sectoral policies may work to the advantage of the environment in developing countries, even if there are good economic grounds for pursuing such policies. For example, beginning in 1983, Ghana attempted to revive its stagnating agricultural sector, and cocoa production in particular, through a combination of devaluations and increases in the producer price of cocoa. Although the result has been a sustained increase in cocoa production and recovery of exports, the unknown effect is the impact on the resource base. On the one hand, the general rise in rural incomes from the revival of smallholder and possibly from all agricultural cultivation may have reduced the motivation, from sheer poverty, for overextension of food production onto more marginal lands. On the other hand, the revival of cocoa's fortunes may have spurred some farmers to clear yet more forest or other environmentally fragile lands for cocoa cultivation (Conway and Barbier 1990).

Trade-environment linkages can involve complex relationships across several countries and trading regions. A good example of this is the "cassava connection" between Indonesia, Thailand, and the European Community (EC), which has implications for upper watershed degradation and deforestation in the two developing countries (Conway and Barbier 1990; Phantumvanit and Panayotou 1990; see also Siamwalla, Chapter 8, this volume). Indonesia and Thailand compete for a share of the EC's total import quota for cassava, most of which is used as feed for intensive pig farming in the Netherlands. For example, only 10 percent of Indonesia's cassava crop is exported, but 97 percent of these exports go to the EC. To maintain or even increase its share of the quota, the government of Indonesia has been procuring a larger share of domestic production for export. The result has been rapid rises in cassava prices and expansion of production in upland areas of Java and on converted forestlands in the Outer Islands. Ironically, donor-funded soil and water conservation projects in the upper watersheds of Java have been trying to discourage monocropping of cassava on erodible upland soils because of its deleterious impacts on soil structure. Concern has also been expressed in both Indonesia and Thailand over the large-scale losses of forestland to cassava production. If domestic cassava prices in Indonesia and Thailand eventually return to near world levels—they have in the past generally followed world market trends—expansion in the area planted to cassava should also level off. But, in the meantime, the "cassava connection" is a concrete reminder of how distortionary trade interventions combined with short-term policy objectives can lead to both economically and environmentally questionable outcomes.

An important challenge for economic analysis is to examine more thoroughly the extent to which trade and macroeconomic policies influence large-scale land use changes and resource degradation. A number of comparative studies have been launched to analyze the main factors behind tropical deforestation. The results are far from conclusive, but they do indicate that macroeconomic and trade policies are only one of a variety of important factors determining this trend.

Studies by Capistrano (1990) and Capistrano and Kiker (1990) examine the influence of international and domestic macroeconomic factors on tropical deforestation. The econometric analysis indicates the role of high agricultural export prices in inducing agricultural expansion and forest clearing, as well as the influence of domestic structural adjustment policies, such as exchange rate devaluation and increased debt servicing ratios. Comparative analysis of 24 Latin American countries also highlights the strong but indirect relationship between population pressure and frontier expansion—increasing numbers of urban consumers raise the demand for domestic production and hence for agricultural land—and the countervailing role of increased agricultural productivity and yield growth in slowing agricultural expansion (Southgate 1991). A statistical analysis by Burgess (1992), covering all tropical forest countries over the 1980–1985 period, did not find the level of debt servicing to be statistically significant in influencing tropical deforestation but did indicate that economic development as a whole (as represented by real gross national product per capita) reduced pressure on the resource. Industrial roundwood production and population pressure were also positively associated with forest clearance in the tropics.

Finally, it may be difficult to determine the full economic implications of trade and macroeconomic policies on the environment because some impacts may prove to be beneficial and others more negative. In Costa Rica, the elimination of export taxes has increased production of perennial tree crops such as beverages (coffee), fruits, and nuts, which in contrast to annual crops are supposedly more beneficial in controlling soil erosion through providing better ground cover and maintaining soil structure. Similarly, in Haiti the combination of removing import restrictions on grains and the export tax on coffee has reversed price distortions that previously discriminated against coffee, again with consequences for soil erosion control (Markandya and Richardson 1990). It would appear that these policies are having a beneficial environmental impact. However, much perennial crop production is intensive in its use of fertilizer and agrochemical inputs, with consequent runoff problems for downstream fisheries, farm production, and water use.[4] Both of these potential environmental benefits and costs of increased perennial crop production must be examined more carefully before a conclusion can be reached on the overall environmental implications of the policy changes.

Agricultural Sectoral Policies

Agricultural output and input policies, including price controls, taxes and subsidies, marketing and infrastructure policies, and credit and interest rate policies, may stimulate or retard excessive resource degradation through their effects on choice of agricultural inputs and outputs, income, rates of time preference, and other economic factors. As these effects are usually indirect, occurring via changes in demand and supply conditions, they are often difficult to discern (see Figure 9.1). Careful analysis of the effects on a case-by-case basis is required to be certain of not only the magnitude of the impact but even the direction of change. In some cases, agricultural subsidies might be contributing to a resource degradation problem; in others, subsidies might be required.

---

4. See Conway and Pretty (1991) for a comprehensive review of the empirical evidence of the impacts of agricultural pollution in developing countries.

The following sections briefly examine the role of agricultural output prices, input prices, and marketing and infrastructure policies in influencing these effects.[5]

Agricultural Output Prices

Changing relative prices can influence the relative returns to different resource activities, thus reducing the incentives for choosing a more resource-degrading activity over another. The main problem is often the unsuitability of the economic activity for given ecological and physical conditions, rather than the unsuitability of the economic activity per se. Also, there is little understanding of aggregate supply responses to increased prices, let alone the resource impacts. Under certain conditions, increasing the profitability of agricultural crops and other commodities may provide incentives for opening new areas for cultivation.

Recent studies in Sub-Saharan Africa suggest that the effect of changes in output prices on the aggregate level of production tends not to be substantial in many countries, but the responsiveness of individual crops to changes in relative prices is highly significant (Bond 1983; Fones-Sundell 1987; Weaver 1989). As relative producer prices change, the increase in individual crop production appears to be accompanied by a reduction in substitute crops.[6] However, in investigating the environmental impacts, the concern should be less with measuring the actual magnitude of small-scale farmer supply response to price incentives than in determining how they choose to respond. It should be remembered that increasing agricultural production does not necessarily translate into environmental degradation—it is the way in which the extra cultivation is being carried out that is important. The expansion of agricultural production may be achieved through

1. a more efficient and sustainable use of existing factors of production (for example, improved cropping patterns, land management schemes);
2. increased use of land and other inputs in an environmentally sound manner (for example, extensification of agricultural land onto slopes using sustainable agroforestry techniques and investing in structural conservation works); or
3. expanding unsustainable agricultural production practices and further degrading the natural resource base.

In the first two cases, the impact of increased production on the environment may be negligible, and could be beneficial if degraded land is "reclaimed."

---

5. See Barbier and Burgess (1992a) for a more detailed review of agricultural pricing and environmental degradation.
6. However, see Ogbu and Gbetibouo (1990) for a critical review of agricultural supply response models in Sub-Saharan Africa.

However, in many developing countries, increased agricultural production has typically been accompanied by environmental degradation. Nevertheless, the relationships between agricultural pricing policy, production responses, and environmental degradation are rarely straightforward, often involving many important additional economic and social factors.

For example, since 1979 Malawi has gone through a period of rapid macroeconomic adjustment, including extensive agricultural pricing and marketing reform for the smallholder subsector. The objective was to stimulate smallholder maize and export crop production, as well as to increase overall agricultural growth. There has been limited success in achieving this objective: although farmers may have been responding to changes in relative prices by shifting their cropping pattern, the impact of pricing policy on their aggregate response is less certain. Moreover, the recent increases in agricultural output have been achieved by extensification of agriculture onto marginal lands rather than by improving the yields on existing cultivated land (Barbier and Burgess 1992b). The reasons for this are predominantly structural:

1. Rapid population growth and the corresponding fast decline in the land-person ratio has led to increased land pressure and the opening of more marginal areas for cultivation.
2. The pricing and marketing reforms have achieved little for the majority of smallholders cultivating less than 1 hectare, mainly because the severity of the land constraint and low yields preclude production of net marketable surpluses. Thus the main income benefits of these reforms are limited to the relatively better-off producers.
3. The food security of many food-deficit households may actually deteriorate as the prices of maize and other food crops increase, thus limiting the ability of these households to diversify out of own-food production and to take risks.
4. Consequently, over the past five years there has been little change in the average yield for any of the main maize varietal groups—local, composite, or hybrid—despite markedly higher rates of hybrid adoption and fertilizer use. The low productivity of maize has in turn exacerbated the land constraint.

The relationships governing farmer responses to relative crop prices are very complex and depend on various factors such as household wealth and income, tenure security, attitudes toward risk, access to off-farm employment, labor and capital constraints, and intrahousehold allocation of labor.[7] Nevertheless, the limited evidence does indicate that farmers respond to higher relative prices for erosive crops by seeking short-run economic rents from erosive crop cultivation, which may cause long-term land degradation. This

---

7. See the studies cited in Barbier and Burgess (1992a) and Chapter 10 in this volume.

result holds mainly for sedentary farmers cultivating rainfed plots in areas with predominantly "closed" agricultural frontiers (that is, areas where agricultural extensification is reaching or has already reached its limit). In frontier agriculture, farmers will open new areas to cultivation when the returns from the new land exceed those from existing land under cultivation (Southgate 1990; Burgess 1992). Higher relative prices and returns to erosive crops and systems will not only accelerate degradation on existing land but also, as a consequence, induce a more rapid expansion into new areas and increased land clearance.

A study in Thailand highlights the complex linkages between agricultural crop prices, the relative returns from different crops, and the demand for land (Phantumvanit and Panayotou 1990). In Thailand, approximately 40 percent of the increase in cultivated land in recent years has been met by converted forestland. The most important factors affecting the demand for cropland, and thus forest conversion, appear to be population growth followed by nonagricultural returns, although agricultural pricing also has a significant influence. Higher aggregate real prices may have a slightly positive influence on the demand for cropland, and thus increased forest clearing. However, this direct effect may be counteracted by the indirect impact of higher agricultural prices on raising the productivity of existing land and increasing the cultivation of previously idle land, thus reducing the demand for new land from forest clearing. Changes in relative prices also influence the demand for new cropland by affecting the relative profitability of land-saving as opposed to land-extensive cropping systems.[8]

In all sectors, the relative weight that pricing policies as opposed to other economic variables and "noneconomic" factors (for example, population growth, tenure security, regulations, binding contracts) have in influencing problems of environmental degradation are important analytical issues that need to be resolved. In Indonesia and Malaysia, government pricing and export policies to encourage the switching from raw log to processed timber exports are alleged to have led to substantial economic losses, the establishment of inefficient processing operations, and accelerated deforestation (Repetto and Gillis 1988). Others allege that in Southeast Asia short-term timber concession rights and leasing agreements, coupled with the lack of incentives for reforestation, are the predominant factors leading to excessive and rapid depletion of timber forests (Paris and Ruzicka 1991).

Agricultural Input Prices

Inappropriate pricing of agricultural inputs (for example, irrigation, pesticides, fertilizers, credit) can bias choice of inputs and lead to excessive

---

8. The authors also examined the effects of relative price changes on land productivity and the cultivation of previously idle land but found this relationship more difficult to estimate in such an aggregate analysis.

degradation. In some cases, the problem is one of unnecessary subsidies leading to wasteful use or inappropriate choice of economic activities. However, careful analysis is also required of the income, labor, and other constraints influencing the economic behavior of households. Under some cases, input subsidies to improve distribution and access may actually improve the productivity of economic activities sufficiently to reduce degradation. On the whole, less analysis of the impacts of input as opposed to output pricing on environmental degradation has been conducted.

The analysis of land clearing in Thailand discussed earlier illustrates some of the potential linkages that need to be explored. For example, the study showed that the relative returns to land-saving cropping systems can also be affected by the relative costs of inputs (for example, fertilizer, seed, credit, irrigation, agrochemicals) when these differ between land-saving and land-extensive systems. More important, investments in land productivity will also be affected by the costs of these inputs. Thus the Thailand case study suggests that lower input prices generally would reduce the demand for new cropland and forest conversion both directly and indirectly by making previously idle land more attractive to cultivate. Changes in relative input prices could also make a difference for agricultural extensification by affecting the relative returns to land-saving cropping systems.

If input prices only affected the choice between land extensification and intensification, then the case study from Thailand would suggest a strong rationale for subsidizing agricultural inputs, and perhaps even tying such subsidies to land-saving cropping systems. However, there is also widespread evidence indicating that many negative environmental impacts are associated with input subsidies.

Government policies maintaining low input prices through subsidies to encourage adoption and expanded agricultural production have resulted in the misuse and overuse of agricultural inputs in many developing countries, with serious implications for the environment. For instance, short-run increases in land productivity through increased input use may actually lead farmers to neglect problems of soil erosion that have longer-term implications for land productivity and returns. High and excessive uses of irrigation also cause long-run salinization and waterlogging problems. Off-site environmental costs may also result from soil erosion, agrochemical, and fertilizer runoff.

For example, in Indonesia there is strong evidence indicating that the high fertilizer subsidies encourage excessive and inefficient use of fertilizers by lowland irrigated rice farmers in Java. At the same time, the subsidies appear to be a disincentive, at least in the short run, for upland farmers to face the full economic costs of declining soil fertility from erosive cropping practices (Barbier 1989, 1990b).

The lessons from the fertilizer subsidy in Java are not necessarily applicable in other countries and regions. The structural economic problems and

TABLE 9.2 Irrigation charges and costs for six Asian countries, 1987

Country	Actual Irrigation Charge	Total Cost of Operation and Maintenance (Moderate Estimate)	Irrigation Charge as a Percentage of Total Cost
	(US$ per hectare)		
Bangladesh	3.75	375.00	1.0
Indonesia	25.90	191.00	13.5
Korea	192.00	1057.00	18.2
Nepal	9.10	126.00	7.2
Philippines	16.90	75.00	22.5
Thailand	8.31	151.00	5.5

SOURCE: Repetto 1988.

incentives constraining the ability of smallholders to control land degradation in Malawi were noted earlier. The government's policy of encouraging small-holder uptake of fertilizer through subsidies for credit expansion in the short term may actually mitigate some of these problems, although in the long run there is a policy commitment to eliminate the subsidy as uptake and distribution improve. On balance, the benefits of increased productivity and poverty reduction from the fertilizer subsidy policy appear to exceed the impact of fertilizer runoff on water pollution, soil conservation disincentives, and land degradation in Malawi. However, improved targeting of fertilizer credit to poor, especially female-headed, households is necessary to improve its effectiveness. Also, the policy of increased fertilizer use has not been adequately integrated with overall conservation and land management planning. In fact, too much emphasis has been placed on the role of fertilizer alone without sufficient attention to complementary improvements in cropping patterns and systems and conservation investments to boost long-term land productivity (Barbier and Burgess 1992b).

The complexities and trade-offs encountered in fertilizer pricing policies also occur when designing appropriate pricing policies for other agricultural inputs. For example, irrigation subsidies have been used as a means of encouraging land settlement, crop production, and regional development. However, underpricing of irrigation water has resulted in extravagant use and has led to problems of waterlogging, salinization of land, and soil erosion. In addition, the failure to recover costs undermines long-term operation and maintenance of supply systems (Table 9.2). The combination of inefficiencies and misuse has led to water supply scarcities in many regions and the tendency to finance more irrigation investments rather than improve existing networks. Because irrigation water significantly raises land productivity, its inefficient and wasteful use has a particularly high opportunity cost. For example, in Thailand increasing irrigation has a positive impact on agricultural land productivity, with a 10 percent increase in irrigation leading to a 3 percent increase in land productivity (Phantumvanit and Panayotou 1990).

Other input subsidies may also be playing an important role in environmental degradation. For example, there may be a direct link between pesticide subsidies and the adverse environmental and human health consequences of agrochemical runoff (Repetto 1985; Conway and Pretty 1991). Similarly, government credit and capital subsidies in the Brazilian Amazon are thought to be a significant factor in tropical deforestation (Browder 1985; Binswanger 1989a; Mahar 1989).

Marketing and Infrastructure Policies

Improved marketing and value-added processing can increase the potential of new cropping systems (for example, agroforestry) that are less environmentally degrading or more land-saving and the potential of new crops (such as nontimber forest products) that can increase the returns from resources. However, care must be taken to ensure that marketing margins are realistic but not punitive to producers. Overcoming infrastructure and marketing bottlenecks may also require innovative policies for directing credit and other inputs to poor farmers in remote areas whose livelihoods are most threatened by resource degradation.

In many instances, excessive marketing margins arise out of monopolistic practices that artificially reduce the economic incentives for producers. This was certainly the case in Sudan for gum arabic for many years, as the government maintained a low producer price for gum to capture a larger share of the export returns for itself and the parastatal Gum Arabic Company. This policy was relaxed somewhat when production of gum fell drastically (IIED/IES 1990). Similarly, in Java the small relative share to producers of the overall returns from perennial crops has slowed their incorporation in upland cropping systems, although poor postharvest processing and marketing infrastructure appear to be just as much at fault as monopolistic pricing (Barbier 1989).

Overcoming transportation and marketing bottlenecks may require short-term policies of subsidizing credit and fertilizer, coupled with long-term policies of improving the marketing infrastructure itself, including the road system. In the case of Malawi, it was noted that the credit and fertilizer policy operates essentially as a subsidy to help smaller farmers overcome the high costs of transport and the poor distribution of fertilizer, seeds, and other inputs (Barbier and Burgess 1992b). Similar constraints are faced by the poor farmers in the hills of Nepal. An appropriate policy approach there might be to establish a transport subsidy for fertilizer distribution in the hills and to extend credit schemes for fertilizer to small farmers in remote areas (Pearce, Barbier, and Markandya 1990). However, such policies are no substitutes for long-term efforts to improve rural marketing infrastructure and credit institutions and for ensuring that complementary improvements in land management and cropping systems also take place.

Public Investments and Resource Degradation

Many public investments in developing countries unnecessarily increase resource degradation through the failure to account fully for their environmental impacts. The result is an unintended loss in economic welfare, in positive distributional effects, and in long-run development benefits. As noted earlier, public infrastructure investments may indirectly promote resource degradation by opening new areas to uncontrolled development.

For example, analyses by Schneider et al. (1990) and Reis and Margulis (1991) emphasize that road building encourages small-scale frontier settlement by providing an "outlet" for population pressure and increasing agricultural rents. In the northern Brazilian Amazon, the total road network (paved and unpaved) increased from 6,357 to 28,431 kilometers over 1975–1988. A simple correlation between road density and the rate of deforestation shows that as road density increases, the rate of deforestation increases in larger proportions (Reis and Margulis 1991). Schneider et al. (1990) argue that this factor encouraging frontier agriculture—"nutrient mining"—far outweighs the more publicized impacts of fiscal incentives for cattle ranching. A statistical analysis by Southgate, Sierra, and Brown (1989) of the causes of tropical deforestation in Ecuador indicates that colonists clear forestland not only in response to demographic pressure but also to "capture" agricultural rents and to safeguard their tenuous legal hold on the land. Again, road building is a key factor driving the opening of new forestland.

Other large-scale public investment projects and programs, such as hydroelectric dams, irrigation schemes, and commercial agricultural development schemes, also have significant environmental impacts. Some of these impacts may impose additional costs on society. Given such costs, to appraise the net benefits of the investment project or program in terms of its direct costs and benefits alone would be a misrepresentation of its economic net worth to society. The foregone net benefits associated with any environmental impacts must also be included as part of the opportunity costs of the development investment.

Frequently, appraisal of the environmental impacts of major public investments has shown that the investments should be modified and in some cases should not proceed. For example, Barbier, Adams, and Kimmage (1991) conducted an analysis of the net benefits of the Hadejia-Jama'are flood plain in northern Nigeria, which is under threat from upstream irrigation development investments, such as the Kano River Project. The analysis shows that the economic benefits of the floodplain system are considerable, particularly in comparison with the irrigation project, which would suggest that the opportunity cost of diverting water to upstream developments could be high.

Not all public investments necessarily have negative impacts on the environment. Moreover, some investments can raise agricultural productivity and income, reduce poverty, and thus indirectly improve the incentives for natural resource management. This will be the case particularly if the income and wealth effects of greater public investment lead to more efficient and sustainable use of existing factors of production (for example, improved cropping patterns and land management schemes).

Conclusion

Macroeconomic, trade, and sectoral policies have important implications for resource degradation in developing countries. However, these effects are often complex and difficult to discern. Moreover, they vary considerably in terms of not only magnitude but also direction, depending on the situation. Careful analysis is required to derive policy implications.

Macroeconomic and trade policies used to control the economy often have a much wider economic context and influence than protection of the environment. These broader policy tools can have important environmental impacts but are generally more difficult or even dangerous to manipulate expressly to affect resource use. Even at the sectoral level, manipulation of pricing and other sectorwide economic instruments can have many counterproductive and unintended side effects. Caution is warranted in the use of such instruments for environmental protection or improvement, especially when more specific policy interventions such as taxes, charges, or targeted subsidies are available.

Priority should be given to the reform of government policies that appear to be both environmentally damaging and detrimental for economic welfare and social equity. Counteracting such policy failures will require complementary institutional reforms and possibly additional microeconomic interventions. Failure to account for the environmental impacts of public investments can also have major implications for resource degradation and economic welfare. Proper valuation and consideration of environmental costs and benefits associated with these investments are required. For all environmental problems in developing countries, improved economic analysis of both the impacts and the causes underlying environmental degradation will become crucial in the years ahead, as will the further integration of environmental objectives in policymaking.

10 Policy Analysis of Conservation Investments: Extensions of Traditional Technology Adoption Research

THOMAS REARDON AND STEPHEN A. VOSTI

A central contention of this volume is that many developing countries are forced to pursue rapid agricultural growth to keep up with increasing food and fiber demand from growing populations, urbanization and industrialization, and foreign exchange needs. Yet this growth needs to be done in such a way that poverty is alleviated and the productive capacity of the natural resource base sustained or enhanced. Hence agricultural research needs to seek land use technologies that raise agricultural productivity at a rate that meets growth objectives and that conserve the natural resource base to sustain that growth—what we term "overlap technologies."

These overlap technologies are central to the pursuit of sustainable agricultural intensification, a concept that appears frequently in recent debate (for example, Chapters 3 and 20 in this volume). An equivalent of the concept of sustainable intensification can be found in Boserup (1965a). She posits that, under population pressure and increasing constraints on arable land (which is the case in much of the developing world), as farmers intensify by cropping more on the same land, they can protect the land with land improvements such as terraces and bunds, and sustain soil fertility by use of fertilizer and manure. Such improvements can greatly increase yields and reduce degradation.[1] The generation of such technologies in the public sector is dealt with in Chapter 12 and elsewhere in this volume. Here we address technology adoption.

Policies (macroeconomic, sectoral, institutional, infrastructural, research, and extension) can strongly affect the desire and capacity of households and communities to undertake land improvements, what we term conservation

The authors thank Samuel K. Dapaah, Julie Witcover, Scott Swinton, and two reviewers for comments on earlier drafts. An earlier version of this chapter appeared as Reardon and Vosti (1992).

1. For example, Clay et al. (1995), for Rwanda, found large yield impacts from soil conservation measures, as do the studies on Thailand cited in de Haen (Chapter 3, this volume), Lopez-Pereira et al. (1994) for Honduras, or Tiffen et al. (1994) for Machakos, Kenya.

investments (such as investments in bunds and terraces and changes in land use practices, such as contour plowing), as well as more narrowly productivity-enhancing investments such as fertilizer, animal traction, and irrigation. Barbier (Chapter 9, this volume) illustrates the many ways that policies can affect natural resource use on farms and in the commons and open-access areas.

But Barbier, as well as Siamwalla (Chapter 8, this volume), caution that broad trade and macroeconomic policies have complex effects on overall economic activity and, in turn, on the natural resource base. Policies targeted narrowly at the rules and incentives for natural resource use are more efficient and predictable instruments, but even these can have complex and unforeseen effects.

There also appear to be hierarchies in policies at the national, community, and household levels. Developing country governments face short-run political pressures to put growth goals first. They appear willing to compromise growth for environmental goals only to a limited degree. For Africa, Idachaba (1987) makes this point strongly by noting that "sustainability," from the policy-makers' perspective, mainly means avoiding slowdowns in growth, and that the environment is a "second generation" issue for many poor countries.

Similarly, de Haen (Chapter 3, this volume) notes that poor rural households put immediate food security and income objectives first, possibly relegating environmental enhancement to second tier. Hence it is not certain that households will necessarily want or be able to take longer-term measures to sustain the resource base; this is reflected in rapid degradation in many rural areas, caused by infrequent or insufficient spontaneous investment (outside government or donor programs) in resource conservation.

In this chapter we focus on rural households and communities as the primary actors responsible for conservation investments, if they are to take place. Households and communities act within a complex policy, socioeconomic, and physical environment. We focus on how to conceptualize the effects of this complex environment on their investments in resource conservation. Our discussion places such investments in the broader context of household and community economic behavior in the commons and open-access lands, in agricultural lands, and in nonagricultural activities, because policies' effects on investment are generated via their effects on the full set of economic decisions. We discuss the following three issues in order:

1. How do conservation investments differ (in nature and determinants) from the "productivity investments," about which much was written during the technology adoption and Green Revolution debates in the 1970s and 1980s? That is, is there any reason to treat conservation investments as a new type of technology adoption question?

2. What drives farmers and villages to make (or refrain from making) conservation investments? How should the particularities of conservation investments affect how one analyzes policy impacts?
3. What are the policy issues and lessons specific to the promotion of conservation investments? Are new policy prescriptions or agents responsible for their promotion required—that go beyond those usually set out for the adoption of Green Revolution technologies (more roads and credit, better prices, and so on)?

Similarities and Distinctions between Productivity Investments and Conservation Investments

In the 1960s and 1970s, agricultural research focused on creating Green Revolution technology packages (new seeds combined with fertilizer and irrigation) that could rapidly boost productivity of land and labor, mainly in agroclimatically favorable zones. In the late 1970s and 1980s, the focus shifted to extending Green Revolution technologies to favorable zones where they had not yet been adopted and to finding technologies to raise productivity in agroclimatically unfavorable zones with risky agriculture. Most recently the quest has been to raise the sustainability of Green Revolution technologies in favorable zones and seek methods to conserve the resource base and stabilize yields in unfavorable zones (CGIAR/TAC 1989). There is a new (or, in some areas, reemerging) emphasis on conservation investments that complement and sustain the "traditional" Green Revolution technologies.[2]

During the past three decades, a large literature developed on the determinants of farmer adoption of productivity-enhancing Green Revolution technologies (Feder, Just, and Zilberman 1985). But it is not obvious what part of the adoption literature applies to the new questions regarding farmer and community investments in resource conservation—what drives them, what policies would spur them, what are their consequences.

This section addresses the following: (1) Are there types of "polar" investments and practices that are clearly either productivity-enhancing or conservation-enhancing, and is there an overlap set? (2) How do the polar types of investments compare in terms of input requirements and effects on agricultural productivity and environment? We begin with a typology of investments, then compare them.

Typology: Agricultural and Environmental Effects

We classify technologies (embodied in practices or physical capital, or both) by yield and environmental effects—a continuum from mainly productivity-

---

2. By agroclimatically favored zones, we mean zones that are well watered (by rain or irrigation) and have reasonably fertile soils. By unfavored we mean the contrary.

enhancing to mainly conservation-enhancing where the former boost short-term yields and the latter protect the resource base.[3] These categories are

1. technologies that increase productivity but damage the resource base (for example, a modern variety that exhausts soil nutrients, deep plowing that reduces soil integrity, irrigation methods that salinize or waterlog the soil);
2. technologies that increase productivity but with ambiguous effects on the natural resource base (for example, fertilizer use);
3. technologies that improve the natural resource base and increase productivity (for example, tied-ridging that prevents fertilizer runoff and conserves topsoil, or nitrogen-fixing high-yielding varieties); and
4. technologies that improve the natural resource base but with ambiguous effects on productivity (for example, some crop rotation and agroforestry schemes).

Note that a given practice can be classified in different ways, depending on how and where it is done; few technologies are inherently (in every situation) good or bad for the environment. For example, the classification of fertilizer use along this continuum partly depends on the intensity of use and the type of soil and aquifer. Figure 10.1 shows the hypothetical residual traces of nutrients in the soil from fertilizer use. At low levels of use, crops are extracting more nutrients than fertilizer is replenishing, thereby depleting soil nutrients. This first zone is in category 1. Increased fertilizer use beyond point B, but before (say) point C, covers crop nutrient requirements and leaves residual nutrients, enhancing the soil. This second zone would fall in category 2. For some types of fertilizer and for some soil and aquifer types, fertilizer use beyond (say) point C pollutes the resource base.

Comparison of Productivity Investments versus Conservation Investments

The technologies over the continuum described are similar in some basic requirements:[4] they all require household or community expenditures on vari-

---

3. There is, of course, inherent ambiguity in such categories. For example, a bund can stop topsoil removal and immediately raise yields on a plot; another conservation investment, agro-forestry, may have more delayed and less easily observed productivity effects. Moreover, sustaining the resource base means that it will continue to be productive or will lose productivity at a slower pace. But the conceptual value of establishing these classifications will be more apparent when we discuss differences in requirements and effects between the "polar" investment types.

4. The relevance of the similarities (and distinctions, for that matter) may begin to erode over time, when interregional or intersectoral linkages are allowed to play out. For example, productivity-focused investments can eventually conserve the resource base because they alleviate poverty (see Reardon and Vosti, Chapter 4, this volume). But agricultural growth does not automatically increase the incomes of all the rural poor. Moreover, the better off also suffer from wind and water erosion, salinization, and so forth in degrading areas, and many do not currently use sustainable practices. In addition, some productivity investments can exhaust, leach, and erode the soil and pollute groundwater in irreversible ways *before* the effects of increased incomes have time to affect farming practices (Ohm and Nagy 1985).

FIGURE 10.1 Stylized nutrient presence and fertilizer use curve

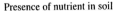
Presence of nutrient in soil

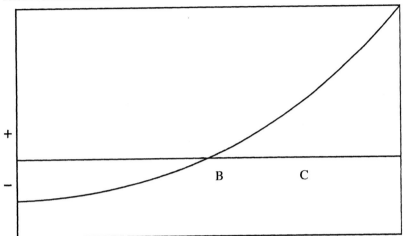

Fertilizer use per hectare

able inputs (labor and nonlabor); and most require external inputs of goods and services from the private sector and the government (technical and socio-economic research, extension, manufacturing and distribution of inputs, credit, market institutions, and hard infrastructure).

These shared requirements highlight, however, the possible competition between these two kinds of investments and between both types of agricultural investments and other investment and consumption expenditures (education, food consumption, and so forth)—not only at the farm and community level but also at the level of institutions of research and extension and in public infrastructure expenditures.

Nevertheless, productivity investments and conservation investments can be very different from one another in their specific requirements, and how these requirements and the benefits derived from them are perceived by farmers, in the following ways.

1. Households and communities might perceive the returns to conservation investments (for example, agroforestry or fallowing) to be both riskier and slower than those derived from investments that have more reliable and immediate impacts on productivity (for example, fertilizer or animal traction use).

2. Timing of input requirements can differ. Conservation investments often need (for reasons linked to the nature of the investment) to be made in the dry season, when, for example, building bunds can compete with migra-

tion and local off-farm activity, and sometimes must be made in the rainy season, when, for example, labor on alley cropping can compete with fertilizer application or weeding. The opportunity cost of labor time and capital for conservation investments to the farm household in either season can be high (Reardon and Islam 1989; Kerr and Sanghi 1992b; Lowenberg-DeBoer and Abdoulaye 1994).

3. Externalities associated with conservation investments can produce disincentives to private action. For example, if one farmer constructs bunds but his or her neighbor does not, the runoff from the second farm can overwhelm the conservation measures of the first. Or watershed management investments by a given farmer might obstruct soil deposition efforts by another (Kerr and Sanghi 1992b).

4. Many conservation investments are difficult to undertake incrementally and therefore require substantial expenditures of labor, cash, or both at particular times during the agricultural cycle, thereby potentially crowding out other menial activities. They often require much more than changes in agronomic practices.

5. Some conservation investments require specific and often scarce equipment for which there is no market; an example is tied-ridgers. Such equipment might be unaffordable for most households or even communities.

6. Many conservation investments require maintenance. Resources to support such maintenance might not be available, and planning for cash and labor to do so may require a longer planning horizon than is typical of farm households in risky, fragile areas.

Implications of the Special Nature of Conservation Investments for Analysis of Investment Determinants

The point of departure is the household investment or adoption model synthesized from the farm investment and adoption literature, including the conservation investment literature,[5] presented in detail in Reardon and Vosti (Chapter 4, this volume). All investments depend on three things: (1) incentives to invest (net returns and risks relative to alternative farm and nonfarm investments) and the household-specific discount rate; (2) capacity to invest (household wealth and on-farm complementary assets such as a well that provides water to maintain a live windbreak); and (3) external conditioning

---

5. For example: Seitz and Swanson 1980; Ervin and Ervin 1982; Bultena and Hoiberg 1983; Feder, Just, and Zilberman 1985; Feder and Onchan 1987; Norris and Batie 1987; Roth and Barrows 1988; Southgate 1988; Christensen 1989; Pagoulatos, Debertin, and Sjarkowi 1989; Barbier, 1990b; Thampapillai and Anderson 1991; Heady and Vocke 1992; Kerr and Sanghi 1992b; Fujisaka 1993; Miranowski and Cochran 1993; Anderson and Hazell 1994; Reardon, Crawford, and Kelly 1995.

variables (technologies, institutions, climate, infrastructure, and community watershed management infrastructure such as dams and culverts).

Rather than work through the specifics of a model of conservation investments, we discuss what additions or emphases would be most important to this general "traditional" investment model to treat this new type of investment. Two household strategies that go beyond resource conservation per se, but influence these investments, merit highlighting.

Off-farm income activities are often very important to farm households in fragile areas as a means of risk management and coping. But these off-farm activities often occur in the dry season (when conservation measures such as bund building or maintenance are done) and often are an important source of cash for conservation investments. The competition between migration and bund building and maintenance in the dry season can be important in the semi-arid tropics. Using cash to hire labor to build terraces versus to start off-farm businesses is an example of such competition. It is often in the most fragile areas, where conservation measures are most needed, that the desire to diversify incomes off-farm (especially into activities less connected with the local agricultural economy, such as activities undertaken during migration away from the local area or in the local town) is strongest, and hence the competition can be the strongest (Reardon and Islam 1989).

Second, crop mix strategies can also have important effects on whether farm households can or want to make conservation investments. Reardon, Crawford, and Kelly (1995), in a synthesis of agricultural productivity case studies in Africa, found that farmers usually apply the bulk of fertilizer, mulch, manure, and soil conservation infrastructure to cash crop fields, either because the profitability is much higher than for subsistence crops or because cash crop schemes often provide credit or inputs. The latter is important where there are missing or underdeveloped local credit markets. Even where credit markets are developed, conservation investments are not typically objects of loans and apparently are perceived as less creditworthy. Moreover, some crop mixes (such as a high share of perennials) or land use patterns (such as a high share of pasture and fallow) are substitutes for conservation investments (Clay et al. 1995).

Hence analysis of conservation investments needs to go beyond the physical characteristics of farm plots to incorporate characteristics of the entire household economy, including demographic characteristics, income from farm and nonfarm sources, crop mix, and human and physical capital variables. A conservation investment on a given plot fits into the general income, investment, and consumption strategy of the farm household. Policy affects that overall strategy, and via that strategy, a specific investment. Likewise, the effects of policy on the natural resource base occur via policy effects on land use strategies and farm investments. The same point can be made for productivity investments, but these considerations are even more important for conservation investments, given their resource-intensive and long-term nature.

This crucial intermediate link (from policy to household overall economic behavior to investments) is relatively rare in the literature on policy impacts on the environment in developing countries. Usually the focus is on how a given price or regulation change affects use of a single resource (for example, land or water), without putting it in the context of effects on overall household behavior, in order to understand the rationale and context of the resource use change. Understanding the household strategy context can be quite important in explaining changes in use of a resource in response to a policy change. For example, a policy change that increases costs of using rangeland may not change the grazing practices of poor households because they lack income alternatives. (For examples of such analysis in developed country agriculture, see Heady and Vocke [1992].)

Incorporation of interaction *among* households is particularly important in analysis of conservation investments. Farmers sometimes do not face the full costs or receive the full benefits of their production activities. Externalities associated with erosion, silting, overgrazing of common lands, and so forth allow farmers to rationally reap short-term gains at the cost (often to someone else) of future production. Because defining and policing these sorts of property rights issues can be costly and often untenable, redressing these incentives via policy or institutional reform will be difficult in many areas of the developing world in the near future (Miranowski and Cochran 1993).

Moreover, the distribution within a watershed of particular types of private investments can affect a given farmer's conservation investment decision. Kerr and Sanghi (1992b), in their analysis of watershed management in India, note that whether others in the watershed are investing in contour bunds can affect downhill farmers' decisions to so invest—if the chain of bunds is broken by one or more farmers, the water will break through and erode fields of neighbors who invested in bunds.[6]

The existence of complementary public investments in the watershed or community can also affect private conservation investment patterns. For example, the presence of a public culvert next to a farmer's field can affect the maintenance costs of a bund on that field. Or a public well can determine whether nearby farmers' live windbreaks will survive the first dry seasons.

Labor and cash available to a given household may not suffice to make a particular conservation investment, and the household may need to hire or borrow. This may also be the case for large productivity investments (such as animal traction equipment), but it is especially true for building bunds and terraces. Hence the degree of development of the labor and credit markets (including inflows of labor and credit from outside the village) can be important determinants of whether or not conservation investments are undertaken.

---

6. On the other hand, Kerr and Sanghi (1992b) note that some Indian farmers deliberately allow erosion of fields on upper slopes to deposit silt on their fields downslope (to build topsoil).

There may be discontinuities in the relation between conservation investments and environmental quality over time. That is to say, environmental degradation may limit the profitability of some conservation investments once critical ecological thresholds have been exceeded. Similarly, before a certain level of degradation is reached (where, for example, loss of topsoil poses no threat to output), there may not be a private financial reason to make conservation investments aimed at retaining soil.

Implications for Promoting Conservation Investments

Overcoming the constraints facing farmers and communities to make conservation investments requires innovative policies. Macroeconomic and sectoral policies that make agricultural activities profitable may be necessary but not sufficient to induce a farmer or village to make conservation investments central to sustainable natural resource management. Farmers require a sufficient net profit, especially relative to other activities, to invest in conservation measures. Policies (such as currency devaluation) that increase average return but do not reduce price or institutional risk sufficiently, or that do not reduce investment costs sufficiently, may also not induce investments. Risk is especially important in unfavorable zones, where investments in cropping yield low and uncertain returns and investments in soil conservation are even worse. When farmers are poor and risk averse, and conservation investments appear to have only long-term payoffs that are perceived as more uncertain than productivity or income diversification investments, then conservation measures will be ranked quite low among farmers' investment priorities.

Collective action or local participation programs can be successful in helping to promote conservation investments, if they address underlying constraints that households and communities face in pursuing their primary objectives—food security and avoiding income shortfalls. Moreover, Barbier (Chapter 9, this volume) and others have stressed the need for resource pricing policies to move actual prices closer to "true scarcity values." Dapaah (1992) has noted, however, that laws that promote this alignment exist but are often not implemented for reasons of weak administrations, high implementation costs, and politics. Moreover, if natural resource prices are increased but the price increase does not translate into sufficient new farmer income to make conservation investments, such policies will not promote them.

Even if returns are sufficiently high and stable to induce conservation investments, other constraints may be present and need policy change to address them. Infrastructure and institutional policies have special significance. Household conservation investments often require complementary infrastructural investments by villages, nongovernmental organizations, or national governments. (Recall the examples of culverts and wells in the preceding section.) These may be constructed through local food-for-work projects if communities lack sufficient financial resources (von Braun, Teklu, and Webb 1991). In addition, public interventions that demonstrate to farmers the practical payoff from conservation investments are critical to reducing the perception of riskiness (Swindale 1988).

Community institutional arrangements to reduce environmental externalities undermining private incentives to investment are important. Chopra and Rao (Chapter 21, this volume) describe one such action in a community in India where the state facilitated conservation investments by undertaking complementary infrastructure investments.

Some evidence points to the assurance of long-term use rights (land tenure) as important for conservation investments such as bunds and agroforestry, although in many cases such secure access to land seems less important for short-term soil fertility management (see, for example, Blarel 1989; Place and Hazell 1993; Clay et al. 1995).

Research (private and public) has the difficult task of seeking appropriate and affordable resource conservation techniques, especially to reduce the cost of large, one-time investments such as tied-ridges, bunds, and drainage. Many technologies and practices are "on the shelf" but need to be adapted to the needs of the farmers in both form and cost (Matlon 1985).

There is a need for improved extension services associated with conservation practices. Extension is costly, and shrinking resources impose hard choices: should an extension agent devote time to showing farmers how to build bunds and terraces, how to apply fertilizer, or how to build irrigation canals? If cash and labor constraints preclude bigger projects (bunds and terraces), agents may choose to focus on the simpler techniques of plant spacing, timing of activities, and fertilizer selection. To succeed, the state will need to create a special cadre of "sustainability extension agents" for the larger conservation investments and to couple such efforts with special credit programs (Wright 1985). But such extension can pay off, especially when the conservation practices are new techniques and promise to be appropriate to the local conditions (see Clay et al. 1995 for Rwanda).

Some new practices are not, strictly speaking, capital investments at the farm level (for example, integrated pest management) and may be relatively cheap (in cash) for the farmer. However, even these will be adopted only if there are prior outlays by the community or the state (Reardon and Islam 1989).

Research and policy action are needed to address the problems related to gaining credit for conservation investments. Credit markets in many environmentally fragile areas are quite underdeveloped. Interest rates are high, and access for smallholders is often limited (Binswanger 1986). Even where formal (or informal) credit markets are developed, there may be special constraints for getting credit for conservation investments, for several reasons. The loan size to construct large items such as bunds or terraces or to establish perennial tree crops might exceed the capacity of local creditors or even village credit groups (Swindale 1988), especially if many households require loans at once. Increased riskiness of conservation investments due to upstream action (or inaction) of other farmers can undermine a farmer's ability to get credit for such investments. Creditors may not perceive (and indeed there may not be) a clear short-term cash payoff from conservation investments, hence the risk of default may appear greater.

Productivity investments often require, but also create, loan collateral (for example, animal traction equipment). This is generally not so with conservation investments (for example, creditors cannot reclaim bunds or windbreaks!). A notable exception might be the establishment of orchards that raise land values, but unfortunately (from the lender's viewpoint) these orchards may not serve as collateral as they cannot be appropriated. For example, some tree-cropping schemes require mass production of seedlings, and few banks are willing to lend for such activities (Ohm and Nagy 1985).

Finally, if local credit markets cannot supply enough funds to overcome household-level cash constraints, then some conservation investments may have to be made by the village or the state (Swindale 1988).

Conclusions

In this chapter we identified some key characteristics of conservation investments that differ from traditional Green Revolution productivity investments. These characteristics imply special constraints on conservation investments and warrant innovative policy approaches. "Getting prices right" at the macroeconomic or sectoral level is necessary but not sufficient. Innovations that aim at the riskiness and affordability of conservation investments and at farmers' incentives and capacity to undertake them are important—especially in the domain of infrastructure, credit, and institutional policy. Complementary public expenditures to make conservation investments attractive, affordable, and compatible with household food security objectives are crucial.

This chapter suggests an important agenda for policy research that goes beyond but complements research on resource conservation techniques. Adoption of conservation investments must be examined in the context of the overall household economy and community, and the household's income diversification and land use strategies must be explicitly considered.

11 "Exogenous" Interest Rates, Technology, and Farm Prices versus "Endogenous" Conservation Incentives and Policies

MICHAEL LIPTON

Many authors in this volume (for example, Barbier, Chapter 9) attribute much resource degradation in developing rural areas (DRAs) to market failure and policy failure—failure, in each case, to "reflect environmental values." Other authors (for example, Reardon and Vosti, Chapter 10) attribute much resource degradation to incorrect domestic policies affecting relative prices. This chapter suggests, instead, that most resource degradation in DRAs responds to the *success* of domestic markets and policies. They succeed in communicating to rationally maximizing agents (households, firms, managers of common property) that changes in prices (especially real interest rates) and in technical options increasingly favor accelerated resource degradation.

Indeed, accelerated resource degradation in DRAs is mainly the cumulative consequence of developed country policies that have led to (1) a tripling of world real interest rates between 1945–1974 and 1979–1993, and, in the longer term, (2) falling and unstable relative farm prices, and (3) labor-displacing technical progress. In this chapter I set out reasons for believing that these international effects have been paramount.

In addition, I contend here that these technology and price incentives responsible for much resource degradation in DRAs (1) depend more on technology than on price; (2) inasmuch as they depend on price, depend substantially on interest rates; and (3) in both these respects, are largely exogenous to agents in developing countries. Economic agents in DRAs are in the great majority of cases *price takers* for interest rates and other environmentally critical prices, and also "*product takers*" for the technology mix. All this suggests that, although the explicit or implicit policy recommendations appearing throughout this volume are reasonable enough, their impact on rates of resource degradation in DRAs will be small, without appropriate changes in policy by the interest rate "price makers" and technology mix "product makers" in the developed world.

High (and Exogenously Set) Rates of Interest

It will now be shown that DRA resource depletion is in significant part caused by developed country policies that raise real long-term interest rates and that it could be moderated or reversed if these policies were. This interest rate argument asserts that rates of interest in the 1980s were excessive in the sense that they increased resource degradation by worsening the structures of investment, production, consumption, and resource management, and that these rates should therefore be reduced.

In May 1991 the World Bank summarized the position: "In the prosperous 1950s and 1960s, real [long-term prime] interest rates [for prime borrowers] stood at some 1 to 1.5 percent and short-term rates were even lower." After an aberrant period of negative real rates during the rapid inflation of 1973–1977, "real [long-term prime] interest rates have hovered between 4 and 5 percent, and they appear set to remain at these levels or to climb even higher"; they have fully met that prediction in the 1990s (World Bank 1991a:33). Such high rates appear to be historically without precedent.

Public policy by the principal developed country governments since about 1979 has accepted, and probably caused, this interest rate upsurge. These governments, reacting against an inappropriately Keynesian response to the first (1973) oil price shock, decided to squeeze out inflation (and inflationary expectations) after the second (1978) shock. Around 1978–1984, this squeeze was attempted mainly by restraining the growth of the money supply, which led to increases in the nominal rate of interest. At the same time, the United States public sector deficits (and perhaps those in some other developed countries) added market-based upward pressure on interest rates. Rates charged by leading public institutions to borrowing governments—even on *old* loans—since the late 1970s have responded quickly to market conditions. There is no reason to doubt that these changes are passed on to final borrowers, especially in view of pressures by donors upon developing country governments to phase out interest rate subsidies.

Rising real rates of interest, transmitted to LDCs and to their DRAs, are likely to cause rising rates of resource degradation, via private incentives and public capacities. A simple example will demonstrate this point.

Suppose a farmer is choosing between a "sustainable" way to manage land, which generates a net return of y_1 each year forever, and an "exhaustive" way, which generates a higher return, y_2 each year for n years, after which the land has been destroyed and yields nothing. It can easily be shown that the "sustainable" path yields a higher present value if, and only if

$$\frac{y_2}{y_1} < 1 - \frac{1}{(1-r)^{n+1}},$$

where r is the real interest rate for an n-year loan. For example, if $r = 10$ percent and $n = 15$ years, the sustainable path is chosen only if it produces at least

78 percent as much, forever, as the exhaustive path produces for 15 years before destroying the land. If $r = 5$ percent, the sustainable path needs to produce less, namely, 54 percent of "exhaustive" net returns, to be preferred. Clearly, the rise in real long-term rates of interest, if transmitted to DRAs, must have had enormous incentive effects on resource management, shifting it away from sustainability.

If risk is allowed for, the interest rate incentive to deplete is probably sharpened. Higher interest rates reduce the present-value burden of long-term-future downside risks, relative to that of near-term risks (and costs). The land use patterns are therefore shifted toward activities with long-term risks, such as possible long-term resource degradation.

Therefore, if one focuses on choices in resource management—for example, between various levels of water use or between nutrient cycling and mining—it becomes impossible to miss the powerful resource-depleting incentive created by higher real interest rates. Costly credit undoubtedly shifts the *composition*—of inputs, outputs, techniques, investments, consumption, and savings—sharply in a resource-depleting direction. It is only the effect of costly credit on degradation via *investment levels* (taken up later in this sub-section) that remains in doubt.

Apart from pushing incentives—to managers of state, private, and common property—away from conserving future production capacity, high real interest rates also reduce resources available for conservation spending. Whether or not conservation requires higher public investment, it certainly requires public spending (1) to reduce the extent to which resource degradation is induced by poverty, population growth, and underpolicing of common property; (2) to develop nondepleting technical options; and (3) to compensate or subsidize poor, or politically powerful, losers from conservation. Yet rising interest rates have slashed public resources for such purposes.

In 1972, interest payments were 5.6 percent of central government spending (plus its lending, minus capital repayments: hereafter SLCR) in non-oil developing countries; the proportions were a little higher in South and East Asia than elsewhere. By 1983 the proportion had risen to 11.9 percent, and by 1988 to 18.7 percent—and more than 28 percent in Latin America and the Caribbean. This extra interest rate burden was not relieved by extra net financial flows. On the contrary, net financing from abroad, which had covered 2.3 percent of non-oil developing countries' central government SLCR in 1972 and 4.6 percent in 1983, fell back sharply, reaching only 1.4 percent in 1989 (IMF, various years). The sharp rise in private flows in the 1990s was confined to a very few developing countries and may have done little to improve public-sector resources (let alone inducements) to act against resource deregulation.

How did those governments respond? Central government expenditure in non-oil developing countries appears to have risen from below 20 percent of gross domestic product (GDP) in the early 1970s to a fairly stable 23–25 percent in 1983–1989. However, net of interest payments, this represents a big fall in central governments' expenditure as a share of GDP.

Partly as a result of the incentive effects considered earlier, this decrease in noninterest government spending by developing countries fell disproportionately upon activities that might reduce rates of resource degradation. In 1975, agriculture received 7.9 percent of central government expenditures in non-oil developing countries. This share then appears to have fallen in every single year, reaching 4.5 percent in 1988. Total government investment fell almost continuously in non-oil developing countries, from 19.2 percent of central government expenditure in 1972 to 11.4 percent in 1988. For all developing countries taken together, rises in the share of private investment in GDP offset public sector falls, but this did not happen in most individual countries. In 1980–1989, total gross domestic investment rose by 9.8 percent yearly in China and India but rose only by 1.5 percent yearly in other low-income countries and fell by 8.9 percent per year in Sub-Saharan Africa and by 2.3 percent in Latin America and the Caribbean (World Bank 1991b).

The decline in real agricultural expenditure by governments, which is matched by trends in the sectoral structure of international flows (Paarlberg and Lipton 1991), weakens the main policy lever to reduce rates of resource degradation. If less is being done to help poor rural people to improve their sustainable access to food and income, then growing populations are under increasing pressure to "mine" natural resources instead. Also, public investment offers a chance to structure public goods capital in ways that correct possible private tendencies toward myopic rates of resource degradation and that embody new technology to conserve resources (issues to be taken up later).

In sum, high real interest rates (1) encourage private and public decisionmakers to increase rates of resource degradation and (2) deprive public decisionmakers in developing countries of resources with which countervailing measures might be taken.

Finally, if the tripling of interest rates from 1945–1975 to 1979–1993 is so important a cause of sapped incentives and capacities for prevention of resource degradation, why is the fact not generally recognized? The main reason is the following belief (Markandya and Pearce 1988:abstract and p. 30):

> Low discount rates may imply less *direct* natural resource use, but [also] more investment, which in turn requires more natural resources to be exploited. . . . Moreover, many of the investment projects that need a low discount rate to be acceptable are . . . potentially damaging to the environment, [e.g.,] irrigation projects. . . . High rates may well . . . slow down the general pace of development [by] depressing the level of investment. Since natural resources are required for investment, the demand for natural resources is generally less at high discount rates. [These] also discourage development projects that compete with existing environmentally benign land uses.

Even if higher rates of interest do significantly reduce levels of total investment, this belief assumes "that resource-using investment is dominant. There is little evidence for this assumption" (Pezzey 1989:30), even though it is shared by the 1992 *World Development Report* (World Bank 1992b:3). Indeed, there is no general—let alone necessary—mechanism linking lower investment to slower resource degradation.

However, there is another reason why economists have resisted the argument that real market rates of interest have greatly worsened resource degradation in DRAs. The reason is that the proponents of the argument just described sometimes confuse it with arguments for manipulation downward of shadow rates of interest in benefit-cost analysis—that is, for pretending that the opportunity cost of capital is less than it really is. The practice is neither sensible nor the best means to check resource degradation (Markandya and Pearce 1988; Pezzey 1989).

Exogenous World Farm Prices

The level of world farm prices also affects the scale and level of impact from developing country domestic policy upon resource degradation or renewal in DRAs. With marked fluctuations, world prices for most main crops have been falling in real terms for 40 years (World Bank 1989a). Farmers anticipating continued price declines will shift toward adding value by farm production now at the cost of production later. Accelerated resource degradation results. This price-induced shift toward resource degradation is attributable to exogenous factors.

It is policies in developed countries that have produced the bigger, more pervasive, more durable, and worsening "price twists" against developing countries' farm prices, thereby encouraging developing country farmers to discount the future capacity of their resources to sustain output. Farm policy in the European Community (EC), and for some products in the United States (sugar, tobacco, cotton) and Japan (rice), lowers the trend line of world farm output prices by (1) stimulating overproduction; (2) subsidizing huge stock overhangs that depress prices further, and arguably by subsidizing exports as well; and (3) greatly stimulating developed country farmers' demand for research, which generates a pipeline of technical progress that leads to further incentives to overproduce.

There is another price-related effect of EC (and probably other OECD) farm policies on the incentive to degrade resources in DRAs. These policies reduce the impact of higher (or lower) world prices upon EC farmers' incentives to raise (or lower) output and thereby destabilize world prices of major agricultural commodities (Koester 1982). This further encourages farmers in developing countries, whenever prices are temporarily high, to increase output even at the cost of mining natural resources.

Finally, developing country governments have often ill-advisedly intensified this price decline via trade regimes, parastatal monopolies of farm inputs or monopsonies of farm outputs, and so forth (Lipton 1977; Schultz 1978; Krueger, Schiff, and Valdés 1991).

Exogenous Technical Progress

In the long run, at least in the more vibrant regions of developing country farming, technology probably affects farm-level incentives more than prices do. For example, the productivity levels of land, labor, fertilizer, and irrigation in rice or wheat production in the Indian Punjab have probably changed faster over the 1964–1992 period than their respective input/output price ratios. Farmers' selection from an available set of generated production technologies determines whether their response to the joint pressures of population and changing prices will be resource-enhancing or resource-degrading.

Those developing countries with capacity and markets large enough to render some degree of research self-sufficiency plausible may escape the impact of "imported" changes in technology. However, there has been little attempt to design the generation, selection, or availability of techniques "formally" supplied by international agricultural research in ways that increase the likelihood of resource-preserving outcomes as rural populations grow. This is partly because the problem has not been posed in these terms. It is mainly, however, because the process of technology generation in agriculture remains exogenous to most of the developing countries and is not driven significantly by their resource-saving, or other, requirements.

Promising lines of research on different crop mixes, areas, methods, and so forth (for example, rotations and agroforestry) may have substantially different effects on rates of agrochemical extraction from the soil, on soil erosion, or on groundwater removal and recharge. But are there ways to compensate for changes in the type, quantity, and timing of outputs generated by these methods vis-à-vis traditional cropping patterns? Answering such questions is costly and time-consuming. For conventional and emerging technologies, agricultural research should try to specify the extent to which higher yields are due to more inputs, to better plant partitioning efficiency, to better plant conversion efficiency, or to higher—and perhaps nonsustainable—rates of nutrient and water extraction by plant populations.

Agricultural research outputs may also skew the benefits of technical change toward farm systems based on private property and away from those based on common property resources (CPRs), as well as skewing the balance among innovations produced for CPRs. Partly for demand-side reasons, the rate of technical progress "delivered" by agricultural research has been much faster for privately owned resources than for CPRs. This must have accelerated privatization of CPRs, but with what effect on resource degradation rates?

Also, the research balance must have affected the management of existing CPRs: again, with what impact on sustainability? Finally, there is a serious problem about research outputs that do improve productivity on CPRs. For example, will better pasture or more conversion-efficient beasts increase the incentive to overgraze—particularly in circumstances where the forces that normally prevent "tragedies of the commons" are weakening (Lipton 1985)? If so, better techniques on the commons can soon bring worse outcomes for resource degradation rates.

These issues for international agricultural research may point to an underlying problem. Is the technical progress made available to farmers in developing countries as exogenously determined as the real rate of interest? Selection by farmers from the menu of techniques (innovation), and the generation by a region's researchers of locally attractive additions to that menu (invention), are largely determined by that region's food requirements (Boserup 1965b), land and labor availabilities, and relative prices (Ruttan and Binswanger 1978; Hayami and Ruttan 1985). All these incentives would, in turn, be affected by rates of resource degradation, so that induced innovation—and induced invention via research—would tend to save, or to discover, resources otherwise tending to be degraded.

But how much power do farmers, or even governments, in developing countries have over the direction of research outputs affecting the farmers' capacity to respond to changes in demand or resource availability? On a global scale, agricultural research responds not to the needs of workers or smallholders experiencing rapid growth of person-land ratios (and degrading food-growing resources), but to those of large farmers (not only in developed countries [Grabowski 1981]) seeking to save labor and of research scientists seeking intellectual satisfaction and security by catering to the better-endowed and better-understood problems, environments, and crops of such farmers.

Research outputs apart, the very structure of agricultural research is changing in response to the needs and demands of wealthy farmers, consumers, and researchers. It is well known that biotechnology has raised the returns (and prospects) for internalizing the gains from research to the companies that undertake it and increased the net outflow of scientists from public to private agricultural research. Yet agricultural biotechnology is concentrated mainly on the products, conditions, and factor intensities of big Western farmers. This, and similar trends in other areas of agricultural research, threatens to substantially reduce the proportion of research resources devoted to the farm products, labor intensities, and local resource degradation threats that most concern smallholders in poor countries. All this provides exogenously structured incentives (and funds) for international and national agricultural research systems that do *not* focus on reducing the rate of resource degradation in developing rural areas.

Conclusion

To recognize partial exogeneity is not to counsel despair. Plenty of improvement in natural resource management is possible through national and global research and investments undertaken by existing private and public institutions. Also, developed country firms, consumers, and governments are certainly not to blame for all woes in the developing world. But such attribution has much justice regarding the determination of the real interest rate on long-term loans; world farm price trends and fluctuations; and the pattern, emphasis, and end-products of global applied research. Unfortunately, it is these three topics that do most to determine the rate of resource degradation in DRAs. If there is no change in developed countries' policies for any of the three topics, even great improvements in developing country governments' policies can achieve only modest, though locally still significant, advances in agricultural sustainability.

12 Research Systems for Sustainable Agricultural Development

PETER ORAM

Technological change in agriculture is fundamental to economic growth, food security, and family welfare in developing countries. Substantial progress has been made in raising agricultural productivity, especially in Asia and South America, enabling countries to maintain or slightly increase per capita food intakes despite fast population growth. But it is proving difficult to sustain technical advances in those regions, even in favorable agroecological zones. In Sub-Saharan Africa and West Asia–North Africa food production has generally failed to keep pace with population growth rates.

The challenge facing policymakers and scientists in developing countries is to develop agricultural technology that can raise food production without compromising the sustainability of the natural resource base. If those goals are to be compatible, it will be necessary (1) to find ways of increasing productivity without using agricultural chemicals at levels that aggravate environmental pollution; (2) to improve the effectiveness of input use; (3) to develop systems of land use to match varying agroecological potentials, market requirements, and demographic situations; and (4) to induce farmers to adopt environmentally sound practices by demonstrating to them the appropriateness and value of the practices.

The task is difficult and complex, requiring new concepts and approaches to resource management in the tropics, transcending the conventional chemical- and mechanical-based agricultural technology originally developed for temperate latitudes. The main burden of developing sustainable new technology acceptable to potential users will fall on the institutions responsible for research and technology transfer. Those institutions must work closely with policymakers to create a flexible national strategy for agriculture and natural resource management, as well as with local communities so that research can be adapted to specific ecological and social needs.

Many institutions are concerned with technical change: national planning agencies; the research system (public sector institutes, universities, and the private sector); the knowledge-transfer system (research, extension, nongovernmental organizations [NGOs], the media); support services (seed, credit, marketing); and local government and people's organizations. Failure to sustain a key component, or poor linkages among them, may jeopardize the whole. In this chapter I discuss not only national research capacity to develop sustainable technology, but also the sustainability of the technology transfer system, including the role of international research and development institutions. I examine three issues: (1) the problems that need to be addressed to develop sustainable technology and natural resource management; (2) the institutional capacity to address those problems; and (3) the sustainability of the institutions.

Problems Facing Agricultural Research Institutions in Developing Sustainable Agricultural Technology

National and international agricultural research systems, which have been concerned mainly with increasing production, are now faced with an expanded set of research imperatives related to sustainable agricultural technology and land use. These include:

1. developing systems of agroecological characterization to help determine optimal land use systems and to identify technologies and input levels appropriate to those systems;
2. examining the links between social and demographic situations and ecological conditions to develop technology that is environmentally appropriate and acceptable to potential users;
3. evaluating and monitoring the technological, economic, social, and demographic factors contributing to environmental degradation, including poverty, uncertainties over property rights, loss of biodiversity, and possibly global warming;
4. initiating macrolevel studies to understand the impact of policy on land use, technology adoption, resource management, and environmental sustainability and to shed light on which policies have been most beneficial and why;
5. assessing environmental externalities associated with agriculture;
6. evaluating and conserving plant and animal genetic resources, both internationally and nationally;
7. raising efficiency of chemical inputs (fertilizers, herbicides, pesticides) to improve cost-effectiveness and avoid environmentally damaging overuse or misuse;
8. evaluating the technical and economic viability of "environmentally friendly" farming systems and techniques of production—alley cropping, "organic" farming, integrated pest management, drip irrigation, low-input agriculture, and so forth—in different ecological and social situations;

9. understanding social and economic constraints at the farm or village level that might limit the adoption of sustainable innovations; and
10. establishing complementary physical and social infrastructure to support sustainable farming systems.

A critical need is to link research on monitoring the technological and social causes of losses or gains in environmental sustainability to evaluation of their economic impact. This may involve measurement of sources of loss or gain as they affect the nature and value of the resource base, agricultural productivity, incomes, and human welfare, both in the area concerned and in other areas via externalities.

Although it would be unjust to suggest that agricultural scientists have neglected sustainability, the long list of "new" research needs, the widespread failure of efforts to introduce "improved" technology to farmers (Carr 1989; Lele 1989), and the abandonment of subsidized practices adopted by farmers once the subsidies are withdrawn all suggest that much more attention must be given to sustainability.

Factors Influencing the Capacity to Develop Sustainable Technologies

Strategies for developing technologies to meet food needs will require institutional flexibility and interdisciplinarity. However, institutional capacity to respond to these challenges may be limited for several reasons.

First, the influence of the evolution of agricultural education and technology in the developed countries on the research and training strategy pursued by expatriate scientists and technical assistance staff working in developing countries has led to a narrow and unbalanced disciplinary composition of national agricultural research systems (NARSs) and extension staff in developing countries. This hampers their capacity to deal with the wider research and advisory needs of sustainable technological change and natural resource management.

Second, the planning and management structure in most developing countries is not conducive to a holistic view of the agricultural resource base and the way it should be managed to achieve an optimum marriage of productivity and sustainability.

Third, the sustainability of the institutions responsible for the generation and transfer of improved technology is threatened by internal weaknesses and financial constraints.

The Influence of Developed Country Technology, Technical Assistance, and International Agricultural Research on Developing Countries

Over the past 200 years, farming in the industrialized countries has evolved from a largely self-contained, organically and biologically based, labor-intensive pattern to one that is chemically and mechanically based, labor-saving, and market-oriented. This change has enabled these countries to feed an increasingly urbanized population with a shrinking farm labor force and to meet changing demand for food generated by rising incomes. Advances in science led to sharp increases in productivity in industrialized countries after World War II, at a time when food production in the newly independent developing countries was falling seriously behind population growth, generating a need for food aid, famine relief, and technical assistance.

The scientists and technicians sent to help developing countries found that farmers used little chemical fertilizer or pesticides, failed to control weeds, planted unimproved varieties, and lacked adequate draft power and organic manure because they kept few large animals. It seemed logical to transform traditional agriculture by following the same paradigms that had proved so successful in temperate countries and that appeared to show great promise in the tropics.

The success of this strategy in the densely populated food deficit countries of South and Southeast Asia led to the Green Revolution, to the creation of the International Maize and Wheat Improvement Center (CIMMYT) and the International Rice Research Institute (IRRI), the first two international agricultural research centers (IARCs), and subsequently to the establishment in 1971 of the Consultative Group on International Agricultural Research (CGIAR).

Since then, the CGIAR has supported the establishment of 16 new IARCs, of which 9 are primarily commodity oriented, with a strong emphasis on genetic improvement for higher yields, pest and disease control, and fertilizer technology. Resource-oriented centers dealing with fertilizer development, insect physiology, soil resources, irrigation management, aquatic resources, agroforestry, and mountain development were also established outside the CGIAR system: those working on irrigation management, aquatic resources, and agroforestry are now part of the CGIAR.

While a commodity-oriented strategy does not run counter to sustainability, especially where genetic improvement is the focus, "high-yielding" varieties and their technological packages have not been widely adopted in semi-arid, rainfed areas of Sub-Saharan Africa, West Asia, North Africa, and Latin America, nor in the difficult soils of the wet tropics, which are more suited to forests or perennial crops. Lack of appropriate and sustainable agricultural technology for these problem areas is leading to deforestation, soil mining, erosion, and desertification. Moreover, even where the new technologies have been successful, increasing expenditures on maintenance research is necessary to hold on to the gains. Consequently, most of the commodity-oriented IARCs are seeking to move "upstream" into biotechnology to raise yield ceilings of existing cultivars, to reduce yield maintenance research needs, and to improve stress tolerance in difficult environmental situations (CGIAR 1990).

TABLE 12.1 CGIAR operational expenditures for essential activities, 1983, 1987, 1989, and 1991

	1983		1987		1989		1991 (proposed)	
	Expenditure (US$ thousands)	Share of Research Expenditures (percent)	Expenditure (US$ thousands)	Share of Research Expenditures (percent)	Expenditure (US$ thousands)	Share of Research Expenditures (percent)	Expenditure (US$ thousands)	Share of Research Expenditures (percent)
Research								
Cereals	37,192	40.4	33,260	40.0	39,870	39.8	54,000	40.0
Food legumes	11,159	12.1	10,810	13.0	12,100	12.0	14,590	10.8
Roots and tubers	10,654	11.6	6,590	7.9	10,000	9.9	12,770	9.6
Livestock and pastures	10,834	11.8	15,820	19.0	21,700	21.3	29,820	22.1
Natural resources/ farming systems research	14,651	15.9	12,590	15.1	12,700	12.7	18,950	14.0
Food policy	4,459[a]	4.8[a]	4,130	5.0	4,280	4.3	4,820	3.6
Miscellaneous	3,094[b]	3.4[b]						
Subtotal	92,043 (50.6)	100.0	83,200 (44.2)	100.0	100,650 (44.8)	100.0	134,950 (48.9)	100.0
Strengthening NARSs								
Information, communications, libraries, and documentation	8,354		10,220		12,810		15,690	
Institution building	11,849		11,680		14,580		17,720	
Training and conferences	14,263		16,560		16,580		20,320	
Subtotal	34,466	(13.5)	38,460	(20.4)	43,970	(19.7)	53,230	(19.3)
Research support	25,083	(13.0)	20,300	(10.8)	22,220	(9.9)	25,320	(9.2)
Management and operations	40,000[c]	(22.0)	46,310	(24.6)	57,310	(25.6)	62,650	(22.6)
Total operations	191,592	(100.0)	188,250	(100.0)	223,820	(100.0)	276,150	(100.0)

SOURCES: 1983: Pineiro and Moscardi 1984; 1987 and 1989: CGIAR 1990; 1991: CGIAR Secretariat.

NOTES: Figures in parentheses are shares of total CGIAR expenditures. Blank cell indicates not applicable.

[a] Includes other socioeconomic research.

[b] Genetic conservation.

[c] No 1983 figure cited by authors. Amount given is imputed at about the 1987–1991 administrative costs of the system.

Across the CGIAR centers, there has been limited change in recent years in either the allocation of spending to commodity research compared with other budgetary components, or in the distribution of resources among commodities, although support to strengthening national systems via institution building, training, and information has risen (Table 12.1). While it is difficult to detect any clear trend toward research on the range of sustainability-related issues outlined earlier, several IARCs are proposing to expand research on resource management in absolute terms (although not necessarily relative to overall resource allocations). This seems mainly to imply an increase in farming systems research. There is little indication of increased research emphasis on social issues, and support for policy research declined in relative terms during the late 1980s, although it has risen in the mid-1990s. Generally, the focus of the IARCs has been on the supply side of research rather than on issues related to demand.

A review of IARCs' work on sustainability by Craswell (1989) concludes that, although progress had been made in the 1980s, especially through the establishment of the resource-oriented institutes outside the CGIAR and their expanding links with the commodity centers, a good deal remains to be done to tackle the new imperatives discussed earlier in this chapter.

Gaps in research identified by Craswell include land use and policy-related issues, forestry and agroforestry, groundwater hydrology, water resource inventory, salinity in irrigated and rainfed land, soil erosion research, monitoring impacts on the natural resource base of high- and low-input technologies, and economic analysis of the importance of the resource-related constraints so that research priorities can be assigned.

In addition to research gaps, international agricultural research activities related to natural resource management overlap and lack uniformity in approach, for example, with respect to agroecological characterization (Bunting 1988). This applies to both IARCs' own research and the ways in which they work with national programs.

The decision to admit the International Irrigation Management Institute (IIMI), the International Centre for Research in Agroforestry (ICRAF), and the International Center for Living Aquatic Resources Management (ICLARM) to full membership in the CGIAR, and to establish a new Center for International Forestry Research (CIFOR) to complement and reinforce national forestry research, should do much to heighten understanding of the issues affecting the sustainability of agricultural systems.

The economically measurable successes of the CGIAR centers have been primarily related to their commodity research, particularly with wheat and rice, but also to a less dramatic extent with maize, sorghum, cassava, potato, and grain legumes. These are the world's key staple food crops, especially important to the poor, although the spillover effect of the CGIAR research on genetic improvement has also contributed significantly to increased productivity of wheat and rice in developed countries (Pardey et al. 1996). Nothing in the outlook for those commodities in the next 20 years, even allowing for some income-induced shifts in dietary preferences, suggests that demand for them will diminish. There has been some narrowing of the gap between on-farm and experimental yields of rice and wheat, which gives cause for concern about a yield plateau. Average farm yields of most other key staples remain well below the potential of well-managed farms, let alone experimental ceilings. The first problem indicates a need for strategic research on rice and wheat to raise yield ceilings. The second suggests that much remains to be done to modify existing technologies or the incentives and constraints farmers face to improve adoption rates and the efficiency with which technologies are used.

Holding the line on existing yields against pests, diseases, and climatic variability, while at the same time introducing environmentally friendly techniques such as conservation tillage, integrated pest management (IPM), and organic agriculture, poses a further challenge to commodity researchers. Evidence from the introduction of such practices in developed countries suggests that they are management intensive and that there may be lengthy learning periods during which yields may actually decline before eventually increasing.

These problems suggest that research to increase productivity of the main food and export commodities of developing countries should not be relaxed. However, this does not necessarily mean that a narrow crop-by-crop research focus is the best strategy. A strong scientific nucleus for crop improvement through biotechnology and plant breeding for yield stability, nutritional quality, stress tolerance, and pest and disease resistance must be maintained at the commodity-oriented centers. But it must be accompanied by innovative research on improved management of the resource base to conserve soils, build up soil nutrients, enhance water-use efficiency, increase the efficiency of pesticide use, and develop complementary measures to minimize potentially harmful effects of agricultural chemicals through misuse or overuse. Such measures would indicate residue management, crop rotation, IPM, plant nutrient cycling, and timeliness of operations.

This strategy implies a systemic approach to agricultural research within the CGIAR that will require greater cooperation between commodity-based, resource-based, and ecoregional centers (the latter combine elements of both of the others). The need for systemwide planning to apportion responsibility for research on management of natural resources between these three types of centers to avoid unnecessary duplication and to ensure that the best-equipped institute plays the lead role in a given situation has been recognized since 1993. The CGIAR has developed systemwide initiatives on major problems within a matrix framework that will clarify the role of the CGIAR within the global research system (CGIAR 1996). Increased interinstitutional teamwork will be essential if this research is to be cost-effective. Moreover, donors must be prepared to accept that the benefits of the results may be more difficult to attribute to individual centers.

As a result of the broader and (to some extent) competing demands it now faces, the CGIAR system is at a crossroad in its history. Apart from the trade-offs between resource allocation to commodity research and research on management of natural resources, there is the further issue of "upstream versus downstream" research. In other words, to what extent should the CGIAR system focus on ground-breaking basic or "strategic" research, and to what extent concentrate on applied research to develop technology that NARSs and farmers can adapt for specific ecological situations?

Both of these issues have been waiting in the wings since the CGIAR was first established in 1971. Some of its founders hoped that the scientific expertise of the centers would lead to further Green Revolution–type breakthroughs not only in wheat and rice, but also in other crops and in geographical regions other than South and Southeast Asia. This expectation has been only partially fulfilled. Others feared that the CGIAR centers' efforts would be frustrated by the weakness of the national systems unless they worked closely with NARSs. This fear led to decentralization of the center's work, with international staff being outposted to work with national programs on an increasing scale, and eventually to the establishment of the International Service for National Agricultural Research (ISNAR). Consequently, strengthening NARSs rose from 13.5 percent of the total CGIAR core operating expenditures in 1983 to 18.5 percent in 1991. The new demands being placed on NARSs by the growing popular concerns about environmental degradation suggest that this emphasis will need to continue, at least in the near term.

Zoning for Sustainability

The idea of defining and mapping major regions of the world in terms of climate, soils, and natural vegetation as an aid to agricultural planning is not new. Systems of classification developed by Koppen and Geiger (1936), Troll and Paffen (1965), and Papadakis (1975) have been available for many years and have proved useful to the international centers.

However, the need for sharper tools to assist development planners in identifying research priorities and allocating resources to agricultural research, and the enhanced global interest in environmental issues, and especially in sustainable management of natural resources, have given new impetus to agroecological zoning. It can be valuable in determining the size and nature of the problems likely to be encountered in managing natural resources within a given zone of a country, and in understanding their magnitude across countries and the possibilities and potential benefits of research spillover between similar zones among countries (Davis, Oram, and Ryan 1987). Where sufficient georeferenced local data are available, a social dimension such as the distribution of poverty can also be related to agroecological zones (Broca and Oram 1991).

To increase understanding of the nature of the problems that have to be faced in managing natural resources for agricultural production, the likely consequences of mismanagement, and the techniques required for sustainable development, the CGIAR adopted "continental agroecological zones," a modified and more aggregated version of the agroecological zone methodology of the Food and Agriculture Organization of the United Nations (FAO). If agroecological zoning is to be adopted and used effectively as an aid to both planning and implementation, it will require much closer collaboration between physical, biological, and social scientists than is the case in most NARSs. It may also require restructuring of NARSs, IARCs, and extension services to reflect the ecoregional priorities identified by the zoning.

While many developing countries currently lack the requisite expertise to undertake comprehensive research programs based on ecological zones, the IARCs may assist in identifying broad agroecological zones with relatively limited variability across subregions or with intransigent problems of sustainable resource management probably involving costly long-term research. On the other hand, research requirements of ecologically heterogeneous areas may be very location-specific. This situation suggests that a careful division of labor is required between international and national research institutions, taking into account the contribution that NGOs, bilateral donor staff, technical assistance agencies, and the private sector might also make.

Because the success of bilateral and international development assistance depends heavily on characterization of the resource base and the social setting in the areas where projects are located, there is increasing emphasis on definition of agroecological zones. However, this task is too big to be undertaken by the relatively small international center staff with expertise in this field and the limited resources of the majority of the NARSs. Donors should therefore contribute both expertise and financial support to national and international efforts and should also place more emphasis on training staff of developing countries in the requisite techniques.

Areas where developed-country expertise would be valuable include remote sensing and its application to zonal characterization; the identification of areas of environmental degradation, deforestation, overgrazing, and desertification; assistance to developing countries in the establishment and application of geographical information systems (GIS); and scientific collaboration with IARCs and NARSs in the development of techniques for the monitoring and evaluation of natural resources and their sustained management for forestry or agriculture.

THE CAPACITY OF NARS TO DEAL WITH FUTURE NEEDS. To some extent, especially in Asia and South America, there have been notable advances in national capacity to undertake advanced research and to collaborate more effectively with the IARCs in applied and adaptive research. However, in other major geographical areas agricultural research remains weak, for example, in most of Sub-Saharan Africa, Central America, the Caribbean, the Arabian Peninsula, and the South Pacific. They are mostly small countries, and many of them are economically disadvantaged. Thus a major challenge facing the CGIAR system is to enhance the capacity of these small developing countries to do effective research without spreading CGIAR resources too thin and weakening the centers' own capability to tackle difficult problems of major environmental and economic importance requiring strategic research for their solution. The narrow conceptual and disciplinary focus that has pervaded international agricultural research strategy and technical assistance for more than two decades has inevitably had its impact on the direction of research and research capacity of NARSs in developing countries. The IARCs have pursued a praiseworthy policy of training national staff in their methods and techniques and of building information services to help NARSs keep up with the latest developments in their field. However, the long-run effect has been to skew research capacity in NARSs toward the disciplines that predominate in the IARCs. To a considerable extent, the same is true of teaching and graduate training emphasis at universities, especially agricultural universities, thus extending into the future the current disciplinary imbalances in the scientific cadres of the NARSs and the extension services.

The overall seriousness of this problem can be gauged from the disciplinary composition of staff shown in Table 12.2. While the data are mainly from the mid-1980s, it is unlikely that the situation has changed greatly, given the time involved in training new staff to meet emerging challenges. A detailed breakdown at the national level shows:

1. The disciplinary balance in the NARSs strongly favors plant sciences, especially breeding, genetics, pathology, and entomology.
2. Disciplines related to natural resource management are less well represented and mainly confined to conventional plant nutrition and irrigation management, with little provision for climatology, ecology, plant physiology, resource evaluation, or land use.
3. Technology (both mechanical and postharvest) is poorly represented.
4. Farming systems research is receiving increasing attention but with only a modest staff commitment; little effort is devoted to developing complementarities in land use *among* agroecological zones and farming systems.
5. Social science—including economics—receives a meager share of resources, and the emphasis of NARSs is on supply of technology. Not surprisingly, capacity to do good policy research is very limited.
6. Livestock research is poorly served compared with crops (Bennell 1986), with resources divided fairly evenly between veterinary medicine and livestock improvement. However, with respect to the latter, the emphasis in the CGIAR system is on management and feeding for production and draft power, whereas in many NARSs it is on breeding with limited

TABLE 12.2 Distribution of NARS research staff by disciplinary category for 92 developing countries, by region

Disciplinary Area	Sub-Saharan Africa		Asia (S/SE/E)		West Asia/North Africa		Latin America		All Developing Regions	
	Number of Scientists	Percentage of Total	Number of Scientists	Percentage of Total	Number of Scientists	Percentage of Total	Number of Scientists	Percentage of Total	Number of Scientists	Percentage of Total
1. Crop sciences	2,168	43.0	4,469	28.2	3,556	51.3	1,820	22.2	12,013	33.3
2. Resource management	501	9.9	2,051	13.0	1,121	16.1	1,084	13.2	4,757	13.2
3. Technology	250	4.9	949	6.0	322	4.6	595	7.3	2,116	5.9
4. Social sciences	348	6.9	1,324	8.4	230	3.3	466	5.7	2,368	6.5
5. Animal sciences	715	14.2	2,272	14.3	940	13.5	1,265	15.4	5,192	14.4
6. Fishery sciences	286	5.7	1,772	11.2	285	4.1	1,249	15.2	3,592	10.0
7. Forestry	595	11.8	2,812	17.8	291	4.2	1,654	20.1	5,352	14.8
8. Miscellaneous	178	3.4	187	1.1	203	2.9	67	0.9	635	1.7
Total	5,041	100.0	15,836	100.0	6,948	100.0	8,200	100.0	36,025	100.0

NOTES: Data are the most recent available after 1980.
1. Plant breeding and genetics; entomology, pathology, weed science; biochemistry, physiology, botany; agronomy; horticulture.
2. Soils and plant nutrition, chemistry, physics; irrigation and water management; ecology, climatology, geography.
3. Harvesting, processing, engineering, farm mechanization, seed technology.
4. Extension, information sciences, economic statistics, sociology, human nutrition, marketing.
5. Breeding and genetics, animal management, range and pasture, physiology and nutrition, veterinary, economics.
6. Marine, inland, fish biology, economics and management of fish production, fish unspecified.
7. Tree breeding, processing, forestry unspecified.
8. Management and general administration.

164

attention to feeding and management and little to draft capability. Attention to range and pastures, crop-livestock integration, and social factors affecting the livestock sector is generally meager.

7. Fisheries research receives modest support, but where a breakdown of resources is available, it appears to be focused primarily on oceanic fisheries.

8. Forestry research now appears relatively well supported, but it was not possible to identify disciplinary gaps.

All this suggests that in order to match the new imperatives created by the need to develop sustainable systems of land use, and related environmentally benign agricultural technologies that can maintain the productivity of major agricultural commodities, there needs to be a reappraisal of the research philosophy and the disciplinary composition of agricultural research institutions, both internationally and in the NARSs.

Thus it seems logical to increase the numbers and quality of scientific staff in disciplines that will

1. facilitate agroecological characterization and the determination of sustainable patterns of land use (agroclimatology, geography, ecology, soil science, forestry, agronomy);

2. increase understanding of the social, demographic, and economic factors affecting land use, choice of technology, and farmers' and community behavior, with particular emphasis on the factors affecting demand for technological change (national and sectoral policy, agricultural economics, sociology, agronomy, forestry, animal management, input and output prices and marketing);

3. strengthen the ability of plants and animals to withstand environmental stress and to use inputs more efficiently (genetic conservation and improvement, plant physiology, biotechnology, biochemistry, soil-crop-water relations);

4. reduce the need for agricultural chemicals (legumes and livestock in farming systems; soil microbiology; integrated pest management; biological pest, disease, and weed control; storage technology);

5. improve methodology for monitoring and evaluating technical and physical causes of resource degradation and externalities (soil physics, chemistry, hydrology, engineering, agronomy, computer modeling, economics);

6. alleviate intersectoral conflicts of interest leading to environmental degradation by strengthening macropolicy analytical capacity.

A large training and retraining effort is clearly indicated, involving the training and information programs of the IARCs, the curricula and teaching priorities of national universities, and donor policies and activities in support of higher education and training. The goals should be twofold: to build a disciplinary balance of national research and extension cadres adequately funded and equipped to meet these challenges collaboratively while training them to apply their knowledge to solving problems systematically.

Structural Reorganization of Ministries and Public Institutions in Developing Countries

Most agricultural activities of public institutions are the responsibility of line ministries, but operational responsibilities are often fragmented among several ministries. Crop-related activities are normally located in ministries of agriculture, but livestock may be allocated to a different ministry, forestry to a third, and fisheries to a fourth. Resource management may also be split (some countries have ministries of irrigation), but it is increasingly coming under ministries of environment or natural resources.

Fragmentation can result in large inefficiencies and research gaps. Indeed, one of the most widespread complaints of review missions is the inadequacy of linkages between research and extension services, even where there is only *one* national extension system. A second is the isolation of the universities from the realities of rural life. "Agricultural" universities may or may not be under the ministry of agriculture, but tend to go their own way in both teaching and research (Bennell 1986).

Ministries of finance or planning often seem unable to coordinate effectively the many players in agricultural research and extension. Consequently, agricultural research directors claim that they are being asked to achieve unrealistic targets with inadequate funds, and planners complain that research is a waste of money because it fails to produce tangible results.

A device that has had some success in bridging communication gaps among and within ministries is an agricultural research council, such as the Indian Council for Agricultural Research. But whereas larger systems have resources and flexibility to support such a council, this may be beyond the capacity of smaller countries. Nevertheless, some mechanism, at least within the ministry of agriculture, is essential to plan, coordinate, and allocate resources to priority research and extension activities *across* subsectors and to stimulate and fund interdisciplinary and interinstitutional teamwork, including between the public sector research system, the universities, and the private sector. This is particularly necessary in the case of strategic research (for example, in biotechnology) and for work on natural resource management, both critically important future needs.

A device being used increasingly by the IARCs and technical assistance agencies to assist smaller countries is the research network. This can help build a critical mass of research across countries to tackle problems of common interest and provide economies of scale, although it is not a panacea (Oram 1988b). Unfortunately, there is a growing tendency to oversell the concept: a CGIAR review (Plucknett, Smith, and Ozgediz 1990) lists more than 50 networks in Sub-Saharan Africa, and their number is increasing. There is little liaison among their progenitors, nor are their priorities always of the first order. Care needs to be exercised in the establishment of further networks, as their proliferation can put a heavy burden on the limited scientific resources of small countries (IITA 1990).

Improving the Sustainability of Agricultural Research and Extension Institutions

The need to build strong and well-managed NARSs has been a concern of the CGIAR system since its inception; it is as important to the success of the IARCs as it is to the countries they serve. Thus it is no coincidence that expenditures by the CGIAR centers on training, information, and institution building have risen over time to about 20 percent of the entire CGIAR budget and that they continue to grow. Donor support to research capacity building has also expanded considerably over the 1960s–1980s period but has fallen off substantially since then (Eicher 1989; Pinstrup-Andersen 1994).

Given recent declines in general support for research, there is cause for concern about both the financial sustainability of NARSs and the CGIAR system. This is alarming in light of the changing emphasis of global research goals from a simple focus on increasing productivity to the broader requirements of sustainable growth. These changes imply a longer research horizon than has necessarily been the case in the past and possibly higher research costs. This places a heavy responsibility on donors and national governments to support research steadily over the long haul, avoiding the hand-to-mouth approach that has often been the case in the past. Six potential causes of loss of sustainability need to be addressed.

1. *The growth of research staff has outpaced their financial support.* While the number of scientists has increased exponentially, research expenditures have shown only a linear increase (Pardey and Roseboom 1989). This situation seriously impedes operational efficiency; as research managers try not to reduce staff, the axe falls on operation and maintenance expenditures instead. FAO (1995) reports that in West and Central Africa this funding constraint has resulted in significant underemployment of research staff, with an aggregate real rate of employment of only 43 percent for the 24 countries studied. A further result is low morale and increasing attrition: Bennell (1986) estimates that at mid-1980 rates in Africa of more than 5 percent per year, half of the professional research cadre would be lost to other institutions every decade.

2. *National commitment to agricultural research is both inadequate and inconsistent.* According to Judd, Boyce, and Evenson (1983), research expenditure per scientist in government institutions was lower in the

1980s than in 1962 in 18 of 24 African countries. Pardey and Roseboom (1991) note a decline in support after the mid-1970s in other regions. Judged by the normative target of 1 percent of agricultural gross domestic product (GDP) suggested by the FAO/United Nations Development Programme (UNDP 1984), and the World Bank's (1981b) 2 percent goal for 1995, few developing countries are spending enough on agricultural research. By the mid-1980s, only 20 of more than 120 countries were committing funds equivalent to 1 percent of their agricultural GDP, and only 7 were spending more than 2 percent. Most of those 20 countries were small—only one had more than 300 researchers.

3. *Many NARSs are heavily dependent on donor financing.* Eyzaguirre (1990) lists 18 small countries where such dependency ranges between 21 and 100 percent of the entire research budget; in a majority of cases it is more than 50 percent. This pattern of dependence, however, is not confined to small countries; a number of larger countries—for example, Bangladesh and several eastern and southern African countries—are also heavily dependent on external funding.

4. *Educational standards of national scientists vary greatly.* An IFPRI survey of degree levels in 90 countries in the mid-1980s shows that staff with a master's degree or higher represented less than 50 percent of total research staff in 64 countries and less than 25 percent in 26 countries. The ratio was especially low in Central America, the South Pacific, and Sub-Saharan Africa (Table 12.3). Consequently, some countries were employing a high proportion of expatriates, whose skills are high but costly, and whose tenure may be short, thus threatening the sustainability and continuity of the research. Recent studies indicate that this situation has improved considerably in Sub-Saharan Africa since the 1980s, reducing the overall dependence on foreign staff to under 15 percent (Pardey, Roseboom, and Beintema 1997; FAO 1995). This trend reflects an increase in the proportion of African scientists with a master's degree or higher.

5. *There is a serious shortage of experienced staff.* This is true in both management and operations because of the rapid increase in the number of scientists and high staff turnover. This is compounded by a lack of formal management courses at universities. Thus research directors are having to learn simultaneously how to manage institutes, build staff capacity, and conduct research to produce practical results. Failure to achieve these multiple goals may account for policymakers' dissatisfaction concerning returns on their investment in research and thus for their reluctance to support it financially at an adequate level.

6. *Research resources are highly concentrated in a relatively small number of developing countries.* Two-thirds of all scientists in the developing world are located in 10 Asian countries, each with more than 1,000

TABLE 12.3 Education and nationality of NARS research staff in Sub-Saharan Africa, 1980–1986

Country	Total Researchers	Percentage Expatriates	Percentage of Total Researchers	Percentage Nationals	Scientists with M.Sc., Ph.D., or Equivalent Degrees from Institutions of Higher Agricultural Education
	Research Staff Holding a B.S. or Higher				
			Postgraduates		
	(number)		(percentage)		(number)
West Africa					
Benin	45	7	73	71	26
Burkina Faso	114	48	n.a.	n.a.	42
Cameroon	187	33	n.a.	n.a.	n.a.
Cape Verde	16	19	57	45	0
Chad	28	29	n.a.	n.a.	28
The Gambia	62	27	n.a.	n.a.	0
Ghana	138	6	74	69	142
Guinea	177	n.a.	n.a.	n.a.	n.a.
Guinea-Bissau	8	13	75	71	0
Ivory Coast	201	73	n.a.	n.a.	59
Liberia	33	27	69	57	31
Mali	275	11	29	20	66
Mauritania	12	n.a.	92	n.a.	0
Niger	57	56	n.a.	n.a.	18
Nigeria	1,005	n.a.	n.a.	n.a.	637
Senegal	174	29	n.a.	n.a.	56
Sierra Leone	46	n.a.	n.a.	n.a.	65
Togo	49	24	n.a.	n.a.	21
Subtotal	2,627	31	50	29	1,191
Central Africa					
Burundi	53	43	85	73	17
Central African Republic	n.a.	n.a.	n.a.	n.a.	11
Congo	68	46	n.a.	n.a.	51
Gabon	24	58	71	30	10
Rwanda	34	28	37	5	8
São Tomé and Principe	3	n.a.	n.a.	n.a.	0
Zaire	43	n.a.	23	n.a.	124
Subtotal	225	43	60	59	221
Southern Africa					
Angola	28	46	46	0	n.a.
Botswana	50	56	73	38	0
Lesotho	18	50	67	33	0
Madagascar	83	12	48	40	36
Malawi	80	6	30	26	41
Mauritius	99	n.a.	36	n.a.	17
Mozambique	77	83	83	0	33
Swaziland	11	36	44	17	27
Zambia	111	49	61	24	21
Zimbabwe	153	n.a.	45	n.a.	32
Subtotal	710	41	52	24	207

(*continued*)

TABLE 12.3 (*continued*)

Country	Research Staff Holding a B.S. or Higher				Scientists with M.Sc., Ph.D., or Equivalent Degrees from Institutions of Higher Agricultural Education
	Total Researchers	Percentage Expatriates	Postgraduates		
			Percentage of Total Researchers	Percentage Nationals	
	(number)		(percentage)		(number)
Eastern Africa					
Comoros	14	50	50	0	0
Ethiopia	142	6	43	40	68
Kenya	483	16	45	n.a.	242
Seychelles	7	38	38	0	0
Somalia	31	13	9	n.a.	57
Sudan	206	n.a.	81	n.a.	164
Tanzania	276	22	61	49	168
Uganda	168	n.a.	n.a.	n.a.	56
Subtotal	1,327	17	54	44	755
Total	4,888	29	53	38	2,374

SOURCE: Calculation based on data presented in Jain 1990.
NOTE: n.a. indicates not available. Data are averages for 1980–1986.

scientists (Table 12.4). Conversely, 40 percent of all developing countries have fewer than 100 scientists, with 22 percent having fewer than 50. Small systems are located mainly in the Gulf states, the Caribbean, Central America, the South Pacific, and Sub-Saharan Africa.

Many small countries depend economically on tropical export crops not covered by the IARCs, while help from stronger developing countries is limited by geographic dispersion. Yet the problems small countries face are no less difficult or complex. Regional research institutions established in the Caribbean, Central America, and the South Pacific have done some useful work but have encountered political and financial problems. Helping small countries with limited resources build and maintain viable systems is a challenge to the entire international research community (Eyzaguirre 1990).

Agricultural Extension Systems

Financial support for agricultural research and extension has not grown evenly over time. Before the 1970s, extension tended to be favored, in the expectation that accumulated knowledge could be readily transferred to potential users without a major research effort. When this idea proved illusory, research began to receive increasing support, in recent years outpacing that going to extension (Oram 1991). This trend is threatening the stability of national extension systems. However, "this decline in the importance of extension is only partly the result of new public expenditure priorities. More important, and contributing to resource allocation decisions, has been the declining effectiveness of the extension services" (Howell 1989). This is a serious situation, since the burden on those services is likely to increase with the new demands on their knowledge and skills, which will be required to help farmers —including women—apply environmentally friendly technologies and sustainable systems of land use.

A number of situations undermine the effectiveness of extension in addition to financial reasons.

1. Extension rarely generates innovations de novo. If new knowledge and techniques do not come from the research system, the extension staff has little to offer.
2. The successful adoption of new technology often depends on the viability of institutions besides extension. The availability of improved seed, fertilizer, or other inputs and credit for their purchase may be crucial, yet these are usually beyond the control of extension staff.
3. Extension services are often loaded with regulatory and other duties that detract from their ability to perform their advisory functions, and this is true of both agriculture and forestry (FAO/IFPRI/CIFOR 1993).
4. In many countries, the field extension staff is not highly educated or well trained, especially in subject areas related to natural resource management. Common areas of weakness include integrated pest management, water use, social issues, nutrition, marketing, animal husbandry, and agroforestry.
5. The staff composition of extension services is heavily male-dominated. Not only are there few women extension staff, but they are mainly home economists. Thus women farmers are often poorly served. Women are also discriminated against in access to higher education, which may impose a limit on the number of qualified female candidates for positions in extension services.
6. Extension staff, especially at the village level, lack mobility, telephones, and modern communications equipment. This problem is likely to be particularly serious where the population density is low or migratory.
7. The number of farm families per extension worker can be very large, although this ratio varies greatly. International Food Policy Research Institute data on 90 countries show that the ratio exceeds 1,000 in about 30 countries. In Australia, Japan, North America, and western Europe, the average is around 100.
8. The command structure and organization of extension tends to be fragmented, with "national" services (mainly for food crops); while separate

TABLE 12.4 101 developing countries grouped by numbers of agricultural research scientists

Country Group, by Number of Scientists	South and East Asia		West Asia and North Africa		West and Central Africa	
	Country	Number of Scientists	Country	Number of Scientists	Country	Number of Scientists
More than 1,000 scientists (17 countries; 16.8%)	India	21,400	Egypt	3,553	Nigeria	1,196
	China	18,844	Turkey	1,630		
	Philippines	3,549				
	Pakistan	3,549				
	Indonesia	2,082				
	Taiwan	1,957				
	Thailand	1,828				
	Malaysia	1,367				
	Bangladesh	1,574				
	Korea	1,004				
500–1,000 scientists (7 countries; 6.9%)	Sri Lanka	506	Iran	628		
			Syria	582		
			Iraq	548		
			Morocco	507		
250–500 scientists (14 countries; 13.9%)	Nepal	388	Algeria	267	Senegal	283
	Burma	300			Mali	268
					Ghana	263
					Ivory Coast	254
100–250 scientists (23 countries; 22.8%)	Vietnam	150	Tunisia	237	Zaire	199
			Saudi Arabia	171	Burkina Faso	126
			Jordan	115	Guinea	111
			Yemen Arab Rep.	123		
			Yemen People's Dem. Rep.	101		
50–100 scientists (17 countries; 16.8%)			Libya	82	Congo	94
			Cyprus	60	Niger	68
					Sierra Leone	66
					Benin	58
					Togo	58
					Central Africa	54
Fewer than 50 scientists (23 countries; 22.8%)			Lebanon	28	Liberia	45
			United Arab Emirates	12	Gabon	38
			Kuwait	8	Cape Verde	29
			Qatar	7	Chad	29
					The Gambia	28
					Mauritania	17

NOTE: Data are the most recent available after 1980.

Eastern and Southern Africa		South America		Central America and Caribbean		South Pacific	
Country	Number of Scientists	Country	Number of Scientists	Country	Number of Scientists	Country	Number of Scientists
		Brazil	4,178	Cuba	2,191		
		Argentina	1,146	Mexico	1,573		
Kenya	626	Colombia	771				
Sudan	355	Chile	463	Honduras	327		
Tanzania	353	Venezuela	412				
		Peru	410				
		Ecuador	337				
Zimbabwe	247	Uruguay	222	Guatemala	172		
Ethiopia	229	Bolivia	145	Dominican Rep.	136		
Zambia	212	Paraguay	137	El Salvador	116		
Malawi	193			Costa Rica	114		
Uganda	159			Guyana	109		
Mauritius	119						
Burundi	81			Trinidad	78	Papua New Guinea	99
Mozambique	79			Jamaica	74		
Madagascar	76			Nicaragua	66		
Botswana	62			Panama	64		
Somalia	48			Haiti	37	Fiji	52
Rwanda	43			Belize	31	Western Samoa	29
Swaziland	26			Barbados	30	Solomon Islands	28
Lesotho	18			Guadeloupe	14	Tonga	25
				Kiribati	2		

services may exist for livestock (mainly veterinary), forestry, fisheries, soil conservation, and irrigation; and special vertically integrated commodity services (tree crops, cotton, sugar, and so forth) run by parastatals, which may also do research as well as extension. Some special services have good records, but they are rarely coordinated within any overall plan. This situation is detrimental to sound land use planning, the adoption of sustainable farming systems, and effective feedback from the farm level to research staff and national policymakers. The inability of extension staff to exert influence on national policy is an important underlying cause of this failure.

9. Effective communication of extension staff, with both the research community and the farmers, is hampered by their generally low level of education. In many countries, the bulk of extension personnel have no more than a high-school diploma (FAO 1995), which represents one of the main obstacles to effective communication with researchers (Seegers and Kaimowitz 1989).

Requirements for Increasing the Sustainability of Research and Extension Systems

Although there are important differences in the nature of their operations, a number of parallel actions would improve the ability of both research and extension to deal with the changing needs of the future as well as increase their sustainability.

1. Structural linkages among ministries and other government agencies should be improved to minimize the fragmentation of responsibilities for implementing policy.
2. Better channels of communication are needed among fieldworkers, system managers, and policymakers.
3. Countries must pursue financial stability, especially to maintain recurrent expenditure. National planners and donors alike must grasp this nettle.
4. Reappraisal of training needs and policies is urgently needed as a base for a 10-year internationally supported program. Not only must levels of training be improved, but the balance of disciplines must be changed if future technical and advisory goals are to be achieved. Training in management, as well as in financial and personnel administration, is particularly important (Oram 1985). The need is not necessarily for more, but for better-qualified people.
5. Equipment for research and extension staff should be upgraded. This will have obvious implications for capital and recurrent expenditure but will increase efficiency, precision, and output. Particular attention must be paid to the potential gains from effective use of modern communications and information technology.

6. Research, and the structure of institutions and field stations, should be planned with greater emphasis on ecological factors so as to provide an integrating and practical framework to commodity and disciplinary research.

7. Special services should be established (probably in ministries of agriculture) to monitor the performance of research and extension systems and to evaluate their environmental, social, and economic impact. To support this, more research is required (possibly internationally) to improve methodology and develop impact indicators.

8. Expanded "research on research" is needed. For example, how are the research needs of small countries best met? What combination of research, extension, or other advisory approaches is best suited to different ecological and demographic situations? No single paradigm is likely to be appropriate for all regions or countries (Ewell 1989; Bourgeois 1990).

9. Conditions of service should encourage productive research and extension work and reward performance in the pursuit of national goals.

10. Countries should form stronger linkages with IARCs, technical assistance agencies, and regional organizations (SADCC, CILSS, SEARCO, IICA, ASARECA, and so forth) for research, training, and information. For larger countries, direct collaboration in research may be feasible; for smaller ones, research networks and other approaches to reinforce their more limited capabilities may be the best route. There has been a noteworthy increase in the development of regional research organizations in the 1990s, especially in Africa.

11. Parallel measures should be taken to strengthen institutions and services responsible for seed distribution, input supply, credit, and marketing, including incentives to private sector involvement.

12. Policymakers should respond to these challenges by expanding policy research, so as to create conditions that will increase the sustainability of the institutions responsible for implementing policy, enhance their effectiveness, and provide feedback on the impact of technology and policy on the goals of sustainable resource management.

Conclusion

Even with an increasing focus on natural resource management issues, commodity research will remain a high priority, as improving productivity of key crops and livestock and reducing yield instability and postharvest losses are not only essential to food security but also crucial to minimizing poverty and environmental degradation. The challenge is to set commodity research in the appropriate ecological and social framework so that related technology will be both acceptable to producers and sustainable.

A key problem remaining to be resolved is who will take responsibility for work on aspects of sustainability that transcend the current boundaries of research at the IARCs or in the NARSs, for example, monitoring causes and effects of environmental degradation across national boundaries and evaluating externalities. The IARCs have no comprehensive mandate for this, and NARSs are poorly equipped to undertake it even for their own countries.

There is concern in the IARCs about their future role. Moving upstream into biotechnology is seen as a necessity, although it may involve an unfamiliar jungle of patents, intellectual property rights, and legal issues related to increased cooperation with the private sector. Moving downstream into issues of environmental resource management also involves uncharted waters. Returns to research in resource-poor areas may be slow and unattractive to private business. Solutions may be social rather than purely technical, involving issues of land tenure and common property rights, health and family planning, and nonagricultural employment, requiring new research partners, including NGOs, outside the existing international and national agricultural research community. How much effort should be allocated to those areas versus Green Revolution–type focus on irrigated and higher-rainfall zones is still controversial. How fruitful new research relationships might be forged among IARCs, NARSs, and other institutions with complementary expertise to address these concerns is a further compelling issue.

Links among Sustainability, Growth, and Poverty Alleviation by Agroecological Zone

13 Agricultural Growth, Sustainability, and Poverty Alleviation in the Brazilian Amazon

AÉRCIO S. CUNHA AND DONALD R. SAWYER

The humid tropics of South America lie mainly within the Amazon Basin, an area of 7.8 million square kilometers (44 percent of the continent's territory) shared by eight countries.[1] The focus of this chapter is the Brazilian Amazon, which covers the largest portion of the total Amazonian territory.[2] Although the region shares many physical features with other humid tropical areas of South America, the scope and intensity of its frontier expansion distinguish it as a special case. The efforts put into settling the Brazilian Amazon and the massive destruction that has resulted may provide valuable lessons for all countries with humid tropical areas.

By and large, agricultural expansion into the Brazilian Amazon has sustained yields of agricultural products by continuous incorporation of new land (Sawyer 1984). This expansion may have only marginally contributed to poverty alleviation. The system of incentives designed to promote Amazonian settlement strongly favored overuse of agricultural resources. Three elements in particular account for unsustainable management of agricultural land and other natural resources: policy failures, market failures, and a speculative rush on natural resources, especially land.

Policy failures, such as tax and subsidy policies, road construction in areas not recommended for agriculture, consideration of deforestation as land

1. Bolivia, Brazil, Colombia, Ecuador, Guyana, Peru, Surinam, and Venezuela. Contrary to what is commonly thought, the Amazon is an immensely diverse area with 112 different ecosystems, 400 ethnic groups, and 160 languages (IDB 1992). Although the plight of indigenous populations is often dire and assistance efforts are insufficient, we do not discuss these issues here because of space constraints.

2. For statistical purposes, the Amazon is considered here to be the North region of Brazil, which covers six states, with a total of 3.6 million square kilometers: Rondônia, Acre, Amazonas, Roraima, Pará, and Amapá. Large parts of Maranhão and Mato Grosso could also be considered Amazonian. Tocantins was added to the North region in 1988 but is not included here, because only a small part of it has forest cover.

improvement for titling purposes, and ill-conceived or ill-executed government and private settlement projects have been studied extensively (Mueller 1982; Mahar 1988; Binswanger 1989a; Sawyer 1990). Classical cases of market failure include undervaluation of the resource base due to lack of transportation infrastructure and inadequate appreciation of the full economic potential of resources such as biological diversity. Another market failure results from the large difference between private and social discount rates, aggravated by dubious property rights and countless conflicts over land ownership. Last but not least, as in frontier areas the world over, the rush to control potentially valuable property prevailed over prudent resource use.

In this chapter we show how the Amazon's peculiarly unbalanced resource endowment and its relative competitive disadvantage with respect to the better-endowed and more centrally located regions combine to make land-intensive agriculture the only economically viable form of cultivation. Second, we argue that prospects for sustainability-enhancing technological development in the future could be jeopardized by the conditions just mentioned. Finally, we present evidence of decline in poverty indicators to support the argument that, so far, settlers have been able to adjust to the deteriorating resource base and thus defer the inception of Malthusian checks.

Sustainability

To address the issue of compatibility of agricultural growth and sustainability, one must first deal with the conceptual question of what is meant by "sustainability." Our definition comprises three overlapping dimensions: technical, economic, and social (Conway 1985a,b; Fearnside 1986; Harwood 1990; Homma 1990).

First, the technical dimension concerns preservation of the resource base. Available resources should be managed so as to prevent a long-term decline of average resource yields. The possibility of factor substitution is implied. Reduction of the inventory of any intermediate good, exhaustible or renewable, will not threaten sustainability as long as adequate substitutes or technology are (or become) available at competitive prices.[3]

Second, because of the possibility of substitution among factors implicit in resource management, technology comes into play. In turn, the choice of technology depends on, among other things, relative factor prices and therefore on factor endowment. Economic conditions thus have a bearing on choice of technology and intensity of resource exploitation.

The reverse is equally true. Capacity to sustain yields in a competitive environment, or even to increase them, is crucial for economic sustainability.

---

3. We are referring to "backstop" products or technology (Nordhaus 1973).

With declining yields, the balance between revenue and outlays cannot be maintained. Thus the condition of yield sustainability goes to the very essence of economic sustainability: capacity to maintain at nonincreasing costs.

Third, social stability is also necessary for long-run sustainability. In the Amazon this is tantamount to alleviating poverty. Unless agriculture provides poor settlers with a steady stream of income, they will be forced to use up natural resources or abandon the area. So far their distinct "preference" has been to do both.

The relationship between technical, economic, and social aspects of sustainable agricultural development does not end with the poor "eating up" the resources and moving out, but is more complex. Resource conservation is a form of investment that takes a long time to mature. It requires the wherewithal, a long-term outlook, and a low discount rate—conditions associated with wealth, not poverty. Thus resource conservation is a "luxury" that the poor cannot afford but also cannot do without. This is the core of the dilemma. Unless poverty is alleviated, a fundamental condition for economic viability will not be met.

Unbalanced Factor Endowments

The links between agricultural growth, sustainability, and poverty alleviation in the context of Amazonian settlement are overwhelmingly influenced by two factors: the favorable resource-to-population ratio and the Amazon's disadvantaged position in the national economy. As in most resource frontiers, the Amazon is rich in natural resources and poor in everything else: labor, capital, and infrastructure. Tapping its resources is socially, economically, and environmentally costly and risky, more so because of information and technological gaps. No inventory of resources is available. Of the resources that are known, many have a potential, not an actual, value and will remain in this condition until research advances. The fragile and biologically diverse ecosystem does not lend itself to exploitation by means other than those that mimic its complexity and equilibrium. Monoculture, so well adapted elsewhere, is anathema to Amazonian ecosystems. Until further research closes the information and technological gaps and other more viable alternatives for expansion of agricultural production become available, intense exploitation of Amazon resources will not be economically sustainable.

Infinitely Elastic Supply of Land

With rural population density in the Amazon of slightly more than one person per square kilometer, one of the world's lowest, diminishing returns to fixed resources (land) are a long way off. To put it differently, Amazonian agriculture faces an infinitely elastic supply of land in the relevant range of the supply function. During the life span of one or two generations, natural resource "mining" can be a physically viable path to sustainable agricultural yields at current rates of population growth.

Even though most Amazonian soils are notoriously infertile, it is estimated that 8.4 percent of the Amazon, equivalent to 60 percent of the total area currently cultivated in Brazil, is fit for agriculture (Moran 1984; EMBRAPA 1988). The hitch is that the patches of usable agricultural land are scattered throughout the region, and most are inaccessible without heavy investments in transportation infrastructure (Kyle and Cunha 1992).

The extent to which there is open access to land in the Amazon is debatable. Most of the land is claimed by government or private individuals, even though only a fraction is properly titled. Still, land availability is not a severe constraint, because of the large average size of productive units. The modal-class farms are in the 50- to 100-hectare range. Given the legal provision that 50 percent of each property be preserved, 25–50 hectares are left for cultivation. This is 10–20 times more than the 1–2 hectares that, on average, subsistence farmers cultivate each year.

The favorable ratio of potential to actual land use makes possible the long fallow system, which preserves the soil's regenerative capacity. In contrast to the humid tropics in much of Africa and Asia, diminishing returns to land in the Amazon, even within plots, need not lead to increased poverty as long as opportunities to move out are available.

Opportunity Cost

The task of alleviating poverty and promoting sustainable agricultural growth in the Amazon is more difficult because of the region's absolute disadvantage in the context of the national economy. Inappropriate technology, greater distance to markets, inelastic supply of complementary inputs and services, and general absence of external economies make Amazonian agriculture unable to compete with that of other regions. Furthermore, there are alternatives for expansion of agricultural output elsewhere, especially in the Southeast, where output falls far short of production potential.

The savannas of the Center-West region are another more promising area for agricultural expansion. They have a more resilient environment, a regular weather pattern, and, compared with the Amazon, greater soil uniformity and less susceptibility to pests and plant diseases. Their sparse natural vegetation makes soil preparation far less costly than in the densely forested areas of the humid tropics. The region has considerable urban and transportation infrastructure. Still, out of a total farm area of 116.7 million hectares in the savannas, only 7.8 million (6.7 percent) are presently cultivated (*Censo agropecuario* 1985).

Thus agricultural expansion into the Amazon involves a sizable private as well as social opportunity cost. Expansion occurred in the 1970s and 1980s, in large part because of government incentives. When government funding practically ceased in the late 1980s, so did the flow of people, investments, and material factors of production.

The difficulty Amazonian farmers face in attracting wage workers is a symptom of the lack of competitiveness of the region's agriculture. Although during the height of intense migration rural wages compared favorably with those of the Center-South (Fundação Getúlio Vargas, IBRE, various years), workers were not attracted by higher wages but by prospects of becoming self-employed farmers. Just 4.4 percent of all agricultural workers are permanently employed wage earners (*Anuário* 1990).

Return migration, mushrooming slums in Amazonian towns, and the decline in rural population growth bear witness to the fact that settling in the region compares unfavorably to eking out a living in cities, where at least there are public services such as education, health care, and a judicial system. Settling in the Amazon, at present, is a prospect worth contemplating only for poor farmers facing a critical shortage of alternatives. At the height of Amazon settlement programs in the 1970s, the municipality of São Paulo alone absorbed as many people as the entire North region (Martine 1992). To settlers who venture there, itinerant agriculture can provide a low-level, but stable, means of survival.

Promising commercial agriculture is restricted to a few crops in areas near cities or in the region's southern and eastern fringes. Black pepper, first cultivated by Japanese farmers, is the most noteworthy success story, but it was attacked by disease. Other crops cultivated with limited success are *robusta* coffee, cocoa, papaya, and lowland rice.

Our pessimistic appraisal should not lead to the conclusion that because the Amazon cannot compete, it should be abandoned. Alternatives to Amazon agricultural development belong not to the level of national grandeur, as attempted in the 1970s, but to more modest and realistic handicraft-type management. Under fairly limited conditions, almost any activity can be (and has been) profitably carried out. Current cultivation methods may be upgraded, probably quite inexpensively, and sustainability can be enhanced. Where grandiose schemes fail, myriad small-scale solutions exist, many of which rely on perennial tree cropping (Martine 1990; Sawyer 1991).

Sustainability-Enhancing Technology

Three questions must be asked about technology for sustainable agriculture: (1) Is it available? (2) If not, is it likely to be generated? (3) If yes, is it likely to be adopted?

The answer to the first question is, on the whole, no. Other than "slash-and-burn," there is no system of agriculture that satisfies the requisites for sustainability in the Amazon (Homma 1990). With regard to the other two questions, the already mentioned conditions—perfectly elastic supply of land and lack of competitiveness—increase the odds that the answer will also be negative.

Because of its lack of competitiveness, Amazon agriculture is not a national priority, even for research. There is little economic justification for allocating scarce funds for research on a high-risk activity with low prospective returns. There is even less economic justification for research on land-saving innovations.[4]

One form or another of agronomic research has been carried out in the Amazon since the 1940s. However, it moved up on the priority scale only *after* migration ebbed in the late 1980s and international concern grew over looming environmental disaster. Even so, in view of the location specificity of agricultural technology and the vastness and ecological diversity of the area, progress to date has been far from sufficient.

For the sake of argument, assume that, against all odds, successful research is undertaken and new resource-saving technology becomes available. Would it be adopted? Would there be a demand for it?

In most of the Amazon, abundance of natural resources and scarcity of almost every other factor, including labor and capital, provide no incentive for natural resource conservation. In fact, producers try to maximize returns on the scarce factors, labor and capital, by intensifying utilization of the abundant resource—land. The argument, of course, presumes a short-run outlook; the more fragile the environment, the shorter the outlook. But instability of land tenure combined with the low income level of settlers makes the short-run assumption plausible.

The same reasoning that explains the producers' optimal allocation of resources also explains their choice of technology. Innovations are meant to relieve resource scarcity constraints. This is how innovations can have a maximum impact on output and be most profitable. While natural resource-saving innovations enhance ecological sustainability, labor- and capital-saving innovations are the most sought after by profit-maximizing producers.

Technical innovations, if and when they come, will reflect, rather than change, relative factor scarcities. The market will not induce technology appropriate for long-term utilization of natural resources. In the case of the Brazilian Amazon, one could probably add, neither will the government.

The point is that society's (and the government's) telescope is as defective as that of its members.[5] Governments tend to answer to demands of society; they rarely anticipate them. If there is no demand for land-saving technology, it is unlikely that the government will provide it, especially under the current scenario of dwindling government intervention.

---

4. However, there may be ecological justification for research on land-saving technologies.

5. The reference is to Bohm-Bawerk's famous statement on society's "defective telescope faculty" (Solow 1974).

TABLE 13.1 Area harvested of food staples in Brazil's North region, selected years (thousands of hectares)

Staple	1966	1977	1984	1988	1989	1990
Rice	75	205	275	361	363	252
Maize	55	117	289	431	432	322
Cassava	77	181	262	271	296	323
Beans	12	47	120	159	187	184
Total	219	550	946	1,222	1,277	1,080
Percent Brazil	1.3	2.1	3.9	4.6	5.0	4.9

SOURCE: *Anuário* 1968, 1980, 1990.

Evidence on Agricultural Growth and Poverty

The scant evidence available on both agricultural performance and poverty indicates that Amazon agriculture is able to sustain yields at the present low-intensity, low-yield level of exploration and that degradation of natural resources, insofar as it has occurred, has not led to an increase in poverty. With respect to economic and social sustainability, only indirect evidence is available: yields are lower and costs are higher.[6] This evidence tells us that the Amazon is not able to compete for mobile resources (capital and labor) with other regions. To the extent that degradation of the resource base is not matched by yield-increasing technological progress, the Amazon's inferior competitive position is likely to worsen. As a result, there will be limited room for market-oriented agriculture.

Agricultural Growth

Despite moments of rapid growth, total agricultural activity and output in the Amazon remain modest. The harvested area of food staples seems to have peaked in 1989 at only 5 percent of Brazil's total area for the same crops, compared with 1.3 percent in 1966 (Table 13.1). Not surprisingly, since annual crops are primarily for subsistence, growth in the area harvested is highly correlated with population growth.

Amazonian population grew at an average annual rate of 5 percent in the 1970s and somewhat less (4.6 percent) in the 1980s. Total population of the North region in 1991 was 9.2 million (Table 13.2). Many migrants settled in urban rather than rural areas; the level of urbanization rose from 51.7 percent

---

6. Marketing costs are much higher in the Amazon. The same cannot be said about production costs, as the private opportunity costs of the resources involved (land, family labor) are close to zero. Wage rates are higher and so is the cost of modern inputs, but for this very reason, neither of them is used often.

TABLE 13.2 Total, urban, and rural population in Brazil's North region, by state, 1980 and 1991 (thousands)

State	1980			1991		
	Total	Urban	Rural	Total	Urban	Rural
Rondônia	491	229	263	1,130	658	472
Acre	301	132	169	417	258	159
Amazonas	1,430	857	573	2,088	1,502	587
Roraima	79	49	30	216	139	76
Pará	3,403	1,667	1,736	5,085	2,610	2,475
Amapá	175	104	72	289	234	56
Total Amazon[a]	5,879	3,038	2,843	9,225	5,401	3,825

SOURCE: *Censo Demográfico* 1980, 1990.
[a]See note 2.

TABLE 13.3 Average yields of food staples for the North region and Brazil, selected years (metric tons per hectare)

Staple	Area	1955	1965	1973	1982	1988	1990
Rice	North	0.9	0.9	1.2	1.5	1.4	1.3
	Brazil	1.5	1.6	1.5	1.6	1.7	1.9
Maize	North	0.9	0.8	1.0	1.4	1.4	1.4
	Brazil	1.2	1.4	1.4	1.7	1.9	1.9
Cassava	North	12.5	14.8	11.4	13.1	12.1	13.0
	Brazil	12.9	14.3	12.6	11.3	12.4	12.5
Beans	North	0.7	0.8	0.9	0.6	0.6	0.6
	Brazil	0.6	0.7	0.6	0.5	0.5	0.5

SOURCE: *Anuário* 1957, 1967, 1975, 1984, 1990, 1993.

in 1980 to 58.2 percent in 1991. Rapid decline in rural population growth rates in the late 1980s is strong evidence of the lack of social sustainability of Amazonian agriculture: migrants left rural areas as soon as government support dwindled.

Yields per hectare for the major food crops show no clear trends (Table 13.3). That they have not increased should not be surprising, as modern technology has yet to penetrate the Amazon: only 3.2 percent of the farms use chemical or organic fertilizers, and only 3.6 percent use mechanical traction (*Anuário* 1990). The fact that they have not fallen shows how producers have been able to compensate for soil degradation through fallow-crop rotation and incorporation of new areas. In comparison with Brazil as a whole, the Amazon

TABLE 13.4 Infant mortality rates for the North
region and Brazil, 1980–1988
(deaths under age one per thousand live births)

Year	Brazil	North
1980	75.0	60.9
1981	68.4	56.7
1982	64.5	57.7
1983	66.7	59.5
1984	65.9	60.8
1985	58.1	59.1
1986	53.2	56.8
1987	51.0	56.4
1988	47.5	47.8

SOURCE: Simões 1992:66.

has a small lead in land productivity in the case of cassava and beans (13.0 against 12.5 metric tons per hectare for the first; 0.6 against 0.5 metric tons per hectare for the second). Neither of the two products has seen any technological progress; both are inferior goods, with negative income elasticity of demand. Thanks to expansion of irrigated area, rice yields in Brazil have increased steadily from an average of about 1.5 metric tons per hectare at the beginning of the 1980s to 1.9 metric tons per hectare at the decade's end. Similar gains have been observed in the case of maize, yields of which also reached 1.9 metric tons per hectare in 1989. In the Amazon, maize yields have remained nearly constant, at around 1.4 metric tons per hectare, and rice yields have declined to 1.3 metric tons per hectare, after a peak of 1.5 metric tons per hectare in 1982 (Table 13.3).

Poverty Indicators

Extensive as destruction of natural resources in the Brazilian Amazon may be, it has not had a measurable negative impact on rural poverty. Nor can existing poverty be attributed to environmental degradation. A few indicators are available.

1. *Infant mortality.* There has been a sharp decline in infant mortality in Brazil, the Amazon included (Table 13.4). Starting from very high levels at the beginning of the decade (75 per 1,000 live births in Brazil and 61 per 1,000 live births in the Amazon), rates fell to 48 per 1,000 live births in 1988 in both Brazil and the Amazon.

2. *Malnutrition.* In the Amazon, as in all regions, malnutrition, too, showed remarkable improvement in the 1980s. Since 1975, incidence of malnutri-

TABLE 13.5 Indices of malnutrition, by region, 1975 and 1989
(percent)

Region	1975[a]	1989[b]	Percent Change
North[c]	24.5	10.6	–56.7
Northeast	27.0	12.8	–52.6
Southeast	13.4	4.1	–69.4
South	11.7	2.5	–78.6
Center-West[d]	13.3	4.1	–69.2

SOURCE: Monteiro et al. 1992:47.
NOTE: Data are percentages of children under five years of age with index weight-for-age inferior to two Z-scores.
[a]Estudo Nacional da Despesa Familiar (ENDEF).
[b]Pesquisa Nacional sobre Saúde e Nutrição (PNSN).
[c]Urban areas only.
[d]Urban areas in 1975, urban and rural in 1989.

tion declined by 56.7 percent in the Amazon, 52.6 percent in the poverty-stricken Northeast, and 78.6 percent in the South (Table 13.5).

3. *Food supply.* We have mentioned that agricultural output in the Amazon is closely correlated with total population growth.[7] From 1980 to 1988, production of beans in the Amazon per rural inhabitant rose from 13 to 30 kilograms, that of maize rose from 78 to 160 kilograms, while production per capita of both cassava and rice remained almost constant at around 918 kilograms and 137 kilograms, respectively (*Anuário* 1984, 1990; *Censo agropecuario* 1985).[8]

Much of the improvement in social welfare indicators can be attributed to greater availability of public goods (education, sanitation, health services) and to urbanization, but it may also be due in part to an increased supply of foodstuffs.

Land degradation, with accompanying declining yields, provokes loss that has to be made up for by extra effort. In the Amazon, this means clearing additional pieces of forest. Through incorporation of new land, farmers can forestall decreasing returns to both labor and land. Or they can move to town, as many have done.

---

7. Much of the population counted as urban by the demographic censuses lives in small towns and works, at least part of the time, in agriculture.

8. For comparison, average countrywide demand per capita for food staples was estimated at 70.2 kilograms for rice, 20.3 kilograms for beans, and 192.8 kilograms for maize (Cunha and Mueller 1988:322). Consumption in 1978 was estimated at 47 kilograms for rice, 21.1 kilograms for beans, and 153.8 kilograms for maize (World Bank 1982:49).

Conclusions

Amazon agriculture can rarely compete with that of the rest of the country: profits are low, if positive, so commercial agriculture is restricted to a few crops, such as black pepper, and to a few more fertile and better-located areas. The region has to compete at the national level for both capital and labor. If the laissez-faire ideology that is now sweeping the country and the world prevails, many rural areas of the Amazon are once again likely to recede to a semi-dormant state.

Nevertheless, the Amazon can sustain a reasonably large number of subsistence farmers as long as the intensity of the operations does not surpass the environment's carrying capacity. For these farmers, the opportunity costs of both labor and land are close to zero and the question of competing in the marketplace is not crucial. Even so, the attraction of cities is strong, and, as long as the government remains aloof, the Amazon is not likely to be a magnet for migrants.

As long as natural resources continue to be the predominant type of resource that is available, responsible natural resource management will not be the hallmark of the Amazon. Regardless of environmental implications, private discount rates outstrip, by far, social discount rates, and individuals' short-run interests supersede long-term social objectives.

Natural resource–saving technology, which could simultaneously promote sustainable growth and alleviate the plight of the poor, is not economical. If by means of an exogenous infusion of government funds such technology eventually becomes available, it is unlikely that it would be widely adopted.

It would not be wise policy to use the Amazon's treasure chest of natural resources to alleviate poverty. To do so would mean substituting natural resources for human capital. This would be inconsistent with the goal of economic and social development.

As can be seen from these conclusions, the constraints on Amazonian agricultural development are huge. To alter the competitive position of the region's agriculture in its own favor is beyond the country's financial capacity, in addition to being unsound economics. This does not mean, however, that there is nothing to be done.

To promote sustainable growth and alleviate poverty, there are four top policy priorities.

1. *Creation of stable conditions for development.* Such conditions include land titling, law enforcement, and creation and maintenance of basic infrastructure.
2. *Speculation dampening.* The destructive rush on natural resources must be penalized. Land titling, complemented by a progressive tax on unproductive landholdings and an end to subsidies and incentives for land speculation, is recommended. Four decades of experience with discre-

tionary policies have shown that they rarely work, especially in peripheral regions, and that their results are often the opposite of what was intended.

3. *Upgrading of current methods of production.* Labor is farmers' chief constraint. They adjust by substituting abundant natural resources for scarce labor. Labor-saving technology would not only be eagerly adopted but would also contribute to resource saving and to social welfare.

4. *Planning.* Because of a lack of information on the existence and location of resources, public investments have responded more to political pressure than to economic potential. An inventory of natural resources to assist planning is a research priority. Much of the puzzle concerning what to do about Amazonian development results from ignorance of the Amazon's comparative advantages.

14 Agricultural Growth and Sustainability: Conditions for Their Compatibility in the Humid and Subhumid Tropics of Africa

DUNSTAN S. C. SPENCER AND RUDOLPH A. POLSON

Africa's dismal record of economic growth over the past two decades has been a cause of international concern (World Bank 1984b, 1989b; Altieri and Anderson 1986; Jahnke, Kirschke, and Lagemann 1987; Weber et al. 1988; Atwood 1990). Aggregate output continues to lag behind population growth rates; per capita income has declined steadily; and the export base, a primary source of income, continues to shrink because of deterioration in the terms of trade for primary export commodities (World Bank 1984b; Jaeger and Humphreys 1988). All this is happening at a time when external funding, once important for stimulating domestic economic growth, is decreasing. Poor sectoral management policies, price policies, and trade and exchange rate imbalances have been cited as major causes of declining income (World Bank 1984b; Jaeger and Humphreys 1988; Binswanger 1989b). An insufficient stock of appropriate agricultural technologies has also limited growth (Matlon and Spencer 1984; Spencer 1985; Carr 1989; Vitta 1990).

An alarming dimension of this dismal economic performance is its short- and long-term impacts on the rural poor, the environment, and the long-term sustainability of the production base. In this chapter we explore the links between sustainability, growth, and poverty in the humid and subhumid tropics of Africa (HST). The chapter is divided into five sections. The first section discusses poverty and sustainability in the context of the HST. This is followed by a discussion of the biophysical and socioeconomic constraints to sustainable economic development. We then discuss the issues of growth and sustainability, based on case studies of potential agricultural growth–inducing technologies, and their possible conflicts or compatibilities with long-term sustainability and poverty alleviation. The case studies presented concern (1) policies affecting growth and deforestation in Côte d'Ivoire; (2) the sustainability of maize-based production systems using inorganic fertilizer in the forest-savanna transition zone in Nigeria; and (3) the persistent questions of sustainability even where significant productivity increases have been achieved in the savanna of Nigeria. The next-to-last section examines technology and

191

policy options for making growth compatible with sustainability and poverty alleviation. We conclude with implications of these policies and technologies for regional economic development.

Poverty, Growth, and Sustainability in the Subhumid Tropics of Africa

The World Bank (1990c) defines the poor as those "struggling to survive on less than $370 a year." By this definition, there were 1.1 billion poor people in the world in 1990, 180 million of which lived in Sub-Saharan Africa, representing 39 percent of the region's population. Most of Sub-Saharan Africa's poor live in rural areas, and their poverty stems from their inability to generate sufficient income from their agricultural and nonagricultural activities.

In much of the developing world landlessness is both a cause and a consequence of poverty, but there are very few landless laborers in the HST of Sub-Saharan Africa. The communal land tenure system in Africa gives virtually all rural dwellers access to land. However, land scarcity due to population pressure is changing the land-person ratio, shortening fallow periods, and putting new pressure on traditional laws and customs, which in the past adequately assured land use rights (Migot-Adholla et al. 1991). The resulting changes in the farming systems can reduce investments in the agricultural sector, reduce the equitability of access to land, and reduce output (Atwood 1990). Hence current production systems may not be sustainable.

In discussing sustainability, we emphasize that sustainable economic development must address the economic, social, and institutional problems affecting output and its equitable distribution, as well as issues relating to the short- and long-term integrity of the production base (Barbier 1987; Paul and Robertson 1989). Productivity increases (that is, through intensification and use of yield-increasing inputs), though necessary, are not sufficient nor do they guarantee sustainability. Stability of yield and of net income are also important.

At the cropping systems level, for example, one can define a sustainable system as one in which the output trend is nondeclining and is resistant, in terms of stability, to normal fluctuations of stress and disturbance (Spencer and Swift 1992). Fluctuations in annual climate, impact of pests and diseases, labor availability, and prices are critical constraints to achieving stable and high yields in the HST. The inclusion of stability (predictable yields and low risk of crop failure) introduces new aspects to the measurement of sustainability. How much fluctuation should be permitted? Variations in annual output can be measured by, for example, a coefficient of variation (Conway 1985b). The stability component could thus be confined to a prespecified range of variation.

Emphasis should also be placed on the production of multiple outputs to reduce income risk and improve food security among the poor (Binswanger and von Braun 1991). Faced with food insecurity, the poor may adopt environmentally damaging practices in their efforts to survive. The resulting rural poverty may inhibit the adoption of new agricultural technologies or practices that have the potential to expand the productive capacity of the resource base in the face of rising population pressure (Oram 1988a).

The basic question then is how agricultural production systems in the humid and subhumid tropics should be organized and managed in order to ensure long-term growth, alleviate rural poverty, and protect the production base. It is also important to understand what factors within the system promote or constrain such growth.

The farming system is the scale at which the economic viability of farming operations is determined and the one at which the farmer integrates resource allocation. The catchment is the fundamental unit for the hydrological cycle, which regulates the dynamics of land-based resources such as soil and vegetation. The catchment may thus be regarded as the fundamental unit scale for integrated resource management. At this scale, the concerns of society supersede those of the individual farmer. The critical factors for assessment of sustainability at this scale include such features as the erosion risk for the landscape as a whole and the impact of upslope and upstream activities on lowland environments.

Biological, physical, and economic measures can be merged into a single index. Ehui and Spencer (1990) use a single economic index, total factor productivity (TFP). TFP is defined as "the total value of all output produced by the system during one cycle divided by the total value of all inputs used by the system during one cycle" (Lynam and Herdt 1989). In normal economic practice, the outputs and inputs would be confined to those attributes that are recognized as economic variables: purchased inputs, labor costs, the value of the harvest, and so forth. Ehui and Spencer extend this approach by including the values of natural resources used within the system, such as soil nutrients. If TFP shows a constant or upward trend and does not fluctuate widely, then the system can be called sustainable.

One advantage of TFP is that it relies exclusively on price and quantity data for inputs and outputs, thereby eliminating the need to estimate the underlying production relationships. It can also be applied at different hierarchical levels from cropping to regional systems. One drawback is that prices must reflect scarcity values, which can be difficult to assess for natural resources (Spencer and Swift 1992).

Agroecological Zones and Constraints to Sustainable Development

Table 14.1 gives a synopsis of the biophysical (soil, rainfall) and socioeconomic (population density and market access) factors affecting the production of major crops in the principal agroecological zones of the HST of West and Central Africa. The extensive production systems in the HST are charac-

TABLE 14.1 Soils, population density, and market access of major agroecological subzones of the humid and subhumid tropics of West and Central Africa

| | Forest-Savanna | | |
	Humid Forest Zone	Transition Zone	Moist Savanna Zone
Humid[a] months	>7	7	5–6
Major soils	Oxisols/ultisols	Oxisols/alfisols	Alfisols/ultisols
Population density (persons per square kilometer)	1–15	1–30	16–30
Market access	Poor	Fair	Fair
Total population (million)	37	32	76
Land area (million hectares)	206	136	371
Major crops	Cassava, yams, rice, sweet potatoes, maize	Yams, cassava, rice, maize	Maize, millet, sorghum, peanuts, rice
Fallow period	Long (4–8 years)	Long (4–6 years)	Short (2–3 years)

SOURCE: International Institute of Tropical Agriculture, agroclimatology data (unpublished).
[a]Months when rainfall equals or exceeds potential evapotranspiration.

terized by low crop yields and low levels of purchased input use. Returns to primary resources—land, labor, and capital—are also low (Binswanger and McIntire 1987; Smith et al. 1991). Labor is the most important input into agricultural production systems in HST. For example, it accounts for 67 percent of the total cost of producing gari, a processed cassava product, in the south of Nigeria (Nweke, Ezumah, and Spencer 1988), while labor-capital ratios were about 630 for rice production systems, about 890 for rice milling systems, and 22–48 for small-scale rural nonfarm enterprises and fishing in Sierra Leone (Byerlee et al. 1983). Rural household income and welfare therefore depend on labor productivity. To increase labor productivity, output must increase over time. This requires adoption of new technologies, a process constrained by the lack of capital to invest in existing sustainable capital-intensive techniques, such as the minimum-tillage herbaceous legume rotation system, and shortages of farm labor to use existing labor-intensive techniques, such as composting and alley cropping.

Soils are another major constraint to sustainable agricultural intensification. The major soil types in the agroecological zones (alfisols, oxisols, and ultisols) have low intrinsic fertility. Alfisols, for example, which cover at least 23 percent of the land area of Africa, have poor nutrient and water retention capacities and poor structural stability. While the soils are suitable for production of a wide variety of cereals and root and tuber crops, they suffer from nitrogen and phosphorus deficiencies with prolonged use. Removal of bush cover typical in shifting cultivation, combined with high rainfall intensity, results in rapid and substantial loss in soil organic matter (SOM) from erosion and leaching. Except when special care is taken to prevent soil compaction and erosion, replace SOM (Jones 1971), and prevent the buildup of pests and diseases, sustainable production without a restorative fallow is extremely difficult to achieve on these soils.

As population increases, there is a corresponding increase in the demand for farmland. Because expansion into marginal areas is often costly, a reduction in fallow periods results, and farming systems may decline (Binswanger and McIntire 1987). Farmers also change the crops they cultivate, change cropping patterns or cropping systems, alter tenure arrangements and substitute inputs, change their soil and vegetation management, or migrate (Dvorak 1993). Shortened fallow periods usually mean a reduction of SOM, increased soil degradation, and weed pressure in slash-and-burn systems.

Ironically, low population density can also constrain the use of the sustainable bush fallow system. Clearing of high forest vegetation by hand is very labor-demanding. Where rural households are short of labor, particularly adult male labor, they usually choose areas with low bush or grassland vegetation, with resulting nonsustainable farming systems. Such situations may occur in areas of high outmigration of able-bodied household members. In such situations, households are also unlikely to adopt new labor-intensive sustainable technologies.

Poor physical infrastructure also constrains sustainable development. Resource-poor areas and poor farmers usually have less access to public infrastructure than do wealthier farmers and areas. Compounded by poor input distribution and marketing systems, this leads to very high costs for purchased inputs, such as fertilizer, which boost productivity and slow degradation in many areas of the HST. Furthermore, infrastructure construction costs are usually higher in the HST than in other parts of the world, principally because of the high cost of imported capital and skilled labor. However, recent experience in rural infrastructure projects shows that local institutions can mobilize financial resources and labor for such purposes. They can help to ensure that project benefits reach the poor, that specific local needs are met, and that the projects remain financially viable. Mixtures of institutions—NGOs, private operations, and local groups—have been very effective (World Bank 1990c).

A final constraint is the shortage of appropriate and adoptable sustainable technologies for the small farmers, an issue we discuss in greater detail in the next section.

Growth, Sustainability, and Poverty Alleviation: Potential Conflicts

The importance of the agricultural sector in development and as an engine for growth have long been noted by development planners. Increases in agricultural productivity widen rural markets for industrial goods, produce surplus

TABLE 14.2 Index of agricultural and forestry production in Africa

Year (1)	Food Production (1979–1981 = 100) (2)	Per Capita Food Production (1979–1981 = 100) (3)	Round Wood Production (4)	Forest and Woodland Stock (1961–1965 = 100) (5)
1975	95	110	94	197
1978	96	102	97	96
1979	97	100	100	105
1980	101	101	104	104
1981	102	99	106	104
1982	105	99	109	104
1983	103	94	112	103
1984	103	92	115	105
1985	113	97	118	105
1986	118	98	121	103

SOURCES: Columns (2), (3), and (4): computed from United Nations 1986; column (5): computed from FAO 1975–1990.

output for exports, and generate wage goods for the urban population. A process of savings and investments within firms and farms is set in motion. As profits from export trade are reinvested in industries and domestic markets are expanded, labor becomes specialized and unit costs of production decline. The resulting price reduction leads to increased access to goods and services and hence improved welfare (Vitta 1990). This scenario deviates substantially from the development reality in Sub-Saharan Africa. In areas where growth has occurred, it has not been sustainable, leading to a reduction in the ability to invest in and improve the long-term capacities of production systems. Aggregate statistics on natural resource degradation in Africa are not available, except for deforestation. Table 14.2 shows that forest and woodland stocks have declined, while per capita food production has also declined.

Reviewers of technology and development policies in Sub-Saharan Africa over the past two decades have recognized the failure of the linkage between growth and sustainability (Jahnke, Kirschke, and Lagemann 1987). In this section, we present three case studies that illustrate why programs to stimulate growth may not always be compatible with sustainability and poverty alleviation goals.

Deforestation in Côte d'Ivoire

Tropical forests help maintain soil fertility by regenerating bush fallow, providing moisture, recycling nutrients, and preventing erosion (OTA 1984). When forests are cleared for agricultural purposes, soil organic matter is lost, erosion increases, and soil structure is compromised. If this process is left unchecked, loss of critical soil nutrients results and there is a net loss of carbon (essential for plant growth) to the systems. Eventually, agricultural yields decline as periods of forest regrowth and replenishment of critical nutrients are shortened (Binswanger and McIntire 1987).

Deforestation has resulted in significant erosion of agricultural growth potentials and increased environmental degradation in Côte d'Ivoire (Ehui and Hertel 1989). Early in this century forests covered 16 million hectares. By 1960, total forest cover had declined to 9 million hectares and two decades later had dwindled to 3.6 million hectares. By 1987, the total area of exploitable timber had fallen to 1 million hectares (UNIDO 1986; EIU 1988). Economic growth policies in Côte d'Ivoire have expressly focused on agriculture as an engine for industrial development. The production of the major cash crops (cocoa, coffee, palm oil, plantain, banana, and rubber) has been concentrated in the southern tropical forest zone of the country, favorable for the production of these crops.

Development of the cash crop industry in Côte d'Ivoire occurred in an uncontrolled manner with little regard for environmental management (UNIDO 1986). Efforts to intensify production of the major cash crops have failed, and increased output was obtained mainly by land expansion. Additionally, reforestation programs have not been successful. Only about half of the planned reforestation of 41,000 hectares has been implemented (EIU 1988). In addition to the deforestation brought about by the expansion of cash crop production, commercial logging of forests has been substantial. More than 4 million cubic meters of logs were harvested in 1982 with a value of about 98 billion CFA. While this fell to about 3.1 million cubic meters in 1986, it nevertheless remained quite substantial (EIU 1988). Agriculture's contribution to gross domestic product (GDP) in Côte d'Ivoire fell from more than 43 percent in 1960 to 27 percent in 1983. Correspondingly, the growth rate of GDP declined from a robust 8 percent in 1960–1970 to 3.2 percent in 1986, after posting negative rates for three consecutive years, 1982–1984.

Deforestation has been economically disastrous as well as environmentally damaging. Since the mid-1960s, conversion of forests to cropland has resulted in agricultural growth and significant growth in GDP (Table 14.3). However, by reducing the capacity to produce future outputs, this conversion deprives future generations of better livelihoods. Soil fertility problems have also risen, and crop yields are falling. It is estimated that 30 percent of the urban and 26 percent of the rural population are below the poverty line (World Bank 1992a). Because a majority of farmers depend on cash crops for income, decreasing yield and low prices for these commodities have contributed to growing rural poverty. Thus those who benefited directly from deforestation (loggers) are not those who are now bearing its cost! Ehui and Hertel (1989) estimate that the present forest resource stock in Côte d'Ivoire is less than socially desirable.

TABLE 14.3 Agricultural and forestry production indexes in Côte d'Ivoire

Year (1)	Aggregate Yield (Ideal Index) (2)	Forest Stock (1978 = 100) (3)	Annual Agricultural Production (1969–1971 = 100) (4)	Food Production (1974–1976 = 100) (5)
1965	90	190		
1966	98	184*		
1967	101	172		
1968	102	166*	94	87
1969	96	156	93	94
1970	106	148	101	97
1971	109	141	106	109
1972	102	134	108	107
1973	104	127*	116	84
1974	108	122	117	95
1975	117	116	131	103
1976	109	110	134	102
1977	102	105	137	111
1978	100	100	136	118
1979	104	95	149	130
1980	112	91*	97	138
1981	117	86	107	140
1982	120	82	98	152
1983	108	78	99	141
1984	119	74	106	150

SOURCES: Column (2): Ehui and Hertel (1989). Column (3): derived from Ehui and Hertel (1989). Figures with an asterisk (*) show years for which actual forest stock data are available. Forest stock figures for the other years were estimated by regressing the known values of forest stock on time using a negative exponential model, which tilted the data well. Additional known years of forest stock include 1964 and 1985. Columns (4) and (5): computed from data in FAO 1970–1990.

Sustainability of Maize-Based versus Alley-Cropping Systems in the Forest-Transition Zone of Nigeria

Increased population density and reduced fallows combine to require increases in soil fertility if production levels are to be increased. The use of inorganic fertilizers has been identified as a means of sustaining yield levels in intensified maize-based systems. Long-term continuous fertilizer trials over an 11-year period on alfisols after forest clearing showed 50 percent reduction in SOM in unfertilized plots and 33 percent reduction in SOM in heavily fertilized plots. Maize yields declined from an initial 7.0 to 4.5 metric tons per hectare. The yield of unfertilized plots declined from around 4.5 to 2.0 metric tons per hectare (Kang and Balasubramanian 1990). Also, continuous use of nitrogen fertilizer has been shown to cause serious soil acidity problems and increased problems from weeds such as *Imperata cylindrica*. Heavily fertilized soil is also more likely to lose its structure, become compacted, and, in the worst case, erode.

High doses of inorganic fertilizer might, therefore, increase crop yields and agricultural growth in the short run. However, it is unlikely that high doses will be profitable, and it is not a sustainable approach, as output will decline in the medium term. In addition, high doses are likely to have detrimental effects on groundwater. Furthermore, such high-input technologies may be too expensive for poor farmers, so their adoption (by richer farmers) is not likely to alleviate rural poverty. On the other hand, improved technologies such as alley farming (planting annual crops between rows of multipurpose trees) use few external inputs and are therefore more likely to be adopted by poor farmers and have a greater impact on poverty.

Infrastructure, Extension, Technology, and Sustainability:
The Case of Maize in Nigeria

Maize is an important food crop in HST. Recent survey research in areas of shortened fallows (Smith et al. 1991) have shown increased use of improved maize varieties, fertilizers, and improved management practices, such as animal traction and effective weeding. Farmers assert that they are better off than before, attributing their improved well-being to the greater profitability of farming.

Several elements combined to intensify agriculture and improve profitability in northern Nigeria. A good road network, linking the northern and southern parts of the country, was built with petroleum revenues during the 1970s. During the same period, an agricultural extension program was organized as part of the World Bank–assisted agricultural development project. With an extension system in place to introduce new technologies and supply fertilizer to farmers, and with roads to bring in the inputs and deliver the produce to markets in the populous south, all that remained to trigger growth was the appropriate crop technology.

The traditional cash crops of the north were groundnuts and cotton, but neither was profitable enough to induce farmers to expand production. By the late 1970s, the International Institute of Tropical Agriculture (IITA) had developed a high-yielding maize variety, TZB. In experimental trials, the new variety yielded 150–200 percent more than the local maize variety. Experiments on farmers' fields showed that it yielded 21–115 percent more than the local variety. It was also resistant to rust, blight, and ear rot, and highly adapted to growing conditions in the savanna. Its white color appealed to consumers.

Agricultural development projects introduced TZB to northern farmers and demonstrated how to obtain high yields using fertilizer. When the farmers found that the maize was far more profitable than other cash crops, they began to expand production rapidly.

During the next decade, the spread of maize in the moist savanna was phenomenal. Maize had been grown in that zone as a backyard crop in the 1970s. By 1989, maize had become a major food crop in virtually all villages and a major cash crop in more than two-thirds of them. Most of this maize was the high-yielding TZB—in more than half of the villages almost no local maize varieties were being cultivated.

Sorghum, traditionally the preferred food crop, is still planted over a greater area than maize. However, since TZB outyields local varieties of sorghum and millet, the other staple cereals in the region, TZB can reduce the land requirement for feeding farmers' families. Many farmers have found that by growing TZB for household consumption, they can free additional land for cash crops. With the surplus over food needs being marketed, farmers have increased their cash income, which they can use to reinvest in cash crop production. Thus widespread adoption of maize cultivation has led to poverty reduction, although it is clear that richer farmers have benefited more: maize occupied 21 percent of the farm among the poorest farmers and 37 percent among the richer farmers (IITA 1992).

However, there are concerns about sustainability. Successful maize cultivation is highly dependent on good soil fertility. With the virtual elimination of fallows, the SOM has declined, micronutrient deficiencies are becoming more evident, and weed pressure, especially from the parasitic weed *Striga,* is increasing. Furthermore, fertilizer use is declining as a result of cost increases and reductions in subsidies. To improve sustainability, more biologically sustainable farming systems involving legumes, more nitrogen-efficient maize varieties tolerant to *Striga,* and more effective control methods for *Striga* need to be developed.

Conditions for Compatibility of Growth, Poverty Alleviation, and Sustainability

We now investigate the conditions necessary to make growth compatible with long-term sustainability and poverty alleviation. Binswanger and von Braun (1991) find that as arable land becomes scarce, growth in the agricultural sector will depend more and more on technological innovations. They note, however, that while such innovations leading to growth may improve incomes of the poor, they may also adversely affect the environment, as seen in the case of Côte d'Ivoire.

Improved Technologies

A number of principles for the development of sustainable production systems on HST soils have been identified (IITA 1986). The overriding requirement is to maintain a cover of organic matter on the ground and in the topsoil. This cover mimics and replaces the forest ecosystem in protecting and regenerating the productive capacity of the soil. Organic mulch protects the soil from structural damage, rain, and excessive temperatures, supplies organic matter to replace that lost in microbiological processes, encourages beneficial activity of earthworms and other soil fauna, and reduces nutrient leaching and acidification.

Other important recommendations include the following:

1. limit use of heavy equipment to avoid soil compaction, and select or design farm equipment that exerts low pressure on soil;
2. loosen compacted soils and restore their physical structure;
3. adopt a mixed cropped system with shallow- and deep-rooting species for efficient use of soil nutrients, as opposed to continuous monocropping of shallow-rooted annual crops; and
4. use fertilizer to balance soil nutrients and replace losses, but avoid over-use that can lead to soil acidification and toxification.

Farmyard manure (FYM) has long been shown to be one of the most effective means of providing SOM. Long-term experiments on alfisols showed that application of 12.5 metric tons per hectare per year of FYM for about two decades maintained organic carbon at 82 percent of required levels. In the semi-arid tropics, FYM is used extensively in fields around dwellings. However in the HST, low livestock populations, particularly of cattle, make it impossible to rely on them to supply needed SOM. Alternative sources, such as crop residues, green manures, and fallow vegetation, play a key role in the sustainability of agricultural production systems in the HST.

In all farming systems in the HST, intercropping is traditional. Farmers grow two or more crops—usually a cereal, a root crop, and a legume—in complex mixtures and associations. Tree crops and other nonfood crops are also planted with the food crops, particularly in the forest zone. These complicated farming systems present a rich mosaic of vegetation. Farmers who operate these complex farming systems have varied and complex needs. Research to produce improved technology for these farmers therefore has a major challenge in understanding both dimensions of this diversity—diversity in cropping systems and diversity in farmers' needs due to culture, educational background, aspirations, and so forth.

To meet this challenge, new technologies must improve the productivity of labor, scarce capital, and land. Since labor and capital are the most limiting resources for the small farmers, it is much more important to increase their productivity than it is to increase yield per hectare. This is true even in areas of relatively high population density, such as eastern Nigeria.

Second, new technologies should not degrade the natural resource base on which farmers' immediate livelihood, and ultimately that of the nation, depends. Unfortunately, many of the technologies recommended by research and development institutions today do degrade the natural resource base, particularly the soil.

Third, technologies offered by research institutions must be adoptable by small farmers. To be adoptable, a new technology must be affordable to, and manageable by, farmers. It is no use offering poor farmers technology that is so expensive that they could not hope to acquire it or that is so complicated that they need a trained scientist to make it work. Innovations that require radical changes in farmer behavior or that require substantial investment will be adopted slowly. Farmers feel comfortable with small changes and may not be keen on assuming the risks associated with drastic changes in resource allocation or land use patterns.

Agricultural research institutes in Africa have had limited success in producing new technologies appropriate to the needs of small farmers because of inadequate understanding of small farmers' goals and resource limitations and overreliance on the transfer of technologies from other regions. Farming systems research is an effective way of improving the focus of scientists on the problems farmers face. Interdisciplinary farming systems research groups are needed to ensure that research programs are more effective at taking into consideration the environmental and socioeconomic conditions of poor farmers when designing new technologies (Spencer 1991).

Experience suggests that technology development should focus on internally regulated systems requiring minimum levels of external inputs. Off-farm productivity-enhancing inputs such as fertilizers are either highly subsidized or unavailable. In either case, inefficiencies result that can have substantial negative impacts on agricultural growth. Technologies that require major investments in infrastructure, for example, large-scale irrigation systems, may be incompatible with growth and sustainability.

In sum, increasing the compatibility of growth, sustainability, and poverty alleviation will require technologies that are (1) appropriate, and designed with maximum participation of users—poor farmers, women, and so forth; (2) based on internally consistent systems with little reliance on subsidized external inputs; and (3) simple to adopt and requiring few changes in management practices. Examples of technologies being developed by IITA for the HST that have the potential to meet these criteria are briefly summarized here (IITA 1991b).

ALLEY FARMING. Alley farming is an agroforestry system in which multipurpose trees (usually legumes) are planted in rows and food crops are planted in the "alleys" between the trees. Soil fertility is improved through nitrogen fixation by the tree species. When applied as mulch, the tree prunings increase organic matter, conserve soil moisture, and suppress weeds.

Alley farming provides other benefits, including leaves for animal fodder, stems that can be used as stakes in growing other crops, and much-needed fuelwood. When the hedgerows are planted on the contour lines of sloping land, they can also help reduce soil erosion.

Compared with traditional practices, alley farming on nonacid soils in the forest-savanna transition and moist savanna zones can increase the sustainability of maize and other crops. Long-term alley cropping trials on degraded alfisols in the transition zone over a seven-year period maintained maize yields at about 2.0 metric tons per hectare without fertilizer application. With the addition of 80 kilograms per hectare of nitrogen, maize yields were maintained at about 3.5 metric tons per hectare. Over the same period, yields of continuously cropped plots (without alley farming) declined to less than 0.5 metric tons per hectare (Kang, Reynolds, and Atta-Krah 1990). Alley cropping can, therefore, be a more sustainable as well as economically viable system (Ehui, Kang, and Spencer 1990). By reducing farmers' need to shift continually to new land, alley farming can also reduce the pressure on tropical rain forests.

To introduce, test, and adapt this system across diverse environments throughout Sub-Saharan Africa, a research network—the Alley Farming Network for Tropical Africa (AFNETA)—has been established, with participating scientists from more than 20 countries.

BIOLOGICAL CONTROL. Pests and diseases constitute a major constraint to sustainable food production in the tropics. Natural, that is, nonchemical, methods of control should be given priority, as poor African smallholders cannot afford the relatively high costs of pest control chemicals. Classical biological control and host plant resistance are two promising avenues of research.

Research on classical biological control, in which a parasite or predator is introduced into an area to control an insect pest, was initiated at IITA in 1979 as an urgent measure to combat the cassava mealybug and the cassava green mite, two pests accidentally introduced into Africa from South America in the 1970s. In collaboration with the Centro Internacional de Agricultura Tropical (CIAT) and the International Institute of Biological Control (IIBC), natural enemies were identified, multiplied, and distributed in Africa. Economic analysis of this program has shown a benefit-cost ratio of 149:1 over 25 years, with an estimated benefit of US$3 billion to African farmers (Norgaard 1988) —one of the world's most successful agricultural research projects.

Host plant resistance involves breeding crop varieties that are attacked less by given pests or diseases or that can withstand attack without significant losses in yield. Success has been achieved in maize, cassava, cowpeas, and plantains, to name a few.

New rust- and blight-resistant varieties of maize have been developed that could be profitably grown in the African savanna. These varieties derive their resistance from lowland rust and blight diseases. A long-term research project to develop varieties resistant to maize streak virus has also proven successful. In Nigeria alone, it is estimated that streak-resistant maize varieties are grown on more than 2 million hectares.

Cassava. Cassava is a staple food for as many as 200 million Africans. Because of its adaptation to low fertility, its cultivation is increasing. Also, its canopy is semiperennial and contributes greatly to the sustainability of intercropping systems into which it is incorporated. IITA has successfully bred improved varieties that yield 40–75 percent more than traditional varieties, even when very little or no fertilizer is used, and the crop is interplanted with maize and other cereals (Nweke, Ezumah, and Spencer 1988). The varieties are also resistant to two devastating diseases (cassava mosaic virus and cassava bacteria blight) and have levels of high consumer acceptance.

Cowpeas. Research on cowpeas has focused on breeding for resistance to the bruchid beetle. This storage pest causes losses of up to 30 percent in cowpeas and is normally controlled by the use of pesticides. The use of bruchid-resistant cowpeas is significantly reducing the need for use of pesticides during storage. A private genetic engineering company and IITA have successfully isolated a resistance gene in cowpeas that dramatically reduces damage from insect pests when transferred to other plants.

Plantains. Plantains are an ideal crop for small farmers in the HST because they fit easily into local as well as improved farming systems, their cultivation does not lead to degradation of the ecosystem, and yields are high. In addition, demand for plantains is increasing in Africa. However, black sigatoka disease attacks plantain production worldwide and is having a devastating effect in Africa. Losses can eliminate profits, and there are no resistant varieties. Recent breakthroughs in research suggest that plants resistant to black sigatoka can be developed.

LEGUMINOUS COVER CROP SYSTEMS. Leguminous cover crops in a continuously cultivated plot can be as efficient as (and therefore substitute for) long-term bush fallow in restoring the fertility of soils in the tropics. However, suitable leguminous cover crop systems are very labor-intensive. Live mulch farming systems for continuous cultivation of maize and cassava, in which the herbaceous crop is planted only once and managed without the use of herbicides, seem promising. These systems can maintain and improve soil fertility, reduce the demand for nitrogen, control weeds, and be economically viable as well as sustainable.

IMPROVED SYSTEMS FOR THE INLAND VALLEYS. Totaling tens of millions of hectares of relatively fertile and well-watered soils in West Africa alone, inland valleys represent a major potential for meeting much of West Africa's food needs. Despite their agricultural potential, inland valleys traditionally have been neglected by agricultural researchers and policymakers, as well as by farmers, in favor of the more readily exploitable uplands. If food-crop production could be increased significantly in these valleys in a sustainable way, pressure on upland areas could be greatly reduced. Attempts to develop these valleys for food production focused on the installation of Asian-type irrigation systems for the production of rice. Few were successful. Increased production and productivities in these areas will depend on an improved understanding of factors that limit the use of inland valleys for food production. Appropriate alternative technologies can then be developed.

The Policy Environment

Macroeconomic policies at the regional and sectoral levels have been adopted by most countries in Sub-Saharan Africa to stabilize output and correct domestic and external imbalances in public accounts (World Bank 1989b). These include direct restraints on government expenditures and limits on additional borrowing, market liberalization and public sector reforms, exchange rate reforms, and a reduction in export taxation. These macroeconomic policies directly affect agricultural production and growth through induced changes in input and output prices, and indirectly affect productivity, profitability, and social welfare via (for example) investments in research and extension, infrastructure development, and human capital development (Jaeger and Humphreys 1988; Binswanger 1989b; World Bank 1989b).

The response of African agriculture to macroeconomic policies, especially sectoral reforms and structural adjustment programs, has been mixed. Cleaver (1988) notes that after the interim problems of adjustment, "adjusting countries" grew at 1.5 percent per year, while those not under adjustment posted, on average, a *negative* growth rate of 1.1 percent. There were substantial differences across countries, reflecting different levels of political commitment to policy reform and resource endowments.

At the farm level, the response to price incentives has been sluggish because producers generally cannot change fixed factors in the short run, and there exists a lag period before new information can be transmitted to producers and consumers. In the period 1963–1981, for example, short- and long-run aggregate agriculture price response elasticities for Sub-Saharan Africa averaged 0.18 and 0.21, respectively. Political and infrastructural barriers to regional trade often lead to saturated markets as supplies expand. Agricultural prices eventually fall in the face of inelastic demand. In the absence of export potential, rapid expansion in output may not occur. Contrary to the current situation in Sub-Saharan Africa, for example, rapid expansion in production of cassava in Thailand is directly linked to policies that freed trade with the European Economic Community (Binswanger and von Braun 1991). Thus absence of such export market opportunities for products of Sub-Saharan Africa may lead to stagnant output.

With regard to poverty alleviation, reduced government expenditures and subsidies directly affect those at or below the poverty line. Policies that attempt to stabilize output in the long term may exacerbate rural poverty in both the short and medium term (World Bank 1989b). As stated earlier, the poor may turn to environmentally degrading activities in a bid to survive under the additional economic stress imposed by adjustments. Macroeconomic and sectoral policies may therefore have the following limitations: (1) while economic growth is necessary for poverty alleviation, the poor do not often possess the physical and human assets needed to take advantage of new opportunities;

(2) development might not lead to expanded employment for unskilled workers, who usually have the least access to productive resources; and (3) growth might not be matched by comparable investments in human capital development or infrastructure.

While structural transformation is a necessary prerequisite for growth and efficiency, these efforts may conflict with strategies to achieve growth and reduce poverty in the short and medium term. Structural transformation may require removing price distortions, cutting back programs considered broadly popular domestically (such as food subsidies), and introducing tighter fiscal control and greater efficiency in public resource management. Tighter fiscal policies to curb wasteful expenditures can translate into reduction in, or outright removal of, subsidies for health, education, and other social needs. Streamlining the civil service can lead to unemployment or wage reduction. These policies can have a direct negative effect on the poor. In such a situation, making growth compatible with long-term poverty reduction may require direct short-term interventions to provide "safety nets" during the period of economic transformation.

Food insecurity in HST, whether caused by failed policies, natural disasters, or political instability, endangers the sustainability of gains made in achieving growth or in reducing poverty. Diversifying and modernizing agriculture through promotion of new technologies and removal of distortionary policies would help increase agricultural efficiency and competitiveness. In addition, better management of public funds would free resources for programs that promote growth and benefit the poor.

Agriculture is an important contributor to total economic growth in Sub-Saharan Africa. On average, agriculture contributes about 31.7 percent of GDP. In some countries this is much higher: agriculture value-added contributes more than 71 percent of GDP in Uganda and 54.1 percent in Ghana (World Bank 1992a). Because a majority of the poor are farmers, raising productivity of this sector has direct implications for their welfare.

But Africa's long-term food security has been undermined through a mixture of poor policies, distortionary programs, and public sector over-involvement. Postindependence policies particularly favored investments in industry at the expense of agriculture. Producers' incentives were destroyed through granting subsidies to urban consumers at the expense of producers and the intervention of governments in agriculture to control input and output prices. Additionally, the sector is often dominated by one or two major crops that contribute substantially to export earnings: in Côte d'Ivoire and Ghana, cocoa and coffee; in Mali, Niger, and Burkina, cotton and livestock; and in Gambia, groundnuts. A fall in the prices of these commodities often results in substantial loss of revenue and reduced capacity to continue with both growth and poverty alleviation programs at two levels: (1) the poor, who are dependent on these crops for cash incomes, lose revenue; and (2) governments, encountering serious revenue shortfalls from exports, may contract expenditures on public goods and services that benefit the poor, or reduce investment programs that spur domestic growth.

Making growth strategies compatible with sustainability and poverty-alleviating goals would therefore require (1) instituting temporary programs of relief in health, nutrition, and education; (2) addressing the root causes of long-term food insecurity in Sub-Saharan Africa; and (3) removing public distortions, encouraging greater private sector participation, and diversifying the agricultural base to reduce the risks and the dependency on a narrow band of export products.

Conclusions and Policy Recommendations

We have investigated the critical linkages between agricultural growth, rural poverty, and sustainability in Sub-Saharan Africa. The region has been characterized by declining per capita output, high population growth rates, and general food insecurity. Almost 50 percent of the region's population is classified as poor. About 75 percent of these are rural inhabitants whose poverty derives mainly from their inability to generate enough income from their agricultural and nonagricultural activities. Unlike the situation on other continents, landlessness is not a major factor in poverty in the region.

Constraints to sustainable development in HST include the fragile and inherently infertile soils that are difficult to manage under intensified production using existing technologies. Poor infrastructure and poor public policies compound the problem. Using case studies of agriculture under different technology options and development strategies, we have provided additional evidence of the potential compatibilities (and incompatibilities) between sustainability and poverty alleviation of some production systems undergoing technological change. Sustainably intensifying agricultural production in the HST requires technologies that are (1) appropriate and designed with maximum participation of users; (2) based on internally consistent biological systems with little reliance on subsidized external inputs; and (3) simple to adopt and require few changes in existing management practices.

Policies needed in HST to increase agricultural growth, reduce poverty, and achieve sustainability objectives include (1) agricultural research that leads to the development of appropriate and adoptable technologies for small farmers; (2) pricing policies that encourage the use of production systems that are internally consistent; (3) policies that encourage investment in appropriate rural infrastructure; and (4) policies that encourage investment in human capital development such as education, rural health, and training of personnel with appropriate research and development skills.

15 Agriculture-Environment-Poverty Interactions in the Southeast Asian Humid Tropics

PRABHU L. PINGALI

The humid tropics of Asia are mainly concentrated in Southeast Asia and the southern portions of South Asia. Average annual rainfall exceeds 1,200 millimeters. Crop production can be sustained for more than 270 days of the year. Rice is the staple crop in this zone. Investment in and gains from modern rice technology are apparent, but sustaining past rates of productivity gains is becoming increasingly difficult. For example, growth in total rice production in Southeast Asia fell from 4 percent per year during 1972–1981 to 2.24 percent per year during 1981–1988 (Rosegrant and Pingali 1991). Growth rates of rice yields per hectare during the same period fell from 2.5 percent to 1.6 percent. However, demand for rice in Asia is estimated to be growing at 2.1 to 2.6 percent per year in the 1990s. These contrasting trends indicate a shortfall despite an anticipated income-induced slowdown in demand growth (Bouis 1994).

Opportunities for area expansion in Asia are limited. Thus incremental output growth must come from further intensification of both lowlands and uplands areas and the associated reliance on yield-enhancing technologies. Since upland areas in the humid tropics cannot sustain continuous annual cropping similar to that in temperate environments, lowland areas (the focus of the Green Revolution) have been relied upon to meet food needs. It is becoming apparent, however, that the lowlands are not as resilient as initially believed. Intensive monoculture systems have led to the degradation of the lowland environments. Productivity stagnation or decline is being observed today.

In this chapter I synthesize existing evidence for the humid tropics of Asia on the following issues: (1) the technological options for sustaining permanent cultivation on the uplands and the conditions under which upland degradation

The assistance of Thelma Paris, Roberta Valmonte-Gerpacio, and Maricel Mendoza is highly appreciated. Dennis Garrity and Sam Fujisaka provided valuable comments on an earlier draft.

can set in; (2) the negative externalities imposed on the lowlands by upland degradation, specifically, the impact of soil erosion on irrigation infrastructure; (3) environmental consequences of intensive lowland rice cultivation; and (4) a preliminary assessment of the relationship between environmental degradation and poverty.

Transition to Sustainable Upland Farming Systems

For millennia, forest farmers in Southeast Asia have been practicing a low-technology, yet sustainable, system of shifting agriculture. Small patches of forest are felled and the woody material burned. Crops are planted on the open land, and a series of harvests and replantings are carried out until yields decline substantially or weed and pest invasions become too great (two to three years). The area is then abandoned and allowed to lie fallow. Forest growth takes over as a new plot is felled and planted. If the period of fallow is long enough for the forest to restore soil fertility and develop a tall, closed canopy to eliminate weeds and brush (at least seven years), the forest farmer can return and start the process again (Hamilton 1984).

Today, however, with rapid population growth, better market infrastructure, and better tools for clearing land, the plots are getting larger, the period of fallow is being shortened, and clearing is taking place on steeper, more erodible slopes. Continuous field crop production on most soils of this zone leads to rapid leaching and to soil acidification or erosion, resulting in decline in soil fertility and yields (Allan 1965; Ruthenberg 1980; Kang and Juo 1981; NRC 1982; Sanchez et al. 1982; FAO 1984).

Ruddle and Manshard (1980) provide a comprehensive survey of the human impact on the humid tropical forests across the world. The experience of Zaire is illustrative of the problem. In 1960, 150 acres of Zairean tropical forests were cut down, burned, and uprooted. The soil was deep-plowed and cultivated in a manner similar to that used in the temperate zone. Yields were found to have dropped dramatically by the second year. The reason was that deep plowing impaired soil structure, and the exposed soil was severely leached. The entire area was abandoned after only a few years of cultivation, and 10 years later the area was only thinly wooded (Ruthenberg 1980). There are several other examples of humid tropical forests that were cleared for intensive cultivation and then abandoned in a degraded state: in Ghana (Moorman and Greenland 1980); in Ivory Coast and Nigeria (FAO 1984); in Peru (Sanchez et al. 1982); and in the Philippines (Sajise 1986).

What are the economically viable options for increased food-crop production in the humid tropics? In general, a system of farming that closely mimics the dense natural vegetation of the humid forests will work in the long run. This is exactly what the shifting cultivators tried to achieve in their multistoried cultivation of cleared tropical forestlands (Ruddle and Manshard 1980). For instance, a system of intercropping short- and medium-term crops under a protective cover of trees is feasible since the ground would be covered for most of the year and therefore the detrimental effects to the soil would be minimized (Okigbo 1974; Sanchez and Salinas 1981; Sanchez, Villachica, and Bandy 1983).

Technological Options for Permanent Cultivation of the Uplands

The humid and subhumid tropics are well suited to perennial crops such as bananas and to tree crops such as rubber, cocoa, and palm oil. Once these crops have been established, their canopy reduces the growth of weeds and they demand less of the soil than annual crops. The effects on the soil resemble those of forest and bush vegetation in establishing a closed nutrient cycle (Sanchez 1976; Ruthenberg 1980). The tree cover, moreover, protects the soil from erosion. Food crops can be intercropped during the establishment phase of a tree crop and sometimes on the mature plantation (Ruthenberg 1980).

The principles of sustainable small farmer tree crop plantations have been applied with some success to agrosilviculture. Agrosilviculture is a regulated system of plantation forestry, in which a public authority allocates forestland to shifting cultivators to clear. The cultivators are allowed to plant for a limited time, after which the cultivators are required to plant tree seedlings and to tend them until the trees are large enough to control weed regrowth. This is essentially a form of regulated shifting cultivation, in which the farmer is a short-term tenant or licensee of an area of land owned by a state authority (Norman 1979; Budowski 1980).

In the Philippines, the Integrated Social Forestry Program (ISFP) was launched in 1983 to "maximize land productivity and enhance ecological stability." Under the program, a *kainginero* (shifting cultivator) family of five members is given a 25-year stewardship certificate of contract for continued occupancy of a forest clearing of 3–7 hectares. Specific requirements include protecting the forest ecosystem by maintaining a certain portion of the land under trees. These stewardship contracts can be renewed for another 25 years (Fujisaka and Capistrano 1985; Sajise 1987; EMB 1990). Other examples of such programs can be found in Pragtong (1987) for Thailand.

Agrosilviculture systems are economically feasible in areas where other, more profitable, agricultural systems are unlikely to be established. The marginal lands on the upper slopes and the steeper midslopes are the most likely areas for agrosilviculture. These areas are already under forest cover, and permanent cultivation of field crops is not possible because of high levels of erosion and low soil fertility. The deeper soils of the mid and lower slopes can be cultivated with a combination of perennial and annual food crops and are less likely candidates for agrosilviculture.

In the agroforestry system, annual crops are grown, usually in mixtures, under perennial forest or plantation trees. The home gardens of South and

Southeast Asia and the compound farms of West Africa are the best-known examples of agroforestry. Permanent compound farming represents an intensive management system that approximates the ecosystem of the forest. Lal (1983) points out that such a system can sustain and prolong the productivity of land and minimize degradation of the soil in the humid tropics, even at high population densities. In densely populated central Java, for instance, home gardens account for 22 percent of the total area cultivated (Ruthenberg 1980). Fujisaka and Wollenberg (1991) report on a case from southern Luzon, the Philippines, where the switch from annual cropping on cleared uplands to an agroforestry system led to a reversal of degradation trends. Migrants adapted their techniques to local circumstances, learned about and tried to obtain better local lands and soils, experimented with crops and necessary farm practices, and continually observed the successes and failures of their neighbors. This study suggests that a sustainable dynamic equilibrium can emerge, with farmer innovation overcoming environmental constraints.

Where markets for tree crops and forest products are limited and where rising population density leads to a reduction in fallow periods, the problem of finding a viable farming system for the humid tropical uplands appears. Arable cropping patterns similar to those used in the temperate environment have adverse effects on the soil and therefore cause a rapid decline in yields (Poulsen 1978; Kang and Juo 1981; Lal 1983). The problem is aggravated in sloping uplands, which are highly susceptible to soil erosion. In the mid and lower slopes of the uplands of Southeast Asia, permanent cultivation of rice, maize, and vegetables is common, and so are the associated soil degradation problems. Indigenous and modern options for arresting and perhaps reversing the soil degradation problem in the humid tropics are discussed here.

The terraces of West Java, Indonesia, and Banaue, the Philippines, are famous examples of indigenous techniques for sustaining production on sloping uplands. There are also examples from the Philippines of indigenous alley cropping, use of natural vegetative barriers (Fujisaka 1990), and improved fallow management (MacDicken 1990). Garrity, Kummer, and Guiang (1991) provide a comprehensive assessment of the technological options for sustaining permanent farming systems on the sloping uplands of the Philippines. Options commonly proposed for controlling soil erosion or sustaining fertility are hedgerows, vegetative or grass strips, minimum tillage, and live mulches.

Table 15.1 provides synthesis results from 78 studies on the impact of alternative soil conservation technologies on surface runoff, on erosion and sedimentation, and on upland crop yield. Each of these studies was summarized in Doolette and Magrath (1990). Six studies found that the removal of forest cover for shifting cultivation purposes led to an increase in surface runoff. The increase in runoff and erosion was more than 100 percent in all but one case. Terracing, plantation trees, and vegetative and grass strips decreased surface runoff by up to 100 percent in 17 studies. Five studies gave no

TABLE 15.1 Effects of soil conservation technologies, various slopes

Soil Conservation Technology	Percentage Changes										
	-100 to -75	-75 to -50	-50 to -25	-25 to 0	NSC	0 to 25	25 to 50	50 to 75	75 to 100	> 100	Total
	(number of studies)										
On surface runoff											
Bare soil/bare fallow/ fallowing	0	0	0	0	0	0	0	1	0	4	5
No till/zero tillage/ minimum tillage	1	0	3	1	0	1	0	0	0	0	6
Agroforestry	0	0	0	0	0	0	0	0	0	1	1
Plantation trees	1	0	1	0	1	0	0	0	0	0	3
Terracing	4	2	4	3	4	0	0	0	0	1	18
Vegetative and grass strips	0	0	1	1	0	0	0	0	0	0	2
On erosion and sedimentation											
Bare soil/bare fallow/ fallowing	0	0	0	0	0	0	0	1	0	7	8
No till/zero tillage/ minimum tillage	5	2	0	0	0	0	1	1	0	2	11
Agroforestry	1	0	0	0	0	1	0	0	0	1	3
Plantation trees	8	1	0	0	2	2	0	0	2	4	19
Terracing	16	3	3	3	1	0	0	1	0	1	28
Vegetative and grass strips	5	2	0	0	0	0	0	0	0	0	7
On upland crop yield											
No till/zero tillage/ minimum tillage	0	0	1	2	3	1	2	1	0	0	10
Terracing	0	0	1	2	6	5	4	1	2	0	21
Use of animal manure	0	0	0	0	0	0	1	0	1	0	2
Mulching	0	0	0	1	0	0	5	3	2	0	11

SOURCE: Summarized from results of studies cited in Doolette and Magrath 1990.
NOTE: NSC = No significant change.

significant change in surface runoff using the same options. Two cases indicated that agroforestry and terracing increased surface runoff by more than 100 percent.

Of the 11 instances that examined the impact of the switch from conventional tillage using a mold board plow to zero or minimum tillage, five studies found that erosion and sedimentation decreased 75–100 percent. In contrast, two studies indicated that zero or minimum tillage increased erosion and sedimentation by more than 100 percent. It should be noted that such impacts are influenced by other factors, such as slope of the area, climate, soil type, land use, or species grown in the area.

From the same synthesis, terracing was found to control erosion and sedimentation effectively, as confirmed by results of 16 studies indicating a decrease of 75–100 percent. Only one study stated that terracing led to an increase in erosion and sedimentation by more than 100 percent. These studies compared terracing with unimproved local farming and soil conservation practices such as clean cultivation, up and down slope cultivation, contour farming, or simple unterraced cultivation.

Vegetative and grass strips decreased erosion and sedimentation 50–100 percent in seven studies. These were either in comparison with monthly tilled bare soil, tree plantations, or conventional cultivation. The impact of agroforestry and plantation trees on soil erosion and sedimentation, however, gave varied results. Ten studies found that these options can decrease erosion by up to 100 percent, while five studies showed they increased it by more than 100 percent. These were compared with either bare soil, shifting cultivation, natural cover, undisturbed natural forest, continuous fallow, crop monoculture, or intercropping.

In terms of upland crop yield and productivity, three studies showed no significant difference when a farmer shifts to farming with zero or minimum tillage. Two studies indicated a possible 25 percent decrease in upland crop yields, whereas two other studies indicated an increase of 25–50 percent in the same. These studies compared zero or minimum tillage with either unmulched traditional cultivation, traditional mixed cropping, or conventional tillage.

Terracing was found not to affect upland crop yield significantly in six studies. Twelve studies, on the other hand, found that it increased crop yield up to 75 percent. The impact of terracing was compared with either crop yield of unterraced cultivation or that of traditional mixed cropping.

Two studies on the use of animal manure (specifically cow or poultry manure applied at 4–5 metric tons per hectare) showed an increase in upland crop yield of 25–100 percent. This was compared with applying manure at 2 metric tons per hectare or with applying commercial fertilizers. Similarly, mulching was found to increase upland crop yield by up to 100 percent in 10 studies. One study showed that it decreased upland crop yield by 25 percent. These studies compared mulching with unmulched traditional cultivation and with clean cultivation.

Determinants of Land Use and Degradation in the Uplands

Soil degradation, defined here as soil erosion or a decline in soil fertility, is generally associated with deforestation, intensive cultivation, and overgrazing. Soil degradation is not a universal problem. First, the threat of soil degradation varies by soil type, temperature, rainfall regimes, and slope. It tends to be higher in the humid tropics on shallow soils with slope greater than 18 percent. Second, appropriate land use and land investments can prevent the problem, even on high-risk soils. Therefore, degradation problems are mainly restricted to areas where the rate of return to preventive land investments is low. Incentives for corrective land investments depend on the relative land endowments of the region and on the security of land tenure.

In Southeast Asia, rapid deforestation caused by unchecked logging and poor conservation efforts contributes more to soil degradation than does agricultural intensification. Studies in the hill forests of Malaysia show that sediment production rates increase from less than 100 cubic meters per square kilometer per year in undisturbed tropical rain forests to between 388 and 694 cubic meters per square kilometer per year in recently logged hill forests (O'Laughlin 1985).

Of the 15 million hectares of public forestland (defined as 18 percent slope or steeper) in the Philippines, only 6 million hectares have significant tree cover, and currently fewer than 1 million hectares of old growth forest remain. Cultivated area in the uplands is approximately 3.9 million hectares, or 43 percent of cleared land (Garrity, Kummer, and Guiang 1991).

Upland cultivation per se does not necessarily lead to land degradation. Degradation sets in if proper safeguards for land and soil conservation are not incorporated into the farming system. Conservation investments require the farmer to have a long-term decision horizon, implying long-term and secure access to land.

Without secure long-term rights to land, farmers do not have the incentive to plant trees and perennials (identified in the previous section) for protecting the soil against erosion (Fujisaka and Capistrano 1985). Shifting cultivators threatened by insecure land tenure can take an opportunistic short-term view of land development (Sajise 1987). In societies where the ownership of trees is tantamount to the ownership of the land the trees are on, farmers temporarily occupying the land can even be prevented from planting trees or perennial crops (Noronha 1985). Raintree (1987) documents case study evidence on the importance of tenure security for investment in trees. Where uncertain owner-ship or tenure prevents the planting of trees, degradation is most likely to occur.

In discussing the impact of land tenure insecurity on the degradation of the upland environment, I distinguish tenure security in privately held agricul-tural lands from tenure security in public forestlands. In agricultural societies with steadily growing populations, private rights to land evolve over time. The transition from general cultivation rights to specific land rights with population growth is documented in Miracle (1967); Hopkins (1973); Noronha (1985); Binswanger and Pingali (1987); Dove (1987); and Pingali (1990). The transition to private land rights widens famers' incentives to undertake the investments required for the intensification of production and soil fertility maintenance. Formal land ownership as characterized by the possession of title also helps the farmer in acquiring credit for making the necessary investments in the land.

Chalamwong and Feder (1986) and Feder and Onchan (1987) provide evidence on land ownership and investment for Thailand.

In addition to inadequate rights to agricultural land, uncontrolled access to public forestlands is a major contributor to upper watershed degradation. Commercial loggers (both legal and illegal) first pioneer into public lands and clear primary forests. They are then followed by migrant farmers who rent parcels of cleared timberland from the nominal "owners" (the logging companies) or the "pseudo-landlords" from nearby towns. These migrants tend to maximize short-term returns and follow the logging companies to the next site once soil degradation has set in (ACIAR 1984; Fujisaka and Capistrano 1985).

Governments in the region have made several attempts to improve the tenure security of the migrant upland farmers but with limited success in controlling degradation. In the Philippines, Certificate of Stewardship Contracts (CSC) have been issued to migrant farmers since the early 1980s. However, only 2.5 percent of the upland area has so far been included in the stewardship leases, and there are several limitations to this contract arrangement. In general, migrant farmers have not been able to assert their CSC claim against that of the absentee pseudo-landlords. The lease is nontransferable and hence cannot be used as collateral for loans to invest in farm improvements, and it is only inheritable within the 25-year lease period (DENR 1990a).

Despite secure long-term rights to land, one would expect erosion and degradation to persist in areas where collective action is required for watershed-level investments. Group action for making watershed-level investments in erosion control would be possible only where farmers have an incentive to cooperate or where they are coerced to do so. Incentives for cooperation will be higher in relatively closed communities under severe land pressure. Terraces in West Java are an example of such cooperation (Soemarwoto and Soemarwoto 1984).

Upland Degradation and Poverty

This section contains a cross-sectional comparison of the level of upland degradation (as proxied by deforestation) and poverty for all regions of the Philippines. The following poverty indicators are used by region for the years 1975 and 1988: percentage of population below the poverty line, unemployment rate, net internal migration rate, age dependency ratio, and percentage of income spent on durable goods (Table 15.2). Bicol and the three regions of the Visayas have the highest incidence of poverty, whereas Cagayan Valley and central Luzon have among the lowest. The incidence of poverty is also lower in regions with a greater proportion of irrigated lowlands where the gains of the Green Revolution are concentrated, such as central Luzon and southern Tagalog, relative to regions with predominantly upland cultivation such as Mindanao, or regions with predominantly rainfed cultivation such as Bicol. Upland

TABLE 15.2 Regional deforestation and poverty indicators, the Philippines

Region	Total Land Area (a)	Percent of Land with Slope > 18° (b)	Percent of Land under Forest Cover, 1984 (c)	Deforestation Index, 1987 (d)	Net Internal Migration Rate		Total Poverty Incidence		Unemployment Rate		Age Dependency Ratio		Percent of Income Spent on Durable Goods, 1985 (m)
					1975 (e)	1988 (f)	1975 (g)	1988 (h)	1975 (i)	1988 (j)	1975 (k)	1988 (l)	
	(thousand hectares)				(percent)		(percent)		(percent)				
Ilocos Region	2,157	64.2	21.6	0.6636	-1.3	-3.1	51.6	47.5	3.3	7.6	87.5	76.1	1.4
Cagayan Valley	3,640	62.6	44.7	0.2859	-0.2	-2.0	55.7	48.9	2.2	5.0	92.1	77.8	1.7
Central Luzon	1,823	36.3	16.3	0.5510	0.7	-0.1	43.5	39.6	5.3	9.6	88.7	72.2	1.5
Southern Tagalog	4,756	59.6	27.3	0.5419	0.4	2.3	55.2	49.3	8.0	8.4	88.5	75.1	1.9
Bicol Region	1,763	53.7	5.4	0.8994	-1.0	-4.0	73.5	65.3	0.9	5.7	102.4	86.1	1.1
Western Visayas	2,022	38.9	5.0	0.8715	-0.4	-3.5	73.4	61.8	4.9	7.3	90.0	81.0	1.3
Central Visayas	1,495	58.2	2.9	0.9502	-1.2	-3.2	69.9	54.6	5.0	5.7	89.5	76.5	0.6
Eastern Visayas	2,143	62.2	20.7	0.6672	-0.2	-5.6	70.2	60.5	1.2	6.0	97.5	81.9	0.9
Western Mindanao	1,869	40.2	14.6	0.6368	-1.2	-0.7	63.0	52.0	0.6	5.2	91.6	79.1	1.3
Northern Mindanao	2,833	61.3	38.7	0.3687	1.7	2.6	65.6	51.5	2.5	7.7	94.0	76.4	2.2
Southern Mindanao	3,169	68.6	32.5	0.5262	1.1	1.8	60.2	52.2	1.6	8.1	92.0	76.1	2.3
Central Mindanao	2,329	44.7	20.0	0.5526	-0.9	1.7	63.6	47.1	—	4.7	93.7	78.9	1.5
National averages													
Including M. Manila					1.5	5.9	58.9	49.5	4.2	8.3	88.0	74.8	1.5
Excluding M. Manila	2,519	54.3	21.2	0.6091	-0.2	-1.1	61.9	52.3	2.9	6.8	92.2	78.0	1.5

SOURCES: (a) Philippine-German Forest Resources Inventory Project, DENR 1987. (b) de los Angeles and Lasmarias 1984. (c) Philippine Forestry Statistics, Forest Management Bureau, DENR. (e–m) NCSO 1986 and 1988; NCSO 1988.

NOTES: Blank cell indicates not applicable; —, not available. (1) Deforestation index presented in column d = (1 − c/b). (2) Net internal migration rate (of population five years old and above) in columns e and f is equal to (number of immigrants minus number of emigrants)/total population × 1,000. A negative value indicates outmigration. (3) Available data for total poverty incidence were only for years 1985 and 1988. (4) Age dependency ratio in columns k and l is the ratio of the number of people under 15 and over 65 years old to the number of people between 15 and 65 years old, multiplied by 100. This is the ratio of the number of economically dependent people to that of the economically productive. (5) Data on percentage of income spent on durable goods are available only for 1985.

FIGURE 15.1 Deforestation and poverty incidence in the Philippines, by region

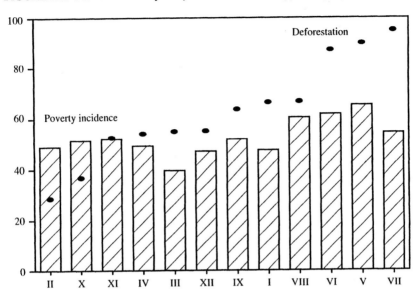

NOTES: Dots represent region-specific indices of deforestation in 1987. Regions I through XII are arranged in ascending order of deforestation. Columns represent percentages of population below the poverty line in 1988.

degradation is measured here by an index of deforestation, which is one minus the ratio of the area under forest cover to the land area with slope greater than 18 percent. Land with slope greater than 18 percent is the most susceptible land for erosion losses. In the Philippines this land is declared public forestland, and in principle private use of this land is regulated. When the deforestation index (column d of Table 15.2) is zero, that is, all land with slope greater than 18 percent is covered by forests, then the potential for degradation is minimal. On the other hand, if the index is one, that is, no land with slope greater than 18 percent is covered by forests, then the potential for degradation is extremely high. Regions can be ranked in terms of their relative levels of degradation by using this index. Environmental degradation, by this measure, is highest in the Bicol and Visayas regions and lowest in Cagayan Valley and northern Mindanao. This does not mean, however, that the latter regions do not suffer from deforestation problems but rather that, in proportion to their forest areas, the problem is smaller.

Incidence of Poverty

Figure 15.1 presents the 12 regions of the Philippines in ascending order of their respective deforestation indices, depicted as dots. In addition, the

FIGURE 15.2 Deforestation and expenditure patterns in the Philippines, by region

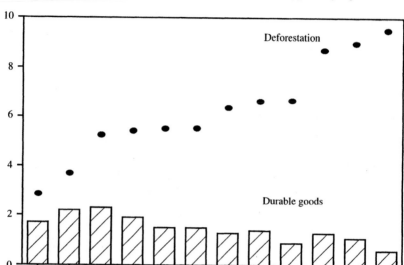

NOTES: Dots represent region-specific indices of deforestation in 1987. Regions I through XII are arranged in ascending order of deforestation. Columns represent percentages of income spent on durable goods in 1985.

figure includes columns that reflect the percentage of regional population falling below the poverty line. The superimposition of poverty levels on deforestation indices suggests a positive link. Average poverty incidence in 1988 for the three regions with the highest level of deforestation was 60.6 percent whereas the average of the remaining regions was 49.8 percent. Poverty incidence in the deforested regions was significantly higher than the national average.

A second indicator of poverty is the percentage of household income spent on durable goods, which is superimposed on the deforestation indices in Figure 15.2. One percent of income, on average, is spent on durable goods in the most degraded provinces, as compared with 1.6 percent for the remaining provinces, suggesting a negative relationship.

Migration, Unemployment, and Dependency Ratios

The availability of areas with low population densities and available agricultural land has been a major factor inducing migration in the Philippines (Garrity, Kummer, and Guiang 1991). The major patterns since 1948 have been twofold: frontier migration, primarily to Mindanao until 1960; and since then a

FIGURE 15.3 Deforestation and migration in the Philippines, by region

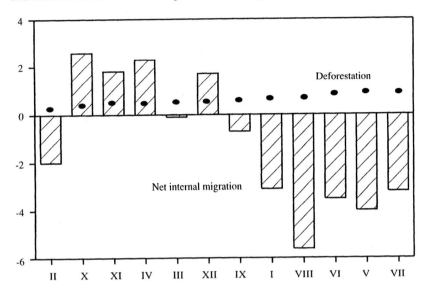

NOTES: Dots represent region-specific indices of deforestation in 1987. Regions I through XII are arranged in ascending order of deforestation. Columns represent net migration rates over the period 1975–1988. Negative numbers indicate outmigration.

movement toward urban areas, particularly the metro Manila area. The rate of migration to metro Manila increased from 1.5 percent in 1975 to 5.9 percent in 1987. Although migration to urban areas has been particularly pronounced since 1960, movement to frontier or upland areas is still continuing (Cruz, Francisco, and Tapawan-Conway 1988). Between 1975 and 1980, almost one-fourth of all interregional migrants had the uplands as their destination.

The upland population was estimated to have reached about 17.8 million by 1988. This includes an estimated population of 8.5 million persons residing on public forestlands. The public forestland population includes 5.95 million members of indigenous cultural communities and 2.55 million migrants from the lowlands (DENR 1990b).

Figure 15.3 depicts deforestation indices and net migration rates. Regions with high levels of degradation experience population outmigration, and regions with low levels of degradation experience population immigration, suggesting an inverse relationship. Outmigration in the highly degraded regions jumped from 0.9 percent in 1975 to 3.6 percent in 1987, while the remaining regions went from marginal immigration (0.01 percent) in 1975 to marginal outmigration (0.3 percent) in 1987.

FIGURE 15.4 Deforestation and unemployment in the Philippines, by region

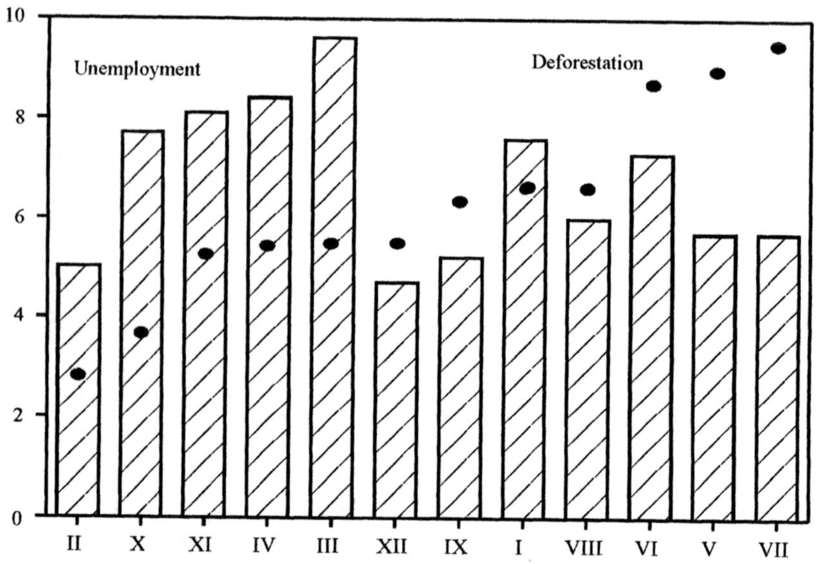

NOTES: Dots represent region-specific indices of deforestation in 1987. Regions I through XII are arranged in ascending order of deforestation. Columns represent unemployment rates in 1988.

Unemployment rates in the degraded regions increased from 3.6 percent in 1975 to 6.2 percent in 1988. As net outmigration seems to take place from regions with higher degradation to regions with lower degradation, unemployment rates, at least in the short term, are relatively higher in the latter (Figure 15.4).

The age dependency ratio is the ratio of population less than 16 years old plus the population over 65 years old, divided by the population that is between the ages of 16 and 65. The larger this ratio, the greater the proportion of non-working population within a region, suggesting a larger proportion of working-age population have migrated out of the region. In 1975, the age dependency ratio was similar across regions (about 92.2), but by 1988, regions with higher levels of deforestation had higher age dependency ratios (81.2) relative to the national average (74.8).

Downstream Effects of Soil Erosion

Literature on upper watershed degradation has generally mentioned the externalities imposed on lowland productivity, especially in terms of sediment flow affecting irrigation infrastructure (see, for example, Cruz, Francisco, and

Tapawan-Conway 1988). The externalities generally cited are soil erosion, sediment buildup in reservoirs, and the increased incidence of flooding. There is no general consensus on the importance of human activity in the uplands as a determinant of the problems created for the lowlands. Some soil scientists argue that soil erosion is largely caused by natural processes (Johnson 1988; Burton, Shah, and Schreier 1989), whereas others implicate human activity more definitely (Sanchez 1976). In any case, it is safe to say that susceptibility to erosion is dependent on soil properties and land management practices (Sanchez 1976).

In this chapter I take the position that, at the margin, human activity in exploiting the upper watershed can have an impact on soil erosion and therefore can impose negative externalities on the lowlands. I focus on the negative impact of upper watershed degradation on irrigation infrastructure through an increase in sediment buildup.

There are several case studies in Asia on the continued reduction in the storage capacities of reservoirs because of excessive sedimentation rates. The Karangkates reservoir in East Java, Indonesia, which has a storage capacity of 0.343 square kilometers of water, has a sediment inflow 18 times more than the design rate, shortening the economic life of the reservoir by 2 percent each year (Brabben 1979). In a study of eight large reservoirs in India, the actual sedimentation rates were found to vary between 1.4 and 16.5 times the expected rates (Dogra 1986).

The Pantabangan watershed in the Philippines demonstrates the potential ravages of soil erosion. It has a total watershed area of 82,900 hectares, 44 percent of which is forested. Grasslands that have taken over formerly forested lands now occupy 44 percent. Croplands take up a mere 12 percent. Prior to dam construction in the late 1960s, sediment flow was estimated to be around 20 metric tons per hectare per year. With widespread forest denudation, this increased to 81 metric tons per hectare per year (Cruz, Francisco, and Tapawan-Conway 1988), implying a loss in the dam's service life by 61 years. Similarly, the Magat watershed has some 83 percent of its 414,300 hectares already under severe to excessive soil erosion. Sediment flow at the dam site was estimated at 20 metric tons per hectare per year during the planning stage (Coloma 1984). This has been exceeded by present rates of up to 34 metric tons per hectare per year (Cruz, Francisco, and Tapawan-Conway 1988). As with other dams similarly affected, Magat dam has lost some 40 years of its service life.

Cruz, Francisco, and Tapawan-Conway (1988) estimate on-site and downstream soil erosion in the Magat and Pantabangan watersheds to be 88 metric tons per hectare per year for open grasslands, and 28 metric tons per hectare per year for other land uses. As topsoil sheet erosion is about 40 percent of the gross erosion rate, gross annual erosion per hectare was estimated to be 219 metric tons for the open grasslands and 71 metric tons for other land uses.

Sedimentation reduces project benefits by shortening reservoir and dam service life and reduces useful storage capacity. For example, massive sedimentation of Ambuklao Dam in Luzon, the Philippines, resulted in the reduction of its useful lifespan from 60 to 32 years, yielding an estimated loss of 500 million pesos in 1985. To these costs should also be added benefits foregone from lost biodiversity with potential economic value, such as food, medicine, fuel, fiber, and material for industrial use (EMB 1990).

Castañeda and Bhuiyan (1988) have shown, for a Philippine watershed, the impact of mining upstream on the quality and quantity of water provided to lowland farmers downstream. The upstream discharge of mine tailings caused abandonment of 24 percent of the system's water conveyance network because of sedimentation and a consequent reduction of about 40 percent of the system's service area. Similarly, Sajise (1986) noted that, after 20 years, the Agno River Irrigation System (ARIS) in the Philippines now operates at only 25 percent capacity because of silting of the intake and canal system. In 1976, losses within ARIS from desilting costs and crop failure amounted to US$4.4 million (Coloma 1984). Doolette and Magrath (1990) provide a comprehensive review of the impact of bare soil, bare fallow, or fallowing on surface runoff, erosion, and sedimentation in four Asian countries. Depending on slope and land use, the practice of bare fallow increased surface runoff, sediment yield, and erosion rate by as much as 38,900 percent.

In India, the United Nations Development Programme/Food and Agriculture Organization of the United Nations estimated that 2,400 million metric tons of silt are carried through the rivers of Bangladesh every year. Vital reservoirs have seen their useful life significantly shortened because of sediment yield from mountain watersheds under human pressure (ADB 1987). Bed levels of the Terai rivers are rising 15–30 centimeters annually. Over 1972–1979, Himalayan torrents and streams have more than doubled in width and rivers have widened by more than one-third through erosion and siltation, reducing the capacity to carry flood water.

De Vera (1992) econometrically related upper watershed degradation to irrigation infrastructure for each region of the Philippines. Specifically, this study estimated the impact of forest production, mineral production, and upland rice production on irrigated area and rice area for both the wet and dry seasons. The extent to which system maintenance can sustain irrigation infrastructure, given the externalities imposed by upper watershed degradation, was also assessed.

A data panel consisting of regional aggregates for each of the 12 regions over the 1979–1988 10-year period was used for the analysis. Forest production and mineral production had statistically significant, negative effects on wet season irrigated area. Upland rice area was statistically insignificant, though the effect may have been stronger if data for all upland crops were available. Maintenance expenditures and regional population density had

TABLE 15.3 Determinants of irrigation infrastructure degradation in the Philippines: estimated elasticities

	Wet Season			Dry Season	
	Service Area	Irrigated Area	Rice Area	Irrigated Area	Rice Area
	(565,058)	(409,277)	(382,424)	(329,974)	(310,740)
Wet season irrigated area (409,277)	—	—	—	0.7686	0.6739
Forest products (5,599,630)	−0.1102	−0.1364	−0.1576	−0.1048	−0.0992
Upland rice area (157,121)	−0.0163	−0.0127	−0.0051	−0.0098	−0.0032
Value of mineral production (13,050,370)	−0.0637	−0.0695	−0.0710	−0.0534	−0.0447
Population density (143.57)	0.0934	0.0788	0.0403	0.0534	0.0643
Real maintenance and operating expenditures (62,149)	0.2465	0.2686	0.2687	0.4589	0.4865
Lag of rice price (919.12)	—	—	0.0697	—	0.0861

SOURCE: De Vera 1992.
NOTE: Figures in parentheses are mean values. Dashes indicate not applicable.

statistically significant, positive effects on wet season irrigated area. In essence, results showed that the degradation of national irrigation systems was influenced by upper watershed destruction in addition to reduced maintenance investments. Increased production of logs, upland agriculture, and mining were among the watershed activities identified to cause irrigation system degradation, the adverse effect of which is a loss in total rice production.

Table 15.3 presents the estimated elasticities from that study. A 1 percent increase in forest product production, mineral production, and upland rice area leads to declines in wet season irrigated area of 0.14 percent, 0.07 percent, and 0.01 percent, respectively. The corresponding declines in wet season rice area are 0.16 percent, 0.07 percent, and 0.01 percent, respectively. To the extent that upland rice area is a small proportion of all upland crop area, that elasticity is underestimated. Meanwhile, a 1 percent increase in real expenditures for maintenance of irrigation infrastructure leads to a 0.27 percent increase in wet season irrigated area and a 0.27 percent increase in wet season rice area.

Since there is no runoff from the upper watershed during the dry season, irrigation infrastructure in the dry season is a function of the wet season infrastructure. A 1 percent increase in wet season irrigated area leads to a 0.77 percent increase in dry season irrigated area and a 0.67 percent increase in dry season rice area. The effects of upper watershed degradation on dry season infrastructure are evaluated through their wet season effects.

The net effect of upper watershed degradation on irrigation infrastructure was evaluated by accounting for the positive effect of real maintenance expenditures. For the Philippines as a whole, upper watershed degradation leads to an incremental loss of 4,200 hectares per year of wet season irrigated land and 2,700 hectares per year of dry season irrigated land. This amounts to a production loss of approximately 24,000 metric tons per year.

Changes in wet and dry season rice area, production, income, and employment during the period 1980–1986 in 16 national irrigation systems in the Philippines (reported in de Vera 1992) support these findings. Over this seven-year period, wet season rice area decreased in 12 systems and increased in 4 systems. Across all systems, wet season rice area increased by 233 hectares, resulting in a net increase of 828 metric tons in rice production and a farm income increase of 365,000 pesos. The net increase in area also resulted in an additional labor requirement of almost 11,000 person-days, which, in turn, translates to an approximately 4-million-peso increase in labor income. Incremental irrigation expansion barely compensated for the loss in area due to degradation.

The data also show that dry season rice area decreased in 10 systems and increased in 6 national irrigation systems. Across all systems, the total effect was a decrease in dry season rice area by 3,380 hectares, despite investments in area expansion. This resulted in a loss in rice production of about 60,000 metric tons and a farm income loss of almost 15 million pesos. Employment opportunities also decreased by 142,456 person-days, thereby reducing labor income by almost 7 million pesos.

Overall, the results suggest that the long-term productivity of the lowlands cannot be viewed independently of upland degradation. On the contrary, increased upland clearing could dramatically diminish lowland productivity, production, and employment. Where upland degradation is not explicitly accounted for, there is an underinvestment of research resources in upland conservation in favor of lowland productivity growth.

Humid Tropical Lowlands: Can Past Rates of Productivity Growth Be Sustained?

The Green Revolution strategy for increasing food output growth in the humid tropics concentrated exclusively on the lowlands. This strategy involved the intensification of lowland land use and increases in yields per hectare through the use of modern high-yielding rice varieties. The positive impacts (especially employment and income effects) of intensification and the adoption of modern seed-fertilizer technology have been examined in great detail by the Green Revolution literature (Otsuka, Cordova, and David 1990). The post–Green Revolution phase of declining productivity and stagnant incomes has been analyzed only recently (Barker and Chapman 1988; Herdt 1988; Pingali, Moya, and Velasco 1990). The current farm-level scenario for Asian rice production can be characterized as follows: (1) a diminished gap between the yield frontier and farmer yields; (2) a rapidly degrading paddy microenvironment resulting from intensive rice monoculture; (3) increased input requirements for sustaining current yield gains; and (4) declining profitability of rice monoculture systems. There is a growing concern about the resilience of the humid tropical lowlands and an increasing understanding that they do not have an unlimited absorptive capacity. In the following section I summarize recent evidence of productivity stagnation for lowland rice cultivation. A detailed assessment can be found in Pingali, Moya, and Velasco (1990).

Is There a Yield Gap between the Technological Frontier and Farmer Yields?

At the time IR-8, the first widely adopted modern rice variety, was released, traditional rice variety yields were 2.0–2.5 metric tons per hectare, implying a yield gap of around 3.5–4.0 metric tons per hectare between the farmer and the experiment station (IRRI 1967). More recent studies estimate the current yield gap at about 1.2 metric tons per hectare and point out that farmers with yields below experiment station levels have poorer access to irrigation water and may be less efficient in the use of modern technology. These differences are structural and cannot be rectified through research alone (Pingali, Moya, and Velasco 1990).

The leveling off of the farmer yields has also been witnessed in other Southeast Asian countries. While national average yields continue to rise in Indonesia and Thailand, average yields in the "traditional rice bowl" provinces of each of these countries have been stagnant for the current decade. For example, since 1982, provincial average yields for Suphan Buri, Indonesia, have been stagnant at under 3.0 metric tons per hectare and for West Java at 4.5 metric tons per hectare.

Stagnant or Declining Technological Yield Frontier

Experiment station data indicate that rice yield potential may actually be declining. When IR-8 was released in 1966, it yielded as much as 10 metric tons per hectare in the dry season and 6 metric tons per hectare in the wet season on IRRI's experimental farm. Following IR-8, 33 rice varieties have been released in the Philippines, many with better insect and disease resistance, shorter crop duration, and to some extent better eating quality than IR-8. However, *none* of these later varieties has been able to match the yield potential of IR-8. Perhaps more disturbing is the observation that the highest yields obtained from the long-term fertility trials are exhibiting a decline (Pingali, Moya, and Velasco 1990). Wet season yield declines are observed for three of the four experiment stations, and dry season yield declines are observed for two of the four experiment stations.

Similar yield declines have been observed in other experiment stations in India, Indonesia, and Thailand. Long-term fertilizer trials on rice conducted in four locations in India from 1972 to 1982 found declining long-term yields in two and stagnant yields in two locations.

For rice-wheat cropping system trials, significant long-term rice yield declines have been found in most sites in India during 1973–1988 (Byerlee 1987). Long-term yield declines have been observed in 11 years of continuous rice cropping at Maros, Indonesia, and 10 years of continuous rice cropping in Chiang Mai, Thailand (Pingali, Moya, and Velasco 1990).

Long-term stagnation or decline in yield potential under intensive irrigated rice production can be attributed to degradation of the paddy environment in association with production intensification. Specifically, paddy environment degradation can be due to increased pest pressure, rapid depletion of soil micronutrients, changes in soil chemistry brought about by intensive cropping, or increased reliance on low-quality irrigation water (Flinn and de Datta 1984; Pingali, Moya, and Velasco 1990).

Long-term degradation of the paddy environment has direct effects on input-use efficiency and the profitability of rice production. Current yield gains can be sustained only with increasing levels of chemical fertilizers, hence a decline in total factor productivity over time. Desai and Gandhi (1989) report that this is particularly true in Asia, where intensive rice production has resulted in nutrient depletion that has not been compensated for by balanced replenishment. There is evidence throughout Asia of growing phosphorus, sulphur, and micronutrient deficiencies (Stone 1986; Tandon 1987; Desai and Gandhi 1989).

The use of purchased inputs for plant protection was unimportant for rice prior to the mass introduction of modern varieties. Farmers had traditionally relied on host plant resistance, natural enemies, cultural methods, and mechanical methods such as hand-weeding. Relatively minor pests—leaffolder, caseworm, armyworm, and cutworm—started to cause noticeable losses in farmers' fields as the area planted to modern varieties increased. The green leafhopper and brown planthopper became major problems (Teng 1990). The growing pest problems in Asian rice production can be attributed to the uniformity of varieties grown, indiscriminate pesticide use, and increasing susceptibility of varieties to resistance breakdown.

These results on the degradation of the paddy environment with intensive rice cultivation have several implications for a post–Green Revolution rice research strategy: (1) quantification of the economic costs of modern rice technology should include production and environmental costs; (2) greater emphasis should be given to understanding the physical, biological, and ecological consequences of intensive rice monoculture systems; (3) crop diversification (for example, a rice-nonrice crop rotation) should be examined as a mechanism for arresting or reversing the long-term stagnation in rice productivity and incomes; and (4) incremental gains in productivity will be achieved only by adopting increasingly knowledge-intensive technologies, so the returns to extension and training programs continue to be high.

Policy Implications

Agricultural intensification and modern technology use impose significant long-term environmental costs on the production system. For the uplands, these costs are increased susceptibility to soil erosion and declining soil fertility. For the lowlands, the environmental costs are nutrient imbalances, increased susceptibility to pest damage, and declining input efficiencies. Upland degradation also imposes a negative externality on the lowlands through increased sediment buildup in irrigation infrastructure.

While unit costs of production fall with agricultural intensification, environmental costs tend to rise and be ignored. In evaluating the returns to intensification and modern technology use, comprehensive economic costs should be considered, including environmental costs. Rates of return to agricultural intensification and the adoption of modern yield-increasing technologies will be overstated if environmental costs are not considered.

Sustaining productivity growth requires grappling with the physical, biological, and ecological consequences of agricultural intensification. When yield per hectare is used as the only measure of productivity growth, environmental costs are ignored and research resource allocation is biased toward improving yields rather than understanding systemic problems causing their stagnation or decline. Sustaining input-use efficiency is closely related to understanding the changes in the paddy system under different levels and types of intensification.

For the irrigated lowlands, the rice bowls of Asia, if the trend in stagnant or declining yields is widespread, the long-run sustainability of intensive irrigated rice monoculture is in question. Crop diversification should be examined as a mechanism to reverse rice yield declines. Wet season rice cultivation will continue because of the high drainage costs for nonrice crop production, but opportunities exist for diversification in the dry season. Diversified cropping patterns in irrigated environments that maximize the carryover effects of inputs from one crop to the next can increase the efficiency of input use. The common example is rice-legume systems that allow for lower levels of nutrient application for the subsequent rice crop. Also rice-nonrice crop rotations could reduce pest carryover from one crop to the next.

Long-term productivity of the lowlands, especially the state of irrigation infrastructure, is not independent of upper watershed degradation. In the design of irrigation systems, estimated siltation rates tend not to consider different upland land use strategies and the different levels and types of watershed degradation associated with them. One therefore tends to overestimate the life of irrigation systems and consequently the returns to irrigation investment, and also to overlook opportunities for extending project life by properly managing upland areas.

The steady decline of investments in real terms for the maintenance of irrigation infrastructure is a cause for concern. For the Southeast Asian countries, donor lending for irrigation infrastructure has declined from US$630 million in 1977–1979 to US$202 million in 1986/87 (Rosegrant and Pingali 1991). Consequently these countries sharply reduced their total spending on irrigation for both new construction and maintenance (Rosegrant and Pasandaran 1990). The full effects of these declines are just beginning to be felt owing to the lags in irrigation construction.

Where upper watershed externalities are not explicitly accounted for, there is an underinvestment of research resources in upland conservation. The Green Revolution strategy of increasing lowland productivity has to a large extent relieved the pressure on the uplands by providing employment opportunities for migrant labor. However, if the current trend toward stagnation or decline in lowland productivity persists, one could expect a decline in employment opportunities in the lowlands and hence increased pressure on the uplands.

Finally, upland resource conservation policies ought to take a holistic view of agriculture, forestry, mining, and human habitation. Agriculture policy alone cannot prevent or reduce soil erosion. Clearly defined access rights to public forestlands are essential for selective clearing and replanting of forests. For land under agricultural production, secure long-term tenure and access to markets for traditional and emerging tree crop products provide the incentive for farmers to invest in soil and forest conservation. Where the returns to private investment in soil conservation are low, government-encouraged collective action is required for watershed-level investments.

16 Agricultural Growth and Sustainability: Prospects for Semi-Arid West Africa

PETER J. MATLON AND AKINWUMI A. ADESINA

The food-crop sector in the West African semi-arid tropics (WASAT) faces a triple challenge: (1) the lack of technical change has led to zero or, in some areas, negative growth in productivity; (2) deepening poverty has forced farmers to employ short-term survival strategies to meet their immediate needs for food and income, but these strategies mine the resource base and thereby reduce future production potential; and (3) the application of many yield-increasing technologies may itself contribute to environmental degradation. In this chapter we consider some of the factors underlying this situation and suggest how research and development efforts might shift to achieve sustainable production growth into the twenty-first century.

Production Trends and Farming Systems

Production and Productivity

The millet and sorghum sectors have performed poorly during the past 30 years, with production for both crops growing slower than rural populations. During the period 1963–1993, statistics from the Food and Agriculture Organization of the United Nations (FAO) suggest that sorghum production grew at an annual rate of 1.4 percent and millet production at a rate of 2 percent. Sorghum productivity was essentially stagnant over that same period, with yields growing from an average of 720 kilograms per hectare during 1962–1965 to only 740 kilograms per hectare in 1990–1993. Millet performance was only marginally better, with yields growing 17 percent over the 30-year period, from 580 kilograms per hectare in 1962–1965 to 680 kilograms per hectare in 1990–1993.

The Natural Environment

Environmental constraints underlie these patterns but vary significantly across the four major agroclimatic zones found within the WASAT. Climatic

TABLE 16.1 Land and population characteristics of the major agroclimatic zones in the West African semi-arid tropics

	Sahelian	Sahelo-Sudanian	Sudanian	Sudano-Guinean
Annual rainfall[a] (millimeters)	<350	350–600	600–800	800–1,100
Total area (percent)	24	30	21	24
Cultivable soils (percent)	29	30	37	42
Population (percent)				
Rural	18	20	56	6
Total	16	19	59	6
Rural population density (persons per square kilometer)				
Cultivable	24	67	51	21
Total	7	20	19	9

SOURCE: World Bank 1985.
[a]0.9 probability isohyets.

constraints are most limiting in the Sahel and decline in importance in the Sudanian and Guinean zones (Table 16.1). These include a short unimodal rainy season, high intraseasonal rainfall variability, and high rainfall intensity. The loamy sands of the Sahelian zone and sandy loams of the Sudanian and Guinean zones are low in phosphorus, nitrogen, and organic matter, are structurally inert, tend to cap, and are susceptible to acidification and erosion under continuous cultivation. These properties result in generally low water-holding capacity and poor fertilizer-use efficiency. Because the climatic and edaphic constraints tend to be closely correlated across agroclimatic zones, technical potential is greatest in the Sudano-Guinean zone and declines systematically moving north.

Farming Systems

Farming systems closely reflect these environmental differences. Extensive migratory livestock rearing is the dominant agricultural activity in the Sahelian zone, with subsistence cropping limited primarily to millet and fonio with little marketable surplus potential. In the Sahelo-Sudanian zone, millet, cowpeas, fonio, and groundnuts are the major upland crops. Sorghum is of secondary importance, grown primarily in lowland portions of the landscape and on upland soils in the more southern margin of the zone. The Sudanian zone is an area of transition between millet- and sorghum-based systems. Maize, groundnut, cowpea, and cotton are also cultivated, representing up to 25 percent of total cultivated area. Cropping systems are most diversified in the relatively high-potential Sudano-Guinean zone, with significant areas sown to marketed crops such as cotton, maize, rice, cowpeas, groundnuts, and vegetables. Sorghum is replaced by maize as the dominant food staple in the southern portion of this zone. Livestock rearing and nonagricultural employment contribute substantial income shares in each zone. A study in Burkina Faso found that 52 percent, 26 percent, and 57 percent of average total farm household income came from noncrop income sources in the Sahelo-Sudanian, Sudanian, and Sudano-Guinean zones, respectively (Reardon, Delgado, and Matlon 1992).

Devolution of Traditional Land Management Systems

With access to ample surplus land in the past, farmers have traditionally employed extensive bush-fallow land management systems that sustained production at subsistence levels. These low-input systems were an efficient means of maintaining the physical and chemical parameters of the soil. Although the vast majority of farmers continue to use such systems, population growth and market penetration during the past several decades are rendering these systems unsustainable. In areas of most rapid population growth, farmers have already reduced fallow periods below levels necessary to maintain soil quality without increasing soil amendments. Without viable options to meet their food needs, the rural poor are expanding cultivation onto less productive and more easily degraded soil types. These factors are contributing significantly to the stagnant yields noted. A more ominous long-term threat is the steady degradation of the land base, a trend that forecasts declining potential over vast areas of the WASAT in the future.

The Emerging Disequilibrium

Population Carrying Capacities

Recent analyses have attempted to locate and quantify the emerging disequilibrium. FAO researchers compared current and projected populations to potential population supporting capacities (PSCs) at several levels of technology (Higgins, Kassam, and Naiken 1982). They found that with low-input technologies, typical of current production practices, 1975 populations had already exceeded carrying capacity in five of eight semi-arid countries in West Africa, as well as in the semi-arid portions of Nigeria. They predicted that seven of the eight Sahelian countries will exceed PSC by the year 2000.

World Bank researchers using a different method reached similar conclusions (World Bank 1985). Regional imbalances and environmental damage were greatest in the Sahelo-Sudanian zone, despite an average population density of only 20 persons per square kilometer in 1980 (Table 16.2). Although these analyses and the precision of their results can and have been challenged, the conclusions are consistent with location-specific evidence of severe land

TABLE 16.2 Sustainable and actual population densities in the major agroclimatic zones of West Africa (persons per square kilometer)

	Sahelian	Sahelo-Sudanian	Sudanian	Sudano-Guinean
Sustainable population[a]				
Crops	5	10	15	25
Livestock	2	5	7	10
Total	7	15	22	35
Actual 1980 rural population	7	20	19	9
Ratio (actual/sustainable)	1.00	1.33	0.77	0.26
Sustainable population based on fuelwood availability	1	10	20	20
Actual 1980 total population	7	23	21	10
Ratio (actual/sustainable)	7.00	2.30	1.05	0.50

SOURCE: World Bank 1985.
[a]Based on traditional crop and livestock systems.

degradation in the 300–600 millimeters annual rainfall belt (Thomas 1980; NRC 1984).

These results have three important implications. First, they challenge the assumption that the WASAT is a land-surplus region where sustainable increases in production are possible through area expansion. Second, if current farming practices persist in the Sahelo-Sudanian and Sudanian zones, where 84 percent of the rural population of the Sahelian states live, production potential is likely to decline further (Higgins, Kassam, and Naiken 1982). And third, rapidly changing factor endowments are fundamentally altering the economic incentives for adopting different production technologies.

The Potential for Technological Change

Sustainability of New Technological Interventions

Sustainability can be defined with respect to (1) technical, (2) economic, and (3) socioinstitutional viability.

1. Technical sustainability means that new technologies result in reducing or maintaining unit production costs over time without incurring major negative externalities outside these systems.
2. Economic sustainability means that net social returns are competitive and that financial profitability is positive and low-risk, given most probable future price and policy conditions. Economic sustainability also requires poverty alleviation such that the mix of farm and nonfarm activities pursued by rural households assures their livelihood and generates

surplus income that can be allocated to additional productivity-enhancing investments.

3. Socioinstitutional sustainability means that the institutional support requirements for technology adoption demand neither major modifications in social behavior nor levels of managerial or fiscal support that are infeasible for national programs to maintain over time.

These criteria can be applied with varying degrees of rigor to assess the viability of a range of crop production technologies available or under development in the WASAT. We evaluate four sets of technical options: (1) yield-increasing technologies, (2) yield-stabilizing technologies, (3) labor-saving technologies, and (4) land-conserving technologies.

Yield-Increasing Technologies

Yield-increasing technologies include those that increase variable input use to reduce the land needed to produce a given output. The benefits from yield-increasing technologies are directly related to the cost of land saved and inversely related to the opportunity cost of the additional capital or labor employed. Thus these technologies are most appropriate where land is scarce and valued in monetary terms, when cash or credit is not a binding constraint, and when labor is not constraining.

Research results demonstrate that existing techniques can increase yields significantly. From base sorghum grain yields of 500–700 kilograms per hectare under farmers' conditions in the Sudanian zone, yields of up to 1,500 kilograms per hectare can be achieved through plowing and fertilization; up to 3,000 kilograms per hectare combining an improved variety with plowing, fertilization, and tied-ridges; and up to 4,500 kilograms per hectare with an improved variety, plowing, fertilization, and irrigation (Matlon 1990). The key issue, however, is not technical potential but whether these techniques reduce unit production costs when farmers' factor endowments and opportunity costs are considered, and their long-term effects on land quality.

IRRIGATION. Irrigation was a necessary precondition to the seed-fertilizer strategy that dramatically reduced unit costs of producing rice and wheat in many parts of the developing world. Within West Africa, however, economic returns to most large-scale irrigation schemes have been negative (CILSS 1980; FAO 1983). Investment costs range between US$10,000 and US$20,000 per hectare, which is more than three times greater than in Asia (CILSS 1980; World Bank 1981a). Production potential is rarely realized because of poor water control, the absence of double cropping, inappropriate technical packages, inflexible water management practices, and the lack of complementary inputs. As a result, large-scale irrigation schemes in the WASAT generally increase unit production costs significantly above those in rainfed systems.

Environmental, health, social, and institutional problems also threaten the sustainability of large schemes. Inadequate drainage and poor water management have led to increased salinization over expanding areas. Well-known practices can alleviate this problem, but the flat landscape of many of these perimeters makes gravitational drainage difficult and costly. Human health problems associated with irrigated agriculture can also be important. Mosquito populations and malaria incidence have risen rapidly in irrigation schemes along the Senegal River Valley and in the Kou Valley of Burkina Faso because of the creation of water habitats within irrigated plots and canals that are conducive to larvae development (Mounier 1986; Carnevale and Robert 1987). Rising cases of schistosomiasis among persons working in irrigation perimeters along the Senegal River Valley (Velayudhan 1991) and in the Niger River Basin in Mali (Madsen, Coulibaly, and Furu 1987) have also been attributed to increasing snail host populations within irrigation canals.

Finally, experience has shown that most large irrigation schemes require a high degree of cooperation among producers (timing of irrigation activities, canal maintenance, and so forth), which departs from the autonomous production behavior of farming units in rainfed systems. Where irrigation is a relatively new technology, and particularly when diverse social groups are present in a single scheme, social conflicts can render the necessary interhousehold coordination unsustainable (Huibers and Diemar 1991).

In an effort to correct some of these technical and socioinstitutional problems, emphasis in the Sahel has recently shifted to the development of smaller-scale village schemes that place greater water management responsibilities in the hands of individual farmers and farmers' groups. Similarly, management in many large schemes is being transferred to farmers' groups to improve flexibility and secure greater participation in system maintenance. Recent experience suggests the improved technical, institutional, and economic sustainability of these systems (Huibers and Diemar 1991).

Inland valleys in the Sudanian and Guinean-savanna zones represent robust ecosystems that can sustain continuous cropping of high-value crops such as rice and vegetables without suffering environmental degradation. Therefore the development of partial water control systems within inland valleys may be one of the most promising methods to intensify and diversify cropping systems sustainably, while at the same time reducing rainfall-related risks and reducing pressure on more fragile upland ecosystems. The major challenge is to develop low-cost approaches that fit local factor endowments and that are compatible with upland farming systems. Experience suggests that intensification of inland valleys is economically viable primarily in densely populated areas or where markets for high-value farm products are assured.

FERTILIZER. Phosphorus and nitrogen deficiencies are the major soil constraints to increased sorghum and millet production in much of the WASAT. In view of the region's low use of chemical fertilizers, this might suggest large potential demand for fertilizer. Regional fertilizer use per hectare has in fact grown from a low base by nearly 12 percent annually during the period 1963–1993. However, although total fertilizer supplies are likely to continue to increase, regional fertilizer prices are also projected to rise rapidly because of market forces (Bumb 1989) and reduced subsidies resulting from structural adjustment policies.

Among the major cereals, technical response to fertilizer applications is greatest for rice, followed by maize, sorghum, and then millet; for example, average incremental grain-to-nitrogen ratios for these crops are 21.4, 20.4, 9.9, and 5.9, respectively (Matlon 1990). Economic incentives to use fertilizer follow the same order if grain prices are roughly similar across crops. This means that as the cost of fertilizer increases in diversified cropping systems, millet and sorghum will be the first crops for which fertilizer use will become unprofitable. A similar argument holds concerning the allocation of fertilizer across agroclimatic zones. Because technical response is greater where soil moisture is more assured, fertilizer-use efficiency is greater in more humid zones (Matlon 1990), where the share of area sown to sorghum and millet is lowest. In short, significant demand for fertilizer is likely primarily in the Guinean and Sudano-Guinean zones, with applications growing most for maize and rice. Only moderate demand for fertilizer is likely in the Sahelo-Sudanian zone, and very little is likely in the Sahel, except in irrigated schemes.

Equally important is whether reliance on chemical nutrients can sustain improved grain yields over time. Long-term fertility trials in several WASAT countries show that continuous applications of nitrogenous fertilizers on upland fields can reduce the production potential of the soil through acidification and associated toxicities (Pieri 1985; Wilding and Hossner 1989). Although manuring can ameliorate acidic soils by improving buffering capacity and nutrient-use efficiency, limited supply and high costs for transport and application constrain manure use well below required levels.

Greater emphasis needs to be placed on alternative fertilizer management practices that are cheaper, more efficient, and economically sustainable. Natural rock phosphate, which is abundant in the region, may hold considerable promise (Bationo, Christianson, and Mokwunye 1987). Problems of high processing costs, low solubility, highly variable returns, and its powdery nature (which makes it difficult to apply) restrict its use. Although the incorporation of crop residues following harvest can improve soil organic matter and soil structure, this practice is limited by high costs of incorporation and by livestock competition for crop residues (Adesina 1992).

HIGH-YIELDING CULTIVARS. Probably less than 5 percent of total sorghum and millet area in the region is sown to modern cultivars. Underlying this record are the generally poor local adaptation of most introduced materials and the inappropriate objectives that marked regional breeding programs in the past (for example, emphasis on yield potential at high-input levels with inadequate attention to stability and postharvest traits). At economic levels of input use under farmers' management, the yield advantage of most improved sorghum and millet cultivars compared with farmers' varieties rarely exceeds 15 percent and is often negative (Matlon 1985; Andrews 1986).

Sorghum and millet improvement programs in the region have diagnosed these problems and are now giving greater priority to production stability by placing greater emphasis on stress avoidance traits and on tolerance to a range of biotic and abiotic yield loss factors. Local germplasm collections are providing sources for many of these characteristics. However, the average production impact of stress-resistant or stress-avoiding cultivars under low-input management is probably quite small in most years. In the short term, this strategy can reduce downside risks, especially during poor rainfall years (Adesina and Sanders 1991), and permit farmers to expand cultivation onto marginal land types and into marginal agroclimatic zones. But in the longer term, such expansion may accelerate land degradation, unless the new cultivars respond better to improved management thereby increasing incentives for using sustainable intensification practices.

LABOR-INTENSIVE CULTURAL PRACTICES. Projected declining real rural wages and rising land costs (Matlon 1990) will provide incentives to intensify labor use over growing areas of the WASAT. Tied-ridging (constructing small dikes across furrows to create small water catchments) is perhaps the most promising method to increase labor use with greater-than-proportional production increments. On-farm tests have shown that, on moderately heavy soils, returns to labor can be substantially increased even under low-fertility conditions (Purdue University 1986). Average yield increments of 50–100 percent have been measured on-farm when tied-ridges are combined with improved soil fertility to exploit the technical complementarity between soil moisture and improved nutrient status. By reducing runoff, an important secondary benefit is the reduction of erosion on gentle slopes. Tied-ridges are most suitable in the Sudanian and Sahelo-Sudanian zones, as soils are too sandy in the Sahel and rainfall is too high in the Sudano-Guinean zone.

High labor requirements are the major constraint to broad adoption of tied-ridges under agroclimatically suitable conditions. Prototypes of animal-drawn equipment that reduce labor costs have been developed by the International Institute of Tropical Agriculture (IITA) and by the International Crops Research Institute for the Semi-Arid Tropics (ICRISAT), but adaptive research is needed before their adoption potential can be assessed. In the absence of such equipment, the current potential for manual tied-ridging is probably limited to maize, which responds best to improved soil moisture, cultivated on small, highly manured plots adjacent to farm dwellings. In the longer run, changing factor endowments in the most populated parts of the Sahelo-Sudanian and Sudanian zones may make manual tied-ridging sufficiently attractive for large-scale adoption in both sorghum and maize systems.

Yield-Stabilizing Technologies

The primary benefits to yield-stabilizing technologies are reduced production variability and increased average yields as the effects of chronic yield loss factors are mitigated. This technology set includes cultivars resistant to the most common biotic and abiotic stresses and management practices, such as tied-ridging, that reduce periodic soil moisture deficits. Binswanger and Pritchard (1987) have argued that although such traits are relevant for all regions, they are more important in land surplus areas (since no additional chemical or labor inputs are required), in arid conditions where fertilizer efficiency is limited by inadequate soil moisture, and where farm-level cash constraints are most binding.

Breeding programs currently placing greater emphasis on incorporating resistance and tolerance traits in improved cultivars are likely to make significant progress in the near term. Advances can be expected for *Striga* resistance in both millet and sorghum, for mildew resistance in millet, and for drought escape as a range of well-adapted, early-maturing cultivars becomes available. Projecting the production impact of such gains is difficult, as very few rigorous yield-loss assessments are available. It is unlikely, however, that such gains would exceed 10–15 percent of aggregate regional production. Moreover, as already observed, more robust varieties may actually encourage expanded cropping in marginal zones and on fragile land types, thereby accelerating land degradation.

Labor-Saving Technologies

Rainfed farming systems throughout semi-arid West Africa display sharply seasonal patterns of labor use, with peaks generally occurring at land preparation and planting and at first weeding. Technologies that reduce labor use in these operations can increase production through improved timeliness and by allowing area expansion. Herbicides and mechanization are the two principal labor-saving technologies.

HERBICIDES. Although herbicides have been promoted for cash cropping in parts of the Sudano-Guinean zone, their adoption has remained marginal. Limited evidence of herbicide use in sorghum systems suggests that, at current factor costs, manual and animal traction weeding are more profitable (Ogunbile 1980). There may be some potential for profitable herbicide use in land surplus areas with high peak-season wages. But over the long run, increases in population-land ratios will reduce land surplus and lower wages relative to land costs, making the future profitability of chemical weed control doubtful. Herbicide use in subsistence agriculture also raises important questions about the modification of genetic variability of existing weed flora, the development of herbicide-tolerant weeds, and dangers to human and animal health.

MECHANIZATION. Tractorization programs have been introduced in several West African countries beginning in the 1950s but with little success. Field evaluations have concluded that most tractor service schemes have been economically unsustainable because of the high foreign exchange share in initial investments and recurrent costs, chronic maintenance problems, and inadequate yield response to power operations. Large subsidies are generally necessary to create adequate farm-level demand.

Although animal draft power represents an attractive alternative power source, the potential gains from animal power vary by region according to agroclimatic and demographic factors (Pingali, Bigot, and Binswanger 1987; Jaeger and Matlon 1989). Because animal-powered weeding can significantly raise labor productivity during bottleneck periods, there is considerable adoption potential in zones where surplus land permits area expansion. The use of both plowing and weeding equipment can be profitable in land-surplus regions, where the rainy season is sufficiently long to permit plowing without delaying planting and where heavy soils give significant yield response to plowing (Jaeger and Matlon 1989; Adesina 1992). The short rainy season and generally light soils of the Sahel and Sahelo-Sudanian zones strictly limit utilization of animal draft power. Potential is greatest in the Sudano-Guinean zone thanks to its longer growing season, heavier soils, and the presence of cash crops that help relieve the cash constraint to adoption.

The introduction of animal traction into WASAT farming systems can have two opposing impacts on system sustainability. Oxen and donkeys can contribute to improved soil fertility through nutrient recycling and by importing recycled nutrients from grazing natural grasslands (Sanford 1987). Animal carts also reduce the cost of carrying manure to distant fields where the marginal productivity is higher compared with more fertile fields around homesteads. On the other hand, the introduction of animal traction may have negative sustainability effects by permitting the expansion of cultivation onto marginal or fragile land types and by accelerating intensification. Equipped farmers tend to move rapidly toward destumping and grass fallows as a means of improving traction efficiency. In the absence of alternative soil fertility management methods, the decline in fallow period can deplete fertility. An inappropriate use of tillage equipment may also lead to soil structure deterioration and reduced infiltration and may contribute to the occurrence of surface water runoff and erosion (Lal 1991). Although zero tillage has been proposed as an alternative practice on the more structurally active soils of the humid tropics, applicability in the WASAT is doubtful because of differences in soil chemistry and structure (Nicou and Charreau 1985; Hulugalle and Maurya 1991). Shortages of crop residues and the questionable profitability of herbicides pose additional constraints to zero tillage in the WASAT.

Land-Conserving Technologies

Households in poverty are more likely to allocate their scarce resources to conservation practices when there are significant short-term gains from doing so and where the short- and long-term benefits can be appropriated by the household itself. In subregions where population densities and cropping intensity have increased slowly over time, farmers have developed methods to maintain soil chemical status and to stabilize yields at a low level by recycling crop residues, manuring, and using legumes in rotation and as intercrops (Prudencio 1983). More problematic is the degradation of soil physical properties through erosion and associated changes in soil depth and texture, which can accompany intensification.

Techniques to arrest and reverse physical deterioration include a variety of runoff management systems. One of the most promising is the use of permeable bunds constructed of rock or crop residues laid out on contours (Wright 1985). Although a principal benefit is to maintain and enhance the long-term productivity of the land base, these systems can significantly increase yields in the short run by reducing runoff loss of topsoil and organic matter and by increasing water infiltration. Moreover, by improving soil moisture, permeable bunds improve fertilizer-use efficiency and provide immediate complementary yield effects when combined with fertilization and input-responsive cultivars.

Farmers' tests have confirmed that short-term benefits to erosion control and water harvesting systems are higher in the Sahelo-Sudanian zone than in the Sudano-Guinean zone. Greater drought stress, more surface water flow (due to the greater proportion of cleared areas), higher population pressure, and more degraded conditions in the Sahelo-Sudanian zone underlie the zonal differences (ICRISAT 1985).

Synthesis of Potential Gains from Technological Change by Zone

The prospects for significant, sustainable gains in productivity differ across the major zones of the WASAT as a function of agroecological potential, the technical fit of current and prospective technologies, and economic incentives. Table 16.3 summarizes where agricultural research and development can have the most important effects by zone and theme.

The Sahel

There is very limited potential for significantly reducing unit production costs of millet on a sustainable basis in the Sahelian zone. Technologies that dampen the impacts of recurrent drought can reduce downside yield risks somewhat. However, the long-term impact of such technologies can be negative by encouraging expanded cropping in this ecologically fragile zone. Popula-

TABLE 16.3 Prospects for different types of technical change in sorghum and millet production in the West African semi-arid tropics

Agroclimatic Zone	Yield-Increasing Technologies	Labor-Saving Technologies	Yield-Stabilizing Technologies	Land-Conserving Technologies
Sahel zone				
Land-abundant regions	−	−	+ +	+
Land-scarce regions	−	−	+ +	+ +
Sahelo-Sudanian zone				
Land-abundant regions	−	+	+ +	+ +
Land-scarce regions	+	−	+ +	+ + +
Sudanian zone				
Land-abundant regions	−	+ +	+	+
Land-scarce regions	+ +	−	+	+ + +
Sudano-Guinean zone				
Land-abundant regions	+ +	+ + +	+	−
Land-scarce regions	+ + +	+ +	+	+

SOURCE: Matlon 1990.

NOTE: − = No potential for adoption and impact; + = low potential for adoption and impact; ++ = moderate potential for adoption and impact; +++ = high potential for adoption and impact.

tion densities in the Sahel are already at the sustainable margin for crop and livestock activities, and cropping would contribute to already severe zonal desertification. Extensive livestock raising would be a more ecologically sustainable alternative.

The Sahelo-Sudanian Zone

The immediate technical priority in this zone is to arrest rising unit production costs caused by land degradation and the expansion of cultivation onto marginal soils. In areas of moderate to high population pressure, emphasis should be placed on low-cost water runoff management systems, such as permeable bunds, which can increase yields in the short run while enhancing the productivity of the land in the long run. Genetically based stress-reducing and stress-avoiding technologies are either now available or likely to be developed soon. However, these technologies will serve primarily to stabilize yields and prevent further declines in productivity. Only in the most highly populated subregions are large productivity improvements likely through high-input yield-increasing technologies, and these only after the introduction of improved water runoff management.

In less populated areas, investments in both yield-increasing and land-conserving technologies will not be attractive to farmers until population densities rise. In such areas, only stress-avoiding technologies to reduce yield variability will have significant adoption potential, and these will result in only limited yield gains. Fertilizer use will remain low for the foreseeable future throughout this zone. In short, only minor productivity gains are possible over the greater portion of this zone in the medium term.

The Sudanian Zone

Land-conserving and yield-stabilizing technologies are appropriate in most portions of the Sudanian zone. However, where population pressure is higher, there is somewhat greater potential for adoption of yield-increasing packages. In such areas, moderate doses of chemical fertilizer and recurrent applications of organic matter combined with input-responsive cultivars can achieve significant productivity gains, particularly on land types with more assured soil moisture. To improve fertilizer-use efficiency, reduce farmers' risk, and expand use of low-input packages to a wider range of land types, these packages must be preceded by the introduction of water runoff management practices. Because of its greater nutrient and moisture responsiveness, sorghum, rather than millet, will benefit most.

In areas of low to moderate population pressure, there are fewer incentives to invest in land-conserving techniques complementary to low-input intensification packages. Mechanized tied-ridging, once developed, may be an appropriate means to improve soil moisture, thereby permitting low-risk and profitable use of yield-increasing packages. Animal traction mechanization of weeding operations offers some short-term potential for area expansion in land-surplus areas. Continued population growth, however, will largely eliminate these potential gains, possibly within the next two decades, as area expansion will be possible only at the expense of manual farmers or onto marginal land types. Biomass recycling through integrated crop-livestock systems will give greater long-term benefits than if animals are used as a power source alone.

The Sudano-Guinean Zone

The most promising technical options for sustainably improving productivity are found in the Sudano-Guinean zone. With lower population pressure, higher and more assured rainfall, a longer cropping season, and generally better soils, either yield-increasing or labor-saving techniques can be profitably adopted, with the choice of technique being a function of local factor endowments. Ironically, the highly diversified cropping systems of this zone also pose the major constraint to substantial improvements in sorghum or millet production. In areas where mechanization has led to area expansion within the Sudano-Guinean zone, as in southern Mali and southwestern Burkina Faso, farmers have found it more profitable to expand the cultivation of cash crops such as cotton rather than sorghum or millet. Where environmental conditions permit, as farmers begin to intensify through improved soil preparation and fertilizer use, they give first priority to maize and cotton rather than to sorghum or millet, which respond less to the improved management. This suggests that as population growth induces intensification, sorghum improvement programs must develop substantially improved input responsiveness if sorghum is to remain competitive.

Priorities for Sustainable Technical Change

Policymakers face difficult decisions in allocating scarce research and development resources among zones, between crops, and among technical themes. Guiding these decisions are (1) efficiency criteria that give priority to interventions for which net benefits are larger and can be achieved earlier, (2) equity criteria that give priority to improving and stabilizing real incomes of the poor and that can be achieved earlier, and (3) sustainability criteria that place greater priority on zones where environmental degradation is most advanced and on interventions that enhance and protect natural resource quality over time.

Zonal Priorities

Applying efficiency criteria alone, the more favorable factor endowments of the Sudano-Guinean zone mean that the largest and most sustainable payoffs from the application of existing technologies as well as from research are most likely to occur in that zone. Regional equity criteria focused uniquely on producer incomes would suggest emphasis on more arid and marginal zones. However, the poorest producers are also generally deficit cereal producers (Reardon, Matlon, and Delgado 1988), and the shares of cereals in food budgets of both the rural and urban poor are extremely high. Thus, from a societal and interpersonal perspective, equity goals may also be best served by investing in the higher-potential areas in order to reduce the real cost of cereals within the region as a whole. Similar arguments would give sorghum higher priority than millet, and rice and maize higher priority than either sorghum or millet.

Sustainability criteria suggest a two-pronged approach. First, priority should be given to productivity-enhancing research and development in more favorable environments and ecosystems, particularly in the Sudano-Guinean zone, where the pressure on natural resources is lowest and the land base less fragile, and in favorable lowland ecosystems of the Sahelo-Sudanian and Sudanian zones. Second, research and development targeting upland land types in more arid zones should aim to arrest and reverse the environmental decline, and create incentives for activities that are more compatible with the fragile natural resource base, such as extensive livestock production and nonagricultural employment.

Integrating Sustainability Concerns

A fundamental reorientation is required toward the development and extension of farming practices that improve productivity in the short term while maintaining or enhancing land quality over time. We can identify three sets of research activities to achieve this.

1. *Diagnosis of sustainability problems.* To define the criteria for measuring sustainability and design corrective interventions, it is necessary first to understand how production systems evolve over time and to identify those factors most susceptible to long-term degradation. This can be done by characterizing and monitoring representative production systems in key sites and by conducting long-term trials to measure the impact of cropping systems on land productivity. Emphasis for these studies should be in high-risk zones, in particular in the Sudanian zone, and in areas of most rapid population growth in the Sudano-Guinean zone, which could come under threat through rural-rural migration.

2. *"Active" or targeting approaches.* Identification and diagnosis of sustainability problems are relatively straightforward for those zones and cropping systems where productivity is visibly declining, where major negative externalities are already evident, or where complementary socio-institutional support systems cease to function. The objective of active sustainability research is to arrest and reverse such breakdowns by developing new technical interventions to correct the causes of system failures. Such research should be concentrated in the Sahelo-Sudanian zone and should target soil erosion, soil fertility management, and deforestation as priority issues.

3. *"Passive" technology screening approaches.* The objective of passive approaches is to avoid the development and release or expansion of new technologies that are not sustainable. This can be done by (1) an a priori exclusion of research on technological themes known to be unsustainable, and (2) systematically testing prospective technologies to eliminate those that violate sustainability criteria.

A PRIORI EXCLUSION OR SELECTION. Diagnostics research has already identified interventions that are not sustainable for either socioeconomic or technical reasons. These include (1) reliance on chemical means to maintain soil fertility and for pest control; (2) large-scale, capital-intensive irrigation schemes; and (3) plowing of highly erodible soils. Experience also demonstrates that sustainable adoption is greater for technologies that (1) exploit on-farm resources and depend less on external inputs, (2) involve incremental changes to current farming systems rather than requiring radical restructuring of factor use and production patterns, (3) employ simple rather than multiple-component packages, and (4) allow farmers to pursue better management strategies. Research should emphasize these characteristics in the development of new technology options.

TESTING FOR SATISFACTION OF SUSTAINABILITY CRITERIA. Where symptoms of system decline are not yet evident, screening technologies for sustainability criteria is difficult because of the long time frame normally required to measure loss of total system productivity. An important output of diagnostic research is the identification of short-term indicators of longer-term sustainability problems. Although various soils measures, such as soil organic measure and soil acidity, have been suggested, much more work is necessary.

Expanding the Policy Alternatives

Although this chapter focuses on agricultural technology, we conclude by emphasizing that poverty alleviation and sustainable rural development in the WASAT cannot be achieved through development of new technologies alone. Policy change is also required to help farm households escape the cycle of impoverishment and resource mining in which they are trapped. Alternative diversified employment opportunities are crucial to generate surplus income and to reduce pressure on cropping in areas of high environmental risk.

Policy actions in four areas should be explored: (1) restructuring agricultural subsidies, (2) generating nonagricultural employment within poorly endowed, high-risk areas, (3) encouraging resettlement of populations from low- to high-potential areas, and (4) improving market infrastructure.

1. *Restructuring subsidies.* Policies on agricultural input pricing and subsidies should be reexamined to bring factor costs more in line with socially optimal resource allocation patterns. Incentives should be reduced for inputs with negative externalities (for example, chemical nitrogen sources that increase soil acidity) and increased for those with positive externalities (for example, rock phosphate, and especially animal carts to lower the cost of organic fertilization and of bund construction). Food-for-work programs to construct bunds during the dry season should also be considered.

2. *Noncropping employment.* Policies to attract labor in high-risk zones *out* of farming and into noncropping employment should also be explored. Incentives for extensive livestock production and nonagricultural employment in the Sahelian and Sahelo-Sudanian zones could include a range of credit, price, and institutional support mechanisms.

3. *Migration.* The low zonal correlation between population densities and production potential suggests that migration from low- to high-potential areas can reduce environmental degradation and increase aggregate production. Although experience in the WASAT demonstrates the costly and complex nature of population resettlement across political and ethnic borders (McMillan, Painter, and Scudder 1990), policies to encourage larger flows of directed migration deserve serious consideration.

4. *Infrastructure.* Finally, major investments to improve rural transport and market infrastructure are urgently required to reduce interzone grain price

differences. Lower prices in traditionally deficit grain-producing zones (which are also at greatest environmental risk) would create incentives to shift resources out of subsistence cropping activities. Higher relative grain prices in grain-surplus areas (which are at low environmental risk) would improve incentives to attract migrants and provide an incentive for the expansion and intensification of agriculture in high-potential zones of the WASAT.

17 Prospects for Pastoralism in Semi-Arid Africa

PATRICK WEBB AND D. LAYNE COPPOCK

Sub-Saharan Africa's semi-arid regions (including the the Sahel, Rift Valley, and Kalahari basin) represent almost one-quarter of the continent's land area and contain the highest density of livestock and agriculturally active people of all ecological zones apart from the humid highlands (Jahnke 1982; Skoupy 1988). At the same time, these regions are characterized by a high concentration of poverty in both socioeconomic and natural resource terms. Almost 60 percent of the continent's absolute poor are located in areas of low and variable rainfall, infertile soils, and sparse vegetation (Broca and Oram 1991).[1] Such conditions severely constrain the potential for growth in crop cultivation (Sivakumar et al. 1991; Matlon and Adesina, Chapter 16, this volume). In this chapter we therefore discuss whether a workable strategy for sustainable growth and poverty alleviation for semi-arid Africa can instead be based on pastoralism.

There are three main reasons for a separate chapter focusing on pastoral issues. First, constraints facing pastoralists differ from those facing farmers and require different solutions. Based on extensive mobility and ecological opportunism, pastoralism is a socioeconomic system in which households derive more than 50 percent of their income from livestock products and a substantial part of their diet from home-produced milk, meat, and blood

We gratefully acknowledge detailed reviews of earlier drafts by Joachim von Braun, Thomas Reardon, Yohannes Habtu, and Girma Bisrat. The authors also thank Rajul Pandya-Lorch for her editorial input.

1. The key characteristics of semi-arid areas in which pastoralism is concentrated include low precipitation (average annual rainfall of 150–400 millimeters), high intra- and interyear fluctuations in precipitation (coefficients of variation of up to 50 percent), a short growing period (usually less than 150 days), shallow soils of low fertility (clay and organic matter content usually less than 1 percent, with limited moisture retention), and a sparse, specialized vegetative cover adapted to each of the above (Matlon 1987; Ellis and Swift 1988; Sollod 1990).

(Monod 1975; Sandford 1983; Ellis and Swift 1988). These systems capitalize on the ability to transform scarce, open-access common property resources into private economic goods and calories via the agency of livestock.[2] Thus policy- or technology-based remedies for low or declining productivity in such systems are often different from those appropriate for populations deriving income primarily from cultivation.

Second, the strengths of pastoralism are being eroded. There is widespread concern that combined effects of drought, population growth, territorial contraction, and inappropriate development have been leading to a conflict over diminishing resources and the breakdown of traditional systems (Hogg 1985; Bonfiglioli 1988; af Ornas 1990; Bascom 1990). The outcome is increased poverty and food insecurity among the poor, increased vulnerability to future climatic and economic shocks, and accelerated environmental degradation that may ultimately compromise sustainability of dryland cultivation and pastoralism (IGADD 1990; Stone 1991). This widely documented transition calls for urgent attention if protecting traditional elements of pastoralism is seen as a policy priority.

Third, the question of whether governments and donors should act to preserve pastoralism as a way of life remains to be settled. Although broad agreement exists on the conditions required for growth and poverty alleviation among farming communities (such as improved market infrastructure, producer incentives, credit support, and crop research and extension), no such agreement exists with regard to pastoral systems. Debate continues over basic issues such as destocking versus restocking policies, land enclosure versus open-access grazing, and sedentarization versus continued nomadism. Thus effective development strategies for pastoral communities remain elusive.

In this chapter we describe the key characteristics of African pastoralism and the underlying pressures that serve to transform such systems and then examine the potential for achieving growth and sustainability through pastoralism. Growth is defined here in terms of an enhanced asset base rather than income. The former, measured as per capita livestock wealth, is an aggregate expression of capital accumulation that fluctuates less than per capita income across seasons and years. The strength of the asset base is, however, a proxy for income and is closely associated with poverty alleviation. Sustainability in this context is a two-pronged goal aimed, on the one hand, at promoting household food security (via stable per capita milk production) and, on the other hand, at guaranteeing the capacity of the natural resource base to support pastoral activities in the long run. Both objectives are interrelated, and the key to both is risk reduction. We argue that it is premature to contemplate sustained

---

2. For present purposes, we include nomadic and semisedentary pastoralists in this definition but exclude agropastoralists (who have a primary interest in farming) and commercial ranchers.

economic growth through pastoralism until current risks to human and biological degradation (both a symptom and a cause of poverty) have been reduced.

Traditional Pastoral Systems

Although husbandry systems vary in cultural and organizational terms, several common features characterize traditional production strategies across semi-arid Africa.

1. Milk production is arguably the central function of pastoral livestock holdings. Milk forms an important part of the diet, its share ranging from 25 to 76 percent of total consumption according to season and ethnic group (Bernus 1980; Donaldson 1986; Grandin 1987). Beyond milk and meat production, livestock are used for traction, fiber and manure production, transport, investment, and insurance, and they are a source of income.
2. Pastoral herds usually include more than one animal species. Large ruminants form the core of most herds, but small ruminants are also kept because of their higher reproductive rates and greater disposability through sale when cash is required (Dahl and Hjort 1979; Wienpahl 1985; Mace 1990). Small ruminants are more disposable because their sale is usually left to the discretion of the individual, whereas the sale of large ruminants can be an event of wider importance to the community that requires consultation before action.
3. Herd mobility is central to both nomadic and seminomadic husbandry systems. Herds seek seasonal vegetative growth, capitalizing on water and grazing when and where these are available (Monod 1975; Jahnke 1982). Alternatively, milk-producing and young animals can be kept at a central point (water sources or enclosures, such as the dispersed "cattle-posts" of Botswana), while older animals graze on long-range loops around that point (Donaldson 1986; Oba and Lusigi 1987; Perkins 1991).
4. Complex systems of collective land and water management have been developed to share limited resources. Although most pastoral territories are communally used, individual access to grazing land is commonly controlled by clan authorities. In other words, the lack of private tenure rights to pastoral land does not imply unbridled exploitation of those lands by individual households. For example, the Fulani and WoDaaBe of Niger and the Borana of Ethiopia allocate "well keepers" responsible for arranging the time schedule and duration of watering periods allowed for each clan and household around an individual well (Cossins 1985; Thebaud 1988).

These features of traditional pastoralism have lent themselves to an opportunistic utilization of resources in regions of relatively low population density. Such low-input, low-output systems rely on few modern technologies, and labor (for herding and watering animals) is often the main factor of production. Of course, they do not operate without constraints. Choices about herd composition, consumption and expenditure patterns, and herd mobility have always taken place within clearly prescribed physical, sociopolitical, and territorial limits (Monod 1975). Physical limits are set by the distributional patterns of resource availability, as well as by the prevalence of parasites and epizootic diseases. Sociopolitical limits are defined by rules set in clan councils as noted earlier. Territorial limits are set by proximity of other pastoral groups and settled agriculturalists.

The greatest challenge facing pastoralists at the end of the twentieth century is how to cope with ever more stringent limits to activity in each of these spheres. The potential for herd mobility is decreasing as a result of competition over land, which forces sociopolitical regulations to become more restrictive. At the same time, competition for and stresses on natural resources within current physical limits appear to be rising (de Haan 1990; Stone 1991). Thus as internal constraints increase, the extensive, low-input features of pastoralism become more difficult to sustain.

Underlying Forces of Change

Three main factors are commonly associated with recent changes in traditional pastoral systems: population growth, resource poverty and drought, and territorial contraction.

Population Growth

Although pastoral communities are believed to experience lower population growth rates than farming communities, many groups find it difficult to match their increasing population with the milk supply necessary for consumption. Their growth rates of 2.0–2.5 percent per year (compared with 3.0–3.5 percent among cultivators) are still 50 percent above livestock growth (INSEE 1973; Ware 1977; Anteneh 1984). Growth in livestock numbers is in turn constrained by ecological limits on forage availability; the net result can be a decline in per capita livestock holdings (Coppock 1994).

Population growth drives other factors, especially urban growth and expansion of the cropping frontier. There has recently been rapid expansion of small towns along roads in semi-arid zones (af Ornas 1990; Coppock 1994). This appears to be driven by a rise in commercial activity among pastoralists (pastoral trade links between Ethiopia, Kenya, and Somalia are strong), a tendency for younger male and destitute adult pastoralists to move to towns for employment (either seasonally or on a more permanent basis), and emigration from adjacent regions of higher population density (usually highlands).

Such growth improves the availability of services and goods to pastoralists and permits a degree of employment diversification (Holden,

Coppock, and Assefa 1991). On the other hand, it also increases local demand for fuel products, which leads to deforestation, soil erosion, and depletion of water tables. It also raises demand for food, thereby encouraging expansion of the cropping frontier and possible loss of grazing lands.

Continued high levels of population growth in areas with limited employment opportunities (either within or outside the pastoral zone) remain one of the key contributors to household vulnerability, which hampers both poverty alleviation and growth.

Resource Poverty and Drought

Ninety-one percent of the roughly 500 million hectares of semi-arid land in Sub-Saharan Africa is classified as having inherent soil constraints for farm production, and an even larger share has water constraints (WRI 1990b). Thus not only is the potential low for expansion of cropped area in such regions, but forage and water resources for livestock are also limited. These constraints are compounded by a harsh and unpredictable climate, which bears its severest expression in drought. The latter hurts pastoralists by further reducing water and grazing during dry years and by facilitating the spread of disease (Sollod 1990; Webb, von Braun, and Yohannes 1992).

Although the extent, trend, and degree of natural resource degradation continues to be debated, it is widely argued that degradation is a serious problem in many dry regions.[3] These debates have been tempered by arguments that in areas receiving less than 300 millimeters of annual rainfall, trends in plant and soil resources are determined more by climatic factors than by human agency, the converse holding true for areas receiving more than 500 millimeters of rainfall (Ellis and Swift 1988; Behnke and Scoones 1991).

This remains an open research question with important policy ramifications, as the role of pastoralists in degradation is highly controversial. Pastoralists have been widely blamed for overstocking, trampling of soils around water points (which reduces soil porosity and increases runoff), destruction of woodland through burning (intended to stimulate green regrowth), and prevention of organic buildup in the soil by feeding crop residues to animals (Lamprey 1983; World Bank 1985; FAO 1987b; OECD 1988; Stryker 1989).

Others argue, however, that traditional systems are well adapted to their environment, are economically efficient given current operating constraints, and are not destructive until put under pressure (Monod 1975; Cossins 1985; Hogg 1992). Although the potentially destructive impact of large, concentrated herds on natural resources is recognized, it is argued that the cause of con-

---

3. Resource degradation can be defined as the decline in biological productivity of a tract of land as characterized by decreased herbaceous cover, increased occurrence of undesired forage species, bush encroachment, soil erosion, depletion of soil nutrients, soil compaction, or falling water table (Glantz 1977; Mortimore 1988; OECD 1988).

centration is population growth, which, in the absence of economic opportunity, contributes to poverty where the resource base cannot be increased.

Competition for resources is heightened during drought, when pastoralists suffer four important setbacks: a reduction in milk supply as water and grazing become scarce; an erosion of their purchasing power through deteriorating livestock-grain terms of trade; capital losses through high livestock mortality; and increasing competition for declining resources from nomadic and transhumant pastoralists based in drier areas who move into relatively moister zones in search of grazing (Moris 1988; Riely 1991).

It is important to note that livestock losses often affect the poor proportionately more than the wealthy, resulting not only in increasing destitution among poorest households but also in a widening gap between upper and lower income groups (Horowitz and Little 1987; Sperling 1987; Webb and Reardon 1992).

Territorial Contraction

Competition over pastoral lands is nothing new. Cropping has encroached into and retreated from pastoral zones for centuries according to prevailing rainfall and political conditions (Caldwell 1975; Monod 1975). However, losses of territory by pastoralists have become increasingly permanent during the past few decades. Even where institutional attempts have been made to safeguard the grazing rights of pastoralists, expansion of the agricultural margin has been difficult to control (Horowitz and Little 1987). For example, loss of grazing lands to cropping has been high around flood-retreat pastures that have become priority areas for irrigation development (World Bank 1985; Swift 1988). According to Moris (1988:13), "virtually all of Africa's major irrigation schemes have been located in what had been critical dry season grazing for pastoralists." Most projects have been designed to increase national crop production, with little regard to the needs of local pastoralists.

In Ethiopia, for example, more than 65,000 hectares of land bordering the Awash and Wabi Shebele Rivers were converted in the 1970s and 1980s from dry season grazing into irrigated farms (Bondestam 1974; Gamaledinn 1987). Some areas were made available to pastoralists wishing to settle and become farmers, but most plots took the form of state and commercial farms. The area lost by pastoralists could have supported some 20,000 units of livestock during the dry season (Bisrat 1990).

Some irrigation projects have been designed to provide distressed pastoralists with alternative sources of income, but few of these have been successful. In northern Kenya, for example, projects have been initiated since the 1960s to reduce the number of people surviving primarily on pastoralism. However, few pastoralists were attracted to such schemes, and the main beneficiaries have been farmers arriving from neighboring regions. This unplanned influx of population resulted in deforestation, expansion of farming into grazing areas, and overgrazing around new wells (Hogg 1988).

Nonirrigated cultivation in marginal lands has also expanded in recent years. In Niger, total area under cultivation increased by more than 1 million hectares between 1976 and 1986, but 40 percent of this expansion was made at the expense of fallow land and pastoral grazing grounds (Niger 1991). Part of this expansion is driven by increasing competition over land among non-pastoral communities. But some of it is linked to the sedentarization of pastoralists through development schemes or pauperization (as in Botswana and Kenya), or where pastoralists adopt cropping as a means of diversifying their sources of food energy (as in Ethiopia).

The result of these trends is that pastoralists are forced to operate within contracting boundaries, changing long-standing migration patterns and concentrating activity around water points as demand for grazing and water rises. This increases conflict over diminishing resources, not only between pastoralists and farmers but among pastoralists themselves (Dahl and Hjort 1979; Stryker 1989).

Pastoral Adaptations to Changing Circumstances

Given these increasing constraints on pastoral activity, what has been the response of households most affected? Many studies have concluded that the coping capacity of many pastoral groups has recently been stretched almost to its limits (Grandin 1987; Walker 1988; Coppock 1994). The combined effects of climatic uncertainties, population growth, and territorial contraction on systems whose capital reserves are especially vulnerable to pressures have been similar in many countries.

First, resource competition causes exploitation of increasingly marginal areas. For example, many groups are now obliged to use traditional "drought reserve" pastures during normal dry seasons because of a lack of grazing (Sollod 1991; Coppock 1994). This restricts resources available for drought years, resulting in higher livestock mortality at an earlier stage of a crisis.

Second, grazing lands are being physically enclosed. This is still a localized phenomenon and is essentially an indigenous response rather than the result of external intervention. Nevertheless, in Zimbabwe, Ethiopia, and Mali, there are signs that small plots, often linked to water sources, are being fenced to protect dry season grazing (Toulmin 1983; Behnke 1986; Thebaud 1988).

Third, livestock diversification is increasing. Although many households traditionally maintain a mix of large and small ruminants, the ratio is widely shifting toward small ruminants and sometimes toward more expensive, but more drought-resistant, camels (Mace 1990; Stone 1991). This action has the advantage of diversifying forage requirements and of making short-term disposal of stock easier.

Fourth, nonagricultural activities are increasingly being adopted, such as trade in cloth, tea, sugar, and even electronic goods by individuals who serve as middle agents between towns and remote rural areas. Of course, trade has always been central to the pastoral economy. Predatory activities (raiding, slaving) and long-distance trade (salt, gold) have long been associated with pastoral societies. Today, local commerce and craft activities predominate, and these take on increasing budgetary significance as towns expand. Some men stay in towns and adopt nonpastoral employment on a permanent basis for want of a more secure income (Snow 1984; Anderson and Woodrow 1990). Women, on the other hand, trade milk and its products from pastoral camps within 20 kilometers of towns (Holden, Coppock, and Assefa 1991). Dairy sales used to be regarded as taboo in many pastoral societies (Dahl and Hjort 1979).

Fifth, farming is becoming a stronger complement or alternative to pastoralism. Most governments discourage the expansion of cultivation in marginal areas, fearing an acceleration of soil degradation that would threaten the long-term sustainability of both pastoral and cropping activities (OECD 1988). However, in favorable areas, agropastoralism has already taken hold. On the Borana plateau of southern Ethiopia, for example, pastoral households cultivate maize and sometimes cowpeas (Coppock 1991; Webb and von Braun 1994). Whereas in the past it was the poorest who turned to farming (with a view to replacing livestock lost during drought), today even wealthy pastoralists adopt agropastoralism on a semipermanent basis (Riely 1991). In Ethiopia, farming has expanded in river valleys where soils are more fertile, the techniques being copied from peri-urban farmers (Coppock 1994). Animal traction (both camel and oxen) has gained currency since the mid-1980s, and some households now seek seeds of improved crop varieties.

These indigenous adaptations have been widely reported, but few of them hold the potential for generating sustainable growth in the long term. Reduced herd mobility based on wet season exploitation of former grazing and water reserves increases the risk of future herd collapse during drought. The provision of fodder from enclosed plots of land, and increasing emphasis on small versus large stock, may sustain existing population levels for a short time (assuming distributional equality in land access and control), but degradation of grazing resources can be expected where population rises. Also, vulnerability to drought is increased because the opportunistic harvesting of food and water by mobile herds becomes restricted.

The shift to urban employment provides a short-term palliative by reducing population pressure within the pastoral system. Yet this option is limited because pastoralists tend to be unskilled and therefore uncompetitive in urban labor markets.

Farming in semi-arid areas also remains a limited option. In the absence of large-scale irrigation development (which has proven costly and often unsustainable in Africa; see Matlon and Adesina, Chapter 16, this volume) and major, as yet unanticipated, gains in millet and sorghum yields, cropping will be restricted to favored valley floors and riverbanks. This restricts the absorptive capacity of cropping activities.

In other words, although indigenous responses to change have allowed pastoralism to survive, albeit in a modified form, the contradictions inherent in these responses underline the uncertainty of long-term survival. Of course, pastoralists are supremely adaptable; they have been coping with pressures on their social and economic systems for centuries (Starr 1987). But traditional coping mechanisms are increasingly overwhelmed by current pressures. The poor, in particular, exposed to herd loss through drought, productivity losses through limitations on resource access, and income loss through large fluctuations in livestock-grain terms of trade, are often less food-secure in the 1990s than they were just two decades ago (IGADD 1990; Stone 1991; Hogg 1992).

This raises the question of what role policy or program interventions might play in reducing such risk, particularly by supporting sustainable growth and poverty alleviation. Is pastoralism a viable vehicle for such aims in semi-arid Africa? In the following sections we consider this question, first with a brief overview of past intervention experiences and then with a discussion of a possible agenda for future interventions.

Past Policy and Program Interventions

The track record of livestock development initiatives in semi-arid Africa is not enviable. There is a consensus that the majority of initiatives between 1960 and 1990 met with limited success at best (Swift and Maliki 1984; Hogg 1985). Indeed, many initiatives are blamed for causing more problems than they solved (Snow 1984; Ellis and Swift 1988). Most interventions can be grouped into three main categories: those designed to introduce new technologies; those aimed at improving the management of rangeland resources; and those intended for promoting alternative uses of pastoral lands.

Technological Approaches

Many policies and projects have been based on the assumption that a significant improvement in livestock and rangeland productivity per capita could be brought about if appropriate technical innovations were introduced to and adopted by pastoralists. A number of such innovations have achieved some success.

1. Vaccination and veterinary campaigns have achieved significant control of major epizootic diseases (such as rinderpest, blackleg, and anthrax) and livestock pests (ticks), opening up underused lands in countries such as Burkina Faso, Nigeria, and Zimbabwe and reducing the risks of previously deadly livestock epidemics (Swift 1988; Barrett 1989).

2. Construction of boreholes, ponds, and wells has been one of the most simple and effective interventions to safeguard and expand access to forage supplies (Bille and Eshete 1983; Sandford 1983).
3. Forage supplements, such as crop residues, grass hay, and cultivated legumes, have shown potential for maintaining and even improving calf nutrition (Coppock 1991; Coppock and Reed 1992).

However, despite proven technical feasibility, few innovations have resulted in large-scale improvements in pastoral productivity. Various reasons for this failing can be cited.

1. Most vaccination and parasite reduction activities have proven to be unsustainable because key products are imported and delivery systems have tended to function well only intermittently. To be effective, such activities need to be supported by extensive delivery, extension, and monitoring services, all of which are constrained by central government funding, limited institutional coordination, and lack of training (UNECA 1985; Brokken and Williams 1990). In Ethiopia, for example, acaricide for dipping against ticks and drugs for vaccination against foot-and-mouth were unavailable for much of the 1980s and early 1990s because of foreign exchange constraints and the limited coverage of veterinary services.
2. Proliferation of closely spaced water points has been criticized for encouraging concentrations of livestock that result in overgrazing, soil compaction, and erosion (Moris 1988).
3. "Drought-proofing" of the pastoral economy has not occurred because most innovations aim to raise productivity rather than reduce risk (Hogg 1992). For example, services tend to be curtailed during severe drought because of other urgent demands on funds and personnel (von Braun 1991a). Although water points provide some assistance during drought, they do not reduce competition for grazing resources, which is equally crucial to livestock survival.
4. The focus of the interventions has tended, until recently, to be on cattle (for meat or export) almost to the exclusion of small ruminants and camels, and on the introduction of exotic animal and browse species rather than on enhancement of indigenous resources (Moris 1988; Swift 1988; Coppock 1994).

Management Approaches

The second category of interventions was designed to improve the management of existing technologies and resources through institution- and incentive-building. This approach assumed that creation of state and semi-autonomous organizations would provide the framework for enabling an improvement in both livestock production and marketing (Sandford 1983).

However, the performance of such statals, parastatals, and extension agencies has been generally disappointing. High marketing costs (largely due to high transportation costs and taxes), governments' inability to provide price incentives for high-quality output, rapid deterioration of abattoir and holding ground facilities, a focus on meat rather than milk production, and lack of consideration of risk reduction in the pastoral system have all played a role in this disappointing performance (UNECA 1985; Swift 1988; Riely 1991).

A further problem has been the scanty public financing provided in support of the commercialization of pastoral livestock production when compared with the cropping sector (Moris 1988; IGADD 1990). This has frequently left the burden of pastoral development to donor agencies, which cannot make sectoral policy decisions required in support of their projects.

The other major thrust of the "improved management" approach has been encouragement of better management of existing rangeland resources by the households that use them. This has taken two forms: (1) creation of herders associations or grazing groups that regulate stocking rates, rotational grazing systems, and use of grazing blocks or cells (UNECA 1985; Lawry 1987); and (2) a focus on land tenure issues.

The enclosure of rangeland and its allocation to individuals or groups have been components of many projects (Oxby 1982; Behnke 1985a). This idea derives from Hardin's (1968) elaboration on the potential contradiction between group and individual interests wherever pastoral resources are held in common but animals are privately owned. The "tragedy of the commons" theory has influenced practitioners for two decades to embrace the idea of "privatizing the commons."

Yet, despite considerable effort, few projects based on enclosure, fencing, or private land tenure have been successful (Behnke 1985a; Bromley and Cernea 1989). Because different pastoral clans lay claim to tracts of "common" land, "common" property regimes do not preclude the functioning of community rules governing resource management; that is, an open-access regime cannot be equated with free-for-all access to grazing and water resources (Brown and Harris 1992).

There is now a strong current of thought that opposes the private enclosure principle (Bennett, Lawry, and Riddell 1986; Ellis and Swift 1988; Bromley and Cernea 1989). According to McCay and Acheson (1987), the tragedy theory fails to differentiate between common property as a hypothetical condition in which institutionalized mechanisms for controlling users do not exist and common property as a social asset managed by recognized rules of social interaction. Bhattarcharya (1990) also argues that the "tragedy" model inadequately reflects the real problem because it does not "deal with the complexities involved in multiperson [relationships]." It is therefore argued that traditional tenure and access rights should serve as the foundation for any program of rangeland management (Swift 1991; Hogg 1992).

Alternative Land Use Approaches

The third category of interventions has been the promotion of alternative, nontraditional systems of land use. One alternative has been the development of wildlife reserves. Many countries pursue wildlife conservation through the demarcation of zones from which pastoralists are excluded. Ethiopia, following the lead of Kenya and Zimbabwe, has established 12 wildlife reserves and 8 national parks. The problem is that few employment alternatives are made available to displaced pastoralists whose territories are further limited (Pratt and Gwynne 1977; Gamaledinn 1987; Bisrat 1990).

The same displacement effect occurs when grazing lands are developed for irrigated agriculture (Bondestam 1974; Hogg 1985). Although some schemes attempt to involve former pastoralists, many do not. In addition, investment and running costs of irrigation projects in Africa have proven to be very high and frequently unsustainable (von Braun, Puetz, and Webb 1989; Webb 1991).

Another approach has been the development of commercial ranching. There is a long history of commercial ranching in less arid regions of southern and eastern Africa, where capital-intensive beef production has been established for urban consumption and export needs (Jahnke 1982). This production option, long favored by policymakers concerned with productivity growth and foreign exchange earnings, underlines the incongruence between national and local (pastoral) development objectives. The use of cash income generated by livestock sales as an indicator of growth does not match the pastoralists' emphasis on risk reduction through capital accumulation.

But few large ranches have registered good performances, largely because of marketing constraints, exchange rate disincentives, export quotas, and droughts (Behnke 1985b). By contrast, recent studies have confirmed the relative economic efficiency of traditional pastoralism when compared with modern ranching if the full value of livestock products and services is accounted for (Behnke 1985b; de Ridder and Wagenaar 1986; Scoones 1992). There is therefore a question mark over the long-term viability of capital-intensive livestock enterprises in drier areas, regardless of equity issues involved (Jahnke 1982; Moris 1988).

In sum, agricultural growth based on conventional development interventions aimed at increased meat commercialization has not been effective. Few attempts at changing production technologies, management techniques, or land use have succeeded in either raising overall productivity or reducing poverty among pastoralists. The result of such failure, in conjunction with human population growth, has been increased, rather than decreased, food insecurity among pastoralists. This points to the need for a new approach to the development of semi-arid lands based more than in the past on the benefits of low-input, low-output pastoral systems that reduce risk and promote food security.

Prospects for a Pastoral Future

Pastoralism is likely to remain the primary economic activity of drier semi-arid zones for the foreseeable future. No simple, high-impact technologies exist that can make semi-arid environments more productive in the short term. This is a reality that should guide policymaking for the next several years. The question is how to achieve poverty alleviation, growth, and sustainability in such apparently unpromising conditions.

The answer requires a rethinking of objectives. If it is accepted that some form of pastoralism should be supported in order to maintain a relatively large number of people within dry, semi-arid regions, then new policies and programs must focus on reducing the risk of output losses, even at current levels of productivity, rather than on increasing productivity and commercial value per unit of animal. Projects that increase the live-weight of calves or fatten animals to maximize meat production or sales are not necessarily a priority for herders, whose food security strategies generally preclude animal sales except in times of need. Pastoralists commonly accord higher priority to milk production, calf survival, enhanced endurance of mature stock, and improved terms of trade between livestock and grain in their search for household food security.

These local goals can be assisted through policy- and technology-based initiatives. Policy efforts should concentrate on (1) improving household food security; (2) supporting a flow of people out of pastoralism to alternative employment; (3) ensuring long-term sustainability of the natural resource base (upon which both pastoral and nonpastoral activities depend); and only then (4) encouraging economic growth in the pastoral system. All four steps are interrelated, but they need to be addressed in sequential fashion.

Household food security can be assisted by (1) improving the terms of trade between livestock and grain through improved, freer, interregional trade in foodgrains and improved marketing systems for livestock; (2) raising the sensitivity of famine early warning and emergency relief systems to indicators of pastoral stress; (3) decentralizing control over emergency grain reserves in drought-prone regions; (4) improving the poverty-targeting of development project initiatives; (5) increasing credit opportunities for investment in productivity enhancement and in consumption stabilization among the usually illiterate poor; and (6) encouraging improved integration of crop and livestock systems where cropping is appropriate.

The control of population pressures within pastoral systems must have a long-term perspective. Investment in human capital development in pastoral areas is one goal (improvements in vocational training as well as in formal education), and employment creation in both urban and settled agricultural areas is another. The adoption of labor-based approaches to infrastructure creation, and the intensification of cropping through technological change and commercialization, are both prerequisites for this to succeed. A third goal must be the promotion of family planning and female education, difficult tasks that must be accompanied by effective health care interventions.

Policies for sustaining the resource base should focus on the reconstitution of drought grazing reserves (facilitated by lowering human population pressures) and on reestablishing land and water tenure rights based on local norms, control of agricultural expansion in marginal lands via the enforcement of tenure rights, and control of charcoal production. Restriction in the size of the nonmilking portion of herds would also have a positive effect on soil and water resource availability and quality.

Closely combined with these policies, investments should be made in technological developments that concentrate in two areas: (1) reducing the risk of productivity decline (in terms of milk per capita) and asset loss (as livestock wealth per capita); and (2) offering the possibility of productivity gains.

Reducing risk can be aided by better calf survival through improved calf-feeding management (based on hay and legume supplements) and by improved veterinary services aimed at lowering disease-related calf and cow mortality. Potential productivity gains are associated with technologies (such as acaricides) that reduce parasitic infestations. Animal nutrition improvements are also associated with grazing supplementation, such as cowpeas and hay, while the dissemination of draft animal technology can ensure that the output of other fodder crops such as legumes can be increased.

None of these options is easy or cheap to implement. What is more, the effects of each intervention will vary considerably by locality, pastoral management system, and prevailing climatic and economic conditions. Yet each can have a positive effect on poverty alleviation by lowering household risks of food insecurity, on natural resource sustainability by controlling long-term pressures on those resources, and ultimately on aggregate agricultural growth.

Conclusions

A new strategy focusing on increasing inputs to, rather than outputs from, pastoralism is needed. Traditional low-input, low-output pastoral systems are relatively well adapted to the marginal environments in which they function. However, such systems are well adapted only if their mobility and access to resources are unhindered. This is now rarely the case because constraints to growth and sustainability lie as much outside as within pastoral systems. Thus productivity gains in semi-arid pastoralism remain elusive. Pastoralism needs higher inputs just to maintain its current low output.

The key to the survival of pastoralism, and therefore to poverty alleviation in semi-arid Africa, rests on a refocusing of policy on human productivity rather than on animal or biomass productivity. Despite decades of failed projects and programs, investment in pastoralism should continue because it represents the only viable short-term economic security for most inhabitants of drier areas. But economic growth objectives should be subservient to human food security objectives, and indicators of food security, rather than levels of commercial livestock output, should become the measures of successful development. Food (and environmental) insecurity translates into pastoral destitution and the loss of human assets. Reducing the loss of such assets, which includes the cultural and technical wisdom embodied in traditional pastoral systems, is as much an issue of sustainability as reducing losses in the economic and environmental spheres. By extension, a successful refocusing of pastoral development on the human element (and its associated needs) will constitute the basis for future growth more closely tied to other sectors of the economy.

18 Agricultural Sustainability, Growth, and Poverty Alleviation in the Indian Semi-Arid Tropics

MERI L. WHITAKER, JOHN M. KERR, AND P. V. SHENOI

The semi-arid tropics of India (ISAT) account for an estimated 170 million hectares (54 percent of India's land area), supporting more than 400 million people. For those crops grown mostly in the ISAT, annual growth in yields has increased somewhat between 1949–1965 and 1967–1989: from 1.29 percent to 1.34 percent for coarse grains, from –0.77 percent to 0.74 percent for pulses, and from 0.13 percent to 1.70 percent for oilseeds (India, Ministry of Agriculture 1990). Yet these gains have been dwarfed by increases in yields of crops cultivated in non-ISAT areas. There is a widespread feeling that the productivity of soil and water in the ISAT has not been increasing. Per capita rural incomes in dryland India are a fourth of the national average (Swindale 1984). The problem of poverty in India is related to the problems of increasing crop yields and improving sustainability in the ISAT; there are strong indications that India is placing increased priority on improving the natural resource base in semi-arid areas.

In this chapter we explore the links between increasing agricultural productivity, enhancing agricultural sustainability, and alleviating poverty. We first describe the climate and natural resources, incomes, population pressure, and policy environment of the ISAT. Then we discuss ways of increasing agricultural productivity and the threats to sustainability, including degradation of soil and water resources. Finally, we present recommendations for agricultural policy and research.

The ISAT Environment and Smallholder Agriculture

The ISAT has low rainfall with high inter- and intraseasonal variability. Average annual rainfall ranges from 400 to 1,200 millimeters. Rainfall variability tends to be inversely correlated with quantity (Virmani, Willey, and Reddy 1981). Irrigation potential is low relative to other regions of India. Aquifer characteristics determine short- and long-term availability of groundwater; these are highly location-specific.

The soils vary widely in agricultural potential, often even over small distances, because of spatial heterogeneity in soil type and quality and in erosiveness (Naga Bhushana, Shankaranarayana, and Shivaprasad 1983; Dvorak 1990). Soils are mostly red (alfisols) and black (shallow vertic soils and deep vertisols).

The major rainfed crops in the ISAT region are coarse grains (sorghum and pearl millet) and grain legumes (pigeonpea and chickpea). Crop yields are lower, on average, and higher in variability than in other regions of India. In addition, rainfall uncertainty at the time of planting causes great variability in area cropped from year to year and causes actual cropping patterns to vary from intended cropping patterns (Walker and Ryan 1990).

Most farms are smaller than 2 hectares. For many small farm households, their own production is not sufficient for household consumption needs. Although agricultural production is primarily for subsistence, many households sell some of their rainfed crops and, if they have irrigation, sell high-value irrigated crops. Off-farm income is increasingly important. Incomes are low, and incidence of poverty is high relative to other regions of India (Put and van Dijk 1989).

Over the past 30 years, rapid population growth has led the government to promote rapid agricultural growth with the stated objective of "efficiency with equity." Yet past investments in agriculture have concentrated on high-potential areas of assured rainfall or good irrigation potential. Price and subsidy policies for inputs and outputs have favored irrigated crops more than the major ISAT crops. Per hectare returns to the traditional subsistence crops have been lower than to crops such as paddy, wheat, sugarcane, cotton, horticultural crops, and groundnuts. As a result, less human and bullock labor, chemical fertilizer, manure, and irrigation are used on traditional crops (Jodha and Singh 1982). Interregional inequities in agricultural growth and rural incomes and poverty have grown.

Increasing Land Productivity in ISAT Agriculture

The Need to Increase Productivity

Despite some spectacular successes over the past 30 years in India's more favorable agricultural environments, population growth has nearly kept pace with the growth in India's foodgrain production; hence per capita consumption of foodgrains has risen only slightly. Average per capita intake of calories remains well below the Asian average. Projections for the next decade predict continued rapid population increase and rising domestic demand for food, feed, and industrial crops. Thus a recent five-year plan for agriculture again stresses the need for substantial growth in agricultural productivity. Most reasonable projections of output from India's high-potential regions indicate that future demand for agricultural products cannot be met from these areas alone. Agricultural productivity in the ISAT region must also be increased significantly (Singh 1984; Kalkat 1986; Sarma and Gandhi 1990).

India has little potential for increasing production through expansion of area under cultivation. Increased production needs to come from increasing yields through technical change and from intensification of input use on land already under cultivation. For traditional crops of the ISAT, technical change has resulted in yield increases only in the more favorable environments of the ISAT, and intensified use of agricultural land has hastened the degradation of soil and water resources.

Jodha (1990:55) offers an operational definition of sustainability as the "ability of a system (or subsystem) to maintain a well-defined level of performance (output, and so forth) over time, and to enhance the same if required." Yet the ISAT faces trade-offs between, on the one hand, technical change and intensification of land use for increasing yields and, on the other hand, the long-term physical sustainability of its agricultural resource base.[1]

Agricultural Research

Until the 1970s, few resources were put into research on the rainfed subsistence crops of the ISAT. In the early 1970s, in response to growing regional inequalities, the All-India Coordinated Research Project for Dryland Agriculture (AICRPDA) was established by the Indian government, and the International Crops Research Institute for the Semi-Arid Tropics (ICRISAT) was established as part of the Consultative Group for International Agricultural Research. Both institutions had as their purpose to identify cropping systems and management practices appropriate for semi-arid environments.

ICRISAT's research in India has focused on the higher-potential areas within the ISAT. AICRPDA, now the Central Research Institute for Dryland Agriculture (CRIDA), has focused on poorer soil and lower rainfall environments. Government research directorates and a university-level network for crop research on the major dryland crops have directed most of the national cropping research.

Constraints on Increasing Agricultural Productivity

Why has it been so difficult to increase the productivity of ISAT crops? The difficulty is due partly to the severe agroecological constraints on farming and partly to the failure of researchers and policymakers to understand the complexities of the traditional farming systems they seek to improve. This

---

1. The relationship between intensification and sustainability is not always clear. For example, after sinking a well a farmer raises the application of farmyard manure and fertilizer to the irrigated fields. He builds better bunds to manage the water and keep the manure on the field. In this case, intensification is consistent with sustainability. On the other hand, increased groundwater irrigation in the ISAT carries the threat of unsustainable use of groundwater resources.

failure has led to low adoption rates for technical innovations, which under the conditions of the research station showed great promise for increasing yields (Put and van Dijk 1989).

The low and uncertain rainfall and the fragile soils in the ISAT often limit the potential for large yield increases from either technical change or intensified use of other resources. In some areas, improved management of soil and water resources to assure adequate soil moisture and nutrients for agricultural production is much more critical to increasing yields than are improved cropping systems. In other areas, improved resource management and cropping systems are highly complementary.

With high spatial and temporal variability in the environment for agricultural production, traditional farming systems have responded with "well-adapted cultivars with varying attributes, mixed farming involving crops and livestock enterprises, mixed cropping combining crops of divergent attributes, a range of crop and resource specific agronomic practices. . . . These elements vary according to agroclimatic conditions of specific tracts. Traditional farming systems have been resource extensive, involved low input use, and had low productivity" (Jodha 1986b:235). Moreover, traditional systems can adjust flexibly to unexpected conditions, especially high or low rainfall. Yet new technology is not often targeted at specific niches and does not allow management flexibility, nor has much attention been paid to how improved cultivars will fit into crop and livestock systems (Jodha 1983; Walker and Ryan 1990).

Traditional subsistence crops (coarse grains and grain legumes) are well suited for traditional farming systems of the ISAT because they are low-risk, require little investment, resist stresses, fit well in mixed or intercropping systems, and provide more fodder than higher-value crops. In contrast, "improved cultivars" are often more costly, require more purchased inputs and more management, are less resistant to drought, pests, and diseases, and provide lower-quality fodder. Because they require expensive inputs, farmers do not use them in mixed or intercropping systems where input efficiency would be diluted. The "improved cultivars" often increase yield variability and, because they are more costly, increase income risk. As a result, improved cultivars have been adopted widely only in the most favorable locations (Jodha 1979).

Furthermore, because coarse grains survive under adverse conditions (poor soils, poor rainfall, or low inputs), farmers typically use them on their poorest land, on good land in poor years, and with fewer inputs than other crops. Under those conditions yields remain far below their potential.[2]

---

2. See Jodha and Singh (1982) and Bapna, Jha, and Jodha (1979) for data on relative yields. Differences in yields of the major coarse grains between national and world averages, and between state averages for different Indian states, indicate that there is significant potential for increasing productivity.

Possibilities for Increasing Agricultural Productivity

Appropriate strategies for increasing productivity vary by agroecology (distinguished by characteristics of soil and rainfall). Alfisols are the poorer soils of the ISAT and have low moisture storage capacity and high susceptibility to erosion and runoff. On alfisols with relatively low rainfall, the major rainfed cropping season is the rainy (*kharif*) season. Because a farmer plants a rainy-season crop before seasonal rainfall is known, crop mixtures are commonly employed to insure against weather vagaries. In medium rainfall areas, intercropping in the rainy season could increase land use intensity and hence productivity (El-Swaify, Walker, and Virmani 1983). Similarly, land use intensity could be increased on deep alfisols with high rainfall by double cropping in the rainy season and post-rainy (*rabi*) season (Singh 1984).

But for most alfisols, there is limited potential for significant increases in productivity without first assuring more soil moisture through better management of soil and water. When use of more groundwater can be sustained, the expansion of well irrigation brings the highest increase in productivity.

Black soils, including shallow vertic soils and deep vertisols, have good moisture storage capacity and moderate susceptibility to erosion. On vertic soils, a single rainfed crop or intercrop in the rainy season is possible. On the vertisols, farmers have traditionally held land fallow in the rainy season and planted sole crops in the post-rainy season on stored moisture. In low rainfall areas this is done because of risk of drought in the rainy season, and in high rainfall areas it is done because of drainage problems. Overcoming drainage problems enables farmers to increase land use intensity by cropping in the rainy season as well as the post-rainy season.

In both low- and high-potential areas of the ISAT, farmers move from subsistence to commercial farming when possible, while continuing to rely on some subsistence production until markets in the ISAT are far better developed.[3] Thus increased productivity of traditional subsistence crops, from improved cropping systems that use cropland more intensively and from better management of soil and water, is likely to be a major source of yield gains as well as enhanced sustainability. The other major source of yield gains will be from the intensified use of land and other resources where irrigation is introduced.

In the higher-potential areas, the development of improved cultivars for intercropping, and fast-maturing cultivars to allow for both a rainy-season and a post–rainy-season crop, offer promise for increasing yields of traditional subsistence crops. To the extent that new commercial crops can be introduced into traditional rainfed cropping systems, these may lead the way to investments in irrigation and increased intensification of resource use (Singh et al.

---

3. This chapter does not develop the issue of the weaknesses of markets for inputs and outputs in the ISAT.

1990). In the longer term, for the higher-potential areas of the ISAT, "comparative advantage is synonymous with oilseeds, cotton, pulses, and coarse grains, but with an increasing demand for alternative uses such as fodder and animal feed" (Walker and Ryan 1990:356).

In the lower-potential areas, improved varieties offer promise for moderate increases in yields without significant intensification of resource use. In the longer term, "comparative advantage resides in non-arable farming activities," such as farm forestry and extensive livestock production (Walker and Ryan 1990:356).

Not surprisingly, in both low- and high-potential areas, the greatest potential gains in productivity come from the introduction of irrigation. Both land use and cropping intensity tend to increase. On irrigated land, farmers typically produce two or even three crops each year; use of nonland inputs is higher per unit of cropped land; and adoption of hybrid varieties and fertilizer is much higher.[4]

Threats to Sustainability of ISAT Agriculture

Degradation of Water Resources

Plots irrigated by tanks and wells have provided farmers with stable and relatively high production in the otherwise unfavorable conditions of the ISAT. Tanks and wells are thus crucial. Recently, however, threats to their sustainability have become clear.

Village tanks are an ancient feature of the south Indian landscape. Historically, there were elaborate management systems for sharing water and assigning maintenance responsibilities among the many farmers who used each tank. Shallow dugwells are another traditional source of irrigation, but on the whole groundwater was a poorly exploited resource until the introduction of modern pumps.

In recent years, the area irrigated by wells has skyrocketed, while that under tank irrigation has fallen. Figure 18.1 shows that groundwater is India's fastest growing source of irrigation. Three main factors have caused this transition. First, technological improvements for digging borewells and pumping water have made wells increasingly attractive. Second, price policies have encouraged profligate groundwater use. Pump users pay a low, flat rate for electric power, so the marginal cost of well irrigation is almost zero. In addition, price policies for fertilizer and outputs favor the cultivation of water-

---

4. Most fertilizer used in the ISAT goes on wheat, paddy, and other irrigated crops, plus high-value rainfed crops such as cotton, groundnuts, and chillies. High-yielding varieties of sorghum and millet grown on irrigated land receive high levels of fertilizer, but the same is not true under rainfed conditions (Bapna, Jha, and Jodha 1979).

FIGURE 18.1 Area under irrigation by source, India, 1951–1986

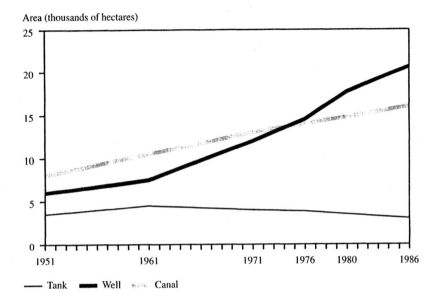

Area (thousands of hectares)

Tank ▬▬ Well ░░ Canal

SOURCE: Government of India.

intensive crops such as sugarcane. Third, wells are controlled individually (or in very small groups), removing the need for cooperation on a large scale as is needed with tanks. Irrigation decisions can thus be made independently, avoiding the costs of coordination and negotiation associated with group decisions.

Area under tank irrigation, on the other hand, has declined. This decline is partly due to legal changes that removed traditional tank management institutions without providing an effective replacement and partly due to the emergence of wells as a viable alternative. Encroachment on catchment areas has led to erosion, which deposits silt into tanks, reducing their capacity. Encroachment on tank beds has caused conflicts between command and catchment area farmers. Management problems have been the inevitable result, and maintenance has been neglected.

The transition from tank to well irrigation has led to a steady deterioration in groundwater resources. Intensive pumping has caused the water table to drop. Water percolation has decreased owing to tank siltation and the increased runoff and decreased infiltration associated with erosion.

Declining groundwater has been especially serious where aquifer recharge is lowest and erosion highest. Most of peninsular India rests on hard rock, and many aquifers are characterized by localized fissures and cracks that trap water. These aquifers, tapped by borewells, recharge at such slow rates that they are essentially nonrenewable. Where dugwells predominate, ground-water is increasingly scarce because of the proliferation of wells. However, as yet there is no evidence of depletion per se, as the water table is recharged each year by the monsoon.

Soil Degradation

On ISAT soils, higher land use intensity can also lead to degradation of soil resources, including both erosion and loss of nutrients. Land pressure increases when marginal lands are brought into cultivation, improved cropping systems are introduced, and fallow rotations disappear on small farms that can no longer afford to leave land idle (Jodha 1979). However, preliminary research indicates that farmers' investments in conservation and replenishment of the soil increase with irrigation and more profitable land use (Kerr and Sanghi 1992a).

Soil erosion, which reduces infiltration and inhibits deep percolation by silting tanks, also varies by location. Its main determinants are socioeconomic. Although erosion potential is greatest where land is steepest, rainfall is highest, and soil is deepest, actual erosion is most severe on farms whose owners have comparatively little interest in or ability to control erosion. These include tenants and absentees, for example, and farmers with limited household labor (Kerr and Sanghi 1992a; Pender and Kerr 1996).

The effect of tenancy on soil erosion results from a combination of market and policy failures. Short-term tenants have little incentive to invest because they will not reap the long-term benefits of their efforts. Indian tenure laws in most states restrict tenancy to the short term because long-term tenants are entitled to claim ownership.

Poor farmers say they do not invest in soil conservation because they lack the resources. However, field observations indicate the need to discern whether investment is limited by lack of liquidity or a perception that is not profitable. If liquidity is the problem, the banking system is not poised to help, as no institutional loans are available for soil conservation, except under a few model projects.

Degradation of Common Property Resources

Common property resource (CPR) management is an ancient institution in India. CPRs have traditionally provided grazing land, fuelwood, and non-timber forest products from common lands, and irrigation water and fish from community-managed tanks. However, in recent years they have been subject to serious degradation. Jodha (1991a) found in a sample of 82 villages that the average area of common lands declined by 31–55 percent between 1950 and 1985. Moreover, physical degradation of what remained reduced its productivity (Jodha 1991a). That CPRs are degraded is not surprising, as the private costs of exploiting the commons are lower than the social costs: an individual can use the commons and capture the benefits, but spread the costs among all the users. This is the classic "free rider" problem; where it is operative, it creates a major disincentive to production and conservation investments in the commons (Olson 1965; Dasgupta 1982).

Degradation of the commons has implications for farming systems. Needs formerly met by products of the commons must be satisfied from production on private land. This change can lead to increasing pressure on marginal croplands and shifts in the output mix. For example, if less fodder is available from the commons, it must be grown on private land.

In India, two types of government policies have increased degradation of CPRs. First, ownership of many common lands and irrigation tanks lies not with the villagers who have always used them but rather with the central, state, and local governments. Government licenses are frequently granted to outside contractors to harvest the produce of the commons. Villagers do not have secure tenure over CPRs and do not control the produce of these areas; therefore their incentive to protect them and invest in their productivity is reduced.

Second, institutional loans are rarely available for groups of investors at the village level, further hampering investment in the commons. Although long-standing institutional credit programs have offered loans to formal co-operatives, there has been no such provision for informal, village-level groups. However, these are the managers and potential investors of the commons, so credit programs must be developed for them. Awareness of this need among bank officials seems to be increasing.[5]

The market and policy failures that cause inefficient and unsustainable use of common property resources also have adverse equity impacts. This is because poor rural people depend disproportionately on common property resources for their livelihoods. Table 18.1 shows that the poor depend on the common lands more than the wealthy. The poor have thus suffered the most with the decline of the commons.

Productivity, Sustainability, Adoptability: Recommendations for Agricultural Policy and Research

Balancing Agricultural Growth with Environmental Protection

How can agricultural growth be balanced with environmental protection? In a region of poor farmers, how can policies or innovations to protect the environment succeed unless they also improve the short-term welfare of the adopters? Solutions are further complicated by the variety of links between

---

5. MYRADA, a nongovernmental organization active in rural resource management, has set up a group loan program with the National Bank for Agriculture and Rural Development.

TABLE 18.1 Extent of dependence of poor and wealthy households on common property resources (CPRs) in dryland India

State	Household Category	CPR Contribution to			
		Income	Fuel Supplies	Animal Grazing	Days of Employment per Household
		(percent)	(percent)	(percent)	
Andhra Pradesh	Poor	17	84	—	139
	Wealthy	1	13	—	35
Gujarat	Poor	18	66	82	196
	Wealthy	1	8	14	80
Karnataka	Poor	20	—	83	185
	Wealthy	3	—	29	34
Madhya Pradesh	Poor	22	74	79	183
	Wealthy	2	32	34	52
Maharashtra	Poor	14	75	69	128
	Wealthy	1	12	27	43
Rajasthan	Poor	23	71	84	165
	Wealthy	2	23	38	61
Tamil Nadu	Poor	22	—	—	137
	Wealthy	2	—	—	31

SOURCE: Jodha 1991a.

technical change and intensified resource use, productivity, and degradation, which depend on the local agroecological environments.

These difficulties are addressed in the Eighth Five-Year Plan, which calls for increased agricultural productivity and sustainable management of resources through "agroclimatic regional planning," integrated watershed development, and soil and water conservation, as well as appropriate provision of inputs, credit, and price incentives and supports. For research on resource management, CRIDA promotes a strategy to "conduct lead and strategic research for improving the productivity of natural resources, develop techniques and systems for long-term conservation and efficient utilization of dryland environmental resources, . . . develop strategies for improving productivity and sustainability of crop production under dryland farming" (CRIDA 1988:1).

Similarly, ICRISAT's mandate is to "develop improved farming systems that will help to increase and stabilize agricultural production through more efficient use of natural and human resources in the seasonally dry semi-arid tropics. . . . Identify constraints to agricultural development in the semi-arid tropics and evaluate means of alleviating them through technological and institutional changes" (ICRISAT 1990:4).

ICRISAT recognizes the need to develop technology that enhances productivity "without threatening the resource base on which food supplies depend" (ICRISAT 1990:33).

Obviously the results of policy and research are seldom independent of each other. Policy and research can be used most effectively to minimize the trade-offs between agricultural growth and resource degradation if they focus on (1) assessing the productivity and sustainability of potential technologies across different environments; (2) developing improved farming systems for heterogeneous environments; (3) improving management of groundwater resources; (4) integrating points (2) and (3) in watershed development; and (5) improving the policy and institutional environment for ISAT agriculture. In the following subsections we address these five objectives.

Assessing the Productivity and Sustainability of Potential Technologies across Different Environments

For researchers studying the productivity and sustainability of alternative cropping systems, Lynam and Herdt (1989:385) suggest that the best measure of sustainability is total factor productivity, "defined as the total value of all output produced by the system over one cycle divided by the total value of all inputs used by the system over one cycle of the system." They also assert that the "sustainability of a system cannot be feasibly measured without a prior determination of the factors likely to make that system unsustainable." Such factors are "almost invariably either some aspect of the soil resource or the creation of an imbalance in the pathosystem."

Technologies already exist to halt and reverse the effects of many forms of soil and water degradation in the ISAT. These include measures to control erosion, to increase moisture infiltration and retention, and to compensate for losses of soil nutrients. But researchers need a better understanding of the relationship between degradation and sustainability in order to assess the importance of technologies that affect degradation.

Collecting experimental data to assess the productivity and sustainability of potential agricultural technologies for the ISAT region is an expensive proposition. Long-term multilocation trials are required to measure productivity in diverse environments over time. Computer-based crop growth simulation models provide an economical way to extrapolate experimental results. These models can simulate multiple seasons of field trials and a wide variety of agroecological conditions, particularly soil characteristics and weather. For instance, ICRISAT has a research program evaluating the productivity and sustainability of alternative cropping systems using a multilateral index of intertemporal and interspatial total factor productivity. The research uses price and quantity data for inputs and outputs from long-term experimental trials at one location to study the effects of soil quality, pests, and disease on crop yields (Whitaker 1990).

Developing Improved Farming Systems for Heterogeneous Environments

On both red and black soils of the ISAT, increasing land use and cropping intensity with improved farming systems is critical to raising productivity. For such innovations to be sustainable and adoptable, more research on the performance of farming systems in diverse environments is required. Research should begin with descriptions of farmers' environments and problems (by agroecological zone and farming system), also distinguishing economic, social, and technological contexts. Geographic information systems (GISs) can be a useful tool for collecting and analyzing the information.

Such information can help researchers develop cultivars for heterogeneous environments, such as cultivars resistant or tolerant to drought and to pests and diseases, or develop cultivars especially useful for their grain yields, fodder, or both. It can also help researchers characterize the diversity in farmers' preferences for new technology. By responding to the needs of different environments, breeders may be able to break current adoption ceilings (Walker and Ryan 1990).

Research is only one step toward developing improved farming systems for heterogeneous environments. India's national testing and release process for new cultivars is based primarily on grain or fodder yield performance under optimal conditions. Changes in testing and release policies to broaden definitions of yield performance to incorporate response to stresses, and to give more opportunities for the release of dual-purpose varieties, would strengthen research initiatives on crop improvement for heterogeneous environments.

Improving Management of Small-Scale Irrigation

Making small-scale irrigation sustainable in the ISAT requires rehabilitation and maintenance of tanks and regulation of groundwater use. Tank rehabilitation involves three steps: (1) removing silt from the tank bed to increase its capacity; (2) undertaking soil conservation measures in the catchment area to reduce the future flow of silt into the tank; and (3) developing and strengthening institutions for managing the tank so that it does not quickly revert to disrepair. This last requirement is the least understood and potentially the most difficult.

The most urgent priority for efficient, sustainable groundwater use is price policy reform, as the current flat-rate pricing regime offers no incentive to conserve. Government attempts at indirect regulatory measures, such as credit restrictions and spacing requirements between wells, have had little effect. However, political pressures might prevent price reform.

In the absence of rationing via the price mechanism, efficient groundwater management requires cooperation among users. For an open-access resource such as groundwater, management institutions are difficult to establish and maintain because the resource has no clearly identifiable boundary and its users do not necessarily form a well-defined group. Communication becomes costly, and free riding is difficult to control.[6]

Protecting Soil Resources

Improved policies could increase private investment in soil conservation. Particular efforts are needed to address erosion on the fields of short-term tenants and nonpracticing or absentee landlords. One option is to subsidize soil conservation investments by tenants. But policymakers can and should encourage longer-term tenancy, selectively discourage absenteeism by large landowners (perhaps by means of a land tax), and encourage remaining absentees to plant perennial vegetation on their land. Likewise, to encourage farmers to plant more trees, policymakers should relax laws that restrict harvesting and transporting trees from private land. Continued research on farmer adoption patterns is needed to supply policymakers with information necessary to help design precise policies.

Institutional credit for soil conservation might also promote investment. It should be available for indigenous technologies as well as recommended conservation structures (such as contour bunds). Preliminary findings suggest that effective indigenous technologies exist. Also, many farmers are unlikely to accept loans if they are required to use contour bunds, which are not always appropriate for small farms because they take up too much space, create awkward corners that hamper farming operations, and cause soil beneath the bund to be lost to farmers down the slope (Kerr and Sanghi 1992a).

Researchers must continue to develop new, less expensive soil conservation technologies that make soil and water conservation profitable and encourage busy, upwardly mobile farmers to invest more. An example of such an effort is the World Bank's recent promotion of vetiver grass, which, in favorable growth conditions, is inexpensive to plant and maintain. It is also compatible with ISAT farmers' preferences for boundary-based soil conservation technology that concentrates soil at the lower end of the field. However, it is unrealistic to think that vetiver—or any other technology—is likely to be the best option for every situation. For example, research suggests that, in the ISAT, maintenance costs of vetiver are very high owing to the dry conditions (Sivamohan, Scott, and Walter 1993). Researchers should experiment with other vegetative soil conservation measures that are also valued for other uses, such as fodder, fuel, and fruit. The best soil conservation measure from farmers' points of view may not be the one that conserves soil most effectively.

---

6. Common property resources are owned and controlled by a well-defined group, usually with some rules about rights and responsibilities. Open-access resources are not owned by anyone and have no rules. This is so usually because they have no recognizable physical boundaries and people cannot be excluded from using them.

Improving Management of Common Property Resources

At least two policy reforms are needed to promote CPR management that is efficient, sustainable, and equitable. First, to extend their planning horizons, CPR users should be given secure tenure. In recognition of this problem, several states of India have enacted legislation for joint management of forests by the state and the villagers (Poffenberger 1990). Under this arrangement, the government and villagers share both the output of common lands managed by the Forest Department and the responsibility to protect it. This approach needs to be strengthened and expanded.

Second, innovative banking schemes should be introduced and expanded to redress liquidity constraints faced by the poor. Such loans should be available for investment in CPRs. Credit can assist poor people to become better off, and it will reduce the pressure they put on the environment by providing them with livelihoods that do not depend directly on natural resources.

Some new, experimental loan programs are being introduced selectively for this purpose. The Grameen Bank in Bangladesh has served as the model for several such programs. The Grameen Bank has been very successful in giving small loans on a group basis. Group pressure, rather than collateral, is used to encourage repayment.

One tempting policy response is privatization of the commons. However, privatization may not be as attractive as it first appears. Irrigation tanks and forest areas are not easily owned by a single person in the South Asian context. Dividing grazing pastures into private parcels has had mixed success in raising productivity and sustainability, but it has denied access to the landless poor who rely on them for their livelihoods (Jodha 1983; Agarwal and Narain 1991).

There remain many questions about how best to promote CPR management. Numerous attempts have been made to formulate general conditions for successful management of the commons, but with little success (Wade 1986; Chambers, Saxena, and Shah 1989; Chambers 1990; Shah et al. 1991). Policies affecting credit and tenure must be accompanied by efforts to build and strengthen village-level institutions for common management. The conditions for success ultimately will be site-specific. Managing CPRs will likely remain a challenge as opportunities for profitable individual investments expand in rural areas, creating attractive alternatives to investment in the commons.

Watershed Technology

Watershed development is widely hailed as the best way to develop India's dryland agriculture. Watershed development is an attractive strategy because in principle it presents no trade-off between sustainability and productivity. However, because it has had limited adoption to date, its contribution to sustainability has been small.

A watershed is a continuous area whose runoff water drains to a common point, so it facilitates water harvesting and moisture concentration. Integrated watershed management focuses on combining improved farming practices with soil and water conservation and appropriate land use. At the watershed level, increased infiltration and percolation increase groundwater levels, supporting well irrigation. At the farm level, soil and water conservation make the land more productive and more suitable for improved farming practices. As a result, watershed development is considered to increase productivity in a sustainable manner through the interactive effects of improved practices and soil and water conservation.

Watershed programs have been disappointing, despite success on research stations. Adoption and maintenance have been low for several reasons. The first and most important reason is related to scale. Watershed technologies transcend farm boundaries, and their costs and benefits are distributed unevenly among those affected by them. On the research station or in large-scale agriculture, such uneven distribution is acceptable as long as overall productivity rises sufficiently. In smallholder Indian agriculture, however, it means that some people gain from watershed technology and others do not. Those situated where central waterways are constructed, for example, lose, as do those with contour bunds cutting through their fields. As a result, farmers have been known to plow over bunds introduced on their fields. If one section of a contour bund is not maintained, the entire structure becomes useless, since water flows through the breach and none is conserved. In general, watershed technologies are likely to fail if they divide benefits unevenly but require near-universal cooperation to make them work. In this case, equity becomes a prerequisite to efficiency (Sanghi 1987).

The second reason for poor adoption of watershed practices has been that programs have tried to impose standardized technologies on diverse locations with widely varying conditions. Soil conservation structures are built with materials used on the research station, not necessarily those that are cheapest and most abundant locally. Likewise, the agencies responsible for their implementation often act individually, without coordination. For example, soil conservation officials often build structures without regard to their impact on production, making it unlikely that they will satisfy farmers.

A third problem of watershed programs is heavy subsidization of improved farming practices, including inputs. Farmers have been known to accept watershed technologies simply to gain access to subsidized inputs, after which they fail to maintain other aspects of the watershed package, such as soil conservation measures. However, implementing agencies remain blind to farmers' rejection of some aspects of the technology, despite the fact that maximum productivity enhancement and sustainability require adoption as a package (Chandrakanth 1988; Kerr and Sanghi 1992a).

Some Indian nongovernmental organizations (NGOs) concerned with dryland agriculture have recognized the problems of watershed programs and devised innovative approaches to overcome them (Mascarenhas, Jangal, and Prem Kumar 1991; Shah et al. 1991). Their initial success has prompted replication by a small number of government programs. The NGOs' approach has had three main components. First, they plan watershed programs with full participation of farmers in order to recognize and address sustainability-productivity trade-offs and barriers to adoption during implementation. Second, they secure coordination among concerned implementing agencies to ensure that their actions do not contradict each other. Third, they promote a modified watershed technology based on farm boundaries instead of contour lines in order to avoid conflicts among affected farmers. Boundary-based watershed development is second best from a technical perspective, but may prove to be best from the standpoint of adoption and overall effectiveness.

The major policy response on the national level is the restructured National Watershed Development Project for Rainfed Areas (NWDPRA), a watershed approach to developing agriculture in areas with little access to assured irrigation. The NWDPRA begins with detailed surveys of local soil, water, and agronomic and socioeconomic conditions in order to promote land use appropriate to farm conditions. Central features include partnership with farmers in planning, an interagency approach to cut down on "turf problems," and promotion of soil conservation through engineering and biological barriers (India, Ministry of Agriculture 1991).

Conclusions

In this chapter we have examined the links among growth, equity, and sustainability in the agriculture of the Indian semi-arid tropics. Agriculture in the ISAT faces tremendous constraints to increased productivity, including low rainfall with high inter- and intraseasonal variability, low irrigation potential, heterogeneous soils, small and fragmented farms, and adverse pricing policies for inputs and outputs. Traditional farming systems addressed problems of resource poverty, risk, and uncertainty, but at low levels of investments and yields. Equity problems arise from the collapse of traditional institutions for common property resource management and collective action, credit restrictions, unfavorable price policies for "poor people's crops," and soil degradation, which particularly hurts those who depend on the land the most. There are also major constraints to sustainability, including rising pressure on land and groundwater, and deterioration of tanks and other CPRs.

Opportunities exist to overcome these problems, however. Collaborative research between the International Crops Research Institute for the Semi-Arid Tropics and the Indian Council for Agricultural Research has led to strategies to alleviate these constraints and risks. Specific technologies, such as high-yielding varieties and hybrids, have been developed for several broad niches with diverse soil characteristics and moisture and temperature regimes. Improved, watershed-based management approaches incorporate soil and water conservation, better management of irrigation potential, and appropriate use of marginal lands. Using these technologies, the government of India has launched a special dryland development campaign.

However, still more awareness is needed of the importance of variability of agroecological and socioeconomic niches in technology development. Participatory research methods offer promise in bridging the gap between development of technologies for broader niches and the often highly specific needs of farmers.

Moreover, the importance of policy and institutional changes more favorable to ISAT agriculture cannot be overstated. In the area of price policy, input and output price reforms are needed to boost incentives to ISAT agriculture. Conversely, scarcity pricing for energy is needed to promote efficient and sustainable groundwater use.

Institutional reforms are also needed to promote agricultural productivity and sustainability. For example, tenure laws should allow more flexible tenancy on private land and give control and ownership to the users of common land. Credit should be provided for both investments in indigenous soil conservation technologies and those that enhance the productivity of common property resources.

Another area for institutional development concerns technologies and production systems that distribute benefits and costs unevenly. Watershed management is a prime example; it cannot succeed without securing the cooperation of those who do not benefit from it. This can be done by encouraging transfers from winners to losers or by modifying the technology to create more even distribution. More generally, a better understanding is needed of enabling conditions for collective action.

In the Indian semi-arid tropics, the goals of agricultural sustainability, growth, and poverty alleviation are intertwined. Today there is a greater awareness of the complexity of this relationship and evidence of greater commitment to all three goals on the part of research and development institutions in India.

19 Agricultural Growth and Sustainability: Conditions for Their Compatibility in the Rainfed Production Systems of West Asia and North Africa

RICHARD N. TUTWILER AND ELIZABETH BAILEY

The region of West Asia and North Africa (WANA) includes some of the world's most extensive arid zones and is characterized by high population growth rates, large and rapidly increasing food deficits, highly variable income levels both within and between countries, and limited natural resources, particularly arable land and water. Climatic features, especially low and variable rainfall, limit the options available to farmers. Crop and livestock production traditionally have been closely interrelated in ways that maintained the growing populations while conserving the resource base. However, recent economic growth, increasing urbanization, and associated rising consumer demand are forcing changes in production practices that threaten the natural resource base. Intensified land use on poor soils in dry areas, the extension of cultivation into agriculturally marginal areas, and overgrazing of natural pastures by an expanding livestock population all threaten the future productive capacity of these resources.

The problems are exacerbated by the prevailing and persistent poverty that exists particularly in the more marginal, less productive zones of the region. It is imperative that development strategies and agricultural policies aimed at increasing agricultural growth and improving the welfare of the rural poor also take into consideration the conservation of the natural resource base upon which sustainable agricultural production depends.

In this chapter we examine the links among agricultural growth, sustainable production systems, and poverty alleviation in the nonirrigated production systems of WANA, reviewing the socioeconomic factors that contribute to resource degradation and identifying strategies for possible solutions.

Of the total land area of WANA, an estimated 14 percent is suitable for rainfed cropping (CGIAR/TAC 1990). Throughout the region, rainfall is highly variable and erratic; in any given location there are substantial variations in both the total annual precipitation and the temporal distribution of rainfall during the rainy seasons. Topography and rainfall determine the major agroecological zones in the region. In the "favored" rainfed lands, those receiving more than 350 millimeters of annual precipitation in winter rainfall areas, wheat in rotation with food and feed legumes and summer vegetables is the basis of the farming system. A substantial area is also planted to high-value horticultural crops (olives, fruits, nuts, and grapes). Potential production is high in these areas, and supplemental irrigation using pumped groundwater is profitable and spreading rapidly.

In the less favored, or marginal, rainfed areas receiving 200–350 millimeters of winter precipitation, barley is the major crop. Barley grain, straw, and residues are used primarily for feeding sheep and goats, which represent the principal economic output. Adjacent to the lowland barley zone are vast areas of seasonal pasture land, generally described as steppe, where rainfall is not sufficient to support permanent agriculture. The steppe traditionally has been an important grazing resource for small ruminant production systems of the barley zone, as well as the nomadic herding populations based in the steppe itself.

Highland areas (mountain slopes, plateaus, and valleys above 1,000 meters) constitute the third major rainfed production zone in WANA, distinguished not so much by rainfall as by topography, elevation, and colder winters. Highland agriculture is diverse. The northern upland plateaus support extensive cereal production, primarily wheat; more than 50 percent of the wheat area in WANA is located in high-altitude areas (Oram 1988c). In mountain areas with steeply sloping land, agriculture is generally based on small-scale cereal cultivation and livestock husbandry, and much of the production is for household or local consumption.

Recent economic and social developments in WANA countries have had an immense impact on the people, production systems, and natural resources of these three rainfed agroecological zones. The rapid demise of traditional systems is a common phenomenon across all zones, but the results vary by zone. Agricultural intensification in high-potential areas is contributing to groundwater depletion, soil erosion on sloping land, and possible long-term damage to soil structure. Expanding animal husbandry practices in the marginal lowland and steppe zone threaten the sustainability of both barley production and rangeland grazing. In the highlands, outmigration coupled with a lack of economic incentives has led to "de-intensification" of production and the neglect of traditional systems of field and woodland maintenance that previously conserved surface water and controlled soil erosion.

Clearly, no one strategy to establish sustainable growth can be applied across all three zones. Each zone needs to be examined as a particular case, with a particular constellation of problems and opportunities, and with specifically designed solutions. In the discussion that follows, each of the three zones will be examined in turn. Each section briefly outlines the impact of regional developments on the strategies being pursued by agricultural producers, the effect of these strategies on agricultural growth and the resource base, and the national policies and programs relating to present problems. The final part of each section suggests new approaches and new strategies that may alleviate resource degradation while sustaining growth in production. To set the regional context of the forces causing the changes that threaten both agricultural growth and maintenance of productive resources, we first review the conditions of recent agricultural growth in WANA.

Conditions of Recent Agricultural Growth in WANA

Agricultural sectors in WANA, historically fragmented and only partially integrated into their respective national economies, have in the past three decades become restructured and, to a greater or lesser extent, dependent on much broader political economies. Significant government intervention in agriculture took place in the 1950s and 1960s in the emergent states, with agrarian reform and large-scale investment projects creating the conditions for modernized agricultural production.

The 1970s were good times for most countries in WANA. Those that were exporting oil realized very large increases in revenues following the 1973 price rises. Those without substantial oil resources found that they shared in the economic boom, either from aid given by the newly rich oil states or through the remittances sent home by workers employed abroad. Foreign aid and loan transfers from the developed world to the non-oil-producing countries of WANA reached unprecedented levels. For the rural, predominantly agricultural population of WANA, the 1970s offered new employment and income opportunities, particularly in the urban construction and service sectors, either in their own countries, in the oil-rich states, or outside the region. Internal and external labor migration became a defining feature of the WANA economic landscape.

As a consequence of increased government spending, rapid urbanization, labor migration, and generally rising incomes, consumer food demand grew rapidly overall and changed in terms of the types of food desired. While demand for basic foodstuffs, such as wheat, rose faster than the rate of population increase, the demand for relatively more expensive items, such as meat, dairy products, fruit, and vegetables, grew at an even faster rate (CGIAR/TAC 1987).

Governments responded to consumer demand with the dual strategy of consumer subsidies to lower the price of basic commodities and producer supports to encourage increased production. The aims were to reduce national spending on food imports, reach self-reliance in food production, and keep the domestic consumers supplied at prices they could afford. Many of the policies and programs instituted to increase national agricultural output were successful. Most WANA countries experienced strong growth in physical output and consequently in agricultural GDP (gross domestic product). The total growth rate of agricultural GDP over the period 1970–1978 in many WANA countries approached, and in some cases exceeded, 20 percent (WRI 1990b). Major advances took place in the techniques and financing of production. Input subsidies, support prices, and the availability of credit encouraged farmers' investments in pump irrigation, machinery, and fertilizer use. Adoption of modern varieties was widespread by the end of the 1980s.

Unfortunately, when oil revenues and labor markets ebbed in the 1980s, national aims of reaching self-reliance in food production had not been achieved. Spending on imports, on food entitlements to consumers, and on producer incentives all had to be maintained in the face of declining revenues and mounting foreign debts. During the 1980s, agricultural growth stagnated, and in some countries agricultural GDP declined (WRI 1990b), though it should be noted that drought was widespread during the first half of the decade. From being a net food exporter in the 1950s, WANA became the world's largest importer of food and feed. Imports of wheat and barley, the most important crops in WANA, amounted to 30 percent of the total supply in 1990, and it is projected that the food gap may double by the year 2000 (CGIAR/TAC 1990).

It is against this background that we will examine the relationships between agricultural growth, resource management, and the development of sustainable production systems. Such an examination must take into account the economic options open to the rural poor. In WANA the most disadvantaged rural populations tend to be located in the less productive and more fragile environments, particularly in the marginal rainfed lands, the steppe, and the highlands. By their very nature, these marginal regions tend not to provide a large agricultural surplus, and thus government research and development efforts have focused on the higher-potential agricultural areas to increase agricultural output.

The Higher-Potential Zone

Intensification and Agricultural Growth in the Higher-Potential Zone

There can be little increase in the area of arable land in the WANA region. FAO (1987a) estimates that only 7 percent of the overall increase achievable in crop production in WANA can be brought about by expanding the area cultivated; the remainder must be achieved through more intensive cropping and increased productivity.

From the 1960s to the 1990s, the function of the high-potential zones has been to provide urban populations with food (wheat, vegetables, fruit, oils, and dairy products) and industrial crops. It is from these areas that national aims of food self-reliance (and particularly self-reliance in wheat) are expected to be realized. Government policies have in general sought to encourage farm output with programs of selective incentives for producers, including provision of interest-free credit, fertilizer and other input subsidies, protected domestic markets, and guaranteed crop purchases at high prices. Incentive instruments are rarely applied across the agricultural sector as a whole. Usually they are selective, directed at encouraging production of particular commodities.

As a result, small producers in the irrigated and higher-rainfall areas have generally followed a direct commercialization strategy. Availability of resources allowed increased cropping intensity and rapid producer response to market forces. Throughout the region, small farmers with access to irrigation have invested in glass or plastic houses for the production of high-value horticultural crops for the growing urban market.

It is for these reasons that most of the agricultural growth achieved during the past two decades has occurred through intensification of production in these more favored zones. But this intensification has been achieved largely through the application of externally derived inputs: fertilizers, herbicides and pesticides, improved varieties, and, increasingly, supplementary irrigation from tubewells. It is questionable how sustainable such systems can be in the long term, given the limitations in raw materials (particularly oil) and water resources on which they depend.

There are signs that intensification and growth in these more favored zones may be slowing down. Off-farm employment opportunities, migration, and the attractions of urban life have led to an increase in absentee or semi-absentee ownership of holdings. Field crops (notably wheat) are being replaced by less labor-intensive and input-demanding tree crops (olives, grapes, other fruits, and nuts). Absentee ownership combined with the growth of contract servicing for many agricultural operations is not conducive to intensification. Absentee landowners who rely on contractors generally invest a minimum of inputs to secure a reasonably guaranteed but low level of production. Alternatively, the land may be leased to sharecroppers who have little incentive or resources to invest in land improvements.

Land tenure reforms and land redistribution were common components of agrarian reform measures enacted in many countries of the region in the 1950s and 1960s. In an attempt to apportion different land types equally, land redistribution frequently resulted in fragmentation of holdings. Population pressure and traditional inheritance laws have in some countries resulted in further fragmented plots, reducing the efficiency of agricultural operations. In other instances, pressure on the land has resulted in a growing body of landless labor.

Impact of Intensification on the Resource Base

Throughout WANA, cultivated land on slopes is commonly divided into narrow strip fields that run up and down the slope and tillage operations are done up and down the slope. The narrow strip fields are often a result of land distribution, the fields running up and down the slope so that different land types were apportioned equally. Plowing up and down the slope is a result of the individuality of farm operations (each farmer manages his own plot) and the narrowness of the plots, which makes tillage operations across the slope difficult, but it results in considerable runoff, contributing to water erosion of what are already shallow soils. Even on the deep soils of the flatter lands, the increase in mechanization, the use of inappropriate equipment and more frequent tillage, and the removal of all ground cover through harvest or grazing may be leading to degradation of soil structure.

The rapid increase in the drilling of wells and the spread of irrigation is having an impact on groundwater resources in many countries of the region. As in the steppe, the problem is one of open access to a common resource and individuals' irrigation strategies. Individuals have no incentive to regulate their use of what is currently regarded as a freely accessible resource. The result has been a rapid depletion of groundwater aquifers, in some instances accompanied by a rise in the water table resulting from overirrigation and inadequate drainage, or salinization of soils.

Improvement Measures for Higher-Potential Zones

The threats to the resource base in the higher-potential zones are less serious than in the more marginal lowland and highland areas. Nevertheless, given their importance as major contributors to the food security of the region, it is imperative that agricultural growth in these zones be maintained and increased, while their dependence on externally derived nonrenewable resources is reduced where possible. There are indications that farmers in these zones, in the absence of adequate information, already apply more fertilizers and other chemical inputs than are necessary for the production of a healthy crop. Surveys of Syrian farmers revealed that the average supplementary irrigation of rainfed wheat greatly exceeded the optimum identified in research trials.

Briefly, technical strategies for increased and sustainable productivity in these zones include (1) the responsible and efficient use of technical inputs (for example, chemical fertilizers); (2) research on integrated pest and disease management, resistance, and control; (3) genetic improvement of principal crops together with maintenance of genetic variability and diversity; and (4) improvements in soil water use efficiency and the efficient use of water for supplementary irrigation.

Such technical interventions must be accompanied by appropriate policy and social interventions. Land management on deep as well as shallow soils could be improved. At one extreme, what are the possibilities of land redistribution or consolidation of fragmented plots? What possibilities exist for group management or for coordination of operations on slopes? Finally, what possibilities exist for alternative tillage or soil conservation systems, such as contour plowing, bunding, ridging, or ditching? Measures such as incentives or sanctions, direct government control, or appropriate pricing of water for irrigation must also be applied to regulate water use and prevent further over-exploitation of aquifers.

The Barley and Steppe Zone

Growth in the Livestock Sector and Feed Deficits

Parallel to the rapidly increasing WANA food deficit, there has emerged a similar shortfall in animal feed. The region experienced a substantial increase in animal numbers in the 1970s and 1980s. By 1985 there were some 355 million sheep and goats, with a projected increase to 490 million by the end of the century (FAO 1987a). For many WANA governments, the problem of finding enough feed for the animal population is becoming almost as acute and politically important as the food security issue.

There are several reasons for the rapid increase in livestock numbers. Livestock producers have been encouraged to increase flock sizes by the increased demand for animal products combined with government policies that tend to allow livestock prices a freer rein than other food commodities in domestic markets. For small producers, the opportunity costs have been lower and expansion of the scale of production has been easier for animal husbandry than for arable farming. Expansion of flock size and number of flocks was particularly noticeable at the drier end of the arable farming spectrum, where more native pasture land and rangelands were open to free grazing.

As livestock numbers have increased, so has the area planted to barley, the principal livestock feed. This growth has been achieved primarily by bringing previously uncultivated land at the steppe margins under the plow and by reducing the area previously left in annual fallow. Only rarely has barley actually replaced another crop. Although growing barley at the margins of cultivation usually results in yields below national averages, area increases have been sufficient to raise regional production levels. Still, this has not been enough to meet feed needs.

In response to the feed deficit, a number of WANA governments instituted feed supply programs in the 1970s and 1980s. Commonly, these programs involved owners' registering their flocks with government agencies or co-operatives and then receiving rationed allocations on a per-animal-head basis of government-imported or locally purchased feedstuffs at stable and some-times subsidized prices. By the end of the 1980s, in some key countries, these feed entitlement programs had assumed major importance in reducing producer costs and holding down consumer prices. However, as with food entitlements, feed entitlements can create major dilemmas in agriculture. Maintaining a balance between feed supply and livestock numbers is crucial, but deciding how to proceed is difficult. Improving the feed supply requires greater efforts to increase domestic feed production, but this decision could result in increased numbers of livestock, which would quickly eat any production gains. Reducing feed demand by decreasing livestock numbers runs the risk of acting against what producers see to be in their best interests.

Changes in Traditional Livestock Production Systems

Traditionally, movements of transhumant flocks were regulated by seasonal forage availability. Animals moved regularly between winter grazing areas in the dry steppe (to graze natural pasture) and summer grazing in the wetter zones (to graze cereal and irrigated crop residues). Such transhumant flocks were distinguished from true nomadic flocks, which moved continuously within the steppe in search of pasture and water. However, they, too, could stay in the steppe only as long as grazing and water were available. In effect, water was the main factor determining the duration of the grazing season in the steppe (Tleimat 1990).

Both systems have been transformed by recent developments. The rapid adoption of vehicular transport by herders in the steppe and steppe margins of Iraq, Jordan, Syria, and other WANA countries has disrupted the traditional grazing cycle and intensified the exploitation of natural grazing. The additional mobility provided by vehicles means that animals can be transported quickly over long distances to take advantage of new pasture. In addition, the ability to transport water to the herds means that they can stay in any given area longer. Thus early grazing and overgrazing are common. Palatable grazing species are not given enough time to regenerate from one year to the next, and the quality of pasture is rapidly deteriorating. Furthermore, feed entitlements, the ability to transport supplementary feed to herds in the steppe, and the drilling of well watering points have encouraged some herders to remain in the steppe year round, increasing their herd sizes while obtaining as much freely grazed roughage from the steppe as possible. In effect, the steppe is supporting a larger number of animals for a longer period of time each year.

Inappropriate policies regarding land use in steppe lands have exacerbated the problem. In most countries in WANA the traditional tribal rights to grazing lands have been abolished, resulting in a system of open access with no corresponding regulatory mechanism to control the extent and intensity of grazing. In some countries, land has been redistributed to individuals and put under cultivation, forcing sheep herders to use the remaining rangeland more intensively. Previously nomadic peoples have been encouraged to settle and now cultivate land around their permanent residences. The combined impact of cultivation and overgrazing is most dramatically illustrated in regions such as southern Tunisia, where previously productive oases are all but buried by windblown sand dunes.

Along the steppe margins and increasingly within the steppe proper, the infusion of money into the traditional system can be seen in the dramatic increases in tractor use and the area sown to barley. By reducing the cost and thus the economic risk to poor farmers of cultivation in low rainfall environments, mechanization has led to removal of the natural ground cover in a way equally destructive to soil and vegetation as overgrazing. Mechanization allows the chance of a significant economic windfall should the rains come in sufficient quantity to produce at least a stand of barley for green grazing or, better yet, a harvested crop.

Impact on the Resource Base

The present situation in the WANA barley and steppe zones has dire consequences for the natural resource base. Continuous barley monocropping is rapidly depleting soil fertility and could stimulate pest development (Cooper and Bailey 1990). Expansion of cultivation into steppe areas, and especially mechanized tillage, has removed pasture species and accelerated erosion processes (Crespo 1988). The adverse consequences of overstocking are perhaps most dramatically witnessed in WANA rangelands. A generation ago a large proportion of the WANA small ruminant population was found in migratory flocks based in steppe rangelands. During the spring, following winter rains, these were joined by transhumant village flocks from the barley-producing zone. Steppe flocks satisfied almost all their feed needs from the native pasture vegetation, and the steppe also served as an important feed bank for village flocks (Bahhady 1981).

Beginning in the 1960s, however, rangelands could no longer provide such a high component of animal feed needs. Supplemental feeding became mandatory for nomadic flocks during winter months. As livestock numbers have grown, so has supplemental feeding, mainly of barley grain, straw, and cotton by-products. The proportion of the contribution of rangeland grazing to the energy diets of steppe-based flocks had, by the end of the 1980s, fallen to 40 percent or less of total requirements (Treacher 1991).

Not only are rangeland resources insufficient to meet current demand, but the absolute level of feed resources available is sharply falling because of overgrazing that causes permanent removal of vegetation and soil erosion. With little time left to regenerate, the remaining forage plants are fewer in number year after year, and there is an increased proportion of unpalatable species (Cocks et al. 1988). The Arab Centre for the Study of Arid Zones and Dry Lands (ACSAD) has classified 70 percent of rangeland in the Arab countries as overgrazed and denuded (El-Kash 1990). Continued degradation can, under certain circumstances, lead to desertification in many areas of North Africa and the Middle East.

Strategies for the Development of Sustainable Production Systems:
Barley Zone

In the arable lands adjacent to the steppe, the most limiting factors are the low and variable rainfall and the poor nutrient status of the soils. Traditionally, barley was grown in barley/fallow rotations, but increasingly, in response to increased demand for livestock feed, the fallow period is being abandoned and replaced by continuous barley production. This trend toward continuous barley monoculture is unlikely to provide sustained increases in production. Results from long-term trials have indicated that yields decline unless fertilizer is applied regularly. Given the production risks inherent in the environment, few farmers are prepared to invest in such costly inputs.

Alternative strategies to improve productivity include replacement of fallow or interruption of barley monoculture with drought-tolerant pasture or forage legumes. Legumes contribute to the soil nutrient status through nitrogen fixation. Inclusion of forage legumes in the rotation obviates the need for nitrogen fertilizer and provides a relatively high-protein feed for livestock. Current constraints to this strategy include (1) the production and distribution of adequate quantities of seed of forage legume species, (2) management of grazing if the crop is to be used as a green fodder source, and (3) problems with harvesting if it is to be used as a stored feed (grain and straw).

In association with introduction of alternative crop rotations, productivity can be increased through the development of barley and legume germplasm with increased yield potential and increased tolerance to drought in particular, but also to cold, heat, and pests. Care must be taken to maintain the current broad genetic base of the crop through the use of land races that are well adapted to their environment. In a system where barley provides the bulk of livestock feed, the selection of improved germplasm must be based not only on grain yield but also on the nutritional quality and palatability of straw.

An alternative to using annual forage crops in the rotation is to use pastures of self-regenerating legumes, especially medics (*Medicago* spp.). Based on the ley farming system of southern Australia, the idea is to reduce costs of annual resowing and harvesting of forage crops by using naturally regenerating medics that are directly grazed rather than harvested. However, the transfer of such an established technology faces many problems, including lack of adapted cultivars, the need for appropriate grazing management, and the lack of appropriate tillage equipment.

In North Africa, fallows are deliberately left weedy to provide fodder for livestock. The application of fertilizers during the fallow phase to stimulate legume production in weedy fallows could lead to a variation of the ley farming system.

The continuous cultivation of shallow soils and the complete removal of crop cover through the hand harvesting and grazing of barley stubbles have increased soil loss through wind erosion. Research on the effects of alternative tillage and stubble management practices will provide data on the effects of conservative management on soil properties and crop yields (Jones 1991). In addition, fodder shrubs may be planted to control wind erosion and provide animal fodder but are less attractive to farmers than the quick returns obtained from an annual crop of barley. One possible compromise is a form of alley-cropping in which barley or other crops would be grown in strips between fodder shrub hedges. Research is under way to investigate the effects of *Atriplex* hedges on barley and food legumes grown in strips between them and to evaluate the productivity of the hedges as feed (ICARDA 1992). Such soil conservation measures, however beneficial in the long term, will be acceptable to farmers only if it can be demonstrated that they are also economically profitable in the farmers' shorter-term time horizon.

Many of the strategies proposed here are aimed at increasing the production of livestock feed in the barley/livestock system. Given that many of the flocks based in the barley-producing zones migrate to the steppe in spring months to take advantage of natural grazing there, any improvement in available feed in the barley zones would also reduce pressure on the threatened resources of the steppe. However, a key issue to be addressed is whether increased productivity from the barley production zones will induce farmers to increase their flock sizes, thus eliminating potential gains in sustainable production.

Strategies for the Development of Sustainable Production Systems: Steppe Lands

Dealing with degradation of the resource base in certain parts of the steppe and developing sustainable production systems are among the most difficult problems facing WANA today. One of the basic conflicts is that rangelands in most countries are open to common use but are grazed by individually owned animals. Conservation under these circumstances is difficult because of individuals' survival strategies. Individuals have no incentive to take conservative action in an open-access system; individual acts of conservation (such as leaving pasture to regenerate) or of investment are not repaid. Resource degradation is accelerated by plowing of rangeland for cereal production, but in many countries in the region plowing of rangeland is a traditional means of land appropriation (Crespo 1988).

Policy measures are needed that establish a system of rational rangeland use and improve livestock productivity and household incomes while conserving the resource base. In developing such policies, careful diagnosis and an understanding of resource users' perspectives are most important. How do those affected by resource degradation perceive the problem, to what do they attribute the cause, and what do they see as solutions? What possibility is there for a concerted communal response? It is also imperative that the resource users fully understand and agree to any measures taken to develop their rangelands, otherwise they will resist or avoid state-sponsored conservation programs because of a lack of clearly perceived personal benefits.

Following Nelson (1989), two types of policies may be expected to influence the behavior of resource users. The first involves finding suitable incentives (pricing, taxing, subsidies, compensation) for practicing sustainable resource management. Previous policy incentives employed by governments have focused on increasing productivity and securing incomes, without due regard to effects on the resource base. The feed subsidies that have been adopted by most countries in WANA have, in Crespo's (1988) opinion, been one of the most efficient ways of increasing rangeland degradation. An adequate balance between prices of animal products and prices of inputs (especially land and water) must be established. "It is clear that when a farmer can purchase 17 to 25 kilograms of feed grains . . . for the price he receives for 1 kilogram live-weight lamb . . . , such an attractive ratio will encourage him to keep as many animals as possible" (Crespo 1988).

Second, where the incentive system is inadequate or inappropriate, it may be accompanied by regulatory policy (zoning, entitlements, licensing, sanctions, and so forth). Regulatory legislation and enforcement are required to support appropriate individual or communal grazing strategies for open-access land. This is most likely to involve some form of land use regulation. One alternative is the creation of cooperatives or other appropriate forms of association in which individuals would have grazing rights, encouraging "block" management of a well-defined number of animals over a well-defined rangeland area (Crespo 1988). In other cases, rangeland privatization may be the best alternative. In both cases, enforcing legislation and policing legislated land are problems and can create conflicts. In most countries, there is no single authority dealing exclusively with rangeland; this hampers enforcement and leads to lack of coordination among different authorities.

Efforts to increase the productivity of rangelands and reverse resource degradation have been carried out in many parts of the region. Proposed improvement measures include fencing off or reseeding degraded rangeland to allow it to regenerate, planting fodder shrubs or trees, and appropriate systems of grazing management. However, many of these measures have been applied without regard for resource users' current strategies and without the support of policy changes discussed here. Such improvement measures have a role to play in rangeland rehabilitation but must be applied in an integrated manner and adapted to local circumstances.

Closing off grazing land may have positive effects on the regeneration of certain types of vegetation, but protecting the land for too long can have negative effects on productivity by favoring the development of more vigorous but unpalatable species that supplant more valuable species such as certain annuals (Crespo 1988). The fencing off of grazing lands can also create antagonism from local range users unless they understand and are involved in the project. Thus grazing lands should be fenced off only for a period necessary to ensure regeneration or to allow newly sown species to be established and then reopened to appropriately controlled grazing as soon as possible. Grazing, if properly managed, is a positive contributor to the improvement of rangeland productivity.

Fodder shrubs and trees can provide important fodder reserves and stabilize areas of degraded rangeland. However, attempts to establish plantations of fodder shrubs or trees have not always been successful. Failure or poor performance of plantations of shrubs can often be attributed to the poor ecological adaptation of selected species that are unable to regenerate by natural reseeding and eventually die out. Inadequate management of grazing, particularly in protected plantations, means that shrubs and trees may attain a size where they are unpalatable or ungrazable.

Encouraging individuals to plant fodder shrubs to provide feed for their animals is also problematic. The shrubs often need two to three years to become established before they can be grazed and may need supplemental irrigation during this period. Farmers must have access to a supply of seedlings and cheap credit to support the costs of establishment. Even when a plantation is established, it requires protection, as other rangeland users may not recognize shrubs and trees as private property and regard it as a freely available grazing source. In the absence of strictly enforced legislation banning cultivation in steppe lands, the investment necessary and long-term nature of returns to planting shrubs may simply not be as attractive to individuals as the short-term returns obtained from plowing and planting barley.

The Highlands

Farmers' Survival Strategies and Changes in Traditional Systems

The income gap between the agricultural population in the more favored environments and that in the less productive environments has been exacerbated because poor people in the latter areas have few alternatives but reliance on their more meager natural resource base. Whereas agriculturalists in favored environments could benefit from intensification of production, diversification of cropping patterns, and commercialization, the scope for such evolution has been much more narrow in the highland and low rainfall environments. Moreover, traditional economic linkages between favored areas and the cities enabled many farm families to augment incomes with nonagricultural pursuits, whereas linkages to nonagricultural sectors and the local economy in the less productive areas remain tenuous.

Populations in highland regions tend to be dispersed and isolated from major economic centers. Historically, they have received little attention from urban-dominated central governments. Because of their relative physical, political, and economic isolation, the less-favored regions receive fewer government services, such as roads, water supplies, schools, and electricity. The strategy followed by poor farmers with limited natural resources in the highlands is somewhat different from that followed in lowland areas.

In steeply sloped mountain areas with a limited growing season or cropping choices, a strategy best termed "de-intensification" has emerged. The key factor is the deployment and use of agricultural labor. Traditionally, mixed farming combining cereals, livestock, and some vegetable and forage crops was practiced on carefully constructed and maintained terraced or banked fields that effectively controlled runoff and soil erosion. Controlling and channeling runoff, maintaining terrace walls, and keeping a level cultivation surface all required substantial labor inputs in addition to those needed to sow, tend, and harvest a crop. Nevertheless, in the absence of alternative sources of livelihood, isolated highland farmers made the labor investment in order to secure their own subsistence.

The opening of migration opportunities for poor farmers in highland Yemen, eastern Turkey, the Atlas Mountains of North Africa, and elsewhere led to a much better quality of life for families remaining at home and receiving remittances. However, the absence of large numbers of young men also raised the local costs of labor needed to maintain the productivity of traditional farming. For those who saved their migrant wages, the opportunities to invest in more capital-intensive agriculture were constrained by the highland environment and especially by the steep slopes that precluded mechanization. Inevitably, markets now supply food bought with remittances, and local production has become less significant in the family diet.

Even though less labor is devoted to maintaining mountainside fields, production of traditional cereal crops continues. This is due not so much to commercialization of field crops as to the continued economic importance of livestock. In fact, livestock is emerging as the key component of production strategies of highland farmers. Two reasons for this can be identified. As in the lowlands, animal products enjoy higher returns than cereals, and, as the composition of the highland agricultural labor force becomes increasingly more female because of male outmigration, women continue their traditional specialization in animal husbandry. WANA highlands are generally poor in natural pastures, and thus cereals continue to provide the bulk of animal feed. However, the decline in maintenance of the mountainside field systems brings into question the sustainability of crop and animal production.

The consequence of migration and the changing composition of the agricultural workforce in the Yemeni highlands are well documented (Tutwiler 1990). Other WANA highland agricultural systems are less well studied, but there appears to be a similar evolution and consequent threat to the resource base in eastern Turkey (Keatinge and Hamblin 1991). Similar problems, particularly erosion, appear to be present in the Moroccan Rif and Atlas Mountains (Ouassou and Baghati 1988).

Strategies for the Development of Sustainable Agricultural Systems

High-elevation areas with cold winters and a limited growing season share a common problem with steppe lands in the limited range of enterprises that the environment allows. The high-elevation plateau areas are dominated by winter cereals in arable areas and the grazing of semimigratory livestock on grazing lands. Opportunities exist for greater integration of the arable and livestock sectors. Given the high demand for animal products in the region, high priority should be given to developing the livestock sector in highland areas. Improved pasture could replace arable cropping in the more marginal areas. Land use could be shifted toward production of feedgrains to support livestock production. However, most Mediterranean barley varieties have limited cold tolerance, while European winter barleys mature too slowly to avoid early summer drought. Improved winter bread and durum wheats have had to be developed for the high-altitude zones; the same may have to be done for barley (Oram 1988c).

In the mountainous areas of high-elevation zones, the opportunities for sustainable agricultural development have yet to be identified. Innovative approaches to the improvement of productivity and the increase of incomes in these areas are needed. These areas suffer from persistent poverty stemming from their physical and economic isolation. Improvements in infrastructure (communications, health, education, markets, and so forth) are essential prerequisites for any agricultural progress. Rural development activities that provide alternative income-earning opportunities are needed to alleviate poverty and prevent the mass depopulation of these areas and the further degradation of the agricultural resource base. Means must be found for encouraging the rehabilitation of terraced lands, perhaps including incentives for communal action. High priority should be given to livestock production, traditionally of importance in these areas. Adapted systems of agroforestry and social forestry may play an important role in these areas, providing timber, forage, and erosion control. Lessons may be learned from similar less-favored areas facing the same problems in western Europe. Too little is known about these areas, and a first requirement for any action is careful local diagnosis of existing systems and the potential for intervention.

Conclusions

Despite frequent predictions that the limited agricultural resource base of WANA countries, the intensification and commercialization of production over the past generation, and the sharply rising opportunity costs of labor will lead to larger farm sizes and a consequent demise of small farmers in the region (CGIAR/TAC 1990), small producers have been surprisingly persistent. They have followed a number of strategies combining different elements in different ways but aimed at the same objective: improved family income and continued involvement in agriculture to a greater or lesser extent. Unfortunately, the economic success that lies behind small-producer persistence may have come at the cost of resource degradation. This is particularly true of the most vulnerable environments: the steppe and steppe margins and the highlands.

Adjustments of existing policy instruments and the introduction of new technologies will not solve these problems. Adaptive research and exploration of policy alternatives are needed, along with a clear acknowledgment of the factors that condition the rural population's activities and determine the way in which they utilize their natural and other resources. In this chapter we have demonstrated that resource mismanagement and rural poverty are inextricably linked in WANA. Producers follow individual strategies they perceive as the best means to maintain their livelihoods, irrespective of implications for the wider community or the long-term impact of their actions. Alternative, sustainable resource management practices will only be adopted if the means are made available and the benefits to rural livelihoods can be demonstrated.

20 Agricultural Growth and Sustainability: Perspectives and Experiences from the Himalayas

NARPAT S. JODHA

In this chapter I discuss the prospects for and problems of sustainable agriculture in mountain (or hill) areas, based on studies in the Hindu Kush–Himalayan (HKH) region undertaken from 1988 to 1991. (For details of the methods and results of the studies, see Jodha [1990, 1991b, 1992a]; Banskota and Jodha [1992a,b]; and Jodha, Banskota, and Partap [1992].) I focus on mountain ecosystems, with illustrations from Nepal, Himachal Pradesh (India), West Sichuan (China), and the NWFP (North-West Frontier Province) and other hill areas in north Pakistan. "Agriculture" in this chapter comprises cropping, horticulture, forestry, agroforestry, and animal husbandry.

I first describe characteristics and problems of most of the HKH region, presenting an integrated picture of its biophysiology, socioeconomics, institutions, technologies, and "mountain specificities" such as fragility, inaccessibility, and diversity. I then evaluate the "sustainability" of production systems in the context of those specificities.

In this chapter, "sustainability" means the ability of a system to maintain or enhance performance (for example, in output, income, and welfare) over time without damaging its long-term potential (Jodha 1990). "Performance" can be more broadly expressed as the range and quality of production and income-generation options (Jodha 1992a). This depends on the ability of the biophysical resource base to handle high levels and complex mixes of inputs, to tolerate disturbances without facing permanent damage or losing regenerative capacities, and to benefit from economies of scale and infrastructure, as well as from intersystem linkages (Jodha 1991b). Links with other systems, in particular, can help the system to be sustained by relaxing input access constraints and absorbing surplus output. The degree to which these intersystem links help system sustainability depend, however, on whether the terms of exchange are extractive or equitable. Institutions, technological innovations, and policies influence the sustainability of a system's biophysical resource base (Pezzey 1989).

Conditions in Mountain Agriculture

Poverty and environmental degradation are common in mountain areas of developing countries and tend to reinforce each other (Jodha 1992a). Agriculture is the main activity in these regions. Since the 1940s, agricultural productivity has declined and the resource base has degraded in the HKH area. Compared with the situation a half-century ago, (1) landslides and riverbank cutting are now more frequent, (2) biodiversity is lower, (3) poisonous and unusable plants in forests and grazing land are more common, (4) water flow for grinding mills and irrigation is lower, (5) topsoil on slopes is more eroded, (6) traditional cultivation of terraces is much less common, (7) diversified and resource (fertility) regenerative farming practices are more difficult to undertake, (8) major crop yields are lower, (9) the interseason food deficit period is longer, and (10) poverty-induced outmigration is more frequent (Jodha 1990, 1992a; Hussain and Erenstein 1992; Liu Yanhua 1992; Shrestha 1992; Singh 1992). Most of these trends promote resource degradation, which in turn fuels those trends in a vicious circle. These trends cause conflict between environmentalists and development promoters and also cause growing pressure on communities to overextract resources.

Taking a "mountain perspective" means understanding and explicitly considering local conditions before designing and implementing interventions in mountain areas. These conditions include inaccessibility (physical isolation, high transport costs, and poor road infrastructure), fragility, marginality, and diversity of niches and human adaptation mechanisms. Some of these conditions are shared by other agroecological zones, especially deserts and marshy coastal areas, but the conditions appear to be most extreme in mountain areas. Transport is more difficult and costly than in flat areas. A watershed of a few hundred hectares can have large variations within it in texture, depth, fertility, and drainage of soils, in average temperature and precipitation, and in vegetation, as one goes from low altitudes to high altitudes within the watershed (often varying from 300 to 7,000 meters in the Himalayas).

Table 20.1 summarizes the conditions of the mountain environment and their effects on sustainability and activity patterns. The table focuses on agriculture, but the concepts could be applied as well to secondary and tertiary sector activities. The conditions limit (1) the capacity of the system to absorb inputs, (2) the production opportunities, and (3) the exposure to and replicability of development strategies from the plains. The scope is quite limited for upgrading and manipulating the resource base (even through infrastructural investment and external support) to increase the intensity of input use. (The potential for a Green Revolution–like change is thus quite limited, except in scattered niches.) Fragility renders land vulnerable to rapid and irreversible degradation following minor disturbances such as indiscriminate tillage. Moreover, verticality contributes to the fragility and marginality of the region.

TABLE 20.1 The sustainability implications of mountain conditions

Mountain Conditions	Sustainability Implications in Terms of:						
	Resource Use Intensity	Input Absorption Capacity	Infrastructure	Scale Economies	Resilience to Shocks	Surplus Generation	Learning from Outside
Inaccessibility (remoteness, distance, closeness)	–	–	–	–	–	–	+ or –
Fragility (vulnerability to irreversible damage, low carrying capacity, limited production options)	–	–	–	+ or –	–	–	–
Marginality (cut off from mainstream, high dependency)	+	–	–	–	–	–	–
Diversity (complex constraints and opportunities) "Niche"	+	+	–	–	+	+	–
(small and numerous activities, use of "niches" beyond local capabilities)	+	+	+	–	+	+	–
Adaptation mechanisms (folk agronomy, ethno-engineering, collective security, diversification, self-provisioning)	+	+	+	–	+	+ or –	+

SOURCE: Table adapted from Jodha 1990.

NOTE: – indicates extremely limited possibilities; + indicates greater scope for sustainability through production performance and linkages with wider systems (for example, upland-lowland interactions). The constraints indicated for the primary production sector also apply to secondary and tertiary sector activities.

Diversity causes location-specificity and favors smaller-scale operation, making it difficult to generate agricultural surpluses (hence limiting primary sector output as well as intermediate input to secondary sector activities such as processing); this difficulty in turn discourages investment in both sectors.

Yet diversity of landscape means opportunity for a diversity of activities. There are areas of high agricultural potential and "niche" activities and products in which the mountain zone has an absolute advantage.

The Traditional System and Sustainability Concerns

Traditional resource-use systems (survival and growth strategies) were mainly in agriculture, with little secondary and tertiary activity apart from some handicrafts and petty trading by some ethnic groups. The system was semiclosed and had low population pressure, and production was oriented toward subsistence. Production, consumption, and exchange were equilibrated among themselves, and each adapted to the limits and potential of the natural resource base; that base was amended as much as possible (for example, using terraces and community irrigation) to meet community needs, and resource management systems focused on resource regeneration, recycling, and conservation (Whiteman 1988; Sanwal 1989; Jodha 1990, 1991b). Land use was diversified, with a mix of land-extensive and land-intensive activities, complementary use of temporal and spatial heterogeneities of resources, and development of niche products for home consumption as well as petty commerce (Allan, Knapp, and Stadel 1988). Through trial and error, low-cost practices (constituting parts of the systems often described as "folk agronomy" and "ethno-engineering") were developed (Jodha and Partap 1993). Social sanctions and collective sharing were used to control extraction of natural resources, use of common property and farmland, and population growth and outmigration (Jochim 1981).

The traditional resource use system was sustainable in that it modestly upgraded the resource base (increasing use options). Nevertheless, the traditional system ceased to be sustainable once change occurred at a rate too rapid for adaptation strategies to cope. The increase in internal and external demands on resources—rapid population growth, increased state intervention, and increased economic integration of the mountain zones of the region with the plain economies—made traditional supply-side control measures inadequate and infeasible. The increase in the population growth rate (due to a reduced mortality rate) came on the heels of improvement in health facilities in the Himalayan region during the last four to five decades (Sharma and Banskota 1992). Outmigration dropped as a result of constraints on absorptive capacity and political developments in receiving areas. As population per hectare of mountain cultivable land increased, land-extensive strategies were undermined. Moreover, it appears that there has been growth in individualistic tendencies and decreases in the effectiveness of social sanctions and informal institutional arrangements for collective sharing and resource conservation.

Rapid population growth led to intensification of farming systems in the region. Intensification, unaccompanied by better resource management and more appropriate production technologies, involved overcropping, overgrazing, cropping on steep slopes, and neglect of traditional diversification and resource regenerative processes. These practices degraded the resource base, affecting the biophysical processes involving regeneration, flexibility, resilience, and material and energy flows. The degradation further impoverished communities, and the pressure to intensify even more was not relieved by reduction in the population growth rate or level. Thus was established a vicious circle of degradation, impoverishment, and degradation.

Development Strategies and Their Sustainability Implications

State interventions have not broken this vicious circle and have even tended to exacerbate it. The government's goals were to (1) intensify food production to feed a growing population and cash cropping (vegetables and fruit, for example) to increase incomes; (2) promote sole cropping and (through biochemical input subsidization and public distribution) increase farmer dependence on external resources; (3) integrate mountain areas with the mainstream plains or urban economies through improvements in physical infrastructure, market links, and legal or administrative processes; and (4) extract mountain "niche" products (for example, hydropower, timber, and tourism services). By contrast, no attention was paid to the need for insulating or protecting the fragile mountain resource base from internal and external demand pressures (Banskota and Jodha 1992a).

Government development strategies for the mountain region—strategies generally developed in nonmountain settings—ignored mountain conditions, which, as noted, require balancing of intensification (for high production) with diversification and local resource regeneration. Even when government development documents recognize these requirements and limitations of the environment, policy decisions and implementation are carried out without regard to these requirements. For example, some plan documents emphasize the need for diversified biomass production and yet promote crops with a focus on high grain yield alone; other documents begin by noting the inaccessibility of the mountain regions and end by promoting activities requiring good access to outside markets (Jodha 1990).

State interventions through legal and administrative controls also marginalized traditional social sanctions and informal community action and alienated the people from resources, which led to overextraction (Guha 1989; Sanwal 1989). With direct state control of resources (for example, nationalization of forests and decrees on access to water resources), the community's role in regulating pressure on resources was eliminated. Moreover, improved physical links and market integration between mountain and plains zones were expected to promote secondary and tertiary sector activity. On the contrary, greater integration reduced the range and quality of economic options for most of the mountain communities. The interventions did enhance employment and income (through intervention's promotion of agricultural commercialization—also aided by increased profitability in general—and downstream linkage activities), but only for a small portion of the population, too small to reverse the move of the population in general to fragile lands. Table 20.2 summarizes state policies and their consequences.

Results of past research at the International Centre for Integrated Mountain Development (ICIMOD 1990a–e); Jodha, Banskota, and Partap (1992); and Jodha (1995a) critique government agricultural policy in the HKH region. First, there has been too much emphasis on food self-sufficiency, especially when food is defined narrowly as foodgrains (Banskota and Jodha 1992b). This emphasis ignores the fact that historically, even with smaller populations, most of the mountain areas were rarely self-sufficient in foodgrains. Instead, access to sufficient food was assured by a combination of foodgrain production on the one hand and on the other a mix of deliberate control of food demand, periodic migration to reduce the number of local consumers drawing on local stocks, and petty commerce in a diverse set of high-value mountain products to purchase foodgrain from the plains economies. Governments' strategies disregarded the value of diversification and thus added to the push of foodgrain production onto steep slopes not suited for annual cropping and the increased use of external inputs, with the environmental degradation consequences already noted.

Second, government programs targeted a narrow set of crops (rice, wheat, and to some extent maize), certain varieties of those crops (those that had proved their yield capacity in the plains' agriculture and that had been released by plains-based agricultural research organizations), and attributes (grain yield as opposed to yield stability or biomass). The production of this targeted set depended on substantial use of external inputs. The programs led to the marginalization of other important local crops and varieties. For instance, in several valleys of the middle mountains of Nepal and the Garhwal hills of India, a dozen varieties of rice used to be produced. Now only two to three varieties, received mainly from the International Rice Research Institute (IRRI), occupy most of the rice-growing area. Similarly, only a few fruits are now widely grown (for example, apples), while formerly a wide variety of mountain fruits were widely cultivated (Shrestha 1992; Singh 1992).

Third, the technologies promoted (for multiple and sole crops, including foodgrains, fruit, and vegetables) involved dependence on chemical inputs. Traditional labor-intensive technologies (for example, nutrition cycling through crop-tree mixes and biological control of diseases and pests through crop

TABLE 20.2 Public intervention strategies and their effects on the sustainability prospects in mountain areas

Key Focus and Mechanisms of Public Interventions	Management of Demand Pressure, Use of Regulation	Resource (Land) Use Systems, Resource Conservation	Diversification Interlinkage, Resource Regeneration
Integration: Linking of the mountain economy to other regions through improvements in infrastructure and markets and through legal, administrative, institutional processes	Uncontrolled external demand on "niche" areas; pressures through commercialization; marginalization of local communities and systems; limited new options	Accessibility and distant market-induced overexploitation; growth of a dual economy with limited prosperous pockets	Market-induced specialization; marginalization of diversified, resource-regenerative options; dependence on subsidies for biochemicals; limited diversified high-payoff options
Extraction: Expansion of mainstream economy (and mountain areas) through exploitation of mountain products (water, timber, hydropower, tourism, horticulture potential)	Overexploitation in response to market signals and revenue needs; siphoning of surpluses at unequal terms; greater focus on external demand	Pace and pattern of extraction adversely affecting fragile resources, people's resource conservation and protection arrangements; combined productivity and protection goals	Limited local multiplier effects of huge projects; marginalization of "niches"; dependent activities
Intensification: Improvement of productivity, growth, welfare, through overextraction, high-input technologies, large-scale operations, infrastructure	Focus on short-term considerations; pressures to produce more using fragile resources; no efforts to manage demand; high-productivity zones overexploited	Disregard of land-extensive options; resource extraction faster than regeneration; intensification where extensification is needed	Specialization, ignoring linkages between resource productivity, regeneration, and diversity of the system; intensification without diversification
Substitution: Replacement of extensive systems by intensive ones, of diversification by specialization, of people's systems by public measures, and of natural processes by biochemical subsidies	Focus on short-term supply aspects, disregarding demand factors; subsidies inducing pressure on land; no resource-use regulations	Incentives for resource intensification ignoring resource degradation, and complementarity of extensive and intensive land uses	Deemphasis on measures conducive to diversification, regeneration, interlinkages, local adaptation mechanisms

SOURCE: Based on Banskota and Jodha 1992a,b, and Jodha, Banskota, and Partap 1992.

rotation) were unable to provide sufficient nutrient input and environmental control to support intensification and yield growth in the way that the external input-intensive technologies could (Yadav 1992). Yet the intensive technologies (1) undermine land use diversity and activity linkages important to resource regeneration and to the balance of productivity and soil conservation and (2) make agriculture dependent on external subsidies (both biochemical and economic). These two problems may conspire to make mountain agriculture unsustainable in this region (Sanwal 1989; Jodha 1991b).

Fourth, diversity and interlinkages of activities in the mountains are ignored not only at the level of production programs in the field but also at the policy and planning levels. Separate departments or agencies treat cropping, animal husbandry, and forestry, so that public investment, project formulation, and foreign assistance are segregated along subsector lines rather than being integrated. This segregation makes the programs and planning ineffective because subsectors are interlinked in the mountain agricultural system, leading to narrow specialization, disregard of interlinkages, and misunderstanding by decisionmakers of the integrated development of mountain areas (Sanwal 1989; Jodha 1992b).

Fifth, agricultural research and development (R&D) policies and programs, as well as extension programs, in the HKH countries exhibit characteristics that generally do not contribute to the sustainable development of these areas. R&D and extension in mountain areas focus on intensification, in line with the policy objectives already discussed. Mountain areas need research on integrated agricultural systems, diversity, flexibility, and local resource regeneration, yet current R&D in mountain areas is largely focused on specific products, adaptation trials of technologies received from the plains, and intensive techniques requiring external inputs, and it tends to ignore the potential for blending traditional and modern technologies (Jodha 1991b; Jodha and Partap 1993). Part of the reason for a "nonmountain perspective" in current mountain research and extension is that the national budget is disproportionately underallocated to mountain research and extension in general, and within the portion allocated to mountains, too little is allocated to research and extension concerning fragile slopes (the majority of areas) and to herbs, vegetables, and fruits. In contrast, too much research and extension are concentrated on easy-access areas and on wheat, rice, and apples.

The Means of Combining Growth and Sustainability in Mountain Areas

Reconciliation of traditional resource-extensive production systems and current resource-intensive systems to meet both growth and sustainability goals would involve combining diversification and intensification (Jodha 1995b). The potential success of this combination is corroborated by some success stories in the HKH region. Preliminary evidence from ICIMOD studies of rapidly transforming areas, including Himachal Pradesh state (India), Ilam district (Nepal), and Ningnan and Miyi counties (West Sichuan, China), shows the importance of the combination. These success stories have several common characteristics: (1) lead sectors and activities based on comparative advantage were identified; (2) R&D, infrastructure, and marketing facilities were provided; (3) production activities complementing the lead activities were promoted, increasing the diversity and quality of production and consumption options; and (4) knowingly or unknowingly, the development interventions took into account the mountain conditions discussed here.

An illustrative success story (although one not without its critics) is the case of Himachal Pradesh. Two decades ago the state focused on horticulture as a lead sector. Investment was made in research and market infrastructure. Fruit trees (for example, apple) were planted on degraded lands. Around the trees were planted high-yielding grasses, which encouraged stall-fed dairying (thus reducing pressure on the land from grazing animals). Beekeeping was promoted to pollinate horticultural crops; the honey earned farmers further profits. Angora rabbits were also introduced and were profitable. Agriculture (in certain areas) became both productive and diversified. Traditional diversification (confined to biomass-centered subsistence activities) was replaced by new forms of diversification that generated more options, including in agroprocessing and marketing, and that induced people to eliminate resource-degrading practices (for example, in several areas land unsuited to cropping was retired to forest). Literacy and skills increased, and the growth rate of population declined somewhat. Some communities were even able to support research and development (Verma and Partap 1992).

Creating technologies that help combine intensification with diversification is an important challenge for R&D. Combining product- and resource-centered research can help, as can combining resource-regenerative technologies with productivity-raising technologies. Incorporating relevant local knowledge will also help, facilitated by local participation. But diversification confined to the primary sector is not enough; there needs to be effort (through trade, marketing, and infrastructure investment policies) to promote secondary and tertiary sector activities. Study of success stories in this regard in other areas in the Himalayas and elsewhere (in the Alps or the East African highlands) can help.

In short, a two-pronged strategy is needed: on the one hand, promote biomass productivity increases and resource regeneration (which would decrease environmental degradation in subsistence areas and strengthen the biophysical base for the rapidly expanding commercial economy), and, on the other hand, promote agribusiness to increase options and sustainability in the long run. A policy framework to develop the two-pronged approach needs to be established.

Conclusions

Agricultural or general development strategies that (1) focus on resource-use intensification (or rather resource extraction) but ignore mountain conditions and (2) concentrate on the primary sector but ignore potential contributions from secondary and tertiary sectors may not ensure sustainable development of mountain agriculture. The challenge is to promote a two-pronged strategy that combines intensification with diversification both within the primary sector and over the primary, secondary, and tertiary sectors by promoting activities that link them (such as agribusiness processing of primary sector output). The means for promotion of this strategy is a mix of development strategies, technologies, institutions, policies, and support systems suited to mountain areas. For more fragile areas, however, it is better to maintain land-extensive activities with generally low (and stable) productivity. The resource base in areas where intensification is appropriate and feasible, and also in fragile areas, requires resource upgrading (for example, through terracing and localized irrigation systems).

Institutional arrangements are also needed for the demand side—to restrict the growth of demand from increased population and market pressure by controlling population growth and regulating markets (Banskota and Jodha 1992a,b). Practical methods might include fixing the extraction rate equal to the regeneration rate of resources, pricing products to reflect real worth (cost), and promoting local off-farm alternative sources of income (to reduce pressure on the resource base).

21 Institutional and Technological Perspectives on the Links between Agricultural Sustainability and Poverty: Illustrations from India

KANCHAN CHOPRA AND C. H. HANUMANTHA RAO

Sustainability of agricultural growth implies complementarity between environmental conservation and development—the "successful management of resources for agriculture to satisfy changing human needs while maintaining or enhancing the quality of the environment."[1] Conway (1985b) notes that agriculture is sustainable if it is "able to withstand stress of a high order." Most definitions seem to be concerned with stabilizing output around an increasing trend and keeping the resource base (in particular, soil and water) intact.

These definitions imply a technical rather than socioeconomic approach to sustainability. Yet sustaining extremely low productivity can hardly be desirable. The system must be productive and efficient enough to sustain livelihoods above the poverty line. To the characteristics comprised in "sustainability" should be added the requirement that agriculture eradicate chronic poverty and ensure the means to fulfill basic needs of food, clothing, and shelter over a long period. Second, sustainable agricultural growth cannot occur alongside a diminishing resource base. High productivity that meets present needs but erodes the resource base is therefore not compatible with sustainability.

Once sustainability is defined with a focus on livelihoods generated, the linkages between degradation and poverty can be seen. Poverty drives people to use the environment purely as a consumer good; present needs are of utmost significance, and time horizons are perceived as short; discount rates are high. In the absence of alternatives, environmental capital is eaten into.[2] As Dasgupta and Mähler (1990) put it, environmental resources are "on occasion

---

1. CGIAR/TAC (1989:3); World Commission on Environment and Development (1987) gives a more general (and more quoted) definition: development that is sustainable "fulfills the needs of the present without jeopardizing the future." For alternative definitions, see Lele (1991) or Ruttan (Chapter 2, this volume).
2. For an in-depth analysis of the relationship between environment and development, see Dasgupta and Mähler (1990).

of direct use in consumption, on occasion in production and sometimes in both." In other words, such resources can be used for consumption in the present or in the future. The mix of the two depends on the discount rate. With heavy discounting of the future due to low consumption levels at present, poverty becomes "the greatest polluter." World Commission on Environment and Development (1987) notes that "close to a billion people live in poverty and squalor, a situation that leaves them little choice but to go on undermining the conditions of life itself, the environment and the natural resources." Moreover, rural poverty creates a large reservoir of labor with very low opportunity cost (Rao 1990). This low opportunity cost reduces the cost of exploiting natural resources (such as forests) to meet increasing demand for these goods in the urban areas; the cheap labor can also be used, however, for investments to redress degradation.

A degraded environment accentuates poverty. Where the poor depend primarily on natural resources, their degradation erodes the poor's entitlements to consumption goods, entitlements that function outside the market. Jodha (1986a), for instance, gives extensive empirical evidence of this dependence for a cross section of villages across India.

There can thus be a mutually reinforcing interaction over time between poverty and degradation. Technology, external demand, and population growth condition this interaction in ways adapted to the agroclimatic region's set of resources, technology, and institutions.[3] Technologies and institutions should in principle adjust to external changes to sustain acceptable livelihood levels in the region. In this chapter we focus on these adjustments with illustrations from semi-arid India. We proceed first by briefly discussing conceptual issues related to the conditioners (technologies, external demand, and population growth) and then present a case study illustrating these interactions.

Technology Strategies

Agriculture using few variable inputs per unit of land (extensive agriculture) can be contrasted with agriculture relying on high levels of variable inputs (intensive agriculture; where the inputs are high-yielding seeds and fertilizer, such technologies are commonly termed "Green Revolution technologies"). Extensive, subsistence agriculture has sometimes been referred to as "sustainable agriculture," but it can actually be unsustainable, leading to degradation when it pushes onto fragile lands and, in turn, increasing poverty.[4] If population growth is controlled, however, such extensive agriculture will not necessarily be degrading.

---

3. Such a co-evolution is somewhat similar to that suggested by Norgaard 1981, 1985.
4. Matlon and Spencer (1984) and Mellor (1988) suggest such a relationship between poverty and sustainability.

Intensive, Green Revolution technology results in high land productivity and improves livelihoods in the short term. But it too can create environmental problems via negative externalities caused by chemical fertilizer and pesticide application, salinization, and secondary waterlogging from irrigation (Chopra 1990). These problems compromise livelihoods in the medium term, but if appropriate price policies and property rights regimes are in place, such intensive agriculture will not necessarily be degrading.

Hence no unique relationship between technological change and degradation can be postulated. In general, a lack of consistency among the type of technological change, the ecological characteristics of the region, and the property rights system can result in the degradation of any resource base, at any level of productivity or intensity of input use.

Demand and Population Growth

Increased demand for natural resource products can come either from within the rural zone (from population growth) or from outside the zone (for example, demand from urban areas for timber). A breakdown of community-based systems of management usually accompanies such shifts in demand. Repetto and Holmes (1983) find in a simulation analysis that resources tend to be degraded most where growth in subsistence demand is reinforced by growth in demand resulting from commercialization and when this joint demand is accompanied by the creation of "open access" to natural resources.[5] Jodha (1985) comes to the same conclusion in an empirical study in western India. The effects of increased external demand—commercialization of production in rural areas and, in turn, deforestation—have many illustrations in developing regions: in plantation areas in South America, in the Himalayan foothills of Asia, and in the forests of Indonesia.

Such increases in demand external to the region often introduce new institutional arrangements. Inappropriate technology, institutions, or simply a very large demand shift can then upset the balanced co-evolution of the indigenous ecosystems and socioeconomic systems; these changes have more far-reaching effects than do increases in local subsistence demand from population growth.

Such upsets can create a downward spiral: livelihoods decline and local labor demand can decrease, creating unemployment and underemployment as population continues to grow. Without further technological or institutional

---

5. Repetto and Holmes (1983) simulate the effect of these factors on degradation, assuming that the biological stock of resources follows a logistic function, the parameters of which stand for the growth rate of stock and carrying capacity of the environment. Growth in demand itself is not as harmful as the creation of open-access situations. Together the two factors lead to accelerated degradation over time.

innovation, endemic poverty can result. This exacerbates the poor's predilection for strategies that focus on immediate survival and increases the rate at which they discount future gains. These survival strategies often mean even greater reliance on natural resources found in the commons and open-access areas, which occasions the well-known "tragedy of the commons" and exacerbates the vicious circle relating poverty with environmental degradation. Such downward spirals are then a symptom of a maladjustment between the socioeconomic system and the ecosystem and can be broken only by interventions in either or both of the systems.

The linkages between sustainable agricultural growth, degradation, and poverty fall into three scenarios.

1. Limited demand scenario: with regulated use of land together with low and regulated demand, a low-productivity, extensive agricultural technology is able to sustain subsistence incomes over long periods.

2. Increased demand scenario: increases in productivity enable improved incomes even when demand is increasing, provided that institutions for land use continue to be regulated. However, once demand increases beyond a certain point or is directed toward the products of common land (or common property resources), it becomes more difficult for private productivity improvements to offset negative effects of demand growth. That is, improved technology can absorb the effect of a breakdown in institutions and increasing demand, but only up to a point.

3. Increased demand with technology and institutional change scenario: a highly productive crop technology may coexist with open-access situations on common lands caused by persistent demand. If improved incomes are to be sustained, technological change has to be accompanied by appropriate institutions for regulated use of private and common land. The intensive crop technology may also degrade the resource base.

Strategies to Counter Poverty and Degradation: Individual Survival Mechanisms and State Programs

Strategies to cope with and redress poverty and degradation occur at various levels—strategies undertaken by individuals, households, and the state, and collective strategies that integrate efforts by individuals and the state by creating institutions for linking technology and social systems.

Individual strategies are often oriented toward survival and are usually labor-intensive and have low capital requirements. As incomes from cropping decline, the rural poor pursue other livelihoods. The poor may diversify into livestock husbandry, especially of small ruminants, as private costs are kept low on account of dependence on common land. Greater pressure on common lands from increased livestock herds can increase degradation of the commons.

The poor may gather fuelwood, carrying it long distances to urban centers, a pattern that is common in India. Gadgil (1989) found that 78 percent of the biomass harvested in a cluster of villages in south India is thus transported and sold in urban areas.

The poor also pursue strategies based on labor sales and migration. They may sell labor to commercial contractors supplying timber to the urban market. They may migrate to urban areas, although mass migration to urban areas is witnessed only at times of extreme stress such as during droughts. Migration to other rural areas has emerged recently as a prominent survival strategy in India.[6] Migration out of the region reduces pressure on common lands by substituting for local livestock husbandry, but often the villagers send fuelwood and small timber for construction to their migrants in cities.

The many pitfalls into which state-initiated schemes for reforestation fall have been documented extensively. Agarwal (1985), in a review of evidence in Africa and Asia, finds that it is common for the tree species in such schemes to be selected in view of their value to commercial enterprises, not in view of their direct interest to the local people. Often the schemes involve fencing land to preclude unwarranted use by local villagers; consequently cooperation of the local population is not common. These problems are widespread and are found in social forestry projects across ecosystems as diverse as Burkina Faso, India, the Philippines, and Trinidad.

Few state-initiated antipoverty programs have ecorestoration as an essential component. Growth that alleviates poverty, for example, induced by Green Revolution programs that create employment, can help in environmental restoration in several direct and indirect ways. If employment increases, the opportunity cost of rural labor increases, possibly reducing the likelihood of their pursuing labor-intensive natural resource–gathering strategies that reduce "environmental capital." Furthermore, if draft power is now provided by tractors, demand for livestock declines and with it pressure on the land. More productive private lands mean more crop residues to feed animals, thus reducing the need for them to graze and browse on common lands. Chopra (1990) examined changes in biomass availability in the Indian Punjab in the wake of the Green Revolution and found that though biomass from agricultural residue increased, the pattern of land use changed such that biomass available from other kinds of land decreased. There was thus not much net increase.

A growth strategy that also aims at ecorestoration, where external demand for natural resources in the zone is growing, requires limiting external demand (say for timber) while increasing the cost of production of forest and land-based products. A part of this can be done by state intervention; another part

---

6. Studies in other parts of the world also suggest that earning income in activities outside cropping is an important survival strategy. See, for example, Reardon, Matlon, and Delgado (1988) for a description of strategies adopted in the Sahelian and Sudanian parts of Burkina Faso.

can be done by changing property rights on community lands, in forests, and for other common property resources. Changing property rights can encourage institutions that determine the use to which environmental resources are to be put.[7]

Strategies to Alleviate Poverty and Promote Sustainability: Institutions, Property Rights, and Technology

More productive technology and effective institutions for resource management must be introduced together to counter the vicious circle of poverty and degradation. There are instances of such adaptation in a variety of agroclimatic regions, albeit at different levels of productivity.

An example is traditional pastoral economies in arid areas of Africa. In a context of traditional technologies, existing social organizations, through regulation of water, labor, and cattle holdings, create a system of authority that ensures the sustenance and interdependence of the group. After a drought, the larger cattle holdings of some members provide a "bank" from which the others can draw. Such adjustments are assisted by interyear changes in the carrying capacity of the rangeland (that varies cyclically with rainfall). Good rainfall years make up in large measure for the degradation that may have occurred in bad years. Moreover, in some such communities, as noted by Livingstone (1986) and Bromley (1991), populations are also controlled. A careful balancing of different parts of the ecosystem and the economic system results in a co-evolution that ensures sustainability over the long run (Norgaard 1981).

In the arid and semi-arid regions of western India, a similar adjustment between socioeconomic systems and ecosystems has been made possible by the interaction of institutions, property rights, and technology, operating fairly efficiently for long periods. In the presence of low and erratic rainfall and highly erodible and infertile soils, a system of management appropriate to the situation has evolved. The local landlord was able to impose a system of levies on the use of common property resources, thereby ensuring their regulated use. Jodha (1985) notes that "traditional management systems prevented rapid population growth from exerting a pressure on the land . . . more levies were imposed on crop producers than on animal raisers." Traditional caste occupations (services and crafts) kept a substantial portion of the village population off the cropland. In other words, the structure of local taxation and subsidies (the major state interventions of relevance to the management of land) was consistent with the natural comparative advantage of crop production, live-

---

7. The well-documented Chipko movement of India, for instance, began with a protest against the cutting of trees to be used in urban small industry.

stock husbandry, and nonagricultural occupations in the environment of that region.

In traditional situations, the cornerstone of management has been a careful understanding of the relative advantage of different sources of livelihood in particular agroclimatic contexts, combined with the development of a social system of control and the management of incremental demand either by population control (as in some African economies) or by diversification of population to non-land-based occupations (as in semi-arid India). Consequently, the extension of cultivation to marginal and submarginal lands arising out of population growth and leading to degradation was preempted. Further, as some of these societies were more or less closed economies, undue exploitation of the environment because of the pressure of demand from outside the system did not take place. Moreover, such systems provided incomes that were at or slightly above subsistence level. Affluence, of the kind to which modern societies aspire, was unheard of, and the average member of such societies could lay claim only to a limited set of entitlements. Considering, however, that these societies were characterized by stagnant technology over long periods, this was to be expected. Improvement could have come only from technical change that was consistent with the conditions of the ecosystem and that produced a simultaneous change in the social system.[8]

Such development of technology did take place historically in large areas of settled agriculture in South Asia. River valleys provided fertile soil, and private property in land was the dominant institution there. The Green Revolution technology was adopted easily. The resultant increases in productivity provided for the population of the region and produced large surpluses as well.[9] With the judicious use of a combination of irrigation and high-yielding varieties of seeds, sustainability and high incomes were attained. This constituted a textbook case of new technology and appropriate institutional structure jointly resulting in development that could absorb rapid population growth.

By contrast, technological or institutional change that is not compatible with the existing ecosystem and socioeconomic systems is not sustainable and accelerates degradation. Witness the investment in water holes in Sahelian Africa. This new technology resulted in concentration of animal herds in particular locations in an ecosystem in which variability in quality of land dictated that migratory practices were appropriate (Livingstone 1986). Such changes are sure recipes for degradation of a fragile environment.

---

8. As Norgaard (1981) puts it, "the gains from development can hardly arise other than from a process of positive feedbacks between the sociosystem and the ecosystem."

9. Chopra (1990) studies the nature of development in Punjab, the northwestern state of India.

Linking Institutional and Technological Strategies:
A Case Study from the Foothills of Northwest India

In this section we describe a case in which simultaneous evolution of technology and institutions produced success defined as improved environment with increased productivity of resources, employment generation, and poverty alleviation to break the vicious circle of degradation and poverty.[10]

Sukhomajri is a village in the foothills of the Siwalik Range of the Himalayas in the northwestern state of Haryana, India. Over a period of decades, the village suffered severe soil erosion, deforestation, and declining land productivity. Since the 1970s, however, the government and the people of the region acted together by adopting an unconventional approach incorporating watershed management and a new participatory institution.

Before the initiation of the new approach, soil runoff from the catchment of the Sukhna River had led over time to accumulated silt in the Sukhna Lake, a recreational area for the city of Chandigarh, and to the loss of fertile soil and forest cover in the foothills of the Siwaliks. About 400,000 cubic meters of silt were deposited in the lake every year. In the uplands the consequence of the degradation was that fodder grass and fuelwood shortages were becoming acute. Yet the people of Sukhomajri, traditional cattle rearers, continued to leave their animals to graze in the uplands; they also increased their goat population and reduced their cattle stock. This was a survival strategy adopted in the face of declining milk and crop yields. As expected, the strategy accentuated the degradation of forest and pasture land.

Like developmental processes in many parts of the world, the early attempts to arrest this environmental degradation were made by the central and state governments. The latter used conventional methods of environmental protection through a Chandigarh-based institution, the Central Soil and Water Conservation Research and Training Institute (CSWCRTI). The methods included wire fencing, contour bunding, planting trees on contour trenches, and construction of check dams.

The villagers reacted indifferently to these governmental measures. Free grazing continued on a large scale. Repeated conventional actions were repelled by counteractions and inaction by the villagers, a typical instance of a repeated game of the noncooperative type that only accentuated degradation and poverty. This chain was broken in 1978 when an agreement was reached between the CSWCRTI and the villagers; the accord stated that if the CSWCRTI built a dam with a storage tank to harvest rain water and supply the community with irrigation, the villagers would stop grazing their animals on the watershed and resort to stall feeding, which they knew would encourage afforestation. Simultaneously, the CSWCRTI, in collaboration with the Forest Department, undertook

---

10. This section draws on Chopra, Kadekodi, and Murty 1990.

a large-scale operation of planting fodder grass and several species of trees with labor contributed by the entire village. Also, irrigation water from the tanks was distributed to village fields, which encouraged hope for increased crop productivity.

An institutional change envisaging higher agricultural productivity (because of the introduction of irrigation) and a protected environment had been initiated. However, a number of stages had to be passed before these goals were achieved.

The second stage was the emergence of conflicts about the distribution of irrigation water and their eventual resolution with the founding of the Water Users Society (in 1981), to which the management of irrigation tanks was transferred. Rules of water distribution such as equal water rights, number of discharges, and water rates were worked out and implemented. This stage can be interpreted as that of creation of ground rules for a new institutional arrangement.

The third stage involved the village "society" in the management of several other common property resources. The Forest Department departed from normal practice and gave exclusive rights to manage fodder and bhabbar grass (*Eulaliopsis binata,* a variety used as an input into the cottage industry of rope making) cutting, distribution, and sales to the village society on a contract basis. The villagers worked out rules of sharing the grasses and the payments to be made to the society. The acceptance of and adherence to all such rules and procedures were almost universal by 1985 when development had reached a mature stage. The creation of a new institutional structure for the management of common property resources such as irrigation water, forests, and common land, which evolved together with the new irrigation-based technology on private land, was now complete.

The process witnessed in Sukhomajri had shown, by 1986, that sustained development was possible with limited financial resources from outside. Initial financial support by the government and persistent leadership (as a catalytic institution), followed by sharing of forest produce between the society and government, saw to it that what would have been a "prisoner's dilemma" with repeated noncooperative actions and retaliations was converted into a cooperative game with sustainable development as its outcome.

A crucial component of the process was agreement on the division of household labor between activities based on private property resources (PPRs), including livestock husbandry and cropping, and common property resource (CPR) use and conservation. This division of labor led to both conservation of CPRs and increased productivity of PPRs. By 1986 the extent of soil runoff had been reduced to 16,000 cubic meters per year (from 400,000 cubic meters before 1960). Crop yields had risen substantially (between 1977 and 1986, wheat yields rose from 2.75 to 5.80 quintals per acre, and average milk yields rose from 2.32 liters per buffalo per day to 3.01 liters). The number of buffalo in the village increased from 136 in 1977 to 182 in 1986. The number of goats declined to zero. Average fuelwood availability increased by more than 30 percent.

Two neighboring villages, in which the model was replicated later, had somewhat different structures of asset ownership than Sukhomajri. Whereas 91 percent of households owned land in Sukhomajri, the corresponding figures in the other two villages were 62 and 41 percent. Households owning milch cattle amounted to 94, 90, and 74 percent in the three villages. The new institutions also varied in terms of their effects on PPR and CPR productivity. Income from PPRs as reflected in within-village income was higher in Sukhomajri, as was average farm income per acre of operational holding. Availability of fodder from CPRs was also higher in Sukhomajri, as indicated by fodder consumed per animal. As might be expected, the levels of income reached were different in each of the villages. However, the poverty-degradation cycle had been broken in each case through a well-considered strategy involving improved technology and villager participation.

Further, the investment in afforestation and water-harvesting structures, along with the creation of participatory institutions, resulted in benefits to the households, the village society, and the government in all three cases. The internal rate of return on investment (at market prices) varied from 19 percent to 36 percent over the three villages. This illustrates that once participatory institutions are initiated by empowering village societies, investments in productivity-increasing resources can become profitable. The combined effect of the two developments is a movement away from the poverty-degradation cycle.

Conclusion

The linkages between environmental degradation and poverty are understood best when one views the environment in its twin roles of providing inputs to production and consumption goods for sustenance. The mix of the two determines (and is, in turn, determined by) prevailing incomes both within and outside the rural sector. It is true that poverty represents a threat to the environment; a world with endemic poverty will always be susceptible to degradation arising from the pressure on resources and the compulsion for consumption in the present. To the extent that growth and new technology increase resource productivity, they relieve the pressure and prevent further degradation. Simultaneously, however, growth may also accentuate environmental degradation; this is growth that adds to demand for resources provided by the environment, while also hastening the breakup of institutions that provide for their regulated use. The notion of sustainability adds a time dimension in that not only present but also future consumption should be kept in view.

Further, the combined effect of technological change and other growth strategies depends on the agroclimatic context and institutional structures;

developing regions are full of instances of adverse consequences of seemingly well-motivated policy intervention. There exist, at the same time, instances of successful co-evolution of technology and institutions in particular agro-climatic regions.

Finally, this case study illustrates how a considered strategy can help in overcoming the poverty-degradation cycle. In such a strategy, the role of the government is best defined as that of an enabling institution. The government can enable the evolution and dissemination of technology and complementary investments that increase resource productivity. It can also enable the creation of a structure of property rights appropriate for strengthening institutions for collective action, which, in turn, ensures environmental conservation while at the same time increasing incomes.

22 Agricultural Growth and Sustainability: Conditions for Their Compatibility in the East African Highlands

AMARE GETAHUN

The East African highlands are environmentally distinct from the rest of tropical Africa and are very important in the national economies of their respective countries. In this chapter I describe these highlands, focusing on the problems and constraints of their farming systems as well as potential conflicts between agricultural growth and sustainability. Examples are used to analyze issues and policies.

Geography, Climate, Soils, and Demographics

The African highlands are those areas (in 20 countries) above 1,500 meters lying within 23 degrees north and south latitude, with rainfall often above 700 millimeters per year, covering 1 million square kilometers, or less than 4 percent of the total landmass of the continent (ILCA 1986). The countries in East Africa with large highland areas include Ethiopia, Kenya, and Tanzania. The highland areas in these and other countries, such as Burundi, Madagascar, Rwanda, and Uganda, are agriculturally important (Figure 22.1 locates the highland areas of Sub-Saharan Africa situated more than 1,500 meters above sea level).[1] The highlands of Ethiopia and other East African countries lying within 17 degrees north and 10 degrees south latitude make up 76 percent of the Sub-Saharan highlands.

These highlands are complex and are the home of diverse languages, cultures, farming systems, and altitudinal zones. These areas are generally free of malaria and tsetse fly and have a nearly ideal climate for both people and domestic animals. They are more humid and warm near the equator (such as in southern Ethiopia, Kenya, and Uganda), and drier and cooler farther from the equator (such as in the subtropical highlands of northern Ethiopia and southern Tanzania).

---

1. Other countries in East Africa with highland areas are Sudan (southwest) and Réunion.

FIGURE 22.1 Highlands of Sub-Saharan Africa

SOURCE: ILCA 1984.

There is great altitude variation in these areas. The high-altitude areas (greater than 3,000 meters) are cold and generally devoted to catchment forestry and some farming, especially in central and northern Ethiopia. Just below this high zone, agriculture consists of barley, horsebean, and oat cultivation and livestock raising (for example, in the Ethiopian highlands), or tea and pyrethrum cultivation and dairying in the tropical zone (for example, in the Kenyan, Tanzanian, and Ugandan highlands). The third altitudinal zone (the next-to-lowest in the highland areas) is well watered and warm and thus a more productive agricultural area dominated by cereals (maize, wheat, teff, sorghum) and pulse and oil crop farming. Livestock is also important in the Ethiopian highlands, whereas coffee, maize, beans, bananas, and potatoes and other root crops dominate in the Kenyan, Tanzanian, and Ugandan highlands. The fourth and lowest altitudinal zone is dominated by sorghum, bean, and millet cultivation; livestock production is also significant. Moisture is often a limiting factor for rainfed agriculture in this lower zone.

Highland soils, with few exceptions (for example, Taita-Taveta, Kenya, Ruwenzori of western Uganda, and the central highlands of Rwanda and

TABLE 22.1 Comparison of sustainability between the two farming systems and environments in the Ethiopian highlands

Parameters	Horticultural–Hoe Farming System[a]	Cereal–Plow Farming System[b]
Settlement age/pattern	Young/dispersed	Old/nucleated village
Human/livestock density	Moderate to high	High
Local topography/drainage	Undulating, rugged/good	Rugged/poor
Climate/rains	Warm/continuous	Cool/intense summer rains
Agriculture	Horticulture	Cereal (grain)
Cultivation	Hoe/fire	Plow (oxen)
Cropping	Mixed (intercropped)	Monoculture/crop rotation (cereal/pulse/oil crops)
Grazing intensity	Normal	Very high
Fallows	Long	Short
Land use (R-value)(percent)	More than 50 percent	Less than 50 percent
Deforestation/erosion	Slight/limited	Complete/considerable
Farmer rural economy	Adequate	Poverty-stricken

SOURCE: Getahun 1984.
[a]South and southwestern Ethiopia.
[b]Central and northern Ethiopia.

Burundi) are of volcanic origin and thus naturally fertile. Local topographics are often steep, and thus there is a high risk of erosion if they are cultivated without adequate physical and biological soil conservation measures. Depletion of organic matter often results in poor agricultural yields, especially when accompanied by depletion of woody biomass.

The highlands that are most degraded (largely from soil erosion) are found in the subtropical highlands production systems that are cereal-livestock based, most of which are found in Ethiopia. Table 22.1 underlines this point by presenting a comparison of sustainability characteristics for Ethiopia between this cereal–plow farming system and one based on horticultural–hoe farming. As Table 22.2 shows (for Ethiopia), the rate of soil loss is highest in croplands as opposed to other types of land cover.

Because of their good rainfall and generally productive soils, the highlands have high agricultural and overall population densities. The rate of population growth has remained high, resulting in declines in per capita arable land. Changes in population density over a 57-year period are shown in Table 22.3 from northeast Tanzania. Similar or higher levels of population density are found in the central (Embu, Meru, and Kikuyu highlands), Kisii, and western highlands of Kenya, in central Rwanda and Burundi, and in the Konso and Gurage highlands of Ethiopia.

TABLE 22.2 Estimated rates of soil loss in Ethiopia

Land Cover Type	Estimated Soil Loss	
	Total Area	Total Soil Loss
	(percent)	(tons/hectare/year)
Cropland[a]	13.1	672
Cropland, currently unproductive[b]	3.8	325
Perennial crops[a]	1.7	17
Forests[a]	3.6	4
Currently uncultivable[b]	18.7	114
Grazing/browsing land[b]	51.0	312
Woodland/bushland	8.1	49
Total country	100.0	1,493

SOURCE: Messerli and Hurni 1990.
[a]Highland.
[b]Highland and nonhighland areas.

TABLE 22.3 Changes in population density in Kilimanjaro, Tanzania, 1921–1978

Year	Average Density	Agricultural Density[a]	Arable Land per Capita
	(persons per square kilometer)		(hectares)
1921	26	48	2.2
1948	50	128	0.8
1957	69	155	0.7
1967	94	220	0.5
1978	140	300[b]	0.2

SOURCE: Messerli and Hurni 1990.
[a]Population density on land available for smallholder agriculture; excludes large-scale commercial farms, grazing land, and agriculturally unusable land.
[b]Estimate.

These high population densities are maintained in the tropical highlands by perennial and intensive farm systems that are productive and sustainable. By contrast, in the subtropical highlands, where cereal-based extensive farming systems predominate, carrying capacity can, at best, be expected to support half the population density of the tropical highlands. These two major ecological zones and their associated farming (land use) systems are discussed in the following sections.

Farming Systems

High-Potential Perennial Farming in the Tropical Highlands

Generally, the highlands lying astride the equator within 4 degrees north and south latitude (but often extending to 6 degrees) exhibit a more intensive farming system characterized by (1) hoe cultivation, (2) horticulture (tree crops, roots and tubers, or vegetable crops), (3) medium to low livestock density, and (4) dispersed homesteads and settlements.

This farming system and region is estimated to be 400,900 square kilometers, with southern Ethiopia, Kenya, and Tanzania (Arusha-Kilimanjaro) contributing the major share of the landmass. This system is often referred to as a hoe–mixed farming system. It is a sustainable and productive system if population growth can be contained. The system has population densities of more than 300 per square kilometer.

Cereal-Livestock Mixed Farming in the Subtropical Highlands

The highlands farther from the equator (usually 6–20 degrees north and south latitude) manifest a disintegrated, yet extensive farming system characterized by (1) plowing with oxen or tractors, (2) cereal, pulse, and oil crops grown in rotation, (3) absence of trees and tree growing, (4) high resident livestock populations (of all types), and (5) old and geographically concentrated (village) settlements. Livestock production is key in the farming system to generate cash, draft power, and dung for domestic fuel.

This farming system has two subtypes showing signs of system disintegration and land degradation. Those with high potential are referred to as high-potential cereal zones, such as the highlands of central Ethiopia and southern Tanzania. Those already degraded (eroded, overgrazed, deforested) are referred to as low-potential cereal zones, such as those of northern Ethiopia. This farming system is also often referred to as an oxen-plow agriculture. Trees are absent from the system and the rural landscape, and cropping is limited to the short rainy growing season of three to four months. Labor use is low, resulting in reduced overall carrying capacity. Land use intensification and improved agricultural technology adoption have not been attempted.

Transitional, Perennial, or Cereal-Livestock System

Lying between these two systems is a transitional or intermediate farming system that exhibits both their features. Most of such areas are the result of southward penetration of the cereal-livestock mixed farming system and are thus more closely related to it. Typical examples are the highlands of southeast Ethiopia (Bale, Arsi, and Harar), the southern highlands of Tanzania (Mbeya), and to a lesser degree the central Burundi highlands and the Achole-Imatong highlands of southern Sudan.

Highland-Lowland Interactions

Traditionally, there has been a product exchange between the settled farmers of the highlands and pastoralists in the lowlands. Pastoralists sell young male cattle and butter to the highlanders and buy maize and sorghum from them. Pastoralists come for dry season grazing and watering to the foothills and drainage valleys of the highland areas, whereas highlanders send a part of their cattle to the lowlands during the cropping season. The highland farmers often cultivate some fields in the lowland valleys and exploit the woodlands for firewood and charcoal during the dry season.

Problems of tenure as well as ethnic conflicts have tended to undermine this interactive system, but when it operates optimally, both groups tend to benefit. A buffer or neutral zone is often needed to maximize this cooperation. At present, outflow from the overcrowded highlands into the traditionally neutral or buffer zones has tended to marginalize the pastoral system, and water resources have been degraded.

Demographic Pressure and Land Use Changes

Carrying capacity, especially in the subtropical zone's subsistence cereal-livestock farming system, is being exceeded, resulting in environmental stress that, in turn, results in drought, crop failure, and famine (Kiros 1991; Rubenson 1991). The economic consequence is a decline in agricultural productivity that leads to increases in food imports and relief programs (for example, Ethiopia), reduction in agriculturally based manufacturing and processing activities, and substantial declines in agricultural (and thus total) exports.

Such negative effects on, for example, the Ethiopian highlands' economy are clearly reflected in low or even negative growth rates in gross domestic product and also in reduced rates of domestic saving and investment. Indeed, Ethiopian agricultural output declined 37.5 percent between 1974 and 1985 (Kiros 1991). Moreover, in the cereal-livestock farming systems of the subtropical highlands, the loss of livestock during drought and famine years is severe and contributes to the difficulty of recovery from such economic and social declines.

By contrast, the *tropical* highlands with their intensive farming system are more stable and sustainable, even at high population densities, than are the subtropical highlands. Table 22.4 outlines the contrasts between the situations in the tropical highlands of Kenya and the subtropical highlands of northern Ethiopia. The main problem in the tropical highlands is a shift toward cereal farming that displaces perennial crop farming—such as replacing coffee (because of the poor global market) with maize, as seen in southwestern Ethiopia and the Kenyan highlands—in the face of rapid population increases.

TABLE 22.4 Agriculture and the rural economy in the tropical and subtropical highlands

Characteristic	Tropical Highlands of Kenya	Subtropical Highlands of Northern Ethiopia
Cash crops	Important (tea, coffee, pyrethrum)	No cash crops, only livestock used as cash source
Food crops	Roots and tubers, grain	Cereals, pulses, oil
Cropping system	Mixed	Monoculture
Livestock	Dairying	All classes for meat
Animal traction	None or minimal	Significant
Hired farm labor	Important	Insignificant
Produce (marketed)	Important (55 percent)	Insignificant
Forestry, game reserve	Highly developed	Insignificant
Nonfarm income	Important	None or insignificant
Development infrastructure	Well developed	Poorly developed
Land improvement efforts (technology program)	High	None
Total income per farmer	High	Very low
Production efficiency (energy return per unit of land)	High	Low

Figure 22.2 summarizes this problem sequence. Given the absence of purchased inputs (fertilizer, lime) and improved seeds, the nonretention of organic residues including farmyard manure, and the lack of farm technology improvement, population increases lead to unsustainable land use patterns. Both increased population and land degradation result in more land required for cropping and grazing to meet food needs.

Thus more forestland is lost and more steep lands are brought under cultivation. The resulting livestock and cropland crises are expected to reach crisis levels by the years 2000 and 2010, respectively, in the Ethiopian highlands (Figure 22.3). But on a regional basis, these crisis levels have already been reached in much of the northern and eastern Ethiopian highlands, which have been the focus of national and international relief and rehabilitation efforts with little progress achieved. Both human welfare and natural resource bases have been undermined over the years, and wars and civil strife have only made matters worse.

Degradation and Resource Depletion

Decline of Soil Fertility and Water Resources

The key problems across all land use systems in the African highlands are declining soil fertility and the destruction of water catchments, especially in

FIGURE 22.2 Major problem sequence in the agroecological system of the western Usambara Mountains

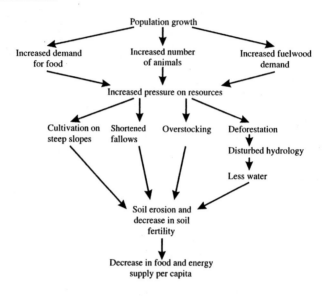

FIGURE 22.3 Likely development of land use in Ethiopia

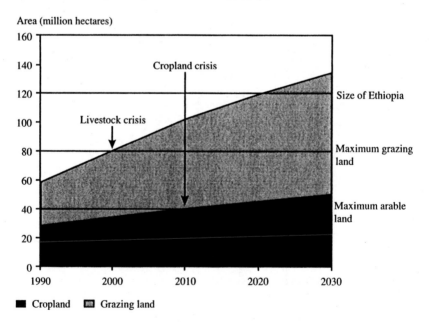

SOURCE: Adapted from Getahun 1990.

the subtropical areas. These problems are caused by continuous cultivation without adequate supplements of nutrients such as chemical fertilizers. The decline is further aggravated by topsoil erosion and the removal of woody vegetative cover, crop residue, and animal manure. The long dry season, short growing season, and intense (erosive) summer rains in the subtropical highlands also contribute to soil degradation.

The loss of productive cropland resulting from soil erosion in the Ethiopian subtropical highlands between 1985 and 2010 (at 3.5 millimeters and 8 millimeters soil depth) is estimated at 4,705 and 9,320 square kilometers, respectively. The loss of grazing land resulting from soil erosion is estimated at 1,011 and 2,275 square kilometers (at 4 and 9 millimeters soil depth). A comparison of estimated production losses attributable to crop residue and dung removal with those resulting from soil erosion indicates that the former exceeds soil erosion–induced losses by a factor of 35 to 80 percent (EFAP 1992).

Economic losses from such degradation would be great. Livestock production foregone was estimated to be equivalent to 2,117,700 tropical livestock units, representing approximately 9.6 percent of the national herd, or a financial loss of 146 million Ethiopian birr (4 percent of the 1990 agricultural gross domestic product). In addition, crop losses totaled 200 million Ethiopian birr, representing 5 percent of the 1990 agricultural gross domestic product (EFAP 1992).

Nearly 2 million hectares of cropland in the Ethiopian highlands are said to have reached irreversible levels of degradation. The cost of this soil damage in 1986 was estimated at US$30 million, 80 percent of which resulted from lost crop production and 20 percent from lost livestock production (Dregne 1990). The results of the production shortfalls are abject poverty, hunger (famine), and underdevelopment, as seen in northern Ethiopia for the last 20 years.

In contrast, the tropical highlands have a long growing season and short dry spells; perennial farming systems and frequent tree planting and maintenance provide good vegetative cover, as do prevailing soil conservation measures, both physical and biological. Cultivation and harvesting is continuous, and crop residues are left in the field, thus minimizing land degradation.

DECLINE OF ANIMAL FEED RESOURCES. Animal feed resources are inadequate in the tropical and especially in the subtropical highlands. This results from a shortage of grazing lands and the reduction or elimination of fallow periods in farming systems (in response to arable land shortages). Animals are an integral part of the farming system in the subtropical highlands where the feed shortage is most critical. Crop residue yields are also low because of crop yield declines.[2]

2. There is a positive correlation between grain yields and crop residue yields. A doubling of grain yields will result in a fourfold or greater increase in crop residue yields.

TABLE 22.5 Farming systems in the western Usambara Mountains, Tanzania

	Economic Benefits	
Farming System	Thousand Shillings per Year	Relative to System 1 (percent)
1. Cropping[a] with no grass strip or macro contours	20,390	100
2. Cropping with grass strip plus dairying	33,545	165
3. Cropping with macro contours plus *Grevillea* trees plus dairying	39,502	193

SOURCE: Pfeiffer 1990.
[a]Main crops grown are maize and beans.

Smallholder dairy farmers in central Kenya, and more recently on the Kenya coast and in the Usambara Mountains (Tanzania), now operate intensive feed gardens using napier, bana grass, and fodder shrubs in association with soil conservation structures such as macro contours. Manure and compost are applied to these fodder and agricultural plots, and the dung is first used to generate biogas. Both crop and fodder yields remain high, and overall farm productivity and revenues are high. Trees such as *Grevillea robusta* are also integrated into these farming systems; the leaf fall is used in livestock bedding before being composted. The practice, popularly known as zero grazing, has been recently evaluated in the Embu (Kenya) and Usambara Mountains (Tanzania), and the practice is ecologically stable and economically sound (Getahun 1990; Pfeiffer 1990). Table 22.5 compares three farming systems. The most profitable is a stall feeding system with fodder grown on soil conservation strips or contours, thus producing manure to fertilize the food-crop plots and fodder strips. The addition of trees in system 3 can provide fuelwood and timber, which makes this system more profitable.

WOOD DEPLETION. There is a general shortage of fuelwood, poles, and construction wood (including timber) in the highlands. This problem is more acute in most farming systems of the subtropical highlands, where complete tree cover removal is generally practiced and where fire is used for land preparation. High-population areas in the tropical highlands with very small landholdings, in particular, the tea and dairy areas, also show acute wood shortages. Elsewhere in the tropical highlands, tree planting is on the increase, especially multipurpose species and those with wide ecological ranges. These are often integrated into crop-livestock farming as well as planted on the homestead. Fruit trees are more common at the lower altitudes (1,500–2,000 meters), while growing subtemperate fruit trees at high altitudes (above 3,000 meters) is less common, especially in the subtropical cereal highlands.

FIGURE 22.4 Sustainable development of farm-household systems

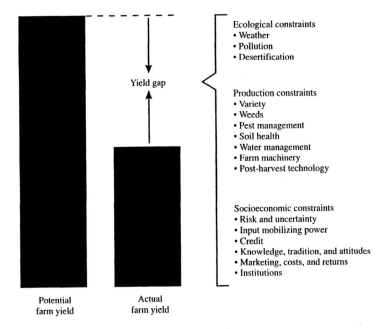

Agricultural Growth and Sustainability: Potential Conflicts

Agricultural growth in the East African highlands can come only through increased yields or through expansion of cropped area at the expense of forest and grazing lands.

In the tropical highlands, much of the agricultural growth has come from increased yields through *intensification,* as can be seen in the Arusha-Kilimanjaro region of Tanzania, the Embu-Meru-Kikuyu highlands of central Kenya, the Kisii highlands of southwestern Kenya, and the central highlands of Rwanda and Burundi. These intensive mixed cropping systems provide for high population densities (more than 800 people per square kilometer), but they cannot be expected to go beyond current levels unless irrigation and more purchased inputs are used along with adoption of other production packages.

In the subtropical highlands, nearly all of the agricultural growth has come from expansion of agricultural area. Crop yields are low, and the gap between the actual and the potential yields is wide. In these cereal-dominated highlands, ecological constraints (drought, pests, diseases, and erosion) have increased, further depressing agricultural growth. This is illustrated in Figure 22.4. This system operates at a low level of efficiency. Thus a population density of only 30–40 people per square kilometer can cause enough ecological stress to break down systems, as seen in most of the northern Ethiopian highlands. As more marginal areas and steep slopes are cultivated, ecological breakdowns are accelerated because of landslides and flash floods. These habitats become more prone to degradation as the years of cultivation increase. Depletion of woody vegetation and organic residues results in large deposits of silt and water in the topographic depressions, which are also rendered less useful as a result of flooding and acidity.

Recommendations

Subtropical highland agriculture can be improved by overcoming the constraints listed in Figure 22.4, but farmers are too poor to purchase these inputs or to forego the use of dung and crop residue for the sake of maintaining the biological regenerative capacity of the land. Indeed, crop yields could be improved three- to fivefold through use of fertilizers, pesticides, improved seeds, and better crop husbandry practices.

Nevertheless, moving to tree crop–based land use systems such as farm forestry and agroforestry practices is the best option for increasing and sustaining yields, even in subtropical highlands. Successful examples are the enset-based and Konso mixed farming systems in southern Ethiopia; the chagaa system of northeastern Tanzania; and the mixed farming systems of eastern, central, and western Kenya.

The following measures would promote agricultural growth, sustainability (ecological stability), and minimization of land use conflicts among crop farming, livestock, and forestry: (1) soil conservation measures; (2) organic matter accumulation through application of compost and mulch, both green manure and crop residues; (3) reduced fallow; (4) integration of trees and animals into cropping system; (5) use of chemical fertilizers (especially on cash crops); (6) increased crop diversity and intercropping; (7) improved markets and marketing; and (8) use of irrigation when available.

Adoption of these measures in the tropical highlands will increase the carrying capacity of the subtropical highlands. The need to bring trees back to the rural landscape in the subtropical highlands is urgent, as is the adoption of soil conservation practices, especially through biological means. Tree browsing and the use of fire for land preparation must also be reduced. Acreage under cereals should also be reduced, but total output should be maintained by increasing yields per unit of land. Certainly the present expansion of the cereal-livestock production system typical of the subtropics into the tropical highlands needs to be minimized and reversed.

Population growth in the highlands needs to be checked if the land use systems advocated here are to operate successfully. Most of the tropical highlands are already overpopulated, but the carrying capacity of the subtropical highlands can be nearly doubled through the recommended land use systems and policy changes (especially land and tree tenure). Increasing the number of rural people, especially in the subtropical highlands, affected by social, economic, and political upheavals means more people living under the increasing threat of food insecurity.

Given the chance and capacity, the rural poor will be the best, most nurturing guardians of their environment (the land) because they depend on it for their survival. Poverty alleviation programs may be needed before rural people can be expected to reduce their mining of the resource base. Increased security of land and tree tenure will encourage long-term planning and promote environmental protection. Poor people are part of a poor environment, and both breed disaster over time.

23 A New Approach to Poverty Alleviation and Sustainability in the Dry Tropical Hillsides of Central America: A Guatemalan Case Study

RAFAEL CELIS, MARIO A. VEDOVA, AND SERGIO RUANO

The structure of economic and legal incentives and the natural resource tenure system in Central America are working against sustainable agricultural development. The region experienced accelerated rates of growth during the 1960s and 1970s, but growth slowed during the 1980s as a result of global recession and domestic political unrest. As elsewhere in the developing world, macroeconomic policies have discriminated against agriculture in favor of an inefficient industrial sector. Additionally, little was done to promote the service sector, one that shows great potential for the region in the 1990s and beyond. Greater openness of the national economies and increased global competition exert additional pressure toward profound social, political, and economic change.

Alongside the expansion and contraction of growth over the past two decades, population growth rates have been among the highest in the world: 3 percent per year. The result has been the worsening of absolute and relative poverty and income distribution accompanied by severe environmental degradation. National and international pressure is mounting to deter what is perceived as an unsustainable expansion of agriculture.

Against this backdrop, policymakers will have to redefine the role of agriculture so that it is itself sustainable and contributes to the sustainability of national and international development. In this chapter we provide an overview of the situation on Central American hillsides and present a case study from one of the most depressed regions, Jutiapa, Guatemala. We conclude by drawing policy and technology lessons.

Sustainability in the Central American Highlands

Hillsides are the prevailing landscape in Central America. As shown in Table 23.1, they represent more than two-thirds of total land area. Although the majority of hillsides are in the humid tropics, it is also common to find hillsides with unimodal, low levels of rainfall typical of dry tropical areas.

328

TABLE 23.1 Land use and population characteristics in Central America, by topographic class

	Lowlands	Hillsides	Total
Total area (thousand hectares)[a]	4,862.6	10,517.9	15,380.5
Annual crops (percent)	6.4	13.9	20.3
Perennial crops (percent)	9.7	14.6	24.3
Forest (percent)	5.5	13.2	18.7
Pasture (percent)	9.3	25.1	34.4
Other (percent)	0.7	1.6	2.3
Total (percent)	31.6	68.4	100.0
Cattle (animals, per square kilometer)	12.9	15.1	14.4
Population (persons per square kilometer)	33.4	69.1	57.2
Illiterate (persons per square kilometer)	6.9	17.0	13.6
Houses without aqueduct (per square kilometer)	2.0	5.3	4.2
Female migrants (per year, per square kilometer)	0.52	0.67	0.62
Male migrants (per year, per square kilometer)	0.47	0.55	0.52

SOURCE: Carter 1991.
[a]Census area excludes unappropriated land, government-owned land, and forest reserves.

The majority of mountain ranges in Central America are under some type of use. The human occupation of the highlands was first driven by early Spanish settlers, who took over the lowlands from native populations, pushing them onto the hillsides. During the coffee expansion of the mid-nineteenth century, forested mountains were converted to cropland. More recently, expanding populations combined with a rapid increase of nontraditional exports have expanded hillside occupation.

Land use patterns on Central American hillsides have features that jeopardize any prospects for sustainable agricultural development. Many of the cleared lands have been so degraded that they are no longer useful, even for forestry. Furthermore, almost half of land suitable for agricultural production on the slopes is devoted to extensive cattle ranching; and, despite the fragility of this land, the total number of animals on the hillsides is about three times larger than in the lowlands (Table 23.1).

Possibilities for modifying these patterns are limited because much of Central America's food supply (about 70 percent) is grown on hillsides. The situation is particularly critical for maize and beans, the two major staples in the region. For example, 80 percent of Nicaragua's maize and 95 percent of its beans are produced on hillsides. In Honduras, 42 percent of all maize and 60 percent of all beans are produced on sloped terrain. Population density on the hillsides is more than double that of lowlands. This translates into higher levels of illiteracy, poor sanitation, and higher levels of both male and female outmigration.

Against this backdrop, it is clear that an operational definition of sustainability requires multilevel and multidimensional approaches. That is to say, while it is necessary to define sustainability at crop, farm, regional, national, and international levels, it is also necessary to incorporate the ecological, economic, social, cultural, and political dimensions of rural life.

Numerous linkages exist between ecosystems within hillside areas and between the hillsides and other agroecological regions, many of which cross national boundaries. For instance, key agricultural inputs (such as water, labor, and credit) and outputs flow within and across hillside areas. Sustainability in these areas, therefore, largely depends on the extent and nature of integration of hillside areas into national economies and the world economic system.

Trade and Sustainability

A great deal of discussion of sustainability has focused on the case of relatively large and closed economies. However, many countries in the tropical world have small and open economies. For instance, all the Central American and Caribbean countries have trade flows (imports plus exports) that range from 30 percent to 90 percent of gross domestic product.

An immediate consequence of this smallness and openness is that production patterns are largely determined by foreign demand. If economic systems undervalue natural resources used in the production of export crops, rapid and widespread environmental degradation can occur. For example, the rapid expansion of banana exports in Central America accelerated deforestation in the lowlands and pushed smallholders onto hillsides.

A second consequence is that production of both tradable and nontradable goods and services is highly dependent on imported capital goods and other inputs. This dependency, combined with the existence of domestic trade distortions, promotes the adoption of technologies that frequently degrade the environment. One example is the production of staples using obsolete machinery and dangerous chemicals, some of which are banned in developed countries. In the context of Central America, then, the concept of sustainability may have to embody the sustained generation of foreign exchange while at the same time securing continuous improvements in human welfare.

Sustainable Development and Policy Reform

Policy reforms under way in the developing world since the beginning of the 1980s and identified under the label of structural adjustment were initially conceived as a set of steps taken to bring domestic economic institutions and policies more into line with world prices, trade patterns, and investment opportunities. This approach frequently neglected the poor and the environment. By the end of the decade, however, it became increasingly clear to governments, bilateral and multilateral agencies, and academicians that two of the most pressing problems in developing countries were poverty and environmental degradation. In the case of

Central America, the persistence of these two problems jeopardizes any prospects for sustainable development in the future (Leonard 1987).

The Critical Links between Poverty and Environmental Degradation

In Central America, as in much of the developing world, poverty and environmental degradation are inseparable. The rate of use of natural resources has accelerated in response to the need to increase income and employment opportunities for a growing population. Some of these countries are falling into the extreme poverty associated with malnutrition, poor health, and low levels of education.

A population increase that is not accompanied by an increase in arable land, or by increases in productivity per hectare, results in the cultivation of marginal lands and fragile areas. Such appears to be the case of Guatemala, where vast areas of dry and humid tropical forest are under increasing pressure by a population that is continually expelled from other zones. In addition, even in cases where population expansion is absorbed by the nonagricultural sectors of the economy, the pressure on arable lands may still be quite high as a result of increasing demand for food, industrial inputs of agricultural origin, and the need to increase foreign exchange revenues through expanded traditional and nontraditional agricultural exports. Costa Rica is a case in point. Such pressures can also lead to the degradation of high-potential areas if conservation investments are not made. Examples of such degradation can be found in the coffee zones of Panama and El Salvador.

In some cases, improved technologies are available, but distorted systems of incentives or institutional and political factors can impede their adoption. A highly skewed distribution of land, for instance, forces the rural poor to move onto and overexploit fragile land and favors a system of extensive use of large farms. The most visible signs of exploitation of fragile lands are the rapid deforestation and soil erosion observed on hillsides all over Central America. As deforestation and soil erosion advance, the rural poor find it increasingly costly to gather firewood, obtain clean water, and hunt wild animals, which in many cases are important sources of protein and cash. The result has been larger demands on scarce family labor—which is distracted from cropping and livestock activities—and high levels of malnutrition and disease incidence, all of which, in turn, push household productivity down, starting a vicious circle of poverty and environmental degradation. This vicious circle has been observed in the Honduran watersheds of Tatumbla, Sabacuante, and Rio Grande and in the semi-arid regions of southeastern Guatemala.

Links among Sustainability, Agricultural Growth, and Poverty Alleviation

Central America faces severe environmental and poverty problems, and the two are linked (Annis 1992). After more than two decades, during which

TABLE 23.2 Trends in land use and agricultural share of gross domestic product (GDP) in Central America (percent)

	Costa Rica	El Salvador	Guatemala	Honduras	Nicaragua	Panama
Change in area, 1981–1987						
Forest and woodlands	–23.0	–36.0	–16.0	–17.5	–23.0	–7.5
Pasture	34.5	0.0	8.0	8.5	12.0	8.5
Crops	6.0	8.5	10.5	6.0	3.0	5.0
Rate of deforestation in the 1980s	6.8	3.2	2.0	2.3	2.6	0.8
Agriculture's contribution to GDP						
1960–1965	23.0	24.0	n.a.	40.0	25.0	17.0
1990	18.0	14.0	n.a.	22.0	21.0	9.0

SOURCE: SIECA 1989.
NOTE: n.a. = Not available.

Central America's policymakers responded with ministries, task forces, and high-level commissions, three inescapable realities remain: (1) poverty has generally gotten worse, not better; (2) the region's physical resources are being depleted at an accelerating rate; and (3) current responses, though positive, are neither reversing poverty nor stemming the degradation of physical assets.

Table 23.2 illustrates the ways natural resources have been used in the countries of the region. Heavy deforestation is the salient feature. Deforestation on hillsides leads to soil degradation. In the seasonally dry zones, 62 percent of the area is highly susceptible to erosion (PIRAMIDE 1990). Conservative estimates put the loss of soil in Guatemala at 1,417 metric tons per square kilometer per year. For Central America as a whole, estimates of soil loss approach 50 million metric tons per year, which, in terms of comparable value of nutrients at market prices, would be considerably higher than the annual federal budgets of all six countries. Not surprisingly, all countries in the region have increased their imports of fertilizers to compensate for crop productivity declines, some of which are clearly evident from Table 23.3.

While it may be difficult to draw conclusions regarding the links between deforestation and changes in crop productivity from aggregate data, some trends seem to emerge from Tables 23.2 and 23.3. Expansion of grassland is greater than that of cropland, which, when combined with expansion of population, suggests a decline in agricultural productivity per worker and hence in real wages.

Jutiapa: A Case Study

One example that illustrates the linkages between sustainability, agricultural growth, and poverty alleviation at the farm and regional levels, and

TABLE 23.3 Percent change in crop yields per hectare in Central America, 1981–1987

	Costa Rica	El Salvador	Guatemala	Honduras	Nicaragua	Panama
Coffee	16.0	n.a.	14.0	32.0	–14.0	n.a.
Sugar	–13.0	3.0	n.a.	15.0	–12.0	n.a.
Cotton	142.0	13.0	–5.0	–5.0	–30.0	n.a.
Bananas	17.0	n.a.	–8.0	13.0	15.0	n.a.
Corn	–18.5	–8.0	14.0	n.a.	69.0	–14.0
Beans	108.0	–30.0	–46.2	–29.0	n.a.	32.0
Rice	–67.0	23.0	12.0	26.0	20.0	22.5
Sorghum	–64.0	n.a.	–45.0	–32.0	n.a.	n.a.

SOURCE: SIECA 1989.
NOTE: n.a. = Not available.

highlights the issues raised so far, is encountered in the hillsides of Jutiapa, in the southeastern part of Guatemala.[1] From a physical perspective, this case is representative of the dry, steep slopes of Central America such as Santa Ana in El Salvador, Choluteca in Honduras, Estelí in Nicaragua, Nicoya and Puriscal in Costa Rica, and the Azuero Peninsula in Panama. It must be stressed that considerable variation exists across these sites from social, economic, political, and cultural perspectives. Therefore, generalizations are limited.

Jutiapa is located at an average altitude of 900–1,100 meters above sea level. Rainfall is less than 1 meter per year and is concentrated during the months of May through October, with a drastic decrease in July, leaving between six and seven dry months. The short rainy season and the irregularity of the rains are the main constraints to agricultural production.

Jutiapa has an agriculture-based economy. Extensive cattle ranching and production of maize, beans, and sorghum are the predominant activities. The structure of land distribution in Jutiapa is similar to that of the rest of the country. Seventy-three percent of farms are smaller than 3.5 hectares, covering just 14 percent of total area (Heer and Celada 1991). Fifty-five percent of the population engaged in agriculture rent land, and more than half of these are landless (CATIE 1990).

Jutiapa is different from the well-known Indian-dominated humid highlands of Guatemala. People in Jutiapa are mestizo, with roots going back to Spanish gypsies. They are of a bellicose character, which has contributed to a traditional climate of violence in the region. As a consequence, inhabitants live

---

1. The situation described here is the result of field observations made during a rapid rural appraisal conducted in Jutiapa in February 1990 and over the following two years during the implementation of a technology validation project.

in clusters to provide safety for their families and cattle. Farms are typically located several hours (walking) from towns.

Seasonal and permanent migration are common in Jutiapa. Seasonal migration occurs during the dry months when people move to the central highlands of Guatemala to harvest coffee and to the coastal lowlands where they engage in sugarcane harvesting or move their cattle to better pasture lands. Permanent migration to the northern lowlands of the Petén in search of opportunities to clear forest and harvest wild plants such as chicle is common. Considerable numbers of people, many of them political refugees, also emigrate to neighboring Mexico and the United States.

Poverty is overwhelming in Jutiapa. Seventy percent of the population are considered very poor, 18 percent are poor, and only 12 percent are classified as nonpoor (Heer and Celada 1991).

A colorful but dramatic socioeconomic and environmental fabric emerges from the arid slopes of Jutiapa. The weaving yarn of this fabric is a tenurial system deeply embedded in Guatemalan society since colonial times. The following is a description of this system derived from multidisciplinary observations.

Landowners in Jutiapa dedicate the highest proportion of their land to raising cattle under harsh conditions that result from shortages of feedstock during the dry season. Herds of Creole cattle raised to satisfy home consumption and local market demand for beef and dairy products are the predominant species. Landowners also devote part of their holdings to maize, sorghum, and beans, yet a sizable part of each farm is rented to other people who use the land to produce the same crops. Rental payments are made in cash or in kind. This is a typical transaction elsewhere in the developing world, but in Jutiapa this transaction yields hidden benefits for both landowners and tenants.

The benefit to landowners is their utilization of crop by-products left in the field by tenants after harvest. By the end of the rainy season, grazing lands are exhausted and cattle are moved to crop parcels and rely on the by-products to survive the long dry season. The market value of this forage (which accrues to landowners) is estimated to be five times that of the grain harvested by the tenant.

But tenants also reap benefits. When the tenants cultivate land, they also gain access to trees, which they trim or cut down for construction and fuelwood use. The market value of these tree products (which accrues to tenants) is estimated to be roughly equal to the value of grain harvested on rented plots.

The environmental consequences resulting from this production system are evident to any visitor to the region: bare mountains, dry rivers and creeks, soil erosion, disappearance of wildlife, declining soil fertility and crop productivity, and increasing poverty and malnutrition. Landowners, tenants, government officers, representatives of local and international nongovernmental organizations, and researchers from international research centers all agree on this gloomy observation.

When landowners are asked why they do not plant trees, their immediate response is: "I am not going to plant trees that the tenants will steal." Similarly, when the tenants are asked why they do not use simple soil conservation practices such as live contours, they answer: "If I do that, next season the landowner will assign me another parcel and use the improved parcel for himself. I am not going to improve land that is not mine." Clearly, incentive incompatibilities generate an unsustainable production scheme.

Many inhabitants of the region still believe, however, that the production system in Jutiapa is sustainable. They point out that the system has been in place since colonial times and people still live there and generate economic rents. Missing from this argument are the declining productivity of land and labor and the increased reliance on chemical fertilizer. Also missing from the argument are the masses of people who have been pushed out to the rain forests in the lowlands and, in many cases, have left the country—the hallmark of an unsustainable social system.

Overlap Technologies for Sustainable Agricultural Development in the Dry Tropical Hillsides

Various local and international institutions have joined together to identify and validate agricultural technologies on farms to deal with threats to sustainability in Jutiapa. The effort is innovative in its cooperation among institutions, its holistic focus, and the degree of farmer involvement in the choice and design of "overlap" technologies, that is, technologies capable of both boosting productivity and reversing environmental degradation. The following is a brief description of these technologies and a preliminary, qualitative assessment of their impact.[2]

Improved Wood Stoves

A new wood stove has been designed to replace open-fire cooking. The stove consists of a long narrow body with three cooking spaces on one end and a chimney on the other. Various types of these stoves have been promoted in the region, and rural families are keen to adopt them, even though their modest cost may put them beyond the reach of many households. Their advantages are not only a large reduction in firewood use, but also the ability to cook three pots at a time with little smoke and increased home safety. The saving of firewood should have a considerable impact on the environment as well as reduce the demand for male labor for gathering firewood.

---

2. These overlap technologies have been promoted by the "Sustainable Agrosilvopastoral Systems for Small Farmers in the Central American Dry Tropics" project, managed by the Tropical Agricultural Center for Research and Training (CATIE).

Improved Varieties of Beans

Mosaic-resistant bean varieties have been introduced by regional research stations. These varieties have met with particular success largely because a mosaic-type disease is spreading throughout the region, seriously affecting yields. The new varieties have substantially increased productivity, reducing the area required to meet family needs. This alleviates pressure on soils while at the same time improving human nutrition.

Soil Erosion Control Measures

Erosion control technologies such as maize straw barriers, live contour barriers of sorghum or sugarcane, and stone contour walls have all been successful. On the basis of simple visual inspection, they seem to greatly reduce soil losses, thus helping to maintain fertility and productivity. No precise measures of soil erosion reduction are yet available. However, these technologies effectively demonstrate how much soil is lost without conservation measures. This type of observation is particularly important, as conservation investments tend to be longer term and the results less visible.

In-Ground Silos and Forage Cones

The prolonged dry season imposes considerable hardship on cattle, leading to cessation of milk production and animal weight loss. In-ground silos and forage cones allow stover and other feed to be stored, thereby providing either a minimum feed supplement for the whole season or a prolonged milking period. While this technology has been adopted by many farmers, its use is limited by the size of the silo and the availability of crop residues. In most cases it only feeds a small herd for about two weeks or fully feeds two milking cows for about one month.

Live Fences and Windbreaks

There is a long tradition of using live trees as fences in the region, and the proposed technology replaces traditional trees with a multipurpose tree that produces fodder and fuelwood. This technology can also be used for subdividing grazing land into paddocks for better range management.

Policy Recommendations

Technologies alone cannot bring about the changes needed in Central America. Policy reforms that promote the adoption of these technologies and secure the spread of the expected benefits to the rest of the economy are needed.

Massive efforts have been made in the region to slow population growth, and without them poverty levels today would be higher and natural resource degradation more severe. However, to further reduce population growth governments should look beyond contraception campaigns and frontally attack the high levels of illiteracy and stimulate female employment.

There are many misconceptions regarding deforestation. For instance, little is known about the demand for timber or the potential substitutes for it in consumption or production. Knowledge of such elasticities of substitution would improve the design of incentives to relieve pressure on forests. In Central America, the border price of timber does not reflect its opportunity cost. Nevertheless, small, "price-taking" countries with severe foreign exchange constraints are forced to wastefully export timber and other forest products. Except for properly established parks and reserves, most Central American forests are now in private hands. Because forests provide water and other services, there are considerable externalities and few incentives to preserve watersheds. Government controls through licensing and the imposition of indirect taxes have accelerated, rather than deterred, logging (Vedova 1996).

The case of Jutiapa might, at first glance, suggest the need for conventional land reform. However, political conditions in Guatemala make this impractical. Furthermore, given the small size of farm holdings and the degradation of the resource base, this is probably not a realistic option. Overlap technologies being tested in the region can improve agricultural land and labor productivity, alleviate poverty, and restore the resource base. But how can their adoption be stimulated in the face of two major constraints?

First, adoption will require large amounts of family labor during the dry season—the seasonal landlords, tenants, and landless peasants usually migrate to other regions to harvest coffee or sugarcane. Therefore, farmers will adopt these technologies only if the net gains derived from improved productivity are greater than the net gains obtained from labor income earned on plantations.

Second, differential benefits accruing to landlords and tenants under the land rental scheme observed in Jutiapa can affect adoption rates, particularly if forage and fuelwood are undervalued. Part of the solution may lie in land taxes, which are potentially important policy instruments in Central America (Strasma and Celis 1992). Land taxes should be instituted and based on land values established with community input. Tax revenues should be earmarked to local governments for use in infrastructure development, soil conservation and reforestation programs, and schools. Such a land tax could also promote decentralization and participatory democracy, while increasing production, improving the resource base, and reducing poverty.

In Jutiapa, a land tax could finance the purchase of land to be preserved as watersheds and biodiversity reserves. It could also help finance soil conservation measures, the adoption of improved stoves, and afforestation and reforestation on communal and private land. What is more important, with investments in improved infrastructure, forage and fuelwood markets would be made more efficient and the processing, storage, and distribution of these two essential commodities enhanced.

24 Conclusions

STEPHEN A. VOSTI AND THOMAS REARDON

This book examines the links among three critical development objectives: agricultural growth, poverty alleviation, and the sustainable use of natural resources in rural areas of the developing world. Four issues are addressed: (1) What is the nature of these links, especially those between poverty and environment, and between growth and environment, about which relatively little is known? (2) How do policies, technologies, institutions, population growth, and climate change condition these links? (3) What policies, technologies, and institutions would increase the compatibility of the three objectives? (4) How do the answers to the first three questions differ over three principal ecoregions of the developing world (humid and subhumid tropics, the arid and semi-arid tropics, and the tropical highlands)?

In this chapter we first summarize, not necessarily in order of importance, the insights this volume has provided on these questions and then discuss agricultural and policy research gaps.

Key Findings Concerning the Nature of the Links and Their Determinants

First, to meet rapid increases in food and fiber needs and alleviate poverty in the developing world, rapid growth in output and yields is imperative. Accelerating and sustaining growth are policymakers' top priorities in poor countries. This growth will need to take place in the face of increasing land scarcity because in most areas the uncultivated land frontier has disappeared or soon will disappear, and populations are increasing rapidly.

Second, agricultural growth, via either intensification or extensification, undertaken without necessary regard for soil and water enhancement and protection can degrade the natural resource base. In most poor countries, soil and water degradation are the main environmental problems; in a few, agricultural pollution has emerged as a problem.

These two findings imply that the issue is *how* growth should occur, not whether it should. As land constraints become generalized, growth will need to take place via the *sustainable intensification* of agriculture. Farmers need to have the incentive and the capacity to maintain soil fertility with fertilizer and manure use, to protect the soil with bunds, irrigation drainage, windbreaks, and other conservation measures, and to avoid extensive practices that mine soil nutrients and other natural resources or push onto the fragile commons. In the long run, sustainable agricultural intensification will be the principal and most effective barrier to environmental degradation, on both private lands and the commons.

One principle should be universally applied: the object of sustainability is not agriculture or forests per se but rural families' livelihoods—income and food security. This security can be based on a mix of cash crops, food crops, livestock, and nonagricultural activities.

General prescriptions advocating sustainable agriculture on the basis of low external inputs are not universally appropriate for meeting all three development objectives. For example, in zones less favored agronomically for foodgrain production, such prescriptions may be environmentally sound, but the low yields and low incomes that result need to be counterbalanced by cash cropping of annuals and perennials and even off-farm activities to meet poverty alleviation objectives. In more-favored zones, promoting low external input agriculture will cause these zones to fall short of growth potential and perhaps even harm the environment as farmers move into common lands or onto hillsides to meet food security needs.

Poverty can cause degradation of the environment: the poor often cannot afford the capital and other nonlabor inputs needed to protect the soil as agricultural intensification proceeds or the off-farm inputs needed to make land improvements not directly associated with intensification. They therefore often need to push farming onto fragile hillsides and into forests to survive. Poverty alleviation should be a priority both for its immediate benefit to peoples' lives and for its long-term potential benefit to the environment on which people depend.

But alleviating poverty does not mean automatic obviation of environmental problems, as richer households often have the means to damage the environment even faster—the machete gives way to the chain saw, small herds of animals to large herds, traditional technologies to the sometimes excessive use of agricultural chemicals.

Degradation of the environment can impoverish—as farm soils are degraded, farmers' yields drop; as forests and bushland disappear, the poor's short-term survival options and the long-term benefits from biodiversity disappear. However, abruptly blocking access to open-access lands can be disastrous to the poor, especially if they do not have adequate alternative income-generating activities.

In the long term, households that deplete the natural resource base and do not discover and invest in alternative, sustainable production activities will suffer increased poverty. Governments that do not make public investments to avoid this end will promote such poverty.

Hence a key challenge to designers of policies, technologies, and institutions is how to promote types of growth, poverty alleviation, and environmental enhancement that are compatible. This may mean wrestling with trade-offs in the short run. The nature of the links determining the trade-offs between objectives will differ over agroecological and policy contexts. Solutions that work in the humid tropics may be inappropriate in the semi-arid tropics; a solution that works where off-farm opportunities are abundant may not work where they are scarce.

Resource-use decisions made by rural households and communities in pursuit of food and livelihood security are typically the main determinants of the links among the three development objectives. Solutions to increase the compatibility of the objectives need to do so from the perspective of these actors and fit their income, investment, and survival strategies. For example, promoting an environmental objective such as protecting biodiversity-rich forests and wetlands, but failing to help farmers to intensify production on the land they farm or identify alternative income sources, will undermine the resource protection goal in the long run as the rural poor skirt forest and wetland barriers to survive.

Nonagricultural activity—often a spinoff of agricultural growth—generates income in ways that increase the compatibility among the three development objectives. First, it provides cash to meet food needs, thereby reducing poverty. Second, nonagricultural income allows rural households to put less pressure on fragile and common lands directly by providing alternatives to low-profit agriculture on these less-favored lands and indirectly by helping farmers purchase improved inputs in order to intensify and focus agriculture on more-favored lands.

Finally, reducing population growth is useful but not sufficient for making the objectives compatible; family planning is a complement to, not a substitute for, rural development.

Implications for Design of Policies, Technologies, and Institutions

A distinction was made in this volume between productivity investments (such as those embodied in Green Revolution technologies) and conservation investments (to protect land), in connection with both the inputs required to undertake each type of technology and the timing and level of economic return farmers can expect. Consequently, different sets of policies may be needed to promote the adoption and effective use of both sets of technologies.

New technologies embodying characteristics that meet both growth *and* environmental objectives (labeled "overlap technologies") need to be developed, and policies capable of promoting their adoption should be designed and implemented. In this volume, a number of promising overlap technologies were identified, but the availability of such technologies is very limited and the obstacles to their adoption worrisome.

Broad policies—trade, macroeconomic, and sectoral—affect the income, production, and investment choices of households and communities and thus are major influences on the links. Such policies affect the costs and benefits of resource use and investments at the farm level and consequently can affect the natural resource base. However, their effects on the environment are often complex and can sometimes be contrary to expectations.

Thus broad policy tools are too blunt (and sometimes dangerous) to use alone in pursuit of specific environmental goals. "Getting prices right" in the macroeconomic or sectoral arena is an incomplete recipe for promoting sustainable intensification of agriculture or the conservation of the natural resource base generally. Broad policy changes are sometimes necessary (to raise incentives) but seldom sufficient to increase the capacity of the actors to adopt overlap technologies or to make conservation investments.

Natural resource policies are generally required to complement and thus improve the effectiveness and predictability of the effects of broad macroeconomic policies on the environment. However, getting natural resource prices "right" is often difficult because of missing markets and high enforcement costs. Much legislation goes unenforced for these reasons. It is most important that natural resource policies be compatible with broad policies that promote growth and poverty alleviation, and indeed they should be viewed as ways of increasing the chances for success of these broad policies.

Given the bluntness and insufficiencies of macroeconomic policies concerning natural resource use, and the difficulties in implementing effective natural resource policies, sets of complementary policies, institutions, and public investments must be identified and implemented. Such policies and investments can make broader policy instruments more effective and predictable and can compensate in cases where the environment is damaged as a result of changes in broad policies.

But complementary policies and investments also help overcome some of the structural impediments to resource conservation and to the adoption of overlap technologies by poor households and communities. These impediments take the form of poor physical infrastructure, insecure access to land and water, limited access to agricultural extension services, and the absence of improved inputs such as fertilizer that complement conservation measures. Some of these impediments can be overcome with local interventions, while others require state, regional, or national action. Better roads, more secure resource tenure regimes, improved access to current information on market prices, and increased community investments in irrigation schemes are all examples of complementary policies and actions that can promote resource conservation.

New institutions and new sets of rules governing interactions within and among them may be required to address natural resource degradation in ways that meet growth and poverty alleviation goals. For example, resource tenure reform and the design of institutions that can implement and enforce such reforms may be important first steps toward sustainability.

Agroecological Zone Considerations

Opportunities for progress on making the three development objectives compatible vary over space. The agroecology of zones defines and in many cases limits technology options and determines the incentives to and capacity of farmers and communities to respond to economic signals as well as to environmental change. The practical implications are that it is difficult to intensify agriculture in fragile, less-favored zones and that it is important to promote sustainable intensification in the more-favored zones. In less-favored agroclimates, foodgrain production will be more costly, suggesting that one should focus on livestock, agroforestry, and other nonstaple production systems better suited to fragile environments. In more-favored zones, agricultural intensification is not only possible but essential to meeting sustainability and poverty alleviation objectives. But development strategies tailored to reflect ecological conditions of particular zones may increase the dependency of rural consumers in less-favored zones on foodgrain markets, which can be worrisome if such markets are underdeveloped or if incomes in less-favored zones fail to rise. Therefore, national policies will be important not only in promoting zone-specific opportunities but also in addressing food security and inequity issues that can emerge as a result of these strategies.

A given agroecological zone contains both more-favored and less-favored regions for agriculture. This heterogeneity must be identified and used appropriately. More-favored regions should be tapped for agricultural growth, and in less-favored regions the focus should be on land protection rather than on large increases in crop yields. This is particularly important in agroecological zones that are less-favored agroclimates, such as the northern tier of the Sahel.

The boundaries of influence of policy (national, state, and district borders) generally do not coincide with agroecological zones or the regions they comprise. This makes inter- and intrazone development planning more difficult and highlights the need for cooperation in promoting sustainable agricultural intensification, especially in areas where the environmental side effects of agricultural change are large.

Environmental degradation and pollution are found in all agroecological zones and regions within them, but the relative importance of the forms of degradation and pollution as well as the obstacles to their resolution may differ across zones. For example, pollution from overuse of chemicals is generally found in the more humid zones where agricultural intensification has been fastest, whereas problems associated with water and soil erosion are found in more arid zones and on hillsides. Controlling chemical overuse can be accomplished by policies that directly affect user incentives. Problems of water and soil degradation generally need to be addressed at the household level as well as the watershed level and often require collective action for effective long-term resolution.

Opportunities for progress will also vary over time in a given zone. The scope for agricultural intensification—including changes in the stocks and qualities of the underlying natural resources—is not immutable but rather is affected by public and private practices and investments. For example, irrigation can transform a desert into a favorable environment for rapid growth, or intensive farming without soil amendments can transform a lush humid area into one with severely degraded soils.

Agroecological zones are linked in the exchange of both outputs and inputs, including labor. Therefore, policies designed to promote sustainability, growth, and poverty alleviation in a given zone must acknowledge and promote these links with other zones.

Agroecological zoning can be an effective aid to spatial planning by providing strategic input into the design of technologies and into agricultural extension policy, economic and environmental policy, and policy implementation. But such zoning needs to be flexible, as economic and physical changes alter the quantity, quality, and usefulness for development of the natural resources they contain.

Given the need for rapid growth in agriculture in ways that conserve the land, water, plant, and animal resources, the challenges appear staggering. What are the specific, practical, affordable technologies that combine growth and sustainability goals? What policies and institutions are practical and needed? How can the private sector be spurred by public action to make the needed investments? Some of these issues are dealt with in this volume, but many gaps in knowledge remain.

Gaps in Knowledge

For decades there has been research on agricultural growth and poverty alleviation. Sustainability research has attained more visibility and volume in the past decade. But research is only beginning on the links among sustainability, agricultural growth, and poverty alleviation and on appropriate policies, technologies, and institutional arrangements to enhance their compatibility. The following are key areas for future research suggested by the work presented in this volume.

First, of the links discussed, the least empirical research has been done on the link between environment and poverty. This volume showed that the nature of this link varies with the level and type of poverty and the environmental problem. The policy, technology, and institutional approaches to making sustainability and poverty alleviation more compatible are a major research challenge. Moreover, there is a large gap between practice and theory. For example, it is a common environmentalist policy at present to limit access to forests to preserve them and to seek alternative income sources for those on the periphery. But these sources are often inadequate to replace what the poor have lost, and their poverty will eventually push them back into the forests to survive. What are practical ways to protect the commons but alleviate poverty in farmlands next to them?

Second, equally pressing is the need to discover technologies that can generate growth at the rate of population growth or more—in many areas, 3–4 percent per year—and yet combine these productivity-enhancing technologies with resource conservation measures that allow such growth to be sustainable. This volume showed that such overlap technologies exist in some areas, but the inventory is still small, and issues related to affordability and enabling conditions for adoption are not well understood.

Third, research on policies and institutions will be particularly important as it pertains to the adoption and effective use of overlap technologies and conservation measures, including the preconditions for spontaneous adoption of such measures. This is in a sense testing the "induced innovation" hypothesis in the resource conservation domain. Research on income and investment patterns and food security strategies (both on-farm and off-farm) of rural households and communities is especially important. Special emphasis in this research should be placed on assessing the effects of changes in policies, technologies, and institutions on farmers' decisions to adopt overlap technologies and conservation measures and the consequences of both adoption and nonadoption of these on the natural resource base. Ultimately, researchers must complete the cycle by examining the impact of human-induced environmental change on human welfare. Issues of access to credit, resource tenure, and off-farm income will be increasingly important in the aftermath of structural adjustment and in the face of rapid growth in population in many areas.

Fourth, research on the design and implementation of innovative, effective, and efficient complementary policies and institutions is needed, and progress is being made. For example, direct government involvement in the control and distribution of irrigation water is being replaced in some areas by innovative schemes that transfer water rights to water users. In other areas, governments are experimenting with new combinations of traditional land rights and formal land-titling schemes in an effort to promote sustainable growth and poverty alleviation and to redress local "negative externalities" such as overgrazing and agricultural pollution. However, the efficiency, sustainability, and replicability of such schemes remains in doubt, as does the potential for modifying them to improve resource use and address equity issues. In all cases, the role of government as a provider of physical and social infrastructure is being questioned. Guidance on where and when governments can and should invest is needed, with special emphasis on the levels at which government action should be taken and on the political economy and public finance issues linked to these actions.

Fifth, the mechanisms for paying for complementary investments are often not in place, and where they are, sometimes they have not been designed in ways to make them sustainable. What should be the roles of the private sector, communities, nongovernmental organizations, the state, and the donor community in financing such investments?

Sixth, biophysical data (such as those provided by remote sensing) are important for depicting natural resource use patterns but fall short of identifying those responsible for resource degradation or enhancement or how changes in policies, technologies, and institutions have (or might) influence resource use. Therefore, remote sensing data are not a substitute for aggregate and micro-level socioeconomic data, but they can be complements, and enhancing this complementarity requires further development of methods.

Seventh, links among agroecological zones, and between more-favored and less-favored regions within them, need to be more clearly understood— and special attention given to establishing links that promote the three development objectives across all zones.

Finally, research is urgently needed on how sustainability issues can be addressed by national and international research institutions without disrupting or displacing fruitful lines of traditional agricultural research (plant breeding and agronomic practices) aimed at raising yields. The latter is crucial for growth and should not be neglected. If agendas (and budgets) of agricultural research are not expanded to incorporate new natural resource management concerns, and there is mere displacement from traditional research to environmental research, the sustainability effort will over time be undermined.

References

ACIAR (Australian Centre for International Agricultural Research). 1984. Soil erosion and management. Proceedings of a workshop held at PCARRD, Los Baños, the Philippines, 3–5 December.

ADB (Asian Development Bank). 1987. *A review of forestry and forest industries in the Asia-Pacific region.* Manila.

Adesina, A. A. 1992. Village-level studies and appropriate cereal technology development in West Africa: A case study in Mali. In *Diversity, farmer knowledge, and sustainability,* ed. J. L. Moock. Ithaca, N.Y., U.S.A.: Cornell University Press.

Adesina, A. A., and J. H. Sanders. 1991. Peasant farmer behavior and cereal technologies: Stochastic programming analysis in Niger. *Agricultural Economics* 5 (1): 21–38.

af Ornas, A. H. 1990. Town-based pastoralism in eastern Africa. In *Small-town Africa: Studies in rural-urban interaction,* ed. J. Baker. Seminar Proceedings 23. Uppsala, Sweden: Scandinavian Institute of African Studies.

Agarwal, A., and S. Narain. 1991. *Towards green villages: A strategy for environmentally sound and participatory rural development.* New Delhi: Centre for Science and Environment.

Agarwal, B. 1985. *Cold hearths and barren slopes: The woodfuel crisis in the third world.* New Delhi: Allied Publishers Limited.

Allan, N. J. R., G. W. Knapp, and C. Stadel. 1988. *Human impacts on mountains.* Totawa, N.J., U.S.A.: Rowman and Littlefield.

Allan, W. 1965. *The African husbandman.* Edinburgh: Oliver and Boyd.

Altieri, M. A., and M. K. Anderson. 1986. An ecological basis for the development of alternative agricultural systems for small farmers in the third world. *American Journal of Alternative Agriculture* 1: 20–38.

Anderson, J. R., and P. B. R. Hazell. 1994. Risk considerations in the design and transfer of agricultural technology. In *Agricultural technology: Policy issues for the international community,* ed. J. R. Anderson. Wallingford, U.K.: CAB International.

Anderson, M. B., and P. J. Woodrow. 1990. Reducing vulnerability to drought and famine: Developmental approaches to relief. *Disasters* 15 (1): 43–54.

Andrews, D. J. 1986. Current results and prospects in sorghum and pearl millet breeding. In *Development of rainfed agriculture under arid and semiarid conditions,* ed. T. J. Davis. Proceedings of the Sixth Agriculture Sector Symposium. Washington, D.C.: World Bank.

Annis, S. 1992. *Poverty, natural resources, and public policy in Central America.* New Brunswick, N.J., U.S.A.: Transaction.

Anteneh, A. 1984. Trends in Sub-Saharan Africa's livestock industries. *ILCA Bulletin* 18 (April): 7–15.

Antle, J. M., and P. L. Pingali. 1992. Pesticides, farmer health, and productivity: A Philippine case study. Paper presented at a workshop on Measuring the Health and Environmental Effects of Pesticides, 30 March–3 April, Bellagio, Italy.

Anuário. Various years. *Anuário estatistico do Brasil.* Rio de Janeiro: Fundação Instituto Brasileiro de Geografia e Estatistica.

Attaviroz, J. P. 1991. Soil erosion and land degradation in the northern Thai uplands. *Contour* 3 (1): 3–7.

Atwood, D. A. 1990. Land registration in Africa: The impact on agricultural production. *World Development* 18 (5): 659–671.

Bahhady, F. 1981. Recent changes in bedouin systems of livestock production in the Syrian Steppe. In *The future of pastoral peoples.* IDRC-175e. Ottawa, Ontario, Canada: International Development Research Centre.

Bandaragoda, J. 1986. Institutional arrangements between the health and irrigation sectors: Present status and suggestions for improvement. In *Proceedings of the workshop on irrigation and vector-borne disease transmission.* Digana Village, Sri Lanka: International Irrigation Management Institute.

Banskota, M., and N. S. Jodha. 1992a. Mountain agricultural development strategies: Comparative perspectives from the countries of the Hindu Kush–Himalayan Region. In *Sustainable mountain agriculture,* ed. N. S. Jodha, M. Banskota, and T. Partap. New Delhi: Oxford and IBH.

———. 1992b. Investment, subsidies, and resource transfer dynamics: Issues for sustainable mountain agriculture. In *Sustainable mountain agriculture,* ed. N. S. Jodha, M. Banskota, and T. Partap. New Delhi: Oxford and IBH.

Bapna, S. L., D. Jha, and N. S. Jodha. 1979. Agroeconomic features of semi-arid tropical India. Paper presented at the workshop on Socioeconomic Constraints to Development of Semi-Arid Tropical Agriculture, 19–23 February, International Crops Research Institute for the Semi-Arid Tropics, Hyderabad, India.

Barbier, E. B. 1987. The concept of sustainable economic development. *Environmental Conservation* 4 (2): 101–110.

———. 1989. *Economics, natural-resource scarcity, and development: Conventional and alternative views.* London: Earthscan.

———. 1990a. Rehabilitating gum arabic systems in Sudan: Economic and environmental implications. *Environmental and Resource Economics* 2 (4): 341–358.

———. 1990b. The farm-level economics of soil erosion: The uplands of Java. *Land Economics* 66 (9): 199–211.

———. 1991a. Environmental degradation in the third world. In *Blueprint 2: Greening the world economy,* ed. D. W. Pearce. London: Earthscan.

———. 1991b. Environmental management and development in the South: Prerequisites for sustainable development. UNCED (United Nations Conference on Environment and Development) workshop on Sustainable Development: From Concept to Action, 6 May, Geneva.

Barbier, E. B., and J. C. Burgess. 1992a. *Agricultural pricing and environmental degradation.* Policy Research Working Papers, Background Paper to the *World Development Report 1992.* Washington, D.C.: World Bank.

———. 1992b. *Malawi: Land degradation in agriculture.* Divisional Working Paper 1992-37, Policy and Research Division, Environment Department. Washington, D.C.: World Bank.

Barbier, E. B., W. M. Adams, and K. Kimmage. 1991. *Economic valuation of wetland benefits: The Hadejia-Jama'are flood plain, Nigeria.* LEEC Discussion Paper 91-02. London: London Environmental Economics Centre.

Barker, R., and D. Chapman. 1988. The economics of sustainable agricultural systems in developing countries. Cornell University, Ithaca, N.Y., U.S.A. Mimeo.

Barrett, J. C. 1989. *Tsetse control, land use, and livestock in the development of the Zambezi Valley, Zimbabwe: Some policy considerations.* ALPAN Network Paper 19. Addis Ababa: International Livestock Centre for Africa.

Bascom, J. B. 1990. Border pastoralism in eastern Sudan. *Geographical Review* 80 (4): 416–430.

Batie, S. 1989. Sustainable development: Challenges to the profession of agricultural economics. *American Journal of Agricultural Economics* 71 (5): 1083–1101.

Bationo, A., C. B. Christianson, and U. Mokwunye. 1987. Soil fertility management of the pearl millet–producing sandy soils of Sahelian West Africa: The Niger experience. In *Soil, crop, and water management in the Sudano-Sahelian zone.* Proceedings of an International Workshop, 11–16 January. Niamey, Niger: International Crops Research Institute for the Semi-Arid Tropics (ICRISAT) Sahelian Center.

Bebbington, A. 1993. Sustainable livelihood development in the Andes: Local institutions and regional resource use in Ecuador. *Development Policy Review* 11 (1): 5–30.

Becker, G., and H. Lewis. 1974. Interaction between quantity and quality of children. In *Economics of the family,* ed. T. W. Schultz. Chicago: University of Chicago Press.

Beckerman, W. 1974. *In defence of economic growth.* London: Jonathan Cape.

Behnke, R. H. 1985a. Measuring the benefits of subsistence versus commercial livestock production in Africa. *Agricultural Systems* 16: 109–135.

———. 1985b. *Open-range management and property rights in pastoral Africa: A case of spontaneous range enclosure in South Darfur, Sudan.* Pastoral Development Network Paper 20f. London: Overseas Development Institute.

———. 1986. *The implications of spontaneous range enclosure for African livestock development policy.* ALPAN Network Paper 12. Addis Ababa: International Livestock Centre for Africa.

Behnke, R. H., and I. Scoones. 1991. *Rethinking range ecology: Implications for rangeland management in Africa.* London: Overseas Development Institute.

Bennell, P. 1986. *Agricultural researchers in Sub-Saharan Africa: A quantitative overview.* Working Paper 5. The Hague: International Service for National Agricultural Research.

Bennett, J. W., S. W. Lawry, and J. C. Riddell. 1986. *Land tenure and livestock development in Sub-Saharan Africa.* AID Evaluation Special Study 39. Washington, D.C.: United States Agency for International Development.

Bernus, E. 1980. Famines et sécheresses chez les Touaregs Saheliens. *Africa* 50 (1): 1–7.

Bhalla, S. 1987. Trends in employment in Indian agriculture, land, and asset distribution. *Indian Journal of Agricultural Economics* 42 (4): 5–60.

Bhattarcharya, R. 1990. *Common property externalities: Isolation, assurance, and resource depletion in a traditional grazing context.* Divisional Working Paper 1990-10, Environment Department. Washington, D.C.: World Bank.

Bille, J. C., and A. Eshete. 1983. *Rangeland management and range conditions: A study in the Medecho and Did Hara areas of the effects of rangeland utilization.* Joint Ethiopian Pastoral Systems Study 7. Addis Ababa: International Livestock Center for Africa.

Binswanger, H. P. 1986. Risk aversion, collateral requirements, and the markets for credit and insurance in rural areas. In *Crop insurance for agricultural development,* ed. P. B. R. Hazell, C. Pomareda, and A. Valdés. Baltimore: Johns Hopkins University Press.

———. 1989a. *Brazilian policies that encourage deforestation in the Amazon.* Environment Department Working Paper 16. Washington, D.C.: World Bank.

———. 1989b. The policy response of agriculture. Proceedings of the World Bank Annual Conference on Development Economics, 26–27 April, Washington, D.C.

Binswanger, H. P., and J. von Braun. 1991. Technological change and commercialization in agriculture: The effect on the poor. *World Bank Research Observer* 6 (1): 57–80.

Binswanger, H. P., and J. McIntire. 1987. Behavioral and material determinants of production relations in land-abundant tropical agriculture. *Economic Development and Cultural Change* 30 (1): 73–99.

Binswanger, H. P., and P. L. Pingali. 1987. The evolution of farming systems and agricultural technology in Sub-Saharan Africa. In *Policy for agricultural research,* ed. V. W. Ruttan and C. E. Pray. Boulder, Colo., U.S.A.: Westview.

Binswanger, H. P., and A. J. Pritchard. 1987. Technology, investment, and institutional priorities for rapid agricultural growth in Sub-Saharan Africa. Draft report. World Bank, Agriculture and Rural Development, Research Unit, Washington, D.C.

Birdsall, N. 1985. A population perspective on agricultural development. In *Proceedings of the Fifth Agriculture Sector Symposium,* ed. T. Davis. Washington, D.C.: World Bank.

———. 1988. Economic approaches to population growth. In *Handbook of development economics,* vol. 1, ed. H. Chenery and T. N. Srinivasan. Amsterdam: North-Holland.

Bishop, J., B. Aylward, and E. Barbier. 1991. *Guidelines for applying environmental economics in developing countries.* LEEC Gatekeeper 91-02. London: London Environmental Economics Centre.

Bisrat, G. 1990. Issues of natural resources management in the Ethiopian rangelands. Paper presented at the Conference on National Conservation Strategy, 22–25 May, Addis Ababa.

Blarel, B. 1989. *Land tenure security and agricultural production under land scarcity: The case of Rwanda.* Washington, D.C.: World Bank, Agricultural Policy Division, Agriculture and Rural Development Department.

Board on Agriculture and Board on Science and Technology for Development. 1992. *Sustainable agriculture and the environment in the humid tropics.* Washington, D.C.: National Academy Press.

Board on Agriculture, National Research Council. 1991. *Sustainable agriculture research and education in the field.* Washington, D.C.: National Academy Press.

Bond, M. 1983. Agricultural responses to prices in Sub-Saharan African countries. *IMF Staff Papers* 30 (4): 703–726.

Bondestam, L. 1974. People and capitalism in northeastern Ethiopia. *Journal of Modern African Studies* 12 (3): 423–439.

Bonfiglioli, A. M. 1988. Management of pastoral production in the Sahel: Constraints and options. In *Desertification control and renewable resource management in the Sahelian and Sudanian zones of West Africa,* ed. F. Falloux and M. Aleki. Technical Paper 70. Washington, D.C.: World Bank.

Boserup, E. 1965a. *The conditions of agricultural growth: The economics of agrarian change under population pressure.* Chicago: Aldine.

———. 1965b. *Conditions of agricultural growth.* London: Allen and Unwin.

———. 1981. *Population and technology.* Oxford: Blackwell.

Bouis, H. E. 1994. The effect of income on the demand for food in poor countries: Are our food consumption databases giving us reliable estimates? *Journal of Development Economics* 44 (1): 199–226.

Bouis, H. E., and L. J. Haddad. 1990. *Agricultural commercialization, nutrition, and the rural poor: A study of Philippine farm households.* Boulder, Colo., U.S.A.: Lynne Rienner.

Bourgeois, R. 1990. *Structural linkages for integrating agricultural research and extension.* Working Paper 35. The Hague: International Service for National Agricultural Research.

Brabben, T. E. 1979. *Reservoir sedimentation study: Karangkates, East Java, Indonesia.* Report OD 22. Hydraulics Research Station, Wallingford, U.K.

Braun, J. von. 1991a. *A policy agenda for famine prevention in Africa.* Washington, D.C.: International Food Policy Research Institute.

———. 1991b. Social security in Sub-Saharan Africa: Reflections on policy challenges. In *Social security in developing countries,* ed. E. Ahmad, J. Drèze, and A. K. Sen. Oxford: Oxford University Press.

Braun, J. von, H. de Haen, and J. Blanken. 1991. *Commercialization of agriculture under population pressure: Effects on production, consumption, and nutrition in Rwanda.* Research Report 85. Washington, D.C.: International Food Policy Research Institute.

Braun, J. von, D. Puetz, and P. Webb. 1989. *Irrigation technology and commercialization of rice in The Gambia: Effects on income and nutrition.* Research Report 75. Washington, D.C.: International Food Policy Research Institute.

Braun, J. von, T. Teklu, and P. Webb. 1991. *Labor-intensive public works for food security: Experience in Africa.* Working Papers on Food Subsidies 6. Washington, D.C.: International Food Policy Research Institute.

Bray, F. 1986. *The rice economies: Technology and development in Asian societies.* Oxford: Blackwell.

Broca, S., and P. Oram. 1991. Study on the location of the poor. Paper prepared for the Technical Advisory Committee to the Consultative Group on International

Agricultural Research. International Food Policy Research Institute, Washington, D.C. Draft.

Brokken, R. F., and T. O. Williams. 1990. *Economic considerations for smallholder cattle, milk and meat production and marketing: Supporting institutions, marketing, and demand.* ALPAN Network Paper 26. Addis Ababa: International Livestock Centre for Africa.

Bromley, D. W. 1991. The commons, common property, and environmental policy. University of Wisconsin, Madison. Mimeo.

Bromley, D. W., and M. M. Cernea. 1989. *The management of common property natural resources: Some conceptual and operational fallacies.* World Bank Discussion Paper 57. Washington, D.C.: World Bank.

Browder, J. O. 1985. *Subsidies, deforestation, and the forest sector in the Brazilian Amazon.* Washington, D.C.: World Resources Institute.

Browder, J. O. 1989. Development alternatives for tropical rain forests. In *Environment and the poor: Development strategies for a common agenda,* ed. H. J. Leonard and contributors. New Brunswick, N.J., U.S.A.: Transaction Books for the Overseas Development Council.

Brown, G., and C. C. Harris. 1992. Natural forest management and the "tragedy of the commons": A multidisciplinary perspective. *Society and Natural Resources* 5 (1): 67–83.

Budowski, G. 1980. Agro-forestry in managing tropical forests. Paper presented at the International Symposium on Tropical Forests, 15–16 April, Yale University, New Haven, Conn., U.S.A.

Bultena, G. L., and E. O. Hoiberg. 1983. Factors affecting farmers' adoption of conservation tillage. *Journal of Soil and Water Conservation* 38 (3): 281–284.

Bumb, B. L. 1989. *Global fertilizer perspective, 1960–95: The dynamics of growth and structural change.* Muscle Shoals, Ala., U.S.A.: International Fertilizer Development Center.

Bunting, A. H. 1988. *Agricultural environments: Characterization, classification, and mapping.* Wallingford, U.K.: CAB International.

Burgess, J. C. 1992. *Economic analysis of the causes of tropical deforestation.* LEEC Discussion Paper 92-03. London: London Environmental Economics Centre.

Burton, S., P. B. Shah, and H. Schreier. 1989. Soil degradation from converting forest land into agriculture in the Chitawan district of Nepal. *Mountain Research and Development* 9 (4): 393–404.

Buttel, F. H. 1991. Knowledge production, ideology, and sustainability in the social and natural sciences. Paper presented at the Conference on Varieties of Sustainability, 10–12 May, Asiomary, Calif., U.S.A.

Byerlee, D. 1987. *Maintaining the momentum in post–Green Revolution agriculture: A micro-level perspective from Asia.* Michigan State University International Development Paper 10. East Lansing, Mich., U.S.A.: Michigan State University.

Byerlee, D., and H. Collinson. 1982. *Planning technologies appropriate to farmers: Concepts and procedures.* El Batarn, Mexico: Centro Internacional de Mejoramiento de Maïz y Trigo.

Byerlee, D., C. K. Eicher, C. Liedholm, and D. S. C. Spencer. 1983. Employment-output conflicts, factor-price distortions, and choice of technique: Empirical evidence from Sierra Leone. *Economic Development and Cultural Change* 31 (2): 315–336.

Cain, M., and G. McNicoll. 1986. *Population growth and agrarian outcomes.* Center for Policy Studies Working Paper 128. New York: Population Council.

Caldwell, J. C. 1975. *The Sahelian drought and its demographic implications.* Overseas Liaison Council Paper 8. Washington, D.C.: Overseas Liaison Council/American Council on Education.

Capistrano, A. D. 1990. Macroeconomic influences on tropical forest depletion: A cross-country analysis. Ph.D. diss., Food and Resource Economics Department, University of Florida, Gainesville, Fla., U.S.A.

Capistrano, A. D., and C. F. Kiker. 1990. Global economic influences on tropical closed broadleaved forest depletion, 1967–85. Food and Resource Economics Department, University of Florida, Gainesville, Fla., U.S.A. Mimeo.

Carlson, G. A., D. Zilberman, and J. A. Miranowski. 1993. *Agricultural and environmental resource economics.* New York: Oxford University Press.

Carnevale, P., and V. Robert. 1987. Introduction of irrigation in Burkina Faso and its effects on malaria transmission. In *Effects of agricultural development on vector-borne diseases.* Edited versions of papers presented at the seventh Annual Meeting of the Joint WHO/FAO/UNEP Panel of Experts on Environmental Management for Vector Control, 7–11 September. Rome: Food and Agriculture Organization of the United Nations.

Carr, S. J. 1989. *Technology for small-scale farmers in Sub-Saharan Africa.* Technical Paper 109. Washington, D.C.: World Bank.

Carter, S. 1991. Análisis geográfico del uso de la tierra en Centroamérica. In *Agricultura sostenible en las laderas centroamericanas: Oportunidades de colaboración institucional.* San José, Costa Rica: Instituto Interamericano de Cooperación para la Agricultura.

Castañeda, A. R., and S. I. Bhuiyan. 1988. Industrial pollution of irrigation water and its effects on riceland productivity. *Philippine Journal of Crop Science* 13 (1): 27–35.

CATIE (Centro Agronómico Tropical de Investigación y Enseñanza). 1990. *Informe de sondeo realizado en la zona de Jutiapa, Guatemala.* Turrialba, Costa Rica.

Censo agropecuario. 1985. Rio de Janeiro: Fundação Instituto Brasileiro de Geografia e Estatistica.

Censo demográfico. 1980. Rio de Janeiro: Fundação Instituto Brasileiro de Geografia e Estatistica.

———. 1990. Rio de Janeiro: Fundação Instituto Brasileiro de Geografia e Estatistica.

Cernea, M. 1987. Farmers organizations and institution building for sustainable development. In *Sustainability issues in agricultural development,* ed. T. J. Davis and I. A. Schirmer. Proceedings of the Seventh Agricultural Sector Symposium. Washington, D.C.: World Bank.

Cernea, M. 1992. *The building blocks of participation: Testing bottom-up planning.* World Bank Discussion Paper 166. Washington, D.C.: World Bank.

CGIAR (Consultative Group on International Agricultural Research). 1990. *1991 funding requirements of the IARCS.* Secretariat Paper ICW/90/IV, September 17, 1990. Agenda Item 11, International Centers Week. Washington, D.C.

———. 1996. *Milestones of renewal: A journey of hope and accomplishment.* Washington, D.C.

CGIAR/TAC (Consultative Group on International Agricultural Research/Technical Advisory Committee). 1987. *CGIAR priorities and future strategies.* Rome: Technical Advisory Committee.

————. 1989. *Sustainable agricultural production: Implications for international agricultural research.* FAO Research and Technology Paper 4. Rome: Food and Agriculture Organization of the United Nations (FAO).

————. 1990. *A possible expansion of the CGIAR.* Washington, D.C.

————. 1992. Review of CGIAR priorities and strategies, Part 1. Washington, D.C.: World Bank.

Chalamwong, Y., and G. Feder. 1986. *Land ownership security and land values in rural Thailand.* Working Paper 790. Washington, D.C.: World Bank.

Chambers, R. 1990. *Microenvironments unobserved.* IIED Gatekeeper Series 24. London: International Institute for Environment and Development, Sustainable Agricultural Programme.

Chambers, R., and G. R. Conway. 1992. *Sustainable rural livelihoods: Practical concepts for the 21st century.* Discussion Paper 296. Brighton, U.K.: Institute of Development Studies, University of Sussex.

Chambers, R., and B. Ghildyal. 1985. Agricultural research for resource-poor farmers: The farmer-first-and-last model. *Agricultural Administration* 20: 1–30.

Chambers, R., N. C. Saxena, and T. Shah. 1989. *To the hands of the poor: Water and trees.* London: Earthscan.

Chandrakanth, M. G. 1988. Dryland watershed management: Are professionals overly ambitious? University of Agricultural Sciences, Bangalore, India. Mimeo.

Chapman, D., and R. Barker. 1991. Environmental protection, resource depletion, and the sustainability of developing country agriculture. *Economic Development and Cultural Change* 39 (4): 723–737.

Chopra, K. 1990. *Agricultural development in Punjab: Issues in resource use and sustainability.* New Delhi: Vikas.

Chopra, K., G. K. Kadekodi, and M. N. Murty. 1990. *Participatory development, people, and common property resources.* New Delhi: Sage.

Christensen, G. 1989. Determinants of private investment in rural Burkina Faso. Ph.D. diss., Cornell University, Ithaca, N.Y., U.S.A.

CILSS (Comité Permanent Inter-Etats de Lutte contre la Secheresse dans le Sahel). 1980. *The development of irrigated agriculture in the Sahel: Review and perspectives.* Paris: Club du Sahel.

Clay, D., F. Byiringiro, J. Kangasniemi, T. Reardon, B. Sibomana, and L. Uwamariya. 1995. *Promoting food security in Rwanda through sustainable agricultural productivity: Meeting the challenges of population pressure, land degradation, and poverty.* Michigan State University Staff Paper 95-08. East Lansing, Mich., U.S.A.: Michigan State University.

Cleaver, K. M. 1988. The use of price policy to stimulate agricultural growth in Sub-Saharan Africa. In *Trade, aid, and policy reform,* ed. C. Roberts. Proceedings of the Eighth Agricultural Sector Symposium. Washington, D.C.: World Bank.

Cleaver, K. M., and G. A. Schreiber. 1994. *Reversing the spiral: The population, agriculture, and environment nexus in Sub-Saharan Africa.* Washington, D.C.: World Bank.

Cleland, J., and J. Hobcraft, eds. 1985. *Reproductive change in developing countries: Insights from the world fertility survey.* New York: Oxford University Press.

Cocks, P., E. Thomson, K. Somel, and A. Abd El-Moneim. 1988. *Degradation and rehabilitation of agricultural land in North Syria.* ICARDA-119. Aleppo, Syria: International Center for Agricultural Research in Dry Areas.

Cohen, J. 1975. Effects of Green Revolution strategies on tenants and small-scale landowners in the Chilala region of Ethiopia. *Journal of Developing Areas* 9 (3): 335–358.

Coloma, A. G. 1984. Management of sedimentation problem in irrigation systems in the Philippines. Honolulu, Hi., U.S.A.: East-West Environment and Policy Institute Paper, July. Mimeo.

Committee on the Role of Alternative Farming Methods in Modern Production Agriculture, Board on Agriculture, National Research Council. 1989. *Alternative agriculture.* Washington, D.C.

Conservation International. 1992. *Annual report 1992.* Washington, D.C.

Conway, G. R. 1985a. Agricultural ecology and farming systems research. In *Agricultural systems research for developing countries,* ed. J. V. Remenyi. Canberra, Australia: Australian Centre for International Agricultural Research.

————. 1985b. Agroecosystems analysis. *Agricultural Administration* 20 (1): 31–55.

Conway, G. R., and E. B. Barbier. 1990. *After the Green Revolution: Sustainable agriculture for development.* London: Earthscan.

Conway, G. R., and J. N. Pretty. 1991. *Unwelcome harvest: Agriculture and pollution.* London: Earthscan.

Conway, G. R., U. Lele, J. Peacock, and M. Pinero. 1994. *Sustainable agriculture for a food secure world: A vision for the Consultative Group for International Agricultural Research.* Washington, D.C.: CGIAR.

Cooper, P., and E. Bailey. 1990. Livestock in Mediterranean farming systems: A traditional buffer against uncertainty, now a threat to the agricultural resource base. In *Risk in agriculture,* ed. D. Holden, P. Hazell, and A. Pritchard. Proceedings of the Tenth Agricultural Symposium. Washington, D.C.: World Bank.

Coppock, D. L. 1991. Haymaking by pastoral women for improved calf management in Ethiopia: Labor requirements, opportunity costs, and feasibility of intervention. *Journal for Farming Systems Research Extension* 2 (3): 51–68.

————. 1994. *The Borana Plateau of southern Ethiopia: Synthesis of pastoral research, development, and change, 1980–90.* Systems Study 5. Addis Ababa: International Livestock Center for Africa.

Coppock, D. L., and J. D. Reed. 1992. Cultivated and native browse legumes as calf supplements in Ethiopia. *Journal of Range Management* 45 (3): 231–238.

Cossins, N. J. 1985. The productivity of pastoral systems. *ILCA Bulletin* 21: 3–7.

Coxhead, I. A. 1993. The distributional impact of technical change in Philippine agriculture: A general equilibrium analysis. *Food Research Institute Studies* 22 (3): 253–274.

Craswell, E. 1989. *Research on natural resource conservation and management in the CGIAR and associated centres.* Washington, D.C.: Technical Advisory Committee, Consultative Group on International Agricultural Research.

Crespo, D. 1988. Some reflections on the degradation and improvement of rangeland productivity in the arid and semi-arid region of North Africa and the Middle East.

Paper presented at the Arab Conference on Rangeland Management, 23–27 October, Damascus.

CRIDA (Central Research Institute for Dryland Agriculture). 1988. *Annual Report.* Hyderabad, India.

Crosson, P. 1986. Soil erosion and policy issues. In *Agriculture and the environment,* ed. T. Phipps, P. Crosson, and K. Price. Washington, D.C.: Resources for the Future.

Cruz, W., H. A. Francisco, and Z. Tapawan-Conway. 1988. *The on-site and downstream costs of soil erosion.* Working Paper Series 88-11. Manila: Philippine Institute for Development Studies.

Cubasch, U., and R. D. Cess. 1990. Processes and modeling. In *Climate change: The IPCC scientific assessment,* ed. J. T. Houghton, G. J. Jenkins, and J. J. Ephraums. Cambridge: Cambridge University Press.

Cummings, R. W. 1989. *Mechanizing Asia and the Near East: Agricultural research in the 1990s.* Washington, D.C.: U.S. Agency for International Development, Bureau for Science and Technology.

Cunha, A. S., and C. Mueller. 1988. A questão da produção e do abastecimento alimentar no Brasil: Diagnóstico regional. In *A Questão da produção e do abastecimento alimentar no Brasil: Um diagnóstico macro com cortes regionais,* ed. M. N. Aguiar. Brasilia: Instituto de Pesquisa Econômica Aplicada (IPEA).

Cure, J. D., and B. Acock. 1986. Crop responses to carbon dioxide doubling: A literature survey. *Agricultural and Forest Meteorology* 38: 127–145.

Dahl, G., and A. Hjort. 1979. *Pastoral change and the role of drought.* SAREC Report R2. Stockholm: Swedish Agency for Research Cooperation with Developing Countries.

Dahlberg, K. A. 1991. Sustainable agriculture: Fad or harbinger. *BioScience* 41: 337–340.

Daly, H. E. 1991. From empty world economics to full world economics: Recognizing an historical turning point in economic development. In *Environmentally sustainable economic development: Building on Brundtland,* ed. R. Goodland, H. Daly, and S. El-Serafy. Environment Working Paper 46. Washington, D.C.: World Bank.

Dapaah, S. 1992. Commentary. In *Agricultural sustainability, growth, and poverty alleviation: Issues and policies,* ed. S. A. Vosti, T. Reardon, and W. von Urff. Washington, D.C.: International Food Policy Research Institute, and Feldafing, Germany: German Foundation for International Development (DSE).

Dasgupta, P. 1982. *The control of resources.* New Delhi: Oxford University Press.

Dasgupta, P., and K. G. Mähler. 1990. The environment and emerging development issues. Paper read at World Bank's Annual Conference on Development Economics, Washington, D.C.

———. 1994. *Poverty, institutions, and the environmental-resource base.* World Bank Environment Paper 9. Washington, D.C.: World Bank.

Davis, J. S., P. A. Oram, and J. G. Ryan. 1987. *Assessment of agricultural research priorities: An international perspective.* ACIAR Monograph Series No. 4. Canberra, Australia: Australian Centre for International Agricultural Research in collaboration with the International Food Policy Research Institute.

de Haan, C. 1990. Changing trends in the World Bank's lending program for rangeland development. Paper presented at the 1990 International Rangeland Development Symposium, 15 February, Reno, Nev., U.S.A.

de Haen, H., and A. Runge-Metzger. 1989. Improvements in efficiency and sustainability of traditional land use systems through learning from farmers' practice. *Quarterly Journal of International Agriculture* 28 (3/4): 326–350.

de Haen, H., and Y. Zimmer. 1989. *Environmental sustainability of technical progress in agriculture: Institutional preconditions, profitability, and diffusion* (in German). Paper presented at the German Agricultural Economics Association (WISOLA) Conference, held in Braunschweig, Germany.

de los Angeles, M. S., and N. C. Lasmarias. 1984. *Handbook on land and other Philippine resources.* Manila: Philippine Institute of Development Studies.

DENR (Department of Environment and Natural Resources, the Philippines). *Philippine forestry statistics.* Manila: Forest Management Bureau.

————. 1987. *Philippine-German forest resources inventory project.* Manila.

————. 1990a. *Master plan for forestry development.* Manila.

————. 1990b. *Philippine strategy for sustainable development: A conceptual framework.* Manila.

de Ridder, N., and K. T. Wagenaar. 1986. Energy and protein balances in traditional livestock systems in eastern Botswana. *Agricultural Systems* 20: 1–16.

Desai, G. M., and V. Gandhi. 1989. Phosphorus for sustainable agricultural growth in Asia: An assessment of alternative sources and management. Paper presented at the symposium on Phosphorus Requirements for Sustainable Agriculture in the Asia and Pacific Region, 6–10 March. Los Baños, the Philippines: International Rice Research Institute.

————. 1990. Phosphorus for sustainable agricultural growth in Asia: An assessment of alternative sources and management. In *Phosphorus requirements for sustainable agriculture in Asia and Oceania.* College, Laguna, the Philippines: International Rice Research Institute.

de Vera, M. V. M. 1992. Impact of upper watershed destruction on the performance of national irrigation systems in the Philippines. Master's thesis, University of the Philippines, Los Baños, the Philippines.

Dixon, J. A., L. M. Talbot, and G. J. M. Le Moigne. 1989. *Dams and the environment: Considerations in World Bank projects.* World Bank Technical Paper 110. Washington, D.C.: World Bank.

Dixon, J. A., L. F. Scura, R. A. Carpenter, and P. B. Sherman. 1994. *Economic analysis of environmental impacts.* London: Earthscan in association with the Asian Development Bank and the World Bank.

Dogra, B. 1986. The Indian experience with large dams. In *The social and environmental effects of large dams,* vol. 2, ed. E. Goldsmith and N. Hildyard. Camelford, Cornwall, U.K.: Wadebridge Ecological Center.

Donaldson, T. J. 1986. Pastoralism and drought: A case study of the Borana of southern Ethiopia. M.Phil. thesis, University of Reading, Reading, U.K.

Doolette, J. B., and W. B. Magrath. 1990. Watershed development in Asia: Strategies and technologies. World Bank Technical Paper 127. Washington, D.C.: World Bank.

Douglass, G. K. 1984. *Agricultural sustainability in a changing world order.* Boulder, Colo., U.S.A.: Westview.

Dove, M. R. 1987. The perception of peasant land rights in Indonesian development: Causes and implications. In *Land, trees, and tenure*, ed. J. B. Raintree. Proceedings of an International Workshop on Tenure Issues in Agroforestry, sponsored by the Ford Foundation, 27–31 May, 1985, Nairobi. Nairobi: ICRAF (International Centre for Research in Agroforestry), and Madison, Wis., U.S.A.: Land Tenure Center.

Downing, T. E. 1991. African household food security: What are the limits of available coping mechanisms in response to climatic and economic variations? In *Famine and food security in Africa and Asia*, ed. H. G. Bohle, T. Cannon, G. Hugo, and F. N. Ibrahim. Bayreuther Geowissenschaftliche Arbeiten 15. Bayreuth, Germany: Naturwissenschaftliche Gesellschaft Bayreuth.

————. 1992. *Climate change and vulnerable places: Global food security and country studies in Zimbabwe, Kenya, Senegal, and Chile*. Research Report 1. Oxford: Environmental Change Unit.

————, ed. 1996. *Climate change and world food security*. Berlin: Springer-Verlag.

Dregne, H. E. 1990. Erosion and soil productivity in Africa. *Journal of Soil and Water Conservation* 45 (4): 431–436.

Dvorak, K. A. 1990. *Indigenous soil classification in semi-arid tropical India*. Economics Group Progress Report 87. Hyderabad, India: International Crops Research Institute for the Semi-Arid Tropics.

————, ed. 1993. *Social science research for agricultural technology development: Spatial and temporal dimensions*. Proceedings of an International Institute of Tropical Agriculture (IITA)–Rockefeller Foundation Workshop, 2–5 October 1990, Ibadan, Nigeria. Wallingford, U.K.: CAB International.

Easterlin, R., and E. Crimmins. 1985. *The fertility revolution: A supply-demand analysis*. Chicago: University of Chicago Press.

EFAP (Ethiopia Forestry Action Program). 1992. *Ethiopia Forestry Action Program*. Addis Ababa: Transitional Government of Ethiopia.

Ehui, S. K., and T. W. Hertel. 1989. Deforestation and agricultural productivity in Côte d'Ivoire. *American Journal of Agricultural Economics* 71 (3): 703–711.

Ehui, S. K., and D. S. C. Spencer. 1990. *Indices for measuring the sustainability and economic viability of farming systems*. RCMP (Resource and Crop Management Program) Research Monograph 3. Ibadan, Nigeria: International Institute of Tropical Agriculture.

————. 1993. Measuring the sustainability and economic viability of tropical farming systems: A model from Sub-Saharan Africa. *Agricultural Economics* 9 (4): 279–296.

Ehui, S. K., B. T. Kang, and D. S. C. Spencer. 1990. Economic analysis of soil erosion effects of alley cropping, no-till, and bush fallow systems in south western Nigeria. *Agricultural Systems* 34 (4): 349–368.

Eicher, C. K. 1989. *Sustainable institutions for African agricultural development*. Working Paper 19. The Hague: International Service for National Agricultural Research.

————. 1991. Building agricultural research capacity for the next generation: Scientific, economic, and political issues. Paper prepared for the Conference on Institutional Innovations for Sustainable Agricultural Development into the 21st Century, 14–18 October, Bellagio, Italy.

EIU (Economist Intelligence Unit). 1988. *Country profile: Côte d'Ivoire*. London.

El-Kash, M. 1990. Wheat and feedstuff production in semi-arid zones of Arab countries. In *Agriculture in the Middle East: Challenges and prospects,* ed. A. Salman. New York: Paragon House.

El-Swaify, S. A., T. S. Walker, and S. M. Virmani. 1983. Dryland management alternatives and research needs for alfisols in the semi-arid tropics. Paper presented at the Consultants' Workshop on the State of the Art and Management Alternatives for Optimizing the Productivity of SAT Alfisols and Related Soils, 1–3 December, International Crops Research Institute for the Semi-Arid Tropics, Hyderabad, India.

Ellis, F. 1993. *Peasant economics: Farm households and agrarian development,* 2d ed. Cambridge: Wye Studies in Agricultural and Rural Development, Cambridge University Press.

Ellis, J. E., and D. M. Swift. 1988. Stability of African pastoral ecosystems: Alternate paradigms and implications for development. *Journal of Range Management* 41 (6): 450–459.

EMB (Environmental Management Bureau), DENR (Department of Environment and Natural Resources). 1990. *The Philippine environment in the eighties.* Philippine Heart Center for Asia Building, East Avenue, Diliman, Quezon City, the Philippines.

EMBRAPA (Empresa Brasileira de Pesquisa Agropecuaria). 1988. *Delineamento macroagroecológico do Brasil.* Rio de Janeiro: Comitê de Publicações do Serviço National de Levantamento e Conservação do Solo (SNLCS).

Ervin, C. A., and D. E. Ervin. 1982. Factors affecting the use of conservation practices: Hypotheses, evidence, and policy implications. *Land Economics* 58: 277–292.

Ewell, P. T. 1989. *Linkages between on-farm research and extension in nine countries.* OFCOR (On-Farm Client-Oriented Research) Comparative Study 14. The Hague: International Service for National Agricultural Research.

Eyzaguirre, P. 1990. *The scale and scope of national agricultural research in small developing countries: Concepts and methodology.* ISNAR Small-Countries Study Paper 1. The Hague: International Service for National Agricultural Research.

Faini, R., and J. de Melo. 1990. Adjustment, investment, and the real exchange rate in developing countries. *Economic Policy* (October): 495–578.

FAO (Food and Agriculture Organization of the United Nations). 1970–1990. *Production yearbook.* Rome.

———. 1983. *Study of irrigation in Africa south of the Sahara.* Investment Center/Land and Water Division. Rome.

———. 1984. Institutional aspects of shifting cultivation in Africa. Rome: Human Resources, Institutions, and Agrarian Reform Division.

———. 1986. *The technology applications gap: Development.* Research Technology Paper 1. Rome.

———. 1987a. *Agriculture: Toward 2000,* rev. version. Rome.

———. 1987b. Guidelines for extensive grazing. Draft report for the *Soils Bulletin.* Rome.

———. 1988. *World agriculture towards the year 2000.* London: Belhaven.

———. 1995. *The national agricultural research systems of West and Central Africa.* Rome.

FAO/IFPRI/CIFOR (Food and Agriculture Organization of the United Nations/International Food Policy Research Institute/Centre for International Forestry Research). 1993.

Report of the regional expert consultation on forestry policy developments and research implications in Asia and the Pacific. RAPA Publication 1993/16. Bangkok: FAO Regional office for Asia and the Pacific.

Fearnside, P. M. 1986. *Human carrying capacity of the Brazilian rainforest.* New York: Columbia University Press.

Feder, G., R., and T. Onchan. 1987. Land ownership security and farm investment in Thailand. *American Journal of Agricultural Economics* 69 (2): 311–320.

Feder, G. R., E. Just, and D. Zilberman. 1985. Adoption of agricultural innovations in developing countries: A survey. *Economic Development and Cultural Change* 33 (2): 255–296.

Feder, G. R., T. Onchan, Y. Chalamwong, and C. Hongladarom. 1988. *Land policies and farm productivity in Thailand.* Baltimore: Johns Hopkins University Press.

Fischer, G., and H. T. van Velthuizen. 1996. *Climate change and global agricultural potential project: A case study of Kenya.* Laxenburg, Austria: International Institute for Applied Systems Analysis.

Fischer, G., K. Frohberg, M. A. Keyzer, K. S. Parikh, and W. Tims. 1991. *Hunger: Beyond the reach of the invisible hand.* RR-91-15. Laxenburg, Austria: International Institute for Applied Systems Analysis.

Fischer, G., K. Frohberg, M. L. Parry, and C. Rosenzweig. 1996. Impacts of potential climate change on global and regional food production and vulnerability. In *Climate change and world food security,* ed. T. E. Downing. Heidelberg, Germany: Springer-Verlag.

Flinn, J. C., and S. K. de Datta. 1984. Trends in irrigated-rice yields under intensive cropping at Philippine research stations. *Field Crops Research* 9: 1–15.

Fones-Sundell, M. 1987. *Role of price policy in stimulating agricultural production in Africa.* Issue Paper 2. Uppsala, Sweden: Swedish University of Agricultural Sciences.

Fresco, L., and S. Kroonenberg. 1992. Time and spatial scales in ecological sustainability. *Land Use Policy* 9: 155–168.

Froment, A. 1990. Biomedical surveys in relation to food and nutrition. In *Food and nutrition in the African rain forest,* ed. C. M. Hladik, S. Bahuchet, and I. de Garine. Paris: UNESCO (United Nations Educational, Scientific, and Cultural Organization).

Fujisaka, S. 1990. Has Green Revolution rice research paid attention to farmers' technologies? Social Sciences Division, International Rice Research Institute, Los Baños, the Philippines.

———. 1993. A case of farmer adaptation and adoption of contour hedgerows for soil conservation. *Experimental Agriculture* 29: 97–105.

Fujisaka, S., and D. A. Capistrano. 1985. *Pioneer shifting cultivation in Calminoe, Philippines: Sustainability or degradation from changing human-ecosystem interactions.* Environment and Policy Institute Working Paper. Honolulu, Hi., U.S.A.: East-West Center.

Fujisaka, S., and E. Wollenberg. 1991. From forest to agroforester: A case study. *Agroforestry Systems* 14 (2): 113–130.

Fundação Getúlio Vargas (FGV), Instituto Brasileiro de Economia (IBRE). Various years. *Preços Pagos pelo Produtor.* Rio de Janeiro.

Gadgil, M. 1989. Deforestation: Problems and prospects. Foundation Day Lecture, Society for Promotion of Wasteland Development, New Delhi.

Gamaledinn, M. 1987. State policy and famine in the Awash Valley of Ethiopia: The lessons for conservation. In *Conservation in Africa: People, policies, and practice*, ed. D. Anderson and R. Grove. Cambridge: Cambridge University Press.

Garcia, M., M. Sharma, A. Qureshi, and L. Brown. 1996. Overcoming malnutrition: Is there an ecoregional dimension? 2020 Vision Discussion Paper 10. Washington, D.C.: International Food Policy Research Institute.

Garrity, D. P., D. M. Kummer, and E. S. Guiang. 1991. *The upland ecosystem in the Philippines: Alternatives for sustainable farming and forestry.* A study commissioned by the National Research Council Project on Agricultural Sustainability and the Environment in the Humid Tropics, Washington, D.C.

Gates, W. L., J. F. B. Mitchell, G. J. Boer, U. Cubasch, and V. P. Meleshko. 1992. Climate modeling, climate prediction, and model validation. In *Climate change 1992: The supplementary report to the IPCC scientific assessment*, ed. J. Houghton, B. A. Callander, and S. K. Varney. Cambridge: Cambridge University Press.

General Accounting Office. 1990. *Alternative agriculture: Federal incentives and farmers options.* US/GAO/PEMD-90-12. Washington, D.C.

Getahun, A. 1984. Stability and instability of mountain ecosystems in Ethiopia. *Mountain Research and Development* 4 (1): 39–44.

————. 1990. Grevillea in East Africa. Mimeo.

Glantz, M., ed. 1977. *Desertification: Environmental degradation in and around arid lands.* Boulder, Colo., U.S.A.: Westview.

Goeller, H. E., and A. M. Weinberg. 1976. The age of substitutability. *Science* 191 (February): 683–689.

Gomez-Pompa, A., A. Kaus, J. Jimenez-Osornio, and D. Bainbridge. 1991. *Deforestation and sustainable agriculture in the humid tropics: A case study of Mexico.* Riverside, Calif., U.S.A.: University of California Press.

Goodland, R. 1991. The case that the world has reached limits. In *Environmentally sustainable economic development: Building on Brundtland*, ed. R. Goodland, H. Daly, and S. El-Serafy. Environmental Working Paper 46. Washington, D.C.: World Bank.

Grabowski, R. 1981. The implications of an induced innovation model. *Economic Development and Cultural Change* 30 (1).

Graham-Tomasi, T. 1991. Sustainability: Concepts and implications for agricultural research policy. In *Agricultural research policy: International connotative perspectives*, ed. P. Pardey, J. Roseboom, and J. R. Anderson. Cambridge: Cambridge University Press.

Grandin, B. E. 1987. Pastoral culture and range management: Recent lessons from Maasailand. *ILCA Bulletin* 28: 7–13.

Gratz, N. G. 1987. *The effect of water development programmes on malaria and malaria vectors in Turkey.* PEEM/7/WP/87.6b. Rome: Joint World Health Organization/Food and Agriculture Organization of the United Nations/United Nations Environment Program Panel of Experts on Environmental Management for Vector Control.

Greer, J., and E. Thorbecke. 1986. *Food poverty and consumption patterns in Kenya.* Geneva: International Labour Office.

Groves, T., R. Radner, and S. Reiter, eds. 1987. *Information, incentives, and economic mechanisms.* Minneapolis, Minn., U.S.A.: University of Minnesota Press.

Guha, R. 1989. *The unquiet woods: Ecological change and peasant resistance in the Himalayas.* New Delhi: Oxford University Press.

Haddad, L. J., and H. E. Bouis. 1991. The impact of nutritional status on agricultural wage productivity: Wage evidence from the Philippines. *Oxford Bulletin of Economics and Statistics* 53 (1): 45-68.

Haddad, L. J., and J. Hoddinott. 1991. *Gender aspects of household expenditures and resource allocation in the Côte d'Ivoire.* Oxford: Oxford University, Centre for the Study of African Economies.

Haggblade, S., P. Hazell, and J. Brown. 1989. Farm-nonfarm linkages in rural Sub-Saharan Africa. *World Development* 17 (8): 1173–1201.

Hamilton, L. S. 1984. *A perspective on forestry in Asia and the Pacific.* EWEPI Reprint 67. Honolulu, Hi., U.S.A.: East-West Center, Environment and Policy Institute.

Hardin, G. J. 1968. The tragedy of the commons. *Science* 162: 1234–1248.

Harwood, R. R. 1990. A history of sustainable agriculture. In *Sustainable agricultural systems,* ed. C. A. Edwards, R. Lal, P. Madden, R. H. Miller, and G. House. Ankeny, Iowa, U.S.A.: Soil and Water Conservation Authority.

Hayami, Y., and V. W. Ruttan. 1985. *Agricultural development: An international perspective.* Baltimore: Johns Hopkins University Press.

Hazell, P. B. R., and C. Ramasamy. 1991. *The Green Revolution reconsidered.* Baltimore: Johns Hopkins University Press.

Hazell, P. B. R., and A. Röell. 1983. *Rural growth linkages: Household expenditure patterns in Malaysia and Nigeria.* Research Report 41. Washington, D.C.: International Food Policy Research Institute.

Heady, E. O., and G. F. Vocke. 1992. *Economic models of agricultural land conservation and environmental improvement.* Ames, Iowa, U.S.A.: Iowa State University Press.

Hecht, S. B. 1984. Cattle ranching in Amazonia: Political and ecological considerations. In *Frontier expansion in Amazonia,* ed. M. Schmink and C. H. Wood. Gainesville, Fla., U.S.A.: University of Florida Press.

Heer, C., and J. E. Celada. 1991. Validación integrada de tecnología en la región suroriental de Guatemala: Un enfoque de sistema con participación interinstitucional. In *Agricultura sostenible en las laderas centroamericanas: Oportunidades de colaboración interinstitucional.* San José, Costa Rica: Instituto Interamericano de Cooperación para la Agricultura.

Herdt, R. W. 1988. Increasing crop yields in developing countries. Paper presented to the 1988 meeting of the American Agricultural Economics Association, 30 July –3 August, Knoxville, Tenn., U.S.A.

Higgins, G. M., A. H. Kassam, and L. Naiken. 1982. *Potential population supporting capacities of lands in the developing world.* Technical report of project INT/75/P13. Rome: Food and Agriculture Organization of the United Nations.

Higgins, G. M., A. H. Kassam, L. Naiken, G. Fischer, and M. M. Shah. 1982. *Potential population supporting capacities of lands in the developing world.* Rome: Food and Agriculture Organization of the United Nations.

Hirsch, P. 1990. *Development dilemmas in rural Thailand.* Singapore: Oxford University Press.

Hladik, C. M., S. Bahuchet, and I. de Garine. 1990. *Food and nutrition in the African rain forest.* Paris: UNESCO (United Nations Educational, Scientific, and Cultural Organization).

Hogg, R. 1985. *Restocking pastoralists in Kenya: A strategy for relief and rehabilitation.* ODI Pastoral Development Network Paper 19c. London: Overseas Development Institute.

————. 1988. Changing perceptions of pastoral development: A case study from Turkana District, Kenya. In *Anthropology of development and change in East Africa,* ed. D. Brokensha and P. D. Little. Boulder, Colo., U.S.A.: Westview.

————. 1992. Should pastoralism continue as a way of life? *Disasters* 16 (2): 31–37.

Holden, S. J., D. L. Coppock, and M. Assefa. 1991. Pastoral dairy marketing and household wealth interactions and their implications for calves and humans in Ethiopia. *Human Ecology* 19 (1): 35–59.

Homma, A. K. 1990. A extração de recursos naturais renováveis: O caso do extrativismo vegetal na Amazônia. Ph.D. diss., Universidade Federal de Viçosa, Viçosa, Brazil.

Hopkins, A. G. 1973. *An economic history of West Africa.* New York: Columbia University Press.

Hopper, W. D. 1987. Sustainability policies, natural resources, and institutions. In *Sustainability issues in agricultural development,* ed. T. J. Davis and I. A. Schrimer. Washington, D.C.: World Bank.

Horowitz, M. M., and P. D. Little. 1987. African pastoralism and poverty: Some implications for drought and famine. In *Drought and hunger in Africa: Denying famine a future,* ed. M. H. Glantz. Cambridge: Cambridge University Press.

Hotelling, H. 1931. The economics of exhaustible resources. *Journal of Political Economy* 39: 137–175.

Houghton, J. T., B. A. Callander, and S. K. Varney, eds. 1992. *Climate change 1992: The supplementary report to the IPCC scientific assessment.* Cambridge: Cambridge University Press.

Houghton, J. T., G. J. Jenkins, and J. J. Ephraums, eds. 1990. *Climate change: The IPCC scientific assessment.* Cambridge: Cambridge University Press.

Houghton, J. T., L. G. Meira Filho, B. A. Callander, N. Harris, A. Kattenberg, and K. Maskell, eds. 1996. *Climate change 1995: The science of climate change.* Cambridge: Cambridge University Press, Intergovernmental Panel on Climate Change, World Meteorological Organization, and United Nations Environment Programme.

Howell, J. 1989. Public investment in Africa's extension services. In *Agricultural extension in Africa,* ed. N. Roberts. Washington, D.C.: World Bank.

Hufschmidt, M., D. James, A. Meister, B. Bower, and J. Dixon. 1983. *Environment, natural systems, and development.* Baltimore: Johns Hopkins University Press.

Huibers, F. P., and G. Diemar. 1991. End of project report, Water management project. Wageningen University, the Netherlands, and West Africa Rice Development Association, Bouaké, Côte d'Ivoire.

Hulugalle, N. R., and P. R. Maurya. 1991. Tillage systems for the West African semi-arid tropics. *Soil Tillage Research* 20: 187–199.

Human Dimensions Programme. 1992. *The case for the study of global land-use and cover change.* Report of an Ad Hoc Committee of the International Geosphere-Biosphere Programme (ICSU) and Human Dimensions Programme (ISSC). Barcelona.

Hurwicz, L. 1972. On informationally decentralized systems. In *Decision and organization,* ed. C. B. McGuire and R. Radner. Amsterdam: North-Holland.

Hussain, S. S., and O. Erenstein. 1992. Monitoring sustainability issues in agriculture development: A case study in Swat in northern Pakistan. Paper presented at the Asian Farming Systems Symposium, 2–5 November, Colombo, Sri Lanka.

ICARDA (International Center for Agricultural Research in Dry Areas). 1992. *Annual report for 1991*. Aleppo, Syria.

ICIMOD (International Centre for Integrated Mountain Development). 1990a. *Agricultural development experiences in Himachal Pradesh*. MFS (Mountain Farming Systems) Workshop Report 1. Kathmandu.

————. 1990b. *Agricultural development experiences in West Sichuan and Xizang, China*. MFS (Mountain Farming Systems) Workshop Report 2. Kathmandu.

————. 1990c. *Agricultural development experiences in Nepal*. MFS (Mountain Farming Systems) Workshop Report 3. Kathmandu.

————. 1990d. *Agricultural development experiences in Pakistan*. MFS (Mountain Farming Systems) Workshop Report 4. Kathmandu.

————. 1990e. Institutions and mountain development. Report of the International Workshop on the Role of Institutions in Mountain Resource Management, 1–4 May, Quetta, Pakistan. Kathmandu.

ICRISAT (International Crops Research Institute for the Semi-Arid Tropics). 1985. *Annual report*. Patancheru, Andhra Pradesh, India.

————. 1990. *Annual report*. Patancheru, Andhra Pradesh, India.

Idachaba, F. S. 1987. Sustainability issues in agriculture development. In *Sustainability issues in agricultural development*, ed. T. J. Davis and I. A. Schirmer. Proceedings of the Seventh Agricultural Sector Symposium. Washington, D.C.: World Bank.

IDB (Inter-American Development Bank). 1992. Demystifying the Amazon: Good economics and good ecology. *The IDB* (May): 4–7.

IGADD (Intergovernmental Authority on Drought and Development). 1990. *Food security strategy study*. Report to IGADD by the Institute of Development Studies, Development Administration Group and Food Studies Group. Djibouti, Djibouti. Mimeo.

IGBP (International Geosphere-Biosphere Programme). 1992a. *Improved global data for land applications*. Stockholm.

————. 1992b. *Report from the START Regional Meeting for Southeast Asia*. Stockholm.

IIED/IES (International Institute for Environment and Development/Institute of Environmental Studies). 1990. *Gum arabic rehabilitation project in the Republic of Sudan: Stage I report*. London: IIED.

IIMI (International Irrigation Management Institute). 1986. *Proceedings of the Workshop on Irrigation and Vector-Borne Disease Transmission*. Digana Village, Sri Lanka.

IITA (International Institute of Tropical Agriculture). 1986. *Annual report*. Ibadan, Nigeria.

————. 1990. *Root crops research collaboration in Africa*. Meeting Report Series 1989/3. Ibadan, Nigeria.

————. 1991a. *Annual report*. Ibadan, Nigeria.

————. 1991b. *Towards sustainable agriculture in Sub-Saharan Africa*. Ibadan, Nigeria.

————. 1992. *Resource and crop management program. Annual Report. Summary and highlights of scientific findings.* RCMP (Resource and Crop Management Program) Monograph 12. Ibadan, Nigeria.

ILCA (International Livestock Centre for Africa). 1984. *Annual report.* Addis Ababa.

————. 1986. *Annual report.* Addis Ababa.

IMF (International Monetary Fund). Various years. *Yearbook of government finance statistics.* Washington, D.C.

India, Ministry of Agriculture. 1990. *Agricultural statistics at a glance.* Ministry of Agriculture, Department of Agriculture and Cooperation, Directorate of Economics and Statistics, New Delhi.

————. 1991. Agenda papers of the National Conference on Agriculture for Kharif Campaign 1991. Ministry of Agriculture, Department of Agriculture and Cooperation, New Delhi.

Indonesia, Ministry of Finance. Various years. *Annual report.* Jakarta.

INSEE (Institut National de Statistiques et des Etudes Economiques). 1973. *Démographie Comparée,* vol. 1. Paris.

IRRI (International Rice Research Institute). 1967. *Annual report.* Los Baños, the Philippines.

————. 1987. *Conclusions and recommendations of workshop on Research and Training Needs in the Field of Integrated Vector-Borne Disease Control in Riceland Agroecosystems of Developing Countries, 9–14 March.* Los Baños, the Philippines.

Ishikawa, S. 1968. *Agricultural development in Asian perspective.* Tokyo: Hitotsubashi.

IUCN (International Union for Conservation of Nature and Natural Resources). 1990. *World conservation strategy: Living resource conservation for sustainable development.* Gland, Switzerland: IUCN, United Nations Environment Program, World Wildlife Foundation.

Jackson, J. H. 1989. *The world trading system: Law and policy of international economic relations.* Cambridge, Mass., U.S.A.: MIT Press.

Jaeger, W., and C. Humphreys. 1988. The effect of policy reforms on agricultural incentives in Sub-Saharan Africa. *American Journal of Agricultural Economics* 70 (3): 1036–1043.

Jaeger, W., and P. J. Matlon. 1989. Utilization, profitability and the adoption of animal draft power in West Africa. *American Journal of Agricultural Economics* (February): 36–48.

Jahnke, H. E. 1982. *Livestock production systems and livestock development in tropical Africa.* Kiel, Germany: Kieler Wissenschaftsverlag Vauk.

Jahnke, H. E., D. Kirschke, and J. Lagemann. 1987. *The impact of agricultural research in tropical Africa: A study of the collaboration between the international and national research system.* CGIAR (Consultative Group on International Agricultural Research) Study Paper 21. Washington, D.C.: World Bank.

Jain, H. K. 1990. Organization and management of agricultural research in Sub-Saharan Africa: Recent experience and future direction. Working Paper 33. The Hague, the Netherlands: International Service for National Agricultural Research.

James, D. E., P. Nijkamp, and J. B. Opschoor. 1989. Ecological sustainability in economic development. In *Economy and ecology: Toward sustainable development,* ed. F. Archibugi and P. Nijkamp. Dordrecht, the Netherlands: Kluwer.

Jayasuriya, S. K., and R. T. Shand. 1986. Technical change and labor absorption in Asian agriculture: Some emerging trends. *World Development* 14 (3): 415–428.

Jeyaratnam, J. 1990. Acute pesticide poisoning: A major global health problem. *World Health Statistics Quarterly* 43: 139–144.

Jeyaratnam, J., K. C. Lun, and W. O. Phoon. 1987. Survey of acute pesticide poisoning among agricultural workers in four Asian countries. *Bulletin of the World Health Organization* 65 (4): 521–527.

Jochim, M. A. 1981. *Strategies for survival: Cultural behavior in ecological context.* New York: Academic Press.

Jodha, N. S. 1979. Some dimensions of traditional farming systems in semi-Arid tropical India. Paper presented at the workshop on Socioeconomic Constraints to Development of Semi-Arid Tropical Agriculture, 19–23 February, International Crops Research Institute for the Semi-Arid Tropics, Hyderabad, India.

———. 1983. Market forces and erosion of common property resources. The proceedings of the International Workshop on Agricultural Markets in the Semi-Arid Tropics, 24–28 October, International Crops Research Institute for the Semi-Arid Tropics, Hyderabad, India.

———. 1985. Population growth and the decline of common property resources in Rajasthan, India. *Population and Development Review* 11 (2): 247–264.

———. 1986a. Common property resources and the rural poor in the dry regions of India. *Economic and Political Weekly* 21 (27): 1169–1181.

———. 1986b. Research and technology for dryland farming in India: Some issues for the future strategy. *Indian Journal of Agricultural Economics* 41 (3): 234–247.

———. 1990. Mountain agriculture: The search for sustainability. *Journal of Farming Systems Research-Extension* 1 (1): 55–75.

———. 1991a. *Rural common property resources: A growing crisis.* IIED Gatekeeper Series 24. London: International Institute for Environment and Development.

———. 1991b. Sustainable agriculture in fragile resource zones: Technological imperatives. *Economic and Political Weekly, Quarterly Review of Agriculture* 26 (13): A-15–A-26.

———. 1992a. Mountain perspective and sustainability: A framework for development strategies. In *Sustainable mountain agriculture,* ed. N. S. Jodha, M. Banskota, and T. Partap. New Delhi: Oxford and IBH.

———. 1992b. Sustainability issues in the mountain context: Emerging scenarios. Paper presented at IHED-ICIMOD (Institute of Himalayan Environment and Development–International Centre for Integrated Mountain Development) Workshop on Approaches to Sustainable Development of the Indian Himalayas, 1–4 August, Manali, India.

———. 1992c. Sustainable land use involving trees in the Himalayan region: Perspectives and policy implications. In *Priorities for forestry and agroforestry policy research,* ed. H. Gregersen, P. Oram, and J. Spears. Washington, D.C.: International Food Policy Research Institute.

———. 1995a. Enhancing food security in a warmer and more crowded world: Factors and process in fragile zones. In *Climate change and world food security,* ed. T. E. Downing. Oxford: Springer-Verlag.

————. 1995b. Environmental crisis and unsustainability in Himalayas: Lessons from the degradation process. In *Property rights in a social and ecological context.* Vol. 2, *Case studies and design applications,* ed. S. Hanna and M. Munasinghe. Washington, D.C.: World Bank.

Jodha, N. S., and T. Partap. 1993. Folk agronomy in Himalayas: Implications for agricultural research and extension. In *Rural people's knowledge, agricultural research, and extension practice.* IIED Research Series, vol. 1, no. 3. London: International Institute for Environment and Development.

Jodha, N. S., and R. P. Singh. 1982. Factors constraining growth of coarse grain crops in semi-arid tropical India. *Indian Journal of Agricultural Economics* 37 (3): 346–354.

Jodha, N. S., M. Banskota, and T. Partap, eds. 1992. *Sustainable mountain agriculture,* 2 vols. New Delhi: Oxford and IBH.

Johnson, R. R. 1988. Putting soil movement into perspective. In *Journal of Production Agriculture* 1 (1).

Jones, M. J. 1971. The maintenance of soil organic matter under continuous cultivation at Samaru. *Nigeria Journal of Agricultural Science* 77: 473–483.

————. 1991. Agricultural sustainability research at ICARDA. A presentation at the Consultative Group on International Agricultural Research Centers Week, Washington, D.C.

Judd, M. A., J. K. Boyce, and R. E. Evenson. 1983. *Investing in agricultural supply.* New Haven, Conn., U.S.A.: Yale University Economic Growth Center.

Kalkat, G. 1986. Role of rainfed agriculture in the Indian economy. In *Development of rainfed agriculture under arid and semi-arid conditions,* ed. T. J. Davis. Washington, D.C.: World Bank.

Kang, B. T., and V. Balasubramanian. 1990. Long-term fertilizer trials on alfisols in West Africa. In *Transactions of the 11th International Congress of Soil Science.* Kyoto, Japan.

Kang, B. T., and S. R. Juo. 1981. Management of low activity clay soils in tropical Africa for food crop production. Paper presented at the 4th International Soil Classification Workshop, 2–12 June, Kigali, Rwanda.

Kang, B. T., L. Reynolds, and A. N. Atta-Krah. 1990. Alley farming. *Advances in Agronomy* 43: 315–355.

Kasperson, R. E., K. Dow, D. Golding, and J. X. Kasperson, eds. 1990. *Understanding global environmental change: The contribution of risk analysis and management.* Worcester, Mass., U.S.A.: Clark University.

Kassam, A. H., H. T. van Velthuizen, G. W. Fischer, and M. M. Shah. 1991. *Agroecological land resources assessment for agricultural development planning: A case study of Kenya, resources, database, and land productivity.* Rome: Food and Agriculture Organization of the United Nations, and Laxenburg, Austria: International Institute for Applied Systems Analysis.

Kates, R. W., and V. Haarmann. 1992. Where do the poor live? Are the assumptions correct? *Environment* 34 (4): 4–28.

Keatinge, D., and J. Hamblin. 1991. Towards improved cereal production in the highland areas of West Asia and North Africa. International Center for Agricultural Research in Dry Areas, Ankara, Turkey. Mimeo.

Kennedy, E. T. 1989. *The effects of sugarcane production on food security, health, and nutrition in Kenya: A longitudinal analysis.* Research Report 78. Washington, D.C.: International Food Policy Research Institute.

Kerr, J. M., and N. K. Sanghi. 1992a. *Indigenous soil and water conservation in India's semi-arid tropics.* IIED Gatekeeper Series 34. London: International Institute for Environment and Development, Sustainable Agriculture Programme.

————. 1992b. *Indigenous soil and water conservation in India's semi-arid tropics.* Gatekeeper Series 34. London: International Institute for Environment and Development, Sustainable Agriculture Programme.

Kiros, F. G. 1991. Economic consequences of drought, crop failure, and famine in Ethiopia, 1973–1986. *Ambio* 20 (5): 183–185.

Knetsch, J. L. 1990. Environment policy implications of disparities between willingness to pay and compensation demanded measures of values. *Journal of Environmental Economics and Management* 18: 227–237.

Koester, U. 1982. *Policy options for the grain economy of the European Community: Implications for developing countries.* Research Report 35. Washington, D.C.: International Food Policy Research Institute.

Koppen, W., and H. Geiger. 1936. *Handbook of climatology.* Berlin: Gerruder Borntrager.

Krueger, A. O., M. Schiff, and A. Valdés. 1988. Agricultural incentives in developing countries: Measuring the effect of sectoral and economy-wide policies. *World Bank Economic Review* 2 (3): 255–271.

————, eds. 1991. *The political economy of agricultural pricing policy,* 3 vols. Washington, D.C.: World Bank.

Kruseman, G., H. Hengsdijk, and R. Ruben. 1993. *Disentangling the concept of sustainability: Conceptual definitions, analytical framework, and operational techniques in sustainable land use.* DLV Report 2. Wageningen, the Netherlands: Agricultural Research Department and Wageningen Agricultural University.

Kuik, O., and H. Verbruggen, eds. 1991. *In search of indicators of sustainable development.* Dordrecht, the Netherlands: Kluwer.

Kumar, S. K., and D. Hotchkiss. 1988. *Consequences of deforestation for women's time allocation, agricultural production, and nutrition in hill areas of Nepal.* Research Report 69. Washington, D.C.: International Food Policy Research Institute.

Kyle, S., and A. S. Cunha. 1992. National factor markets and the macroeconomic context for environmental destruction in the Brazilian Amazon. *Development and Change* 23 (1): 7–33.

Lal, R. 1983. No-till farming: Soil and water conservation and management in the humid and sub-humid tropics. Monograph 2. Ibadan, Nigeria: International Institute of Tropical Agriculture.

————. 1991. Tillage and agricultural sustainability. *Soil Tillage Research* 20: 147–163.

Lamprey, H. 1983. Pastoralism yesterday and today: The overgrazing problem. In *Ecosystems of the world 13: Tropical savannas,* ed. F. Bourliere. Amsterdam: Elsevier.

Lawry, S. W. 1987. *Communal grazing and range management: The case of grazing associations in Lesotho.* ALPAN Network Paper 13. Addis Ababa: International Livestock Centre for Africa.

Lele, S. M. 1991. Sustainable development: A critical review. *World Development* 19 (6): 607–621.

Lele, U. 1989. *Agricultural growth, domestic policies, the external environment, and assistance to Africa.* MADIA (Managing Agricultural Development in Africa) Discussion Paper 1. Washington, D.C.: World Bank.

Lele, U., and S. Stone. 1989. *Population pressure, the environment, and agricultural intensification: Variations on the Boserup hypothesis.* MADIA (Managing Agricultural Development in Africa) Discussion Paper 4. Washington, D.C.: World Bank.

Leonard, H. J. 1987. *Natural resources and economic development in Central America.* New Brunswick, N.J., U.S.A.: Transaction Books.

————. 1989. Environment and the poor: Development strategies for a common agenda. In *Environment and the poor: Development strategies for a common agenda,* ed. H. J. Leonard and contributors. U.S.–Third World Policy Perspectives 11. New Brunswick, N.J., U.S.A.: Transaction Books for the Overseas Development Council.

Leonard, H. J., and contributors. 1989. *Environment and the poor: Development strategies for a common agenda.* U.S.–Third World Policy Perspectives 11. New Brunswick, N.J., U.S.A.: Transaction Books for the Overseas Development Council.

Lipton, M. 1977. *Why poor people stay poor: Urban bias and world development.* London: Temple Smith.

————. 1983. *Poverty, undernutrition, and hunger.* World Bank Staff Working Paper 597. Washington, D.C.: World Bank.

————. 1985. Coase's theorem versus prisoners' dilemma. In *Economy and democracy,* ed. R. C. O. Matthews. London: Macmillan.

————. 1989. *New seeds and poor people.* Baltimore: Johns Hopkins University Press.

————. 1990. Responses to rural population growth: Malthus and the moderns. In *Rural development and population: Institutions and policy,* ed. G. McNicoll and M. Cain. New York: Population Council and Oxford University Press.

————. 1991. A note on poverty and sustainability. *IDS Bulletin* 22 (4): 12–16.

————. 1992. Accelerated resource degradation by third world agriculture: Created in the commons, in the west, or in bed? Paper presented at the conference on Agricultural Sustainability and Poverty Alleviation: Issues and Policies, 23–27 September, 1991, Feldafing, Germany: German Foundation for Internatinal Development (DSE).

Lipton, M., and E. de Kadt. 1988. *Agriculture-health linkages.* WHO Offset Publication 104. Geneva: World Health Organization.

Lipton, M., and R. Longhurst. 1989. *New seeds and poor people.* London and Baltimore: Hutchinson and Johns Hopkins University Press.

Lipton, M., and J. van der Gaag, eds. 1994. *Including the poor.* World Bank Regional and Sectoral Studies. Washington, D.C.: World Bank.

Liu Yanhua. 1992. Sustainable agriculture and people's life in Tibet in the 21st century. Beijing: Chinese Academy of Science, Institute of Geography (a note for limited circulation).

Livingstone, I. 1986. The common property problem and pastoralist economic behavior. *Journal of Development Studies* 23 (1): 5–19.

Lopez, A. D. 1990. Causes of death: An assessment of global patterns of mortality around 1985. *World Health Statistics Quarterly* 43: 91–104.

Lopez-Pereira, M. A., J. H. Sanders, T. G. Baker, and P. V. Preckel. 1994. Economics of soil erosion-control and seed-fertilizer technologies for hillside farming in Honduras. *Agricultural Economics* 11 (2,3): 271–288.

Lowenberg-DeBoer, D. K., and T. Abdoulaye. 1994. *The opportunity cost of capital for agriculture in the Sahel: Case study evidence from Niger and Burkina Faso.* Department of Agricultural Economics Staff Paper. West Lafayette, Ind., U.S.A.: Purdue University.

Loyns, R. M. A., and J. A. MacMillan. 1990. *Sustainable development and agriculture.* Working Paper 90-4. Winnipeg, Manitoba, Canada: University of Manitoba, Department of Agricultural Economics and Farm Management.

Lynam, J. K., and R. W. Herdt. 1989. Sense and sustainability: Sustainability as an objective in international agricultural research. *Agricultural Economics* 3 (4): 381–398.

MacDicken, K. G. 1990. Agroforestry management in the humid tropics. In *Agroforestry: Classification and management,* ed. K. G. MacDicken and N. T. Vergara. New York: John Wiley and Sons.

Mace, R. 1990. Pastoral herd compositions in unpredictable environments: A comparison of model predictions and data from camel-keeping groups. *Agricultural Systems* 33 (1): 1–11.

Madsen, H., G. Coulibaly, and P. Furu. 1987. Distribution of freshwater snails in the river Niger basin with special reference to the intermediate hosts of schistosomes. *Hydrobiologia* 146: 77–88.

Mahar, D. 1988. *Government policies and deforestation in Brazil's Amazon region.* Environment Department Working Paper 7. Washington, D.C.: World Bank.

————. 1989. *Government policies and deforestation in Brazil's Amazon region.* Washington, D.C.: World Bank.

Malthus, A., and D. Pearce. 1988. A summary view of the principle of population. Revision of contribution to *Encyclopaedia Britannica,* Supplement (1824). Reprinted in F. Osborn, ed., *Three essays of population.* New York: Mentor, n.d. (1960?).

Markandya, A., and D. Pearce. 1988. *Environmental considerations and the choice of the discount rate in developing countries.* Environment Department Working Paper 3. Policy Planning and Research Staff. Washington, D.C.: World Bank.

Markandya, A., and J. Richardson. 1990. The debt crisis, structural adjustment, and the environment. Report to the Worldwide Fund for Nature. London Environmental Economics Centre, London.

Marquez, C. B., P. L. Pingali, and F. G. Palis. 1992. Farmer health impact of long-term pesticide exposure: A medical and economic analysis in the Philippines. Paper presented at a workshop on Measuring the Health and Environmental Effects of Pesticides, 30 March–3 April, Bellagio, Italy.

Martine, G. 1990. Rondônia and the fate of small producers. In *The future of Amazonia: Destruction or sustainable development,* ed. D. Goodman and A. Hall. London: Macmillan.

————. 1992. *Ciclos e destinos da migração para areas de fronteira na era moderna: Uma visão geral.* Documento de Trabalho 12. Brasilia: Instituto Sociedade População e Natureza (ISPN).

Mascarenhas, J., J. Jangal, P. D. Prem Kumar, R. Rathod, D. Naik, and R. Maidrappa. 1991. Community organization and participatory learning methods in the watershed context. Summarized in *Farmers' practices and soil and water conservation programs,* ed. J. M. Kerr. Patancheru, India: International Crops Research Institute for the Semi-Arid Tropics.

Mathews, J. T., and D. B. Turnstal. 1991. Moving toward ecodevelopment: Generating environmental information for decision makers. In *WRI Issues and Ideas.* Washington, D.C.: World Resources Institute.

Mathur, V. K. 1988. A dynamic model of regional population growth and decline. *Journal of Regional Science* 28 (3): 379–395.

Matlon, P. J. 1979. *Income distribution among farmers in northern Nigeria: Empirical results and policy implications.* African Rural Economy Paper 18. East Lansing, Mich., U.S.A.: Michigan State University.

———. 1985. A critical review of objectives, methods, and progress to date in sorghum and millet improvement: A case study of ICRISAT/Burkina Faso. In *Appropriate technologies for farmers in semi-arid West Africa,* ed. H. W. Ohm and J. G. Nagy. West Lafayette, Ind., U.S.A.: Purdue University, International Programs in Agriculture.

———. 1987. The West African semi-arid tropics. In *Accelerating food production in Sub-Saharan Africa,* ed. J. W. Mellor, C. L. Delgado, and M. J. Blackie. Baltimore: Johns Hopkins University Press.

———. 1990. Improving productivity in sorghum and pearl millet in semi-arid Africa. *Food Research Institute Studies* 22 (1): 1–43.

Matlon, P. J., and D. S. C. Spencer. 1984. Increasing food production in Sub-Saharan Africa: Environmental problems and inadequate technological solutions. *American Journal of Agricultural Economics* 66 (5): 671–676.

McCay, B. J., and J. M. Acheson, eds. 1987. *The question of the commons.* Tucson, Ariz., U.S.A.: University of Arizona Press.

McGuire, J., and B. Popkin. 1988. The zero-sum game: A framework for examining women and children. *Food and Nutrition Bulletin* 10 (3): 27–32.

McJunkin, F. E. 1982. *Water and human health.* Washington, D.C.: United States Agency for International Development.

McMillan, D., T. Painter, and T. Scudder. 1990. *Land settlement review: Settlement experiences and development strategies in the onchocerciasis control program areas of West Africa.* Binghampton, N.Y., U.S.A.: Institute for Development Anthropology.

Mearns, L. O., C. Rosenzweig, and R. Goldberg. 1991. *Changes in climate variability and possible impacts on wheat yields.* Paper presented at the Seventh Conference on Applied Climatology, 10–13 September, Salt Lake City. Boulder, Colo., U.S.A.: National Center for Atmospheric Research.

Mellor, J. W. 1976. *The new economics of growth: A strategy for India and the developing world.* Ithaca, N.Y., U.S.A.: Cornell University Press.

———. 1988. The inter-twining of environmental problems and poverty. *Environment* 30 (9).

Messerli, B., and H. Hurni, eds. 1990. *African mountains and highlands: Problems and perspectives.* Nairobi, Kenya: African Mountains Association.

Migot-Adholla, S., P. Hazell, B. Blarel, and F. Place. 1991. Indigenous land rights systems in Sub-Saharan Africa: A constraint on productivity? *World Bank Economic Review* 5 (1): 155–175.

Mikesell, R. F. 1991. Project evaluation and sustainable development. In *Environmentally sustainable economic development: Building on Brundtland,* ed. R. Goodland, H. Daly, and S. El-Serafy. Environment Working Paper 46. Washington, D.C.: World Bank.

Mills, A., and M. Thomas. 1984. *Economic evaluation of health programmes in developing countries: A review and selected annotated bibliography.* EPC Publication 3. London: Evaluation and Planning Centre for Health Care, London School of Hygiene and Tropical Medicine.

Mink, S. D. 1993. *Poverty, population, and the environment.* World Bank Discussion Paper 189. Washington, D.C.: World Bank.

Mintzer, I. M., ed. 1992. *Confronting climate change: Risks, implications, and responses.* Cambridge: Cambridge University Press.

Miracle, M. 1967. *Agriculture in the Congo basin.* Madison, Wis., U.S.A.: University of Wisconsin Press.

Miranowski, J., and M. Cochran. 1993. Economics of land in agriculture. In *Agricultural and environmental resource economics,* ed. G. A. Carlson, D. Zilberman, and J. A. Miranowski. New York: Oxford University Press.

Monod, T. 1975. *Pastoralism in tropical Africa.* London: Oxford University Press/International African Institute.

Monteiro, C. A., M. H. D'Aquino Benicio, R. Lumes, N. C. Gonveia, J. A. A. Taddei, and M. A. A. Cordoso. 1992. O estado nutricional das crianças Brasileiras: A trajetória de 1975 a 1989. In *Perfil estatístico de crianças e mães no Brasil: Aspectos de saúde e nutrição de crianças no Brasil, 1989,* ed. M. F. G. Monteiro and R. Cervini. Rio de Janeiro: Fundação Instituto Brasileiro de Geografia e Estatistica.

Moorman, F. R., and D. J. Greenland. 1980. Major production systems related to soil properties in humid tropical Africa. In *Priorities for alleviating soil-related constraints to food production in the tropics.* Los Baños, the Philippines: International Rice Research Institute.

Moran, E. 1984. Amazon basin colonization. *Interciencia* 9 (6): 377–385.

Moris, J. R. 1988. *Interventions for African pastoral development under adverse production trends.* ALPAN Network Paper 16. Addis Ababa: International Livestock Centre for Africa.

Mortimore, M. J. 1988. Desertification and resilience in semi-arid West Africa. *Geography* 73 (1): 61–64.

Mounier, F. 1986. The Senegal River scheme: Development for whom? In *The social and environmental effects of large dams.* Vol. 2, *Case studies,* ed. E. Goldsmith and N. Hildyard. Camelford, Cornwall, U.K.: Wadebridge Ecological Centre.

Mueller, C. 1982. O estado e a expansão da fronteira agrícola no Brasil. In *Anais do seminário expansão da fronteira agropecuária e meio ambiente na América Latina.* Brasilia: Departamento de Economia, Universidade de Brasília.

Naga Bhushana, S. R., H. S. Shankaranarayana, and C. R. Shivaprasad. 1983. Classification requirements of red soil of India for transfer of technology. Paper presented at Alfisols in the Semi-Arid Tropics: A Consultants' Workshop 1–3 December, International Crops Research Institute for Semi-Arid Tropics, Hyderabad, India.

National Academy of Sciences. 1985. *Population growth and economic development.* Washington, D.C.: National Academy Press.

NCSO (National Census and Statistics Office, the Philippines). 1986 and 1988. *Compendium of Philippine social statistics.* Manila.

————. 1988. *Economic and social statistics indicator.* Manila.

Nelson, M. 1989. Policy dimensions in environmental issues papers: A review of experience in the LAC region. Paper presented for the World Bank, Washington, D.C.

Nicou, R., and C. Charreau. 1985. Soil tillage and water conservation in semi-arid West Africa. In *Appropriate technologies for farmers in semi-arid West Africa,* ed. H. W. Ohm and J. G. Nagy. West Lafayette, Ind., U.S.A.: Purdue University, International Programs in Agriculture.

Niger. 1991. *Annuaire statistique: Séries longues.* Niamey: Direction de la Statistique et de la Démographie, Ministère du Plan.

Nijkamp, P., C. J. M. van den Bergh, and F. J. Soeteman. 1991. Regional sustainable development and natural resource use. In *Proceedings of the World Bank Annual Conference on Development Economics, 1990.* Washington, D.C.: World Bank.

Nordhaus, W. D. 1973. The allocation of energy resources. *Brookings Papers on Economic Activity* 3: 529–570.

Norgaard, R. B. 1981. Sociosystem and ecosystem: Co-evolution in the Amazon. *Journal of Environmental Economics and Management* 8: 238–254.

————. 1984. Traditional agricultural knowledge: Past performance, future prospects, and institutional implications. *American Journal of Agricultural Economics* 66 (5): 874–878.

————. 1985. Environmental economics: An evolutionary critique and a plea for pluralism. *Journal of Environmental Economics and Management* 12 (4): 382–394.

————. 1988. The biological control of cassava mealybug in Africa. *American Journal of Agricultural Economics* 70 (2): 366–371.

————. 1991. *Sustainability as intergenerational equity: The challenge to economic thought and practice.* Washington, D.C.: World Bank, Office of the Chief Economist, Asia Region.

Norman, M. J. T. 1979. *Annual cropping systems in the tropics: An introduction.* Gainesville, Fla., U.S.A.: University of Florida Press.

Noronha, R. 1985. *A review of the literature on land tenure systems in Sub-Saharan Africa.* Discussion Paper, Report ARU 43. Washington, D.C.: World Bank.

Norris, P. E., and S. S. Batie. 1987. Virginia farmers' soil conservation decisions: An application of Tobit analysis. *Southern Journal of Agricultural Economics* 19 (1): 79–90.

Norse, D., C. James, B. J. Skinner, and Q. Zhao. 1992. Agriculture, land use, and degradation. In *An agenda of science for environment and development into the 21st century,* ed. J. C. I. Dooge, G. T. Goodman, J. W. M. la Rivière, J. Marton-Lefèvre, T. O'Riordan, and F. Praderie. Cambridge: Cambridge University Press.

NRC (National Research Council), Committee on Selected Biological Problems in the Humid Tropics. 1982. *Ecological aspects of development in the humid tropics.* Washington, D.C.: National Academy Press.

NRC (National Research Council), Advisory Committee on the Sahel, Board on Science and Technology for International Development, Office of International Affairs. 1984. *Environmental change in the West African Sahel.* Washington, D.C.

Nweke, F. I., H. C. Ezumah, and D. S. C. Spencer. 1988. *Cropping systems and agronomic performance of improved cassava in a humid forest ecosystem.* RCMP (Resource and Crop Management Program) Research Monograph 2. Ibadan, Nigeria: International Institute of Tropical Agriculture.

O'Laughlin, D. 1985. *The influence of forest roads on erosion and stream sedimentation: Comparison between temperate and tropical forests.* Honolulu, Hi., U.S.A.: East-West Center, Environment and Policy Institute.

Oba, G., and W. J. Lusigi. 1987. *An overview of drought strategies and land use in African pastoral systems.* Pastoral Development Network Paper 23a. London: Overseas Development Institute.

OECD (Organization for Economic Cooperation and Development). 1988. *The Sahel facing the future.* Paris.

Ogbu, O. M., and M. Gbetibouo. 1990. Agricultural supply response in Sub-Saharan Africa: A critical review. *African Development Review* 2 (2): 83–99.

Ogunbile, A. O. 1980. An evaluation of sole-crop production technology on small farms in northern Nigeria under different power sources: A multiperiod linear programming approach. Ph.D. diss., Iowa State University, Ames, Iowa, U.S.A.

Ohm, H. W., and J. G. Nagy, eds. 1985. *Appropriate technologies for farmers in semi-arid West Africa.* West Lafayette, Ind., U.S.A.: Purdue University, International Programs in Agriculture.

Okigbo, B. N. 1974. *Fitting research to farming systems.* Ibadan, Nigeria: International Institute of Tropical Agriculture.

Olivares, J. 1987. *Options and investment priorities in irrigation development* (final report). The World Bank/United Nations Development Program Interregional Report INT/82/001. Washington, D.C.: World Bank.

Olson, M. 1965. *The logic of collective action: Public goods and the theory of groups.* Cambridge, Mass., U.S.A.: Harvard University Press.

————. 1982. *Economic causes of the rise and decline of nations.* Cambridge, Mass., U.S.A.: Harvard University Press.

Oomen, J. M. V., J. de Wolf, and W. R. Jobin. 1990. *Health and irrigation: Incorporation of disease-control measures in irrigation, a multifaceted task in design, construction, operation,* 2 vols. ILRI Publication 45. Wageningen, the Netherlands: International Institute for Land Reclamation and Improvement.

Oram, P. 1985. Agricultural research and extension: Issues of public expenditure. In *Recurrent costs and agricultural development,* ed. J. Howell. London: Overseas Development Institute.

————. 1988a. Moving toward sustainability: Building the agroecological framework. *Environment* 30 (9): 14–36.

————. 1988b. *Networks as a research modality, Annex II.* Report of the Bellagio Forestry Task Force. New York: United Nations Development Program.

————. 1988c. *Prospects for agricultural production and food deficits in West Asia and North Africa: The role of high-elevation areas.* Washington, D.C.: International Food Policy Research Institute.

————. 1991. *Towards a new agricultural revolution: Research, technology transfer, and application for food security in Africa.* Washington, D.C.: International Food Policy Research Institute and International Service for National Agricultural Research.

Ostrom, E. 1990. *Governing the commons.* Cambridge: Cambridge University Press.

OTA (Office of Technology Assessment). 1984. *Technologies to sustain tropical forest resources.* Washington, D.C.: U.S. Congress.

Otsuka, K., V. G. Cordova, and C. C. David. 1990. *Green Revolution, land reform and household income distribution in the Philippines.* Social Sciences Division Paper 90-08. Los Baños, the Philippines: International Rice Research Institute.

Ouassou, A., and H. Baghati. 1988. Agriculture in the mountainous regions of Morocco. In *Winter cereals and food legumes in mountainous areas,* ed. J. Srivastava, M. Saxena, S. Varma, and M. Tahir. Aleppo, Syria: International Center for Agricultural Research in the Dry Areas.

Oxby, C. 1982. Group ranges in Africa. *Overseas Development Institute Review* 2: 2–13.

Paarlberg, R., and M. Lipton. 1991. Changing missions at the World Bank: The rural poor at risk. *World Policy Journal* (Summer).

Pagoulatos, A., D. L. Debertin, and F. Sjarkowi. 1989. Soil erosion, intertemporal profit, and the soil conservation decision. *Southern Journal of Agricultural Economics* 21 (2): 55–62.

Palladino, P. S. A. 1989. Entomology and ecology: The ecology of entomology. Ph.D. diss., University of Minnesota, Minneapolis, Minn., U.S.A.

Panayotou, T. 1990. Policies, incentives, and regulations: The use of fiscal incentives. Paper presented at the Conference on Environmental Management in Developing Countries, OECD (Organization for Economic Cooperation and Development) Development Centre, 3–5 October, Paris.

Papadakis, J., ed. 1975. *Climates of the world and their potentialities.* Buenos Aires: Published by J. Papadakis.

Pardey, P. G., and J. Roseboom. 1989. A global evaluation of national agricultural research investments: 1960–1985. In *The changing dynamics of global agriculture,* ed. E. Javier and U. Renborg. The Hague: International Service for National Agricultural Research.

————. 1991. *National agricultural research from a regional and agroecological perspective.* The Hague: International Service for National Agricultural Research.

Pardey, P. G., J. Roseboom, and J. R. Anderson. 1991. *Agricultural research policy: International quantitative perspectives.* Cambridge: Cambridge University Press.

Pardey, P. G., J. M. Alston, J. E. Christian, and S. Fan. 1996. Summary of a productive partnership: The benefits from U.S. participation in the CGIAR. EPTD (Environment and Production Technology Division) Discussion Paper 18. Washington, D.C.: International Food Policy Research Institute.

Pardey, P. G., J. Roseboom, and N. M. Beintema. 1997. Investments in African agricultural research. *World Development* 25 (3): 409–423.

Paris, R., and I. Ruzicka. 1991. *Barking up the wrong tree: The role of rent appropriation in tropical forest management.* Environment Office Discussion Paper. Manila: Asian Development Bank.

Parry, M. L. 1990. *Climate change and world agriculture.* London: Earthscan.

Parry, M. L., T. R. Carter, and N. T. Konijn, eds. 1988. *The impact of climatic variations on agriculture.* Vol. 1, *Assessments in cool, temperate, and cold regions;* vol. 2, *Assessments in semi-arid areas.* Dordrecht: Kluwer.

Parry, M. L., P. N. Duinker, J. I. L. Morison, J. H. Porter, J. Reilly, and L. J. Wright. 1990. Agriculture and forestry. In *Climate change: The IPCC impacts assessment,* ed. W. J. McG. Tegart, G. W. Sheldon, and D. C. Griffiths. Canberra, Australia: Australian Government Publishing Services.

Paul, E. A., and G. P. Robertson. 1989. Ecology and the agricultural sciences: A fake dichotomy? *Ecology* 70 (6): 1594–1597.

Pearce, D. W. 1990. Policies, incentives, and regulations: Recent thinking in OECD countries. Paper presented at the Conference on Environmental Management in Developing Countries, OECD (Organization for Economic Cooperation and Development) Development Centre, 3–5 October, Paris.

Pearce, D. W., and J. J. Warford. 1993. *World without end: Economics, environment, and sustainable development.* New York: Oxford University Press.

Pearce, D. W., E. Barbier, and A. Markandya. 1990. *Sustainable development: Economics and environment in the third world.* Brookfield, Vt., U.S.A.: Gower.

Pender, J., and J. Kerr. 1996. Determinants of farmers' indigenous soil and water conservation investments in India's semiarid tropics. Environment and Production Technology Division Discussion Paper 17. Washington, D.C.: International Food Policy Research Institute.

Perkins, J. S. 1991. Drought, cattle-keeping and range degradation in the Kalahari, Botswana. In *Pastoral economies in Africa and long-term responses to drought,* ed. J. C. Stone. Proceedings of a Colloquium, April 9–10, 1990, University of Aberdeen, Aberdeen, U.K.

Pezzey, J. 1989. *Economic analysis of sustainable growth and sustainable development.* Environmental Department Working Paper 15. Washington, D.C.: World Bank.

———. 1992. *Sustainable development concepts: An economic analysis.* World Bank Environment Paper 2. Washington, D.C.: World Bank.

Pfeiffer, R. 1990. Sustainable agriculture in practice: The production potential and environmental effects of macro-contour lines in West Usambara mountains of Tanzania. Ph.D. diss., University of Hohenhein, Federal Republic of Germany.

Phantumvanit, D., and T. Panayotou. 1990. Natural resources for a sustainable future: Spreading the benefits. Report prepared for the 1990 Thailand Development Research Institute Year-End Conference on Industrializing Thailand and Its Impact on the Environment, 8–9 December, Chon Buri, Thailand.

Pieri, C. 1985. Food crop fertilization and soil fertility: The IRAT experience. In *Appropriate technologies for farmers in semi-arid West Africa,* ed. H. W. Ohm and J. G. Nagy. West Lafayette, Ind., U.S.A.: Purdue University, International Programs in Agriculture.

Pineiro, M., and E. Moscardi. 1984. *An analysis of research priorities in the* CGIAR *system.* Buenos Aires.

Pingali, P. L. 1990. Institutional and environmental constaints to agricultural intensification. In *Rural development and population: Institutions and policy,* ed. G. McNicoll and M. Cain. Oxford: Oxford University Press.

Pingali, P. L., Y. Bigot, and H. P. Binswanger. 1987. *Agricultural mechanization and the evolution of farming systems in Sub-Saharan Africa.* Baltimore: Johns Hopkins University Press.

Pingali, P. L., P. F. Moya, and L. E. Velasco. 1990. *The post–Green Revolution blues in Asian rice production: The diminished gap between experiment station and farmer yields.* Social Science Division Paper 90-01. Los Baños, the Philippines: International Rice Research Institute.

Pinstrup-Andersen, P. 1986. Food policy and human nutrition. In *Dry area agriculture, food science, and human nutrition,* ed. D. Nygaard and P. Pellet. New York: Pergamon.

————. 1994. *World food trends and future food security.* Food Policy Report. Washington, D.C.: International Food Policy Research Institute.

Pinstrup-Andersen, P., and R. Pandya-Lorch. 1995. *Agricultural growth is the key to poverty alleviation in low-income developing countries.* Policy Brief 5. Washington, D.C.: International Food Policy Research Institute.

PIRAMIDE (Programa Intensivo de Reforestación con Arboles de Uso Multiple Integrados al Desarrollo). 1990. *Diagnóstico de la región suroriental.* Guatemala City, Guatemala.

Place, F., and P. B. R. Hazell. 1993. Productivity effects of indigenous land tenure systems in Sub-Saharan Africa. *American Journal of Agricultural Economics* 75 (February): 10–19.

Plucknett, D. L. 1993. *Science and agricultural transformation.* Lecture Series 1. Washington, D.C.: International Food Policy Research Institute.

Plucknett, D. L., and N. J. H. Smith. 1976. Sustaining agricultural yields. *BioScience* 36 (1): 40–45.

Plucknett, D. L., S. Smith, and S. Ozgediz. 1990. *International agricultural research, a database of networks.* CGIAR (Consultative Group on International Agricultural Research) Study Paper 26. Washington, D.C.: World Bank.

Poffenberger, M. 1990. Forest management partnerships: Regenerating India's forests. Executive summary of the Workshop on Sustainable Forestry, 10–12 September, Ford Foundation and Indian Environmental Society, New Delhi.

Poulsen, G. 1978. Man and tree in tropical Africa: Three essays on the role of trees in the African environment. Ottawa, Canada: International Development Research Corporation.

Pragtong, K. 1987. Land tenure and agroforestry in forest land in Thailand. In *Land, trees, and tenure,* ed. J. B. Raintree. Proceedings of an International Workshop on Tenure Issues in Agroforestry, 27–31 May, 1985, sponsored by the Ford Foundation. Nairobi, Kenya: International Centre for Research in Agroforesty; and Madison, Wis., U.S.A.: University of Wisconsin, Land Tenure Center.

Pratt, D. J., and M. D. Gwynne. 1977. *Rangeland management and ecology in East Africa.* London: Hodder and Stoughton.

Pretty, J. N. 1990. Sustainable agriculture in the Middle Ages: The English manor. *Agricultural History Review* 3 (1): 1–19.

Price, C. 1991. Do high discount rates destroy tropical forests? *Journal of Agricultural Economics* 42 (1): 77–85.

Prudencio, Y. C. 1983. A village study of soil fertility management and food crop production in Upper Volta: Technical and economic analysis. Ph.D. diss., University of Arizona, Tucson, Ariz., U.S.A.

Purdue University. 1986. *Cereal technology development—West African semi-arid tropics: A farming systems perspective.* International Education and Research. West Lafayette, Ind., U.S.A.: Purdue University.

Put, M., and M. P. van Dijk. 1989. *Semi-arid Indian agriculture: Land, water, and crop management in southern India.* Bulletin 316. Amsterdam: Rural Development Programme, Royal Tropical Institute.

Raintree, J. B. 1987. Agroforestry, tropical land use, and tenure. In *Land, trees, and tenure,* ed. J. B. Raintree. Proceedings of an International Workshop on Tenure Issues in Agroforestry, 27–31 May, 1985, sponsored by the Ford Foundation. Nairobi, Kenya: International Centre for Research in Agroforestry; and Madison, Wis., U.S.A.: University of Wisconsin, Land Tenure Center.

Rao, C. H. H. 1990. Some interrelationships between agricultural technology, livestock economy, rural poverty and environment: An interstate analysis for India. *Golden Jubilee Volume of Indian Society of Agricultural Economics.*

Rapport, D. 1992. Evaluating ecosystem health. *Journal of Aquatic Ecosystem Health* 1: 15–24.

Raup, H. M. 1964. Some problems in ecological theory and their relation to conservation. *Journal of Ecology* 52: 19–28.

Reardon, T. 1995. Sustainability issues for agricultural research strategies in the semi-arid tropics: Focus on the Sahel. *Agricultural Systems* 48 (3): 345–360.

Reardon, T., and N. Islam. 1989. Issues of sustainability in agricultural research in Africa. In the proceedings of the symposium on the Sustainability of Production Systems in Sub-Saharan Africa, NORAGRIC, Agricultural University of Norway, Ås, Norway, 4–7 September 1989. NORAGRIC Occasional Paper Series C.

Reardon, T., and S. A. Vosti. 1992. Issues in the analysis of the effects of policy on conservation and productivity at the household level in developing countries. *Quarterly Journal of International Agriculture* 31 (4): 380–396.

———. 1995. Links between rural poverty and environment in developing countries: Asset categories and "conservation-investment poverty." *World Development* 23 (9): 1495–1506.

Reardon, T., E. Crawford, and V. Kelly. 1994. Links between nonfarm income and farm investment in African households: Adding the capital market perspective. *American Journal of Agricultural Economics* 76 (5): 1172–1176.

———. 1995. *Promoting investment in sustainable intensification of African agriculture.* Michigan State University Staff Paper 95-18. East Lansing, Mich., U.S.A.: Michigan State University Press.

Reardon, T., C. Delgado, and P. Matlon. 1992. Determinants and effects of income diversification amongst farm households in Burkina Faso. *Journal of Development Studies* 28 (January): 264–296.

Reardon, T., P. Matlon, and C. Delgado. 1988. Coping with household-level food insecurity in drought-affected areas of Burkina Faso. *World Development* 16 (9): 1065–1074.

Reardon, T., V. Kelly, E. Crawford, K. Savadogo, and T. Jayne. 1994a. *Raising farm productivity in Africa to sustain long-term food security.* Michigan State University Staff Paper 94-77. East Lansing, Mich., U.S.A.: Michigan State University Press.

Reardon, T., A. A. Fall, V. Kelly, C. Delgado, P. Matlon, J. Hopkins, and O. Badiane. 1994b. Is income diversification agriculture-led in the West African semi-arid tropics? The nature, causes, effects, distribution, and production linkages of off-farm activities. In *Economic policy experience in Africa: What have we learned?* ed. A. Atsain, S. Wangwe, and A. G. Drabek. Nairobi, Kenya: African Economic Research Consortium.

Reis, E., and S. Margulis. 1991. Economic perspectives on deforestation in the Brazilian Amazon. Paper presented at the European Association of Environmental and Resource Economists Conference on Economics of International Environmental Problems and Policies, 10–14 June, Stockholm.

Repetto, R. 1985. *Paying the price: Pesticide subsidies in developing countries.* Washington, D.C.: World Resources Institute.

———. 1988. *Economic policy reform for natural resource conservation.* Environment Department Working Paper 4. Washington, D.C.: World Bank.

Repetto, R., and M. Gillis, eds. 1988. *Public policies and the misuse of forest resources.* Cambridge: Cambridge University Press.

Repetto, R., and T. Holmes. 1983. Role of population in resource depletion in developing countries. *Population and Development Review* 9 (4): 609–632.

Riely, F. Z., Jr. 1991. Drought responses of the Kababish pastoralists in northern Kordofan, Sudan: Implications for famine early warning. Food and Agriculture Organization of the United Nations, Rome. Mimeo.

Rind, D., R. Goldberg, J. Hansen, C. Rosenzweig, and R. Reudy. 1990. Potential evapotranspiration and the likelihood of future drought. *Journal of Geophysical Research* 95 (D7): 9983–10004.

Rosegrant, M. W., and E. Pasandaran. 1990. Irrigation in Indonesia: Trends and determinants. Washington, D.C.: International Food Policy Research Institute. Mimeo.

Rosegrant, M. W., and P. L. Pingali. 1991. *Sustaining rice productivity growth in Asia: A policy perspective.* Social Sciences Division Paper 91-01. Los Baños, the Philippines: International Rice Research Institute.

Rosenfield, P. L., and B. T. Bower. 1978. *Management strategies for reducing adverse health impacts of water resources development projects.* Discussion Paper D-3. Washington, D.C.: Resources for the Future.

Rosenzweig, C., M. L. Parry, G. Fischer, and K. Frohberg. 1992. *Climate change and world food supply.* Oxford: Environmental Change Unit, Oxford University.

Rosling, H. 1987. *Cassava toxicity and food security.* A report for UNICEF. Uppsala, Sweden: Uppsala University, Department of Pediatrics.

Roth, M., and R. Barrows. 1988. *A theoretical model of land ownership security and titling impacts on resource allocation and capital investment.* Madison, Wis., U.S.A.: University of Wisconsin, Land Tenure Center.

Rubenson, S. 1991. Environmental stress and conflict in Ethiopian history: Looking for correlation. *Ambio* 20 (5): 179–182.

Ruddle, K., and W. Manshard. 1980. *Renewable natural resources and the environment: Pressing problems in the developing world.* Dublin: Tycooly International for the United Nations University.

Rudolph, L., and S. Rudolph. 1968. *The modernity of tradition.* Chicago: University of Chicago Press.

Runge, F. 1986. Induced innovation in agriculture and environmental quality. In *Agriculture and the environment,* ed. T. Phipps, P. R. Crosson, and K. A. Price. Washington, D.C.: Resources for the Future.

Runge, C. F., R. D. Munson, E. Lotterman, and J. Creason. 1990. *Agricultural competitiveness, farm fertilizer, chemical use, and environmental quality.* St. Paul, Minn., U.S.A.: University of Minnesota, Center for International Food and Agricultural Policy.

Ruthenberg, H. 1980. *Farming systems in the tropics.* 3rd ed. Oxford: Clarendon House.

Ruttan, V. W. 1971. Technology and the environment. *American Journal of Agricultural Economics* 53:707–717.

———. 1988. Sustainability is not enough. *American Journal of Alternative Agriculture* 3: 128–130.

———. 1989. Why foreign economic assistance? *Economic Development and Cultural Change* 37 (2): 411–424.

———, ed. 1990. *Health constraints in agricultural development.* Department of Agricultural and Applied Economics Staff Paper P90-74. St. Paul, Minn., U.S.A.: University of Minnesota Press.

———, ed. 1992. *Sustainable development and the environment: Perspectives on growth and constraints.* Boulder, Colo., U.S.A.: Westview.

———, ed. 1994. *Agriculture, environment, and health: Toward sustainable development into the twenty-first century.* Minneapolis, Minn., U.S.A.: University of Minnesota Press.

Ruttan, V. W., and H. Binswanger. 1978. Factor productivity and growth: A historical interpretation. In *Induced innovation, technology, and development,* ed. H. Binswanger and V. Ruttan. Baltimore: Johns Hopkins University Press.

Sajise, P. E. 1986. The changing upland landscape. In *Man, agriculture and the tropical forest: Change and development in the Philippine uplands,* ed. J. S. Fujisaka and P. E. Sajise, Bangkok, Thailand: Winrock International Institute for Agricultural Development.

———. 1987. Stable upland farming in the Philippines: Problems and prospects. In *Impact of man's activities on tropical upland forest ecosystems,* ed. Y. Hadi, K. Awang, N. M. Majid, and S. Mohamed. Penang, Malaysia: Faculty of Forestry, Universiti Pertanian Malaysia.

Samarasinghe, M. U. L. 1986. The present malaria situation in Sri Lanka with particular reference to areas where irrigation has recently been introduced. In *Proceedings of the Workshop on Irrigation and Vector-Borne Disease Transmission,* International Irrigation Management Institute. Digana Village, Sri Lanka: International Irrigation Management Institute.

Sanchez, P. A. 1976. *Properties and management of soils in the tropics.* New York: John Wiley and Sons.

Sanchez, P. A., and J. G. Salinas. 1981. Low-input technology for managing oxisols and ultisols in tropical America. *Advances in Agronomy* 34: 279–406.

Sanchez, P. A., J. H. Villachica, and D. E. Bandy. 1983. Soil fertility dynamics after clearing a tropical rainforest in Peru. *Soil Science Society of America Journal* 47 (6): 1171–1178.

Sanchez, P. A., D. E. Brandy, J. H. Villachica, and J. J. Nicholaides. 1982. Amazon basin soils: Management for continuous crop production. *Science* 216: 821–827.

Sandford, S. 1983. *Management of pastoral development in the third world.* Chichester, U.K.: John Wiley and Sons and Overseas Development Institute.

Sanford, S. G. 1987. Crop residue/livestock relationships. In *Soil, crop, and water management in the Sudano-Sahelian zone.* Proceedings of an international workshop, 11–16 January. Niamey, Niger: International Crops Research Institute for the Semi-Arid Tropics (ICRISAT) Sahelian Center.

Sanghi, N. K. 1987. *A modified watershed technology based on interaction between farmers and scientists.* Hyderabad, India: Central Research Institute for Dryland Agriculture.

Sanwal, M. 1989. What we know about mountain development: Common property, investment priorities, and institutional arrangement. *Mountain Research and Development* 9 (1): 3–14.

Sarma, J. S., and V. P. Gandhi. 1990. *Production and consumption of foodgrains in India.* Research Report 81. Washington, D.C.: International Food Policy Research Institute.

Sawyer, D. 1984. Frontier expansion and retraction in Brazil. In *Frontier expansion in Amazonia,* ed. M. Schmink and C. H. Wood. Gainesville, Fla., U.S.A.: University of Florida Press.

———. 1990. The future of deforestion in Amazonia: A socioeconomic and political analysis. In *Alternatives to deforestation: Steps toward sustainable use of the Amazon rain forest,* ed. A. B. Anderson. New York: Columbia University Press.

———. 1991. Campesinato e ecologia na Amazônia. In *Dilemas sócioambientais e desenvolvimento sustentável,* ed. D. Hogan and P. F. Vieira. Campinas, Brazil: Editora da UNICAMP (Universidade de Campinas).

Scherr, S. J., B. Barbier, L. A. Jackson, and S. Yadav. 1995. Land degradation in the developing world: Implications for food, agriculture, and environment to the year 2020. A synthesis of recommendations from an international workshop, 4–6 April, Annapolis, Md., U.S.A. International Food Policy Research Institute, Washington, D.C.

Schmid, A. A. 1987. *Property, power, and public choice: An inquiry into law and economics,* 2d ed. New York: Praeger.

Schneider, R., J. McKenna, C. Dejou, J. Butler, and R. Barrows. 1990. *Brazil: An economic analysis of environmental problems in the Amazon.* Washington, D.C.: World Bank.

Schultz, Paul. 1981. *Economics of population.* New York: Addison Wesley.

Schultz, T. W., ed. 1978. *Distortions of agricultural incentives.* Bloomington, Ind., U.S.A.: Indiana University.

Scoones, I. 1992. The economic value of livestock in the communal areas of southern Zimbabwe. *Agricultural Systems* 39 (4): 339–359.

Seegers, S., and D. Kaimowitz. 1989. Relations between agricultural researchers and extension workers: The survey evidence. ISNAR Linkages Discussion Paper 2. The Hague: International Service for National Agricultural Research.

Seitz, W. D., and E. R. Swanson. 1980. Economics of soil conservation from the farmer's perspective. *American Journal of Agricultural Economics* 65 (5): 1084–1088.

Sen, A. K. 1967. Isolation, assurance, and the social rate of discount. *Quarterly Journal of Economics* (February).

———. 1981. *Poverty and famines.* Oxford: Oxford University Press.

Shah, P., G. Bhardwaj, R. Amerstha, N. P. Gautam, K. Bhai, and R. S. Bhai. 1991. Participatory impact monitoring of a soil and water conservation program in Gujarat.

Summarized in *Farmers' practices and soil and water conservation programs*, ed. J. M. Kerr. Patancheru, India: International Crops Research Institute for the Semi-Arid Tropics.

Sharma, P., and M. Banskota. 1992. Population dynamics and sustainable agricultural development in mountain areas. In *Sustainable mountain agriculture*, ed. N. S. Jodha, M. Banskota, and T. Partap. New Delhi: Oxford University Press and IBH.

Shrestha, S. 1992. *Mountain agriculture: Indicators of unsustainability and options for reversal.* MFS (Mountain Farming Systems) Discussion Paper 32. Kathmandu: International Centre for Integrated Mountain Development.

Siamwalla, A. 1995. Land-abundant growth and some of its consequences: The case of Thailand. In *Agriculture on the road to industrialization*, ed. J. W. Mellor. Baltimore: Johns Hopkins University Press.

SIECA (Secretaría de Integración Económica Centroamericana). 1989. *Series estadísticas seleccionadas de Centroamérica.* Guatemala City, Guatemala.

Simões, C. C. 1992. O estudo dos diferenciais na mortalidade infantil segundo algumas características sócio-econômicas. In *Perfil estatístico de crianças e mães no Brasil: Aspectos de saúde e nutrição de crianças no Brasil, 1989*, ed. M. F. G. Monteiro and R. Cervini. Rio de Janeiro: Fundação Instituo Brasileiro de Geografia e Estatistica.

Simon, J. L. 1981. *The ultimate resource.* Princeton, N.J., U.S.A.: Princeton University Press.

Singh, R. P. 1984. Technology options for increasing crop production·in red and black soils, credit needs, and policy issues. Paper presented at the workshop on Watershed-Based Dryland Farming in Black and Red Soils of Peninsular India, 3–4 October, International Crops Research Institute for the Semi-Arid Tropics, Hyderabad, India.

Singh, R. P., R. C. Kashive, V. Bhaskar Rao, K. G. Kshirsagar, and J. H. Foster. 1990. Production resource management with rapid adoption of a new crop: Soybeans in Madhya Pradesh. ICRISAT Resource Management Program, Economics Group Progress Report. Hyderabad, India.

Singh, S., and J. Casterline. 1985. The socioeconomic determinants of fertility. In *Reproductive change in developing countries: Insights from the world fertility survey*, ed. J. Cleland and J. Hobcraft. New York: Oxford University Press.

Singh, V. 1992. Indicators of unsustainability and their contributing factors and processes: A case study of Garhwal Himalaya. Paper presented at the Institute of Himalayan Environment and Development–International Centre for Integrated Mountain Development Workshop on Approaches to Sustainable Development of the Indian Himalayas, 1–4 August, Manali, India.

Sivakumar, M. V. K., J. S. Wallace, C. Renard, and C. Giroux, eds. 1991. *Soil water balance in the Sudano-Sahelian Zone.* Proceedings of an International Workshop, Niamey, Niger, February. IAHS Publication 199. Wallingford, U.K.: International Association of Hydrological Sciences Press.

Sivamohan, M. V. K., C. A. Scott, and M. F. Walter. 1993. Vetiver grass for soil and water conservation: Prospects and problems. In *World soil erosion and conservation*, ed. D. Pimentel. Cambridge: Cambridge University Press.

Skoupy, J. 1988. Developing rangeland resources in African drylands. *Desertification Control Bulletin* 17: 30–36.

Smit, B., and J. Smithers. 1993. Sustainable agriculture: Interpretations, analyses, and prospects. *Canadian Journal of Regional Science* 16 (3): 499–524.

Smith, J., A. O. Barau, A. Goldman, and J. Mareck. 1991. *Intensification and the role of technology: The evolution of maize production in the Nigerian northern Guinea Savannah*. Ibadan, Nigeria: International Institute of Tropical Agriculture.

Snow, R. 1984. Famine relief: Some unanswered questions from Africa. In *Famine as geographical phenomenon*, ed. B. Currey and G. Hugo. Dordrecht: D. Reidel.

Soemarwoto, O., and I. Soemarwoto. 1984. The Javanese rural ecosystem. In *An introduction to human ecology research on agricultural systems in Southeast Asia*, ed. T. A. Rambo and P. E. Sajise. Los Baños, Laguna: University of the Philippines.

Sollod, A. E. 1990. Rainfall, biomass, and the pastoral economy of Niger: Assessing the impact of drought. *Journal of Arid Environments* 18: 97–107.

———. 1991. Climate-driven development policy for Sahelian pastoralists. In *Pastoral economies in Africa and long-term responses to drought*, ed. J. C. Stone. Proceedings of a Colloquium, 9–10 April 1990, University of Aberdeen, Aberdeen, U.K.

Solow, R. M. 1974. The economics of resources or the resources of economics. *American Economic Review* 64 (2): 1–14.

———. 1991. *Sustainability: Economists' perspective*. J. Seeward Johnson Lecture. Woods Hole, Mass., U.S.A.: Woods Hole Oceanographic Institution, Marine Policy Center.

Sornmani, S. 1987. *Malaria risks involved in slash-and-burn agriculture in A. Dirus infested forests in Thailand*. PEEM/7/WP/87.6c. Rome: Joint World Health Organization/Food and Agriculture Organization of the United Nations/United Nations Environment Program Panel of Experts on Environmental Management for Vector Control.

Southgate, D. 1988. *The economics of land degradation in the third world*. Environment Department Working Paper 2. Washington, D.C.: World Bank.

———. 1990. The causes of land degradation along "spontaneously" expanding agricultural frontiers in the third world. *Land Economics* 66 (3): 93–101.

———. 1991. *Tropical deforestation and agriculture development in Latin America*. LEEC Discussion Paper 91-01. London: London Environmental Economics Centre.

Southgate, D., R. Sierra, and L. Brown. 1989. *The causes of tropical deforestation in Ecuador: A statistical analysis*. LEEC Discussion Paper 89-09. London: London Environmental Economics Centre.

Spencer, D. S. C. 1985. A research strategy to develop appropriate agricultural technologies for small farm development in Sub-Saharan Africa. In *Appropriate technologies for farmers in semi-arid West Africa*, ed. H. W. Ohm and J. G. Nagy. West Lafayette, Ind., U.S.A.: Purdue University.

———. 1991. Institutionalizing the farming system perspective in multi-commodity research institutes: The role of systems-based research groups. *Experimental Agriculture* 27: 1–9.

Spencer, D. S. C., and M. J. Swift. 1992. Sustainable agriculture: Definition and measurement. In *Biological nitrogen fixation and sustainability of tropical agriculture*, ed. K. Mulongoy, M. Gueye, and D. S. C. Spencer. New York: John Wiley and Sons.

Sperling, L. 1987. Food acquisition during the African drought of 1983–1984: A study of Kenyan herders. *Disasters* 11 (4): 263–272.

Starr, M. 1987. Risk, environmental variability, and drought-induced impoverishment: The pastoral economy of central Niger. *Africa* 57 (1): 29–50.

Stiglitz, J. 1987. Some theoretical aspects of agricultural policies. *World Bank Research Observer* 2 (1): 43–60.

Stomph, T. J., L. O. Fresco, and H. van Keulen. 1994. Land use system evaluation: Concepts and methodology. *Agricultural Systems* 44 (3): 243–255.

Stone, B. 1986. Chinese fertilizer application in the 1980s and 1990s: Issues of growth, balances, allocation, efficiency, and response. In *China's economy looks toward the year 2000*. Vol. 1. Washington, D.C.: Congress of the United States.

Stone, J. C., ed. 1991. *Pastoral economies in Africa and long-term responses to drought*. Proceedings of a Colloquium, April 9–10, 1990, University of Aberdeen, Aberdeen, U.K.

Stoorvogel, J. J., and E. M. A. Smaling. 1990. Assessment of soil nutrient depletion in Sub-Sahara, 1983–2000. Study conducted for the Food and Agriculture Organization of the United Nations, Win and Staring Centre, the Netherlands.

Strasma, J., and R. Celis. 1992. Land taxation, the poor, and sustainable development. In *Poverty, natural resources, and public policy in Central America*, ed. S. Annis. New Brunswick, N.J., U.S.A.: Transaction.

Strauss, J. 1986. Does better nutrition raise farm productivity? *Journal of Political Economy* 94 (2): 297–320.

Stryker, J. D. 1989. Technology, human pressure, and ecology in the arid and semi-arid tropics. In *Environment and the poor: Development strategies for a common agenda*, ed. H. J. Leonard and contributors. U.S.–Third World Policy Perspectives 11. New Brunswick, N.J., U.S.A.: Transaction Books for the Overseas Development Council.

Swift, J. 1988. *Major issues in pastoral development with special emphasis on selected African countries*. Rome: Food and Agriculture Organization of the United Nations.

———. 1991. Local customary institutions as the basis for natural resource management among Boran pastoralists in northern Kenya. *IDS Bulletin* 22 (4): 34–37.

Swift, J., and A. Maliki. 1984. *A cooperative development experiment among nomadic herders in Niger*. ODI Pastoral Development Network Paper 18c. London: Overseas Development Institute.

Swindale, L. D. 1984. *Watershed-based dryland farming in black and red soils of peninsular India*. Hyderabad, India: International Crops Research Institute for the Semi-Arid Tropics.

———. 1988. The impact of agricultural development on the environment: An IARC point of view. Consultative Group on International Agricultural Research (CGIAR) Mid-Term Meeting, 15–19 May, West Berlin.

Tandon, H. L. S. 1987. *Phosphorus research and agricultural production in India*. New Delhi: Fertilizer Development and Consumption Organization.

Tegart, W. J. McG., G. W. Sheldon, and D. C. Griffiths, eds. 1990. *Climate change: The IPCC impacts assessment*. Canberra, Australia: Australian Government Publishing Services.

Teng, P. S. 1990. IPM in rice: An analysis of the status quo with recommendations for action. Report to the International IPM Task Force (FAO/ACIAR/IDRC/USAID/NRI). Los Baños, the Philippines: International Rice Research Institute.

Thampapillai, D. J., and J. R. Anderson. 1991. Soil conservation in developing countries: A review of causes and remedies. *Quarterly Journal of International Agriculture* 30 (3): 210–223.

Thebaud, B. 1988. *Elevage et développement au Niger: Quel avenir pour les éleveurs du Sahel.* Geneva: International Labour Organisation.

Thomas, D. 1990. Intrahousehold resource allocation: An inferential approach. *Journal of Human Resources* 25 (4): 635–664.

Thomas, G. W. 1980. *The Sahelian and Sudanian zones of Africa: Profile of a fragile environment.* Report to the Rockefeller Foundation. New York: Rockefeller Foundation.

Tiffen, M. 1989. *Guidelines for the incorporation of health safeguards into irrigation projects through intersectoral cooperation with special reference to the vector-borne diseases.* Geneva: World Health Organization.

Tiffen, M., M. Mortimore, and F. Gichuki. 1994. *More people, less erosion: Environmental recovery in Kenya.* New York: Wiley.

Timmer, C. 1988. The agricultural transformation. In *Handbook of development economics,* vol. 1, ed. H. Chenery and T. N. Srinivasan. Amsterdam: North-Holland.

Tleimat, F. M. 1990. Livestock development strategies in arid lands: The case of the Syrian steppe. Paper presented at the Collège International devenir des Steppes d'Arabie et du Bilad Ach-Cham, 10–13 April, Institut du Monde Arabe, Paris.

Tomkins, A., and F. Watson. 1989. *Malnutrition and infection: A review.* ACC/SCN State-of-the-Art Series Nutrition Policy Discussion Paper 5. Geneva: Administrative Committee on Coordination/Sub-Committee on Nutrition, United Nations.

Toulmin, C. 1983. *Herders and farmers or farmer-herders and herder-farmers?* Pastoral Network Paper 15d. London: Overseas Development Institute.

Treacher, T. 1991. Linkages between the steppe and cultivated areas through livestock systems: Implications for research and development to establish more productive and stable systems. Paper presented at the Colloque International Devenir des Steppes d'Arabie et du Bilad Ach Cham, 10–13 April, Institut du Monde Arabe, Paris.

Troll, D., and K. H. Paffen. 1965. Seasonal climates of the earth. In *World maps of climatology,* 2d ed., ed. H. E. Landsberg and others. New York: Springer-Verlag.

Tutwiler, R. 1990. Agricultural labor and technological change in the Yemen Arab Republic. In *Labor and rainfed agriculture in West Asia and North Africa,* ed. D. Tully. Dordrecht: Kluwer.

UNDP (United Nations Development Programme). 1984. National agricultural research. Report of an Evaluation Study, Joint Study with the Food and Agriculture Organization of the United Nations. Rome: FAO.

UNECA (United Nations Economic Commission for Africa). 1985. *Comprehensive policies and programmes for livestock development in Africa: Problems, constraints and necessary future action.* ALPAN Network Paper 5. Addis Ababa: International Livestock Center for Africa.

UNEP/ISRIC (United Nations Environment Programme/International Soil Reference and Information Centre). 1991. Global assessment of soil degradation, a global perspective. Unpublished draft report. Nairobi, Kenya, and Wageningen, the Netherlands.

UNIDO (United Nations Industrial Development Organization). 1986. *Côte d'Ivoire: Industrial development review.* Vienna.

United Nations. 1986. *Statistical yearbook 1985/86.* New York.

van Bath, S. H. S. 1963. *The agrarian history of western Europe, a.d. 500–1850.* London: Edward Arnold.

Vedova, M. A. 1996. Economic aspects of tree harvesting and processing. In *Interdisciplinary fact-finding on current deforestation in Costa Rica,* ed. E. Lutz and R. Celis. Washington, D.C.: World Bank.

Velayudhan, R. 1991. Report on a visit to the field station of the West Africa Rice Development Association at St. Louis, Senegal, 17 March–1 April. Food and Agriculture Organization of the United Nations, Rome.

Verma, L. R., and T. Partap. 1992. The experiences of an area-based development strategy in Himachal Pradesh, India. In *Sustainable mountain agriculture,* ed. N. S. Jodha, M. Banskota, and T. Partap. New Delhi: Oxford and IBH.

Virmani, S. M., R. W. Willey, and M. S. Reddy. 1981. *Problems, prospects, and technology for increasing cereal and pulse production from deep black soils.* Proceedings of the seminar on Management of Deep Black Soils for Increased Production of Cereals, Pulses, and Oilseeds. Hyderabad, India: International Crops Research Institute for the Semi-Arid Tropics.

Vitta, P. B. 1990. Technology policy in Sub-Saharan Africa: Why the dream remains unfulfilled. *World Development* 18 (11): 1471–1480.

Vosti, S. A. 1990. Malaria among gold miners in southern Pará, Brazil: Estimates of determinants and individual costs. *Social Science and Medicine* 30 (10): 1097–1105.

———. 1993. Reprise of Rio: Will policymakers hear José Carvalho's saw? *Choices* (First quarter): 24.

Vosti, S. A., and W. M Loker. 1990. Some environmental and health aspects of agricultural settlement in the western Amazon basin. In *Environmental aspects of agricultural development.* IFPRI Policy Brief 6. Washington, D.C.: International Food Policy Research Institute.

Vosti, S. A., and J. Witcover. 1993. Gender differences in levels, fluctuations, and determinants of nutritional status: Evidence from southcentral Ethiopia. In *Effects of selected policies and programs on women's health and nutritional status,* ed. E. Kennedy and M. Garcia. Washington, D.C.: International Food Policy Research Institute.

Vosti, S. A., T. Reardon, and W. von Urff. 1992. *Agricultural sustainability, growth, and poverty alleviation: Issues and policies.* Feldafing, Germany: German Foundation for International Development (DSE); and Washington, D.C.: International Food Policy Research Institute.

Vosti, S. A., J. Witcover, and M. Lipton. 1995. The impact of technical change in agriculture on human fertility: District-level evidence from India. Environment and Production Technology Division Discussion Paper 5. Washington, D.C.: International Food Policy Research Institute.

Wade, R. 1986. *Village republics: Economic conditions for collective action in south India.* London: Cambridge University Press.

Walker, P. 1988. Famine relief amongst pastoralists in Sudan: A report of Oxfam's experience. *Disasters* 12 (3): 196–202.

Walker, T. S., and J. G. Ryan. 1990. *Village and household economies in India's semi-arid tropics.* Baltimore: Johns Hopkins University Press.

Ware, H. 1977. Desertification and population: Sub-Saharan Africa. In *Desertification: Environmental degradation in and around arid lands,* ed. M. H. Glantz. Boulder, Colo., U.S.A.: Westview.

Weaver, R. 1989. *An integrated model of perennial and annual crop production for Sub-Saharan countries.* International Economics Department. Washington, D.C.: World Bank.

Webb, P. 1991. When projects collapse: Irrigation failure in The Gambia from a household perspective. *Journal of International Development* 3 (4): 339–353.

Webb, P., and T. Reardon. 1992. Drought impact and household response in East and West Africa. *Quarterly Journal of International Agriculture* 3 (July–September): 230–246.

Webb, P., and J. von Braun. 1994. *Famine and food security in Ethiopia: Lessons for Africa.* London: John Wiley.

Webb, P., J. von Braun, and Y. Yohannes. 1992. *Famine in Ethiopia: Policy implications of coping failure at national and household levels.* Research Report 92. Washington, D.C.: International Food Policy Research Institute.

Weber, M. T., J. M. Staatz, J. S. Holtzman, E. W. Crawford, and R. H. Bernsten. 1988. Informing food security decisions in Africa: Empirical analysis and policy dialogue. *American Journal of Agricultural Economics* 70 (3): 1044–1052.

Weitzman, M. L. 1974. Prices vs. quantities. *Review of Economic Studies* 41: 477–491.

Whitaker, M. L. 1990. Quantifying the relative productivity and sustainability of alternative cropping systems. International Crops Research Institute for the Semi-Arid Tropics. Draft manuscript.

Whiteman, P. T. S. 1988. Mountain agronomy in Ethiopia, Nepal, and Pakistan. In *Human impacts on mountains,* ed. N. J. R. Allan, G. W. Knapp, and C. Stadel. Totowa, N.J., U.S.A.: Rowman and Littlefield.

WHO (World Health Organization). 1980. *Disease prevention and control in water development schemes.* PDP/80.1. Geneva.

———. 1983. *Environmental health impact assessment of irrigated agricultural development projects.* Geneva.

WHO Commission on Health and Environment. 1992. *Report of the panel on food and agriculture.* Geneva: WHO.

Wienpahl, J. 1985. Turkana herds under environmental stress. *Nomadic Peoples* 17: 59–88.

Wilding, L. P., and L. R. Hossner. 1989. Causes and effects of acidity in Sahelian Soils. In *Soil, crop, and water management in the Sudano-Sahelian Zone.* Proceedings of an international workshop, 11–16 January. Niamey, Niger: International Crops Research Institute for the Semi-Arid Tropics (ICRISAT) Sahelian Center.

World Bank. 1981a. *Accelerated development in Sub-Saharan Africa: An agenda for action.* Washington, D.C.

———. 1981b. *Agricultural research: Sector policy paper.* Washington, D.C.

———. 1982. *Brazil: A review of agricultural policies.* Washington, D.C.

———. 1984a. *World Development Report 1984.* New York: Oxford University Press.

———. 1984b. *Toward sustainable development in Sub-Saharan Africa: A joint program of action.* Washington, D.C.

———. 1985. *Desertification in the Sahelian and Sudanian zones of West Africa.* Washington, D.C.

————. 1989a. *Price prospects for major primary commodities,* vol. 2. Washington, D.C.

————. 1989b. *Sub-Saharan Africa: From crisis to sustainable growth.* Washington, D.C.

————. 1990a. Malawi: Review of national parks and wildlife policy. Southern Africa Division. Washington, D.C.

————. 1990b. *Flood control in Bangladesh.* Washington, D.C.

————. 1990c. *World development report 1990.* New York: Oxford University Press.

————. 1991a. *Global economic prospects and the developing countries.* Washington, D.C.

————. 1991b. *World development report 1991.* New York: Oxford University Press.

————. 1992a. *African development indicators.* Washington, D.C.

————. 1992b. *World development report 1992.* New York: Oxford University Press.

World Bank Environment Department. 1991. *Environmental assessment source book,* 2 vols. Washington, D.C.: World Bank.

World Commission on Environment and Development. 1987. *Our common future.* Oxford: Oxford University Press.

WRI (World Resources Institute). 1990a. *Environmental indicators.* Washington, D.C.

————. 1990b. *World resources 1990–91.* New York: Oxford University Press.

Wright, P. 1985. Water and soil conservation by farmers. In *Appropriate technologies for farmers in semi-arid West Africa,* ed. H. W. Ohm and J. G. Nagy. West Lafayette, Ind., U.S.A.: Purdue University, International Programs in Agriculture.

Yadav, Y. 1992. Farming-forestry-livestock linkages: A component of mountain farmers' strategies (Nepal). In *Sustainable mountain agriculture,* ed. N. S. Jodha, M. Banskota, and T. Partap. New Delhi: Oxford and IBH.

Yudelman, M. 1989. Sustainable and equitable development in irrigated environments. In *Environment and the poor: Development strategies for a common agenda,* ed. H. J. Leonard and contributors. U.S.–Third World Policy Perspectives 11. New Brunswick, N.J., U.S.A.: Transaction Books for the Development Council.

Contributors

Akinwumi A. Adesina, an agricultural economist, is social science research coordinator at the International Institute of Tropical Agriculture (IITA), based in Cameroon. He was formerly a senior economist at the West Africa Rice Development Association (WARDA), Côte d'Ivoire.

Elizabeth Bailey, an agricultural economist, is project officer in the office for International Cooperation, the International Center for Agricultural Research in the Dry Areas (ICARDA), Aleppo, Syria.

Edward B. Barbier is a reader in the Department of Environmental Economics and Environmental Management of the University of York, U.K. His main area of research is natural resource and environmental economics applied to developing countries.

Joachim von Braun is director of the Institute of Food Economics and professor of food economics and food policy at Christian Albrechts University, Kiel, Germany.

Rafael Celis is a resource economist and director of Pro Desarrollo, a private research center based in Costa Rica that studies issues relevant to sustainable development.

Kanchan Chopra is professor of economics at the Institute of Economic Growth, University of Delhi, Delhi, India.

D. Layne Coppock is an associate professor in the Department of Rangeland Resources at Utah State University. He was previously a research scientist at the International Livestock Research Institute (formerly the International Livestock Centre for Africa), in Addis Ababa, Ethiopia.

Aércio S. Cunha is professor of economics in the Department of Economics, University of Brasília, Brazil.

389

Hartwig de Haen is the assistant director-general, Economic and Social Department, Food and Agriculture Organization of the United Nations (FAO), Rome.

Thomas E. Downing is program leader for Climate Impacts and Responses in the Environmental Change Unit, University of Oxford, U.K.

Amare Getahun is the director of forestry research at Kenya Equity Management Limited, Nairobi, Kenya.

Narpat S. Jodha is currently a policy analyst at the International Centre for Integrated Mountain Development (ICIMOD), Kathmandu, Nepal. He was formerly the natural resource management specialist in the Social Policy and Resettlement Division of the Environment Department of the World Bank. Prior to that he served as head of the Mountain Farming Systems Division of ICIMOD.

John M. Kerr is a research fellow in the Environment and Production Technology Division of the International Food Policy Research Institute (IFPRI), Washington, D.C. He previously represented Winrock International/ICRISAT (International Crops Research Institute for the Semi-Arid Tropics), India.

Michael Lipton is director of the Poverty Research Unit and professor of development economics at the University of Sussex, Brighton, U.K.

Peter J. Matlon is the director of research at the West Africa Rice Development Association (WARDA), Côte d'Ivoire.

Peter Oram is a research fellow emeritus in the Environment and Production Technology Division of the International Food Policy Research Institute (IFPRI), Washington, D.C.

Martin L. Parry is with the Environmental Change Unit, University of Oxford, U.K.

Prabhu L. Pingali is director of the Economics Program of the International Maize and Wheat Improvement Center (CIMMYT), Mexico City. He was previously an agricultural economist and program leader at the International Rice Research Institute (IRRI), Manila.

Rudolph A. Polson is an economist in the Agriculture and Environment Division, West-Central Africa Department, World Bank, Washington, D.C.

C. H. Hanumantha Rao is with the Centre for Economic and Social Studies, Hyderabad, India.

Thomas Reardon is an associate professor in the Department of Agricultural Economics, Michigan State University, East Lansing, Michigan.

Sergio Ruano is a rural sociologist and director of the Project Centro Maya, Petén, Guatemala.

Vernon W. Ruttan is Regents Professor in the Department of Applied Economics, University of Minnesota, St. Paul.

Donald R. Sawyer is executive coordinator of the Institute for Society, Population, and Nature (ISPN), Brasília, Brazil.

P. V. Shenoi is director of the Institute for Social and Economic Change in Bangalore, India. He was previously affiliated with the International Crops Research Institute for the Semi-Arid Tropics (ICRISAT), India.

Ammar Siamwalla is a Distinguished Scholar at the Thailand Development Research Institute Foundation, Bangkok, Thailand.

Dunstan S. C. Spencer is the managing director of Dunstan Spencer and Associates, Freetown, Sierra Leone. He was formerly director of the Resource and Crop Management Division of the International Institute of Tropical Agriculture (IITA).

Richard N. Tutwiler is the social anthropologist in the Farm Resource Management Program of the International Center for Agricultural Research in the Dry Areas (ICARDA), Aleppo, Syria.

Mario A. Vedova is an economist at the University of Costa Rica and a freelance consultant.

Stephen A. Vosti is a research fellow in the Environment and Production Technology Division of the International Food Policy Research Institute (IFPRI), Washington, D.C.

Patrick Webb is the Joseph G. Knoll Visiting Professor for Developing Country Research at the University of Hohenheim, Stuttgart, Germany.

Meri L. Whitaker was formerly with the International Crops Research Institute for the Semi-Arid Tropics (ICRISAT), India.

Index

Absentee landowners, 282
Absolute poverty, 51, 67
Acaricide, 255
Accommodation, 99, 100t
Achole-Imatong highlands, 319
Acid rain, 116
Active (targeting) approaches to sustainability, 243
Adams, W. M., 133
Africa, 5, 24, 27, 84, 167, 309, 310; conservation investments in, 136, 141; labor-led intensification in, 57; population growth in, 84, 89; sustainability research in, 168. *See also* African humid and subhumid tropics; East African highlands; North Africa; Sub-Saharan Africa; West Africa
African humid and subhumid tropics, 191–207; agroecological zones and sustainability constraints in, 193–95; biological pest and disease control in, 203; improved systems for inland valleys, 204; policy environment in, 205–7; technology in, 199–204
Age of substitutability argument, 27
Agno River Irrigation System (ARIS), 222
Agricultural extension systems, 166, 170–74; in African humid and subhumid tropics, 199–200; requirements for increasing, 174–75
Agricultural growth. See Growth
Agricultural prices. *See* Farm prices
Agricultural productivity: effects of climate change on, 91–94; implications of climate change for, 94–97; in Indian semiarid tropics, 262–66, 271; in West African semi-arid tropics, 229
Agroclimatic conditions, 13

Agroecological zones (AEZs), 13, 14f, 15, 49, 161–66, 343–44; in African humid and subhumid tropics, 193–95; continental, 162
Agroecology, 23
Agroforestry systems, 210–11, 212, 213
Agropastoralism, 253–54
Agrosilviculture systems, 210
Alfisols, 194, 198, 203, 265
Alley-cropping systems: in African humid and subhumid tropics, 194, 198–99, 202–3; in Southeast Asian humid tropics, 211; in West Asia and North Africa, 288
Alley Farming Network for Tropical Africa (AFNETA), 203
All-India Coordinated Research Project for Dryland Agriculture (AICRPDA), 263
Alternative agriculture, 20, 32–33
Amazon. *See* Brazilian Amazon
Ambuklao Dam, 222
Angora rabbits, 302
Animal feed: advances in efficiency of, 25; in Central America, 334; in East African highlands, 323–24; in West Asia and North Africa, 284–85, 286, 287, 288, 289
Animal husbandry, 56, 279; integrated crop-, 23
Animal traction, 238, 241
Apples, 299, 301, 302
Aquifers, 138, 261, 267–68, 283
Arab Centre for the Study of Arid Zones and Dry Lands (ACSAD), 286
Arabian Peninsula, 163
Armyworm, 226
Arusha, 319, 325

Asia, 154; distribution of NARS staff in, 164t; integrated pest management in, 41; irrigation charges and costs in, 131t; population growth in, 84; sustainability research in, 162; trade and environment in, 105. *See also* East Asia; South Asia; Southeast Asia

Asset categories of poverty, 47–48, 49, 50–51, 53, 63, 64

Atlas Mountains, 291

Atriplex hedges, 288

Awash River, 251

Bananas, 197, 316, 330

Banaue, 211

Bangladesh, 75, 83, 222

Barbier, E. B., 133, 136, 143

Barley, 279, 292, 316

Barley zone, 279, 284–90

Baseline reference scenario, 95

Basic Linked System (BLS) world trade model, 95

Batie, S., 20n1

Beans, 187, 188, 316, 329, 333, 334; improved varieties of, 336

Beckerman, W., 82

Beekeeping, 302

Bennell, P., 167

Bhabbar grass, 312

Bhattarcharya, R., 256

Bhuiyan, S. I., 222

Bicol, 215, 217

Binswanger, H. P., 82, 200, 237

Biodiversity, 1–2, 35, 38, 59–60, 295

Biological pest and disease control, 203

Black pepper, 183, 189

Black sigatoka disease, 204

Black soils, 265, 272

Borana, 248, 253

Border taxes, 107

Borewells, 266, 267

Boserup, E., 56–57, 82, 135

Boserup responses, 85, 86

Botswana, 252

Boyce, J. K., 167

Brazil, 83

Brazilian Amazon, 5, 179–90; growth in, 185–87; health and nutrition in, 76–77; input pricing in, 132; poverty in, 187–88; poverty-environment links in, 59–60; road building in, 133; sustainability in, 180–81, 189–90; unbalanced factor endowments in, 181–84

Breast milk, 73

Bromley, D. W., 309

Brown, L., 133

Brown planthopper, 226

Bruchid beetle, 204

Brundtland Commission, 21

Buffalo, 312–13

Bunds, 61, 141, 142, 239, 240, 244

Burkina Faso, 206, 231, 234, 241, 254, 308

Burundi, 315, 317, 319, 325

Buttel, F. H., 21

Cagayan Valley, 215, 217

Camels, 252

Cameroon, 76

Candidate worker children, 81

Capital-led intensification, 57

Carbon, 36, 197

Carbon dioxide, 25, 30, 90, 91, 97, 99; direct enrichment of, 94, 96

Caribbean countries, 148, 149, 163, 170, 330

Caseworm, 226

Cash cropping, 108, 141

Cassava, 76; in African humid and sub-humid tropics, 194, 203–4; biological pest and disease control for, 203–4; in Brazilian Amazon, 187, 188; research on, 159; in Thailand, 8, 111–15, 125, 205

Cassava bacteria blight, 204

Cassava green mite, 203

Cassava mealybug, 203

Cassava mosaic virus, 204

Castañeda, A. R., 222

Caste system, 89, 309

Cattle, 6, 201, 255, 311, 320, 333, 334

Center for International Forestry Research (CIFOR), 159

Central Africa, 167

Central America, 5, 328–38; policy recommendations for, 336–38; sustainability in, 328–31, 335–36; sustainability research in, 163, 168, 170

Central Research Institute for Dryland Agriculture (CRIDA), 263, 270

Central Soil and Water Conservation Research and Training Institute (CSWCRTI), 311–12

Centro Internacional de Agricultura Tropical (CIAT), 203

Cereal-livestock mixed farming, 319

Cereals: climate change and, 95, 96–97; in East African highlands, 316, 317, 319, 326; prices of, 95, 96–97, 111; in West African semi-arid tropics, 242; in West Asia and North Africa, 279, 288, 291, 292

Certificate of Stewardship Contracts (CSC), 215
Chagaa, 325, 326
Chandigarh, 311
Chayanovian response, 82
Chemical erosion, 36, 37t
Chiang Mai, 226
Chickpeas, 262
Children, 70, 72, 76, 81, 86–87
China, 84, 149, 294, 302
Chlorofluorocarbons, 25
Cholera, 71
Chopra, K., 144, 308
Citrus pulp, 115
Climate, of East African highlands, 315–18
Climate change, 13, 25–26, 30–31, 90–102, 116; effects on agricultural productivity, 91–94; health and nutrition influenced by, 74, 75; implications for agricultural production and food poverty, 94–97; planned responses and research needs, 101–2; potential coping strategies, 99–101; projections of, 90–81; sustainability and, 97–99
Climate change and baseline reference scenario, 96–97
Climate change and low economic growth scenario, 97
Cocoa, 124–25, 183, 197, 206, 210
Coffee, 126, 183, 197, 206, 316, 320, 334
Common Agricultural Policy (CAP), 111, 115
Common property resources (CPRs): in India, 312–13; in Indian semi-arid tropics, 268–69, 270t, 274; population growth and, 79, 80, 88–89; technology and, 151–52
Commons, 1, 5, 6, 274; privatization of, 274; tragedy of, 152, 256, 307
Community-level infrastructure, 59
Community-owned resources, 48, 51, 62
Complementary assets, 58
Complementary infrastructure investments, 9, 11, 62, 64, 65, 121, 346; conservation investments and, 142, 143–44
Complementary policy reforms, 121
Compost, 324
Conditioning variables, 49, 50f, 53, 58, 64, 140–41; effects of, 61–62
Conservation farming, 42, 43t
Conservation-investment poverty, 6, 12, 48, 56, 57, 63, 64; conditioning variables and, 61–62, 140–41; welfare poverty versus, 51–53

Conservation investments, 135–45; Brazilian Amazon and, 181; implications for analysis of investment determinants, 140–43; implications for promoting, 143–45; productivity investments versus, 136, 137–40, 141, 142, 145, 341
Conservation tillage, 39
Consultative Group on International Agricultural Research (CGIAR), 157–61, 162, 163, 166, 167, 263; operational expenditures of, 158t
Continental agroecological zones (AEZs), 162
Contraceptive use, 80
Contributors' dilemma, 88
Conventional tillage, 212, 213
Convention on International Trade in Endangered Species (CITIES), 116
Corn gluten, 115
Costa Rica, 126, 331, 333
Cost-benefit analysis (CBA), 67–68, 77
Côte d'Ivoire, 191, 196–97, 200, 206, 209
Cotton, 150, 206, 230, 231, 241–42, 262, 266
Cowpeas, 203, 204, 230, 231
Crawford, E., 141
Credit, 62, 144–45, 269, 274, 282
Crisis response, 99–101
Critical triangle, 2f, 3, 60. *See also* Links among sustainability, growth, and poverty alleviation
Cropping, 56–57
Crop residues, 201, 235, 239
Crop yields: in Central America, 333t; in Southeast Asian humid tropics, 225–26; in West African semi-arid tropics, 233–36, 240–41
Cruz, W., 221
Cutworm, 226

Dairying, 281, 316
Dapaah, S., 143
Dasgupta, P., 304
DDT, 73
Debt servicing ratios, 125–26
Deep vertisols, 265
Deforestation, 36, 38; in Brazilian Amazon, 60, 179–80; in Central America, 332, 337; in Côte d'Ivoire, 191, 196–97; health and nutrition influenced by, 74, 75, 76–77; in India, 306; input pricing and, 132; output pricing and, 129; pastoralism and, 250; road building and, 133; in Southeast Asian humid tropics, 209–10, 214, 215–20; in Thailand, 8, 113–15; trade and, 125–26

de Haen, H., 136
De-intensification, 279, 291
Demand for natural resource products, 306–7
Demographic pressure. *See* Population growth/density
Demographics, of East African highlands, 315–18
Dependency ratios, 218–20
Desertification, 25, 38, 74
Deutsche Stiftung für Internationale Entwicklung (DSE), 4
Developmental sustainability, 33
De Vera, M. V. M., 222
Discount rates, 28, 149, 304, 305
Diversification, 5–6, 297, 298, 299, 301, 302
Donor financing, 168, 228
Douglass, G. K., 20
Drought: in Africa, 309; climate change and, 94; health and nutrition influenced by, 74, 75; pastoralism and, 250–51, 255; in West Asia and North Africa, 281
Drylands, 38–39
Dugwells, 266, 268

Earth Summit, 21
East African highlands, 315–27; conflicts between growth and sustainability in, 325–26; demographic pressure and land use in, 320–21; farming systems in, 319–20; geography, climate, soils, and demographics of, 315–18; lowland interactions with, 320
East African lowlands, 320
East Asia, 25; interest rates in, 148; trade and environment in, 108; wet rice cultivation in, 22–23
Ecological sustainability, 32–33
Economic sustainability, 232–33
Eighth Five-Year Plan (India), 270
El Salvador, 331, 333
Embu, 317, 324, 325
Endogenous population growth, 79
Endogenous technology, 87
Energy, 38
Enset-based farming system, 326
Environment: conservation investments and, 137–38; of Indian semi-arid tropics, 269–71; trade and, 103–18; typology of, 53; of West African semi-arid tropics, 229–30. *See also* Growth-environment links; Poverty-environment links; Trade
Environmental degradation. *See* Resource degradation

Environmental resources. *See* Natural resources
Ethiopia, 75, 315, 316, 317, 319, 320, 321, 323, 326; estimated rates of soil loss in, 318t; likely development of land use in, 322f; pastoralism in, 248, 249, 251, 252, 253, 255, 257
European Community (EC), 28, 111, 113, 115, 125, 150, 205
Evenson, R. E., 167
Exogenous farm prices, 150–51
Exogenous interest rates, 147–50
Exogenous technology, 87–88, 151–52
Export taxes, 126
Extensification, 5, 35, 56, 128, 130
Extension. *See* Agricultural extension systems
Externalities, 65, 121, 345; conservation investments and, 140, 142; human resources and, 67; trade and, 116; typical, 123t; in West African semi-arid tropics, 244
Extraction, 300t, 303

Factor endowments, unbalanced, 181–84
Fallow periods, 40; in African humid and subhumid tropics, 192, 195, 201; historical perspective on, 22; in Indian semi-arid tropics, 268; shortening of, 35; in Southeast Asian humid tropics, 211; in West Asia and North Africa, 287
Farming systems: in East African highlands, 319–20, 326; for heterogeneous environments, 272; in West African semi-arid tropics, 230–31
Farm prices, 1, 24, 146; in African humid and subhumid tropics, 205; climate change and, 95, 96–97; exogenous, 150–51; trade and, 105–7, 111
Fenced land, 110, 252, 256, 289, 308
Fertility rates, 13, 62, 79–81, 86–88
Fertilizers, 5, 24, 35, 41, 135, 138; in African humid and subhumid tropics, 191, 198–99, 201; health and nutrition influenced by, 72t; in humid and semi-humid lowlands, 40; nitrogen, 198–99; phosphate, 25; in Southeast Asian humid tropics, 225–26; subsidies for, 130–31, 282; water degradation and, 38; in West African semi-arid tropics, 230, 233, 234–35, 241; in West Asia and North Africa, 282, 283
Firewood, 56, 76, 308, 335
Fisheries research, 165
Fishing, 194

Floodplain system, 133–34
Floods, 74, 75, 221
Fodder shrubs/trees, 287–88, 289–90, 312
Fonio, 230
Food and Agriculture Organization of the United Nations (FAO), 36, 39, 41, 162, 167, 168, 222, 229
Food availability, 82, 85
Food entitlements, 82, 85
Food-for-work projects, 143–44
Food poverty, 94–97
Food prices. *See* Farm prices
Food security, 128, 136, 206, 247, 258
Food supply, 188
Forage cones, 336
Forestry research, 165
Forest-transition zone, 194t, 198–99, 202–3
Fossil fuels, 25, 38
Francisco, H. A., 221
Frontier settlement, 125–26, 133
Fruits, 279, 281, 299
Fuelwood, 56, 76, 308, 335
Fulani, 248

Gadgil, M., 308
Gambia, 72, 206
Garhwal hills, 299
Garrity, D. P., 211
Gender, 70, 76, 253, 291
General Agreement on Tariffs and Trade (GATT), 116, 117
General circulation models (GCMs), 91
Genetic engineering, 24–25
Geographic information systems (GISs), 162, 272
Geography, of East African highlands, 315–18
Ghana, 124–25, 206, 209
Goats, 279, 284, 311, 313
Grains, 126, 244–45, 264, 266, 299
Grameen Bank, 274
Grapes, 279, 282
Grazing, 251, 252, 256; in East African highlands, 324; in Himalayas, 298; in India, 311–13; in West Asia and North Africa, 285–86, 289–90, 292; zero, 324
Greenhouse gases, 25–26, 90
Green leafhopper, 226
Green manure, 23, 201
Green Revolution, 2, 7, 11, 15, 136, 137, 157, 161; health and nutrition and, 66, 71, 74; in Himalayas, 295; in India, 305–6, 308, 310; population growth and, 83, 85,

86, 88; in Southeast Asian humid tropics, 208, 215, 224, 228
Gross domestic investment, 149
Gross domestic product (GDP), 148–49, 168; of African humid and subhumid tropics, 206; of Côte d'Ivoire, 197; of East African highlands, 320; of West Asia and North Africa, 281
Ground cover, 40, 200–1, 211, 214, 286
Groundnuts, 206, 230, 231, 262
Groundwater, 38; health and nutrition influenced by, 71; in Indian semi-arid tropics, 261, 265, 266–68, 272–73; in West Asia and North Africa, 283
Growth, 1. *See also* Growth-environment links; Links among sustainability, growth, and poverty alleviation; Sustainability-growth links
—in African humid and subhumid tropics, 192–93; compatibility with other goals, 200–7; potential conflicts, 195–200
—in Brazilian Amazon, 185–87
—in East African highlands, 325–26
—in Himalayas, 301–2
—in Indian semi-arid tropics, 269–71
—pastoralism and, 247–48
—in West Asia and North Africa, 280–82
Growth-environment links, 5, 15, 34–46
—complementarities in, 40–42
—extent and type of resource degradation, 36–38
—health and nutrition and, 66–78; conceptual framework for, 68–70; data gaps in studies of, 70; technology in, 70–77
—strategies for minimizing trade-offs, 43–45
—by zone, 38–40
Guatemala, 6, 73, 328–38. *See also* Central America
Guiang, E. S., 211
Guinean zone, 230, 234, 235
Gum arabic, 124, 132
Gum Arabic Company, 132

Hadejia-Jama'are, 133–34
Haiti, 126
Halocarbons, 90
Hard infrastructure, 61
Hayami, Y., 82
Hayami-Ruttan-Binswanger (HRB) responses, 85, 86
Health, 7, 31, 66–78; intrahousehold, household-, and community-level issues in, 70; policy implications for, 77; research on, 77–78; technology and, 70–77

Herbicides, 237
Heterogeneous environment farming systems, 272
Higher-potential zone, 281–84
Highlands: of Central America, 328–31; of East Africa, *see* East African highlands; of West Asia and North Africa, 290–92
High-yielding cultivars, 235–36
Hillsides, 40, 75–76
Himachal Pradesh, 294, 302
Himalayas, 75, 222, 294–303, 306; agricultural conditions in, 295–97; development strategies and sustainability in, 298–301; means of combining growth and sustainability in, 301–2; traditional system and sustainability in, 297–98
Hindu Kush–Himalayan (HKH) region. *See* Himalayas
Holmes, T., 306
Honduras, 329, 331, 333
Hopper, W. D., 19
Horsebeans, 316
Household and village behavior, 49, 50f
Household resource allocation, 53, 54f
Human resource assets, 48, 50–51
Human resources, 66–68
Humid forest zone, 194t
Humid lowlands, 40
Humid tropics. *See* African humid and sub-humid tropics; Southeast Asian humid tropics

Idachaba, F. S., 136
Ilam district, 302
Income-earning strategies, 55–57
Increased demand scenario, 307
Increased demand with technology and institutional change scenario, 307
India, 222, 294, 299, 302, 304–14; caste system in, 89, 309; conservation investments in, 142, 144; crop yields in, 225–26; demand for natural resource products in, 306–7; gross domestic investment in, 149; linking technological and institutional strategies in, 311–13; population growth in, 84, 86, 88–89, 306–7; semi-arid tropics of, *see* Indian semi-arid tropics; strategies to conquer poverty and degradation in, 307–9; strategies to conquer poverty and promote sustainability in, 309–10; technology strategies in, 305–6
Indian Council for Agricultural Research, 166, 276

Indian Punjab, 83, 151, 308
Indian semi-arid tropics (ISAT), 261–77; environment and smallholder agriculture in, 261–62; heterogeneous environment farming systems for, 272; increasing land productivity in, 262–66; policy and research recommendations for, 269–76; small-scale irrigation in, 272–73
Indonesia, 125, 211, 221, 306; crop yields in, 225–26; health and nutrition in, 73; input pricing in, 130; output pricing in, 129
Induced innovation hypothesis, 345
Infant mortality, 187
Infinitely elastic supply of land, 181–82
Infrastructure: of African humid and sub-humid tropics, 195, 199–200; community-level, 59; hard, 61; irrigation, 221, 222–24, 227–28; policies on, 132–33; transport and communication, 58–59; of West African semi-arid tropics, 244–45
Infrastructure investments. *See* Complementary infrastructure investments
In-ground silos, 336
Inheritance rights, 62, 282
Input/output price ratios, 151
Input prices, 129–32, 151
Institutions, 9, 12, 44, 341–43
—incentive-compatible design needed for, 28–29
—in India, 306–7, 309–10; technology linked with, 311–13
—structural reorganization of, 166–67
Integrated crop-animal husbandry, 23
Integrated pest management (IPM), 12, 39, 40, 41, 160, 283; historical perspective on, 22
Integrated Social Forestry Program (ISFP), 210
Integration, 300t
Intensification, 5, 7, 35, 135; capital-led, 57; de-, 279, 291; in Himalayas, 298, 300t, 301, 303; in Indian semi-arid tropics, 263; input pricing and, 130; labor-led, 57; spillover from, 25; technology and, 84–86; in West Asia and North Africa, 281–83
Interest rates, 28, 61, 86, 146; exogenous, 147–50; population growth and, 79, 80, 88
International agricultural research centers (IARCs), 157, 159, 162–63, 165, 166, 167, 170, 175, 176

International Center for Living Aquatic Resources Management (ICLARM), 159
International Centre for Integrated Mountain Development (ICIMOD), 299, 301–2
International Centre for Research in Agroforestry (ICRAF), 159
International Crops Research Institute for the Semi-Arid Tropics (ICRISAT), 236, 263, 270–71, 276
International Food Policy Research Institute (IFPRI), 4, 72, 168
International Institute of Biological Control (IIBC), 203
International Institute of Tropical Agriculture (IITA), 199, 204, 236
International Irrigation Management Institute (IIMI), 159
International Maize and Wheat Improvement Center (CIMMYT), 157
International Rice Research Institute (IRRI), 73, 157, 299
International Service for National Agricultural Research (ISNAR), 161
International Soil Reference and Information Centre (ISRIC), 36
International Union for Conservation of Nature and Natural Resources (IUCN), 20
Intestinal worms, 76
Investments: complementary infrastructure, *see* Complementary infrastructure investments; conservation, *see* Conservation investments; by immigrants, 83–84; land improvement, 58; productivity, *see* Productivity investments; public, 121, 133–34; strategies in, 58–59
IR-8 (rice variety), 225
Iraq, 285
Irrigation, 24, 35, 39, 57; charges and costs for, 131t; floodplain system and, 133–34; health and nutrition influenced by, 71–72, 74; in Himalayas, 297; in India, 311–13; in Indian semi-arid tropics, 261, 266–68, 272–73; input pricing and, 130, 131–32; pastoralism and, 251, 257; small-scale, 272–73; in Southeast Asian humid tropics, 221, 222–24, 227–28; subsidies for, 131–32; in West African semi-arid tropics, 233–34; in West Asia and North Africa, 283
Irrigation infrastructure, 221, 222–24, 227–28
Islam, N., 84–85
Ivory Coast, 191, 196–97, 200, 206, 209

Japan, 28, 111, 150
Japanese encephalitis, 71
Java, 125, 130, 132, 211
Jodha, N. S., 263, 309
Jordan, 285
Judd, M. A., 167
Jutiapa, 332–35, 337, 338

Kalahari basin, 246
Kano River Project, 133
Karangkates reservoir, 221
Kelly, V., 141
Kenya, 36, 41, 315, 316, 317, 319, 320, 324, 325, 326; climate change in, 91–94; pastoralism in, 249, 251, 257; population growth in, 84
Kerala, 84
Kikuyu, 317, 325
Kilimanjaro, 318t, 319, 325
Kimmage, K., 133
Kisii, 317, 325
Konso, 317, 326
Kou Valley, 234
Krueger, A. O., 108
Kummer, D. M., 211

Labor: in African humid and subhumid tropics, 194; in Brazilian Amazon, 59–60; in Rwanda highlands, 60–61; trade and, 108
Labor-capital ratios, 194
Labor-intensive cultural practices, 236
Labor-land ratios, 80, 85, 111
Labor-led intensification, 57
Labor-saving technologies, 237–38
Lal, R., 211
Land: infinitely elastic supply of, 181–82; of Rwanda highlands, 60–61; of Sahel, 60
Land-conserving technologies. *See* Soil protection
Land degradation, 2, 30; in East African highlands, 321–24; extent and types of, 36, 37t; in Indian semi-arid tropics, 268; in Southeast Asian humid tropics, 213–20
Land enclosures, 110, 252, 256, 289, 308
Land improvement investments, 58
Land management, 231, 248
Land ownership, 214–15
Land-person ratios, 75, 89, 128, 192
Land redistribution, 84
Land taxes, 10, 337–38
Land tenure, 62, 144, 192, 282
Land use: climate change and, 91, 92t, 93; in East African highlands, 320–21; in Ethiopia, 322f; pastoralism and, 257; in Southeast Asian humid tropics, 213–15

Latin America, 24; distribution of NARS staff in, 164t; interest rates in, 148, 149; macroeconomic policies in, 125–26; sustainability research in, 157; trade and environment in, 105

Leaffolder, 226

Legume-based cropping systems: in African humid and subhumid tropics, 194, 204; in humid and semihumid lowlands, 40; in Southeast Asian humid tropics, 227; in West African semi-arid tropics, 239; in West Asia and North Africa, 287, 288

Legumes, 159, 264

Limited demand scenario, 307

Links among sustainability, growth, and poverty alleviation, 3–4, 5–13; in Brazilian Amazon, 181; in Central America, 331–35; climate change and, 95; factors conditioning, 7–13; findings on nature and determinants of, 339–41; research gaps in, 344–46. *See also* Growth-environment links; Poverty-environment links; Sustainability-growth links

Lipton, M., 51

Live fences and windbreaks, 336

Livestock: in African humid and subhumid tropics, 206; in East African highlands, 316, 317, 319, 321, 323; in India, 307, 308; research on, 163–65; in West African semi-arid tropics, 231, 235, 240; in West Asia and North Africa, 284–86, 288–90, 291, 292. *See also* Animal feed; Animal husbandry; Grazing; Pastoralism

Livingstone, I., 309

Loans, 62, 144–45, 269, 274, 282

Logging, 214, 215, 337

Low economic growth scenario, 95–96

Lowlands: East African, 320; humid and subhumid, 40; of Southeast Asian humid tropics, 224–26

Low population growth scenario, 95

Luzon, 211, 215, 222

Macroeconomic policies, 7, 8–9, 10, 134; in African humid and subhumid tropics, 205–6; conservation investments and, 143; role in resource degradation, 121; trade policies and, 124–26

Madagascar, 315

Magat watershed, 221

Mähler, K. G., 304

Maize, 36, 128; in African humid and subhumid tropics, 191, 198–200, 203, 204; in Brazilian Amazon, 187, 188; in Central America, 329, 333, 334; climate change and, 93, 94; in East African highlands, 316, 320; in Himalayas, 299; research on, 159; in Southeast Asian humid tropics, 211; in Thailand, 111; TZB variety, 199–200; in West African semi-arid tropics, 230, 231, 235, 236, 242

Malaria, 71, 72, 76–77, 234

Malawi, 128, 131, 132

Malaysia, 73, 110, 129, 214

Mali, 206, 234, 241, 252

Malnutrition, 69, 187–88. *See also* Nutrition

Malthusian theory, 47, 81–82, 84, 86, 180

Manure, 135; in African humid and subhumid tropics, 201; in East African highlands, 324; green, 23, 201; in Southeast Asian humid tropics, 213; in West African semi-arid tropics, 235, 238, 239

Market failures, 119–22, 180

Marketing policies, 132–33

Maros, 226

Matlon, P. J., 57

Measured income, 105, 106, 107, 108, 109

Mechanization, 238

Medicago spp., 287

Meru, 317, 325

Mestizos, 333

Methane, 25, 90

Mexico, 334

Migration: bund building versus, 141; in Central America, 334; in India, 308; population growth and, 82–84; in Southeast Asian humid tropics, 218–20; in West African semi-arid tropics, 244; in West Asia and North Africa, 282, 291. *See also* Outmigration

Mildew resistance, 237

Milk, 248, 312

Millet, 253; climate change and, 94; in East African highlands, 316; in Indian semi-arid tropics, 262; in West African semi-arid tropics, 229, 230, 234, 235–36, 237, 240t, 241–42

Mindanao, 215, 217, 218

Minimum tillage, 212, 213

Mining of resources, 48, 86, 133, 181–82

Ministries, structural reorganization of, 166–67

Miyi county, 302

Moist savanna zone, 194t, 202–3

Molecular biology, 24–25

Monocropping, 42, 43t, 107, 181, 286, 287

Moroccan Rif, 291

Mortality rates, 79; infant, 187
Mosquitos, 234
Mountain areas, 40
Moya, P. F., 225
Mulch, 201, 213

Narrow strip fields, 282–83
National agricultural research systems
(NARSs), 156, 161, 167, 176; capacity to
deal with future needs, 162–66; dependence on donor financing, 168; distribution of research staff, 164t; education and
nationality of research staff, 169–70t
National Watershed Development Project
for Rainfed Areas (NWDPRA), 276
Natural resource policies, 7; failures of,
119–22; impact of trade policies on, 104–
9; reform of for trade purposes, 109–11
Natural resources: categories of, 49, 50f;
degradation of, *see* Resource degrada-
tion; human resources versus, 66–68;
lack of assets, 47–48, 50; valuation of, 43
Negative externalities, 12
Nelson, M., 288
Nepal, 6, 76, 132, 294, 299, 302
Netherlands, 116, 125
Nicaragua, 73, 329, 333
Niche products, 297, 298
Niger, 206, 248, 252
Nigeria, 194, 201, 209, 231, 254; floodplain
system in, 133–34; maize-based systems
in, 191, 199–200; maize-based versus
alley-cropping systems in, 198–99
Niger River Basin, 234
Ningnan county, 302
Nitrates, 38
Nitrogen, 36, 94, 194, 230, 234, 235
Nitrogen fertilizers, 198–99
Nitrogen fixation, 202, 287
Nitrous oxide, 25, 90
Nonagricultural income-earning strategies,
45, 55–56, 341; conservation investments
and, 141; pastoralism versus, 252–53; in
West African semi-arid tropics, 231, 244;
in West Asia and North Africa, 282
Nongovernmental organizations (NGOs),
143, 162, 176, 195, 276
North Africa, 278–93; barley zone of, 279,
284–90; conditions of recent agricultural
growth in, 280–81; distribution of NARS
staff in, 164t; higher-potential zone in,
281–84; highlands of, 290–92; steppe
zone of, 279, 281, 284–90; survival

strategies in, 290–91; sustainability in,
154; sustainability research in, 157
North America, 25
North-West Frontier Province (NWFP), 294
Nutrition, 66–78; intrahousehold,
household-, and community-level issues
in, 70; policy implications for, 77; re-
search on, 77–78; technology and, 70–77.
See also Malnutrition
Nuts, 279

Oats, 316
Off-farm income activities. *See* Nonagricul-
tural income-earning strategies
Off-farm physical and financial assets, 48,
51, 58, 60–61
Oil crops, 316, 319
Oils, 281
Oilseeds, 266
Oil states, 280, 281
Olives, 279, 282
Onchocerciasis (river blindness), 71
On-farm physical and financial assets, 48,
51, 58, 60
Open-access areas, 5, 289, 306
Opportunity costs, 182–83, 305, 337
Optimization models, 91, 93
Outmigration, 13; in Himalayas, 295, 297;
in Southeast Asian humid tropics, 219–20
Output prices, 109–10, 127–29, 151
Overlap technologies, 11–12, 15, 341–42,
345; in Central America, 335–36, 337;
conservation investments and, 135
Oxisols, 194
Ozone depletion, 116

Paddy, 262
Pakistan, 294
Palm oil, 197, 210
Panama, 331, 333
Pantabangan watershed, 221
Papaya, 183
Pardey, P. G., 168
Passive approaches to sustainability, 243
Pastoralism, 6, 246–60; adaptation to chang-
ing circumstances in, 252–54; agro-, 253–
54; alternative land use approaches in, 257;
in East African highlands, 320; manage-
ment approaches to, 255–56; policies for,
254–57; territorial contraction and, 251–
52; traditional systems of, 248–49; under-
lying forces of change in, 249–52
Patamasiriwat, D., 114
Perennial crops, 40, 126, 132, 210, 319

Person-land ratios, 75, 89, 128, 192

Peru, 209

Pest and disease control, 226; biological, 203; integrated, *see* Integrated pest management

Pesticides, 35; bans on, 44–45; health and nutrition influenced by, 71, 72t, 73, 74; in Southeast Asian humid tropics, 226; subsidies for, 41, 42f, 73, 132; water degradation and, 38

Philippines, 209, 210, 211, 214, 215, 221, 222, 225, 308; irrigation infrastructure in, 222–24; migration in, 218; regional deforestation and poverty indicators in, 216t, 217

Phosphate, 235

Phosphate fertilizers, 25

Phosphorus, 36, 194, 226, 230, 234

Physical erosion, 36, 37t

Pigeonpeas, 262

Pingali, P. L., 225

Planned resiliency, 99, 100t

Plantains, 197, 203, 204

Plantation production, 110

Plowing, 233, 288

Policies, 7–10, 341–43; for African humid and subhumid tropics, 205–7; for Central America, 330–31, 336–38; for health and nutrition, 77; for Indian semi-arid tropics, 269–76; infrastructure, 132–33; macroeconomic, *see* Macroeconomic policies; marketing, 132–33; natural resource, *see* Natural resource policies; for pastoralism, 254–57; population, 7; poverty-environment links and, 64–65; price, 44; sectoral, *see* Sectoral policies; for Southeast Asian humid tropics, 227–28; subsectoral, 7; trade, *see* Trade; for West African semi-arid tropics, 244–45

Political capital, 48, 51, 57

Population carrying capacities, 231–32

Population growth/density, 5, 12–13, 62, 345; in African humid and subhumid tropics, 192, 195; in Brazilian Amazon, 185–86; in Central America, 337; in East African highlands, 317–18, 319, 320–21, 325–26; endogenous, 79; in India, 84, 86, 88–89, 306–7; macroeconomic policies and, 125–26; Malthusian theory on, 47, 81–82, 84, 86, 180; migration and, 82–84; output pricing and, 128; pastoralism and, 249–50; policies on, 7; research consensus on, 80–81; resource degradation

and, 79–89; in West African semi-arid tropics, 231–32

Potassium, 36

Potatoes, 159, 316

Poverty: absolute, 51, 67; in African humid and subhumid tropics, 192–93; asset categories of, 47–48, 49, 50–51, 53, 63, 64; in Brazilian Amazon, 187–88; in Central America, 330–31; conservation-investment, *see* Conservation-investment poverty; defined, 192; in Southeast Asian humid tropics, 215–20; typology of, 50–51; ultra, 51; welfare, *see* Welfare poverty. *See also* Poverty alleviation

Poverty alleviation. *See also* Links among sustainability, growth, and poverty alleviation; Poverty; Poverty-environment links

—in African humid and subhumid tropics: compatibility with other goals, 200–7; potential conflicts, 195–200

—in Brazilian Amazon, 181, 189–90

—economic sustainability and, 232–33

—in India, 307–10

Poverty-environment links, 5, 6–7, 15, 43–44, 47–65, 340–41; in Central America, 330–31; determinants of, 53–59; illustrations of, 59–61; in India, 304–5, 307–9; policies for, 64–65; research gaps in, 344–45; typology in, 50–51

Pratong, 210

Pretty, J. N., 23n3

Price makers, 146

Price policies, 44

Price takers, 146, 337

Prisoner's dilemma, 312

Pritchard, A. J., 237

Private property resources (PPRs), 312–13

Privatization: of commons, 274; of research, 24

Productivity. *See* Agricultural productivity

Productivity investments, 9, 136, 137–40, 141, 142, 145, 341

Product makers, 146

Product takers, 146

Property rights, 8, 9, 10, 62, 105, 180; in India, 309–10; population growth and, 83, 89; trade and, 110–11

Public institutions. *See* Institutions

Public investments, 121, 133–34

Pulse, 316, 319

Purposeful adjustment, 99, 100t

Pyrethrum, 316

Rainfall: areas of uncertain, 38–39; climate change and, 91, 93; in Indian semi-arid tropics, 261, 264, 265; pastoralism and, 250; in West Asia and North Africa, 278–79, 286
Rainfed production systems. *See* North Africa; West Asia
Rajasthan Desert, 83
Rao, C. H. H., 144
Reardon, T., 84–85, 140, 141
Red soils, 272
Reforestation, 308
Repetto, R., 306
Research, 44–45; on climate change, 101–2; on conservation investments, 144; gaps in, 64–65, 344–46; on health and nutrition, 77–78; in Himalayas, 301, 302; in Indian semi-arid tropics, 263, 269–76; on population growth, 80–81; on poverty-environment links, 64–65; privatization of, 24; on sustainability, *see* Sustainability research; upstream versus downstream, 161
Resistant cultivars, 203, 237
Resource degradation, 5, 6–7, 119–34. *See also* Growth-environment links
—in Central America, 330–31
—defining the problem, 119–20
—in East African highlands, 317, 321–24
—extent and types of, 36–38
—farm prices and, 146, 150–51
—health and nutrition and, 66–78; conceptual framework for, 68–70; technology in, 70–77
—in Himalayas, 295
—in India, 304–6; strategies to counter, 307–9; technology and, 305–6
—interest rates and, 146, 147–50
—macroeconomic policies and, 121
—market and policy failures and, 119–32
—market and policy success and, 146–53
—pastoralism and, 250–51
—population growth and, 79–89
—public investments and, 133–34
—rural development modalities and, 79–80
—technology and, 146, 151–52
—trade policies and, 124–26, 134
—in West Asia and North Africa, 288–90
—by zone, 38–40
Resource exploitation model, 24
Resource prices, 109–10
Resource-to-population ratios, 181
Rice, 1, 39, 72, 151; in African humid and subhumid tropics, 194; in Brazilian Amazon, 183, 187, 188; climate change and, 94; in Himalayas, 299, 301; integrated pest management for, 41; IR-8 variety, 225; pesticides and, 41, 42f, 73; prices of, 24; research on, 159, 160; in Southeast Asian humid tropics, 208, 209, 211, 222, 224–26, 227; in Thailand, 111; in West African semi-arid tropics, 231, 234, 235, 242; wet cultivation of, 22–23
Rice-legume systems, 227
Rift Valley, 93, 246
Rio Grande, 331
Riparian water resources, 116
Risk, 143
River blindness (onchocerciasis), 71
Road building, 133
Root vegetables, 40
Roseboom, J., 168
Roundwood, 126
Rubber, 111, 197, 210
Ruttan, V. W., 82
Ruwenzori, 316
Rwanda, 57, 60–61, 76, 315, 316, 325

Sabacuante, 331
Sahel, 1, 5, 60, 246, 310
Sahelo-Sudanian zone, 230–32, 235, 236, 238, 239, 242, 244; benefits of technological change in, 240–41
Sahel zone, 230–31, 232t, 234, 235, 236, 238, 244; benefits of technological change in, 239–40
Salinization, 35, 36–38, 43, 130, 131, 234
Schiff, M., 108
Schistosomiasis, 71, 234
Sectoral policies, 7, 8, 10, 126–33, 134; in African humid and subhumid tropics, 205–6; conservation investments and, 143; role in resource degradation, 121
Sedimentation, 211–13, 221, 222
Semi-arid tropics. *See* Indian semi-arid tropics; West African semi-arid tropics
Senegal River Valley, 234
Shallow vertic soils, 265
Sharecropping, 83, 282
Sheep, 279, 284
Shifting cultivation systems, 22, 211, 214
Siamwalla, A., 136
Sierra, R., 133
Sierra Leone, 194
Silos, 336
Slash-and-burn agriculture, 42, 183
Sleeping sickness, 76
Smallholder agriculture, 261–62

Small-scale irrigation, 272–73
Social capital, 51, 59–60
Socioinstitutional sustainability, 232, 233
Soft infrastructure, 61
Soil: of African humid and subhumid
    tropics, 194–95; alfisols, 194, 198, 203,
    265; black, 265, 272; of Brazilian
    Amazon, 59–60; deep vertisols, 265; of
    East African highlands, 315–18; of In-
    dian semi-arid tropics, 262, 264, 272;
    oxisols, 194; red, 272; shallow vertic,
    265; ultisols, 194
Soil acidification, 209, 230, 235
Soil degradation. *See* Land degradation
Soil erosion, 25, 35; in African humid and
    subhumid tropics, 195; in Central
    America, 336; chemical, 36, 37t;
    downstream effects of, 220–24; in East
    African highlands, 317; health and nutri-
    tion influenced by, 74; in Himalayas,
    295; input pricing and, 130, 131; output
    pricing and, 128–29; pastoralism and,
    250; physical, 36, 37t; in Southeast Asian
    humid tropics, 209, 211–13, 220–24;
    water, 36, 37t; in West African semi-arid
    tropics, 230; in West Asia and North
    Africa, 283, 286, 287, 291; wind, 36, 37t,
    287
Soil fertility, 41, 213, 321–24
Soil organic matter (SOM), 195, 201
Soil protection, 42, 239, 273
Soil runoff, 211–12, 239, 291, 311, 312
Solow, R. M., 28
Somalia, 249
Sorghum: in African humid and subhumid
    tropics, 200; in Central America, 333,
    334; climate change and, 94; in East
    African highlands, 316, 320; in Indian
    semi-arid tropics, 262; research on, 159;
    in semi-arid Africa, 253; in West African
    semi-arid tropics, 229, 230, 231, 233,
    234, 235–36, 237, 240t, 241–42
South Africa, 84
South America, 154, 162
South Asia, 24, 210; health and nutrition in,
    70; interest rates in, 148; population
    growth in, 85; sustainability research in,
    157, 161
Southeast Asia, 24, 129, 157, 161. *See also*
    Southeast Asian humid tropics
Southeast Asian humid tropics, 208–28;
    determinants of land use and degradation
    in uplands, 213–15; policy implications
    for, 227–28; poverty and degradation in

uplands, 215–20; sustaining productivity
    in lowlands, 224–26; technological op-
    tions for upland cultivation, 210–13; tran-
    sition to sustainable upland farming in,
    209–10
Southgate, D., 133
South Pacific, 163, 168, 170
Soybeans, 94
Specialization, 107, 109
Speculation, 189–90
Spencer, D. S. C., 57
Spillover effects, 28–29; of intensification,
    25; of sustainability research, 159–60; of
    trade, 104–5, 106, 107
Sri Lanka, 73
Stall feeding system, 324
Steppe zone, 279, 281, 284–90
Striga, 237
Subhumid lowlands, 40
Subhumid tropics. *See* African humid and
    subhumid tropics
Sub-Saharan Africa, 39, 41; distribution of
    NARS staff in, 164t; education and
    nationality of NARS staff in, 169–70t;
    health and nutrition in, 70; interest rates
    in, 149; land degradation in, 36; output
    prices in, 127–29; population growth in,
    85; sustainability in, 154; sustainability
    research in, 157, 163, 167, 168, 170;
    trade and environment in, 105
Subsectoral policies, 7
Subsidies, 126–27, 130–32, 244, 275; for
    animal feed, 289; for fertilizers, 130–31,
    282; for irrigation, 131–32; for pes-
    ticides, 41, 42f, 73, 132
Substitution, 27, 61, 63, 300t
Sudan, 75, 124, 132, 319
Sudanian zone, 230–31, 232, 233, 234, 236,
    242, 243; benefits of technological
    change in, 240t, 241
Sudano-Guinean zone, 230–31, 232t, 235,
    236, 238, 239, 243; benefits of tech-
    nological change in, 240t, 241–42
Sugar, 150
Sugarcane, 262, 267, 334
Sukhna River, 311
Sukhomajri, 311–13
Sulfur, 226
Sulfur dioxide, 90
Suphan Buri, 225
Surface water, 71
Sustainability, 19–33. *See also* Links among
    sustainability, growth, and poverty al-
    leviation; Sustainability-growth links

—in African humid and subhumid tropics, 192–93; compatibility with other goals, 200–7; constraints to, 193–95; potential conflicts, 195–200
— in Brazilian Amazon, 180–81, 183–84, 189–90
—in Central America, 328–31, 335–36
—climate change and, 97–99
—concept of, 4–5
—definitions of, 3n2, 20–22, 32–33
—developmental, 33
—in East African highlands, 325–26
—ecological, 32–33
—economic, 232–33
—in Himalayas, 294, 295, 296t; development strategies and, 298–301; growth combined with, 301–2; traditional system and, 297–98
—historical perspective on, 22–23
—in India, 309–10
—in Indian semi-arid tropics, 263, 266–69, 271
—interest rates and, 147–48
—monitoring global change and, 29–31
—obligations toward future and, 27–28
—overlap technologies and, 135, 335–36
—pastoralism and, 247–48
—research systems for, *see* Sustainability research
—six potential causes of loss of, 167–70
—socioinstitutional, 232, 233
—in Southeast Asian humid tropics, 209–10
—technical, 232
—technology and: in Brazilian Amazon, 183–84; as challenge to, 23–26; in Indian semi-arid tropics, 271; role in widening, 27; in West African semi-arid tropics, 232–33, 242–44
—in West Asia and North Africa, 286–90, 292
—zoning for, 161–66
Sustainability-growth links, 5–6
Sustainability research, 154–76; in Brazilian Amazon, 184; in Central America, 163, 168, 170; donor financing in, 168; educational standards of scientists in, 168; factors influencing capacity to develop technology, 156–67; financial support for, 170–71; improving, 167–70; problems in developing suitable technology, 155–56; requirements for increasing, 174–75; zoning in, 161–66
Syria, 285

Tagalog, 215
Taita-Taveta, 316
Taiwan, 84
Tanks, 266, 267, 269, 272
Tanzania, 315, 316, 319, 324, 325, 326
Tapawan-Conway, Z., 221
Targeting (active) approaches to sustainability, 243
Tatumbla, 331
Tea, 93, 316
Technical assistance, 156–61
Technical sustainability, 232
Technology, 11–12, 23–26, 27, 341–43
—in African humid and subhumid tropics, 199–204
—conservation investments and, 135–45
—endogenous, 87
—exogenous, 87–88, 151–52
—health and nutrition linked to, 70–77
—in India, 305–6, 309–10, 311–13
—in Indian semi-arid tropics, 271
—overlap, *see* Overlap technologies
—pastoralism and, 254–55
—population growth and, 79, 82, 84–86, 87–88
—resource degradation and, 146, 151–52, 305–6
—in Southeast Asian humid tropics, 210–13, 225–26
—sustainability and, *see under* Sustainability
—sustainability research and, 154–67
—in West African semi-arid tropics: potential for change via, 232–39; potential gains by zone, 239–42; priorities for sustainable change, 242–44
Teff, 316
Terai rivers, 222
Terraces, 211, 212, 213, 291, 295, 297
Thailand, 210, 215; cassava in, 8, 111–15, 125, 205; crop yields in, 225–26; input pricing in, 130, 132; output pricing in, 129; slash-and-burn agriculture in, 42; trade in, 110, 111–15
Tied-ridges, 140, 233, 236, 237, 241
Tillage, 39, 212, 213, 238, 287
Time preference rates, 70, 80
Tobacco, 150
Tort law, 104, 105
Total factor productivity (TFP), 193, 271
Tractors, 238, 286, 308
Trade, 44, 103–18; in Central America, 330; impact of given resource policies, 104–9; international policies on, 7–8;

Trade (cont'd)
international policies on environment and, 115–18; macroeconomic policies and, 124–26; open versus closed regimes, 105–9; pastoral, 249; reform of resource policies and, 109–11; resource degradation and, 124–26, 134; sustainability and, 330
Tragedy of the commons, 152, 256, 307
Transitional farming system, 319
Transport and communication infrastructure, 58–59
Tree cover, 40, 200–1, 211, 214, 286
Trees, 210, 211, 213, 302, 324, 326
Trinidad, 308
Tropical rain forests, 76–77
True scarcity values, 143
True welfare, 105, 107, 108, 109
Tuberculosis, 71
Turkey, 291
Typhoid, 71
TZB (maize variety), 199–200

Uganda, 206, 315, 316
Ultisols, 194
Ultra poverty, 51
Unemployment, 218–20, 224
United Nations Conference on Environment and Development (UNCED), 45
United Nations Development Programme (UNDP), 168, 222
United Nations Environment Programme (UNEP), 36
United States, 28, 115, 147, 150, 334
Upstream versus downstream research, 161
Usambara Mountains, 322f, 324

Vaccinations, veterinary, 254, 255
Valdés, A., 108
Valuation of resources, 43
Vegetables, 211, 231, 234, 281, 291
Vegetative and grass strips, 211, 213
Velasco, L. E., 225
Vetiver grass, 273
Visayas, 215, 217
von Braun, J., 200
Vosti, S. A., 140

Wabi Shebele River, 251
Water degradation, 2, 30; in East African highlands, 321–24; extent and types of, 36–38; in Indian semi-arid tropics, 266–68
Water erosion, 36, 37t

Water holes, 310
Waterlogging, 130, 131
Water management: climate change and, 94; health and nutrition influenced by, 72; pastoralism and, 248; population growth and, 85–86; in West African semi-arid tropics, 233–34
Water pumps, 266
Watersheds, 12, 62; conservation investments and, 140, 142; health and nutrition influenced by, 74, 75; in Himalayas, 295; in Indian semi-arid tropics, 270, 274–76; in Southeast Asian humid tropics, 215, 220–24, 228; trade and, 125
Water Users Society, 312
Welfare poverty, 6, 48, 51–53, 62, 63, 64
Wells, 266–68, 283
West Africa, 56, 167, 211. *See also* West African semi-arid tropics
West African semi-arid tropics (WASAT), 229–45; devolution of land management systems in, 231; emerging disequilibrium in, 231–32; farming systems in, 230–31; natural environment of, 229–30; pastoralism in, 246–60; policy alternatives in, 244–45; production and productivity in, 229; technology in, *see under* Technology. *See also* Pastoralism
West Asia, 278–93; barley zone of, 279, 284–90; conditions of recent agricultural growth in, 280–81; distribution of NARS staff in, 164t; higher-potential zone in, 281–84; highlands of, 290–92; survival strategies in, 290–91; sustainability research in, 157
West Bengal, 84
Western Europe, 22, 23, 25
West Java, 211, 215, 225
West Sichuan, 294, 302
Wet rice cultivation, 22–23
Wheat, 151; climate change and, 94; in East African highlands, 316; in Himalayas, 299, 301; in India, 262, 312; prices of, 24; research on, 159, 160; in Southeast Asian humid tropics, 226; in West Asia and North Africa, 279, 281, 282, 283, 292
Wild food gathering, 56
Wildlife conservation, 257
Wind erosion, 36, 37t, 287
WoDaaBe, 248
Women, 70, 76, 253, 291
Wood depletion, 324
Wood stoves, 335
World Bank, 28, 147, 168, 192, 231, 273

World Commission on Environment and
   Development, 305
World Development Report, 150
World Watch Institute, 45

Yemen, 291

Young, A., 84

Zaire, 209
Zero grazing, 324
Zero tillage, 212, 213, 238
Zimbabwe, 84, 252, 254, 257

LIBRARY OF CONGRESS CATALOGING-IN-PUBLICATION DATA

Sustainability, growth, and poverty alleviation : a policy and agroecological perspective /
  edited by Stephen A. Vosti and Thomas Reardon.
      p. cm.
  Includes bibliographical references and index.
  ISBN 0-8018-5607-8 (alk. paper)
      1. Agriculture—Developing countries. 2. Agriculture—Environmental aspects—
  Developing countries. 3. Agriculture and state—Developing countries. 4. Agriculture—
  Economic aspects—Developing countries. 5. Poverty—Developing countries.
  I. Vosti, Stephen A. II. Reardon, Thomas Anthony. III. International Food Policy
  Research Institute.
  S482.S87 1997
  333.7'09173'4—dc21   97-1816
                                                                         CIP